Airline Operations

Written by a range of international industry practitioners, this book offers a comprehensive overview of the essence and nature of airline operations in terms of an operational and regulatory framework, the myriad of planning activities leading up to the current day, and the nature of intense activity that typifies both normal and disrupted airline operations.

The first part outlines the importance of the regulatory framework underpinning airline operations, exploring how airlines structure themselves in terms of network and business model. The second part draws attention to the operational environment, explaining the framework of the air traffic system and processes instigated by operational departments within airlines. The third part presents a comprehensive breakdown of the activities that occur on the actual operating day. The fourth part provides an eye-opener into events that typically go wrong on the operating day and then the means by which airlines try to mitigate these problems. Finally, a glimpse is provided of future systems, processes, and technologies likely to be significant in airline operations.

Airline Operations: A Practical Guide offers valuable knowledge to industry and academia alike by providing readers with a well-informed and interesting dialogue on critical functions that occur every day within airlines.

Peter J. Bruce spent nearly seventeen years as an operations controller in airline operations and has considerable first-hand experience and expertise in this environment. His PhD focused on operational decision-making in airlines and he has presented his work at domestic and international forums and conferences. Besides being chief editor of *Airline Operations: A Practical Guide*, he has written and published four other texts, including *Understanding Decision-making Processes in Airline Operations Control* (Ashgate, 2011). He is Deputy Chair in the Department of Aviation at Swinburne University of Technology, where he is an active researcher in the areas of airline operations, controller selection and training strategies, operational decision-making, and airline safety. He instigated and developed the highly popular Aviation Study Tour at Swinburne, conducting the first six global tours which took groups of students to visit key aviation organizations. Peter's teaching areas focus on aviation business and strategy, and airline planning and operations.

Yi Gao is the Aviation Undergraduate Course Director in the Department of Aviation, Swinburne University of Technology. As a researcher, his principal research areas include airline operations optimization, aviation safety, pilot selection, and pilot learning/cognitive styles. As a senior lecturer, he is currently teaching Aviation Regulation and Operation and the undergraduate capstone research project. As an aviation enthusiast, he holds an FAA Private Pilot license.

John M. C. King established a consultancy providing government relations services for airlines and the tourism industry after a twenty-year career in the airline industry. He also conducted several aviation sector reviews for international organizations including The World Bank, UNDP, and the UN World Tourism Organization. He has been Chairman of a stock exchange-listed company in the tourism sector, Chairman of the Travel Compensation Fund (a co-regulator of the travel agency industry), and he served for three and a half years as a Commissioner of the International Air Services Commission. John is involved in delivering postgraduate courses at Swinburne University of Technology and has served on the Board of Advice of the Institute of Transport and Logistic Studies at the University of Sydney. John is also a fellow of the Royal Geographic Society.

Airline Operations
A Practical Guide

Edited by Peter J. Bruce, Yi Gao, and John M. C. King

Routledge
Taylor & Francis Group

LONDON AND NEW YORK

First published 2018
by Routledge

2 Park Square, Milton Park, Abingdon, Oxfordshire OX14 4RN
52 Vanderbilt Avenue, New York, NY 10017

Routledge is an imprint of the Taylor & Francis Group, an informa business

First issued in paperback 2020

British Library Cataloguing-in-Publication Data
A catalogue record for this book is available from the British Library

Library of Congress Cataloging-in-Publication Data
Names: Bruce, Peter J., editor. | Gao, Yi, 1982- editor. | King, John M. C., editor.
Title: Airline operations : a practical guide / edited by Peter J. Bruce, Yi Gao and John M. C. King.
Description: First Edition. | New York : Routledge, 2018. | Includes bibliographical references and index.
Identifiers: LCCN 2017019779| ISBN 9781472478177 (hardback) | ISBN 9781315566450 (ebook)
Subjects: LCSH: Airlines--Economic aspects. | Airlines--Management.Classification: LCC HE9776 .A38 2018 | DDC 387.7068--dc23
LC record available at https://lccn.loc.gov/2017019779

ISBN: 978-1-4724-7817-7 (hbk)
ISBN: 978-0-367-66985-0 (pbk)

Typeset in Bembo
by HWA Text and Data Management, London

The opinions expressed in this publication are those of the authors only and do not represent the views, expressed or implied, of any government, employer or organization.

Contents

Figures

Tables

Contributors

Editors

Peter J. Bruce   PhD (Swinburne University of Technology, Australia) spent nearly seventeen years in the airline industry, nearly all of which was as an operations controller in TAA/Australian Airlines. His interests in improving operational situation awareness and decision-making led to the completion of a PhD investigating decision-making in airline operations, and he published his fourth book *Understanding Decision-making Processes in Airline Operations Control* a few years ago. He is a current researcher in this area and presents internationally to airlines and conferences. Peter is currently Deputy Chair of the Department of Aviation at Swinburne University of Technology where he teaches Airline Operations and a number of other aviation courses. He is a member of both the Airline Group of the International Federation of Operational Research Societies and the Air Transport Research Society.

Yi Gao   PhD (Swinburne University of Technology, Australia) is the Aviation Undergraduate Course Director in the Department of Aviation, Swinburne University of Technology. His principle areas of research include airline operations optimization, aviation safety, pilot selection and pilot learning/cognitive styles. As a senior lecturer, he is currently teaching Aviation Regulation and Operation and the undergraduate capstone research project. As an aviation enthusiast, he holds an FAA Private Pilot license.

John M. C. King   (Aviation and Tourism Management, Australia) established a consultancy providing government relations services for airlines and the tourism industry after a twenty-year career in the airline industry. He also conducted several aviation sector reviews for international organizations including The World Bank, UNDP and the UN World Tourism Organization. He has been Chairman of a stock exchange-listed company in the tourism sector, Chairman of the Travel Compensation Fund (a co-regulator of the travel agency industry) and served for three and a half years as a Commissioner of the International Air Services Commission. He has served on the Board of Advice of the Institute of Transport and Logistic Studies at the University of Sydney and is also a fellow of the Royal Geographic Society.

Authors

Stephen Angus (Airservices Australia, Australia) has an operational and leadership background in aviation commencing as an air traffic controller in 1989. In 2005 Stephen joined the Airservices Australia Executive Team in roles including Airspace Regulation, National Operations and Safety and Assurance. In 2014 Stephen joined Inmarsat Global as a Senior Director Policy. He also has worked in the resources industry and with the Flight Safety Foundation before rejoining Airservices Australia in July 2016 as the Executive General Manager, Air Navigation Services. Stephen has a Master of Business Administration from Melbourne Business School (Mt Eliza) and is a fellow of the Australian Institute of Company Directors.

Paul Avery BEng(Aero) (Aircraft Load Control Consultants, UK) has over thirty years' experience in aircraft weights engineering and load control systems development and certification. This experience is from both an airline perspective, providing critical support in the centralization of Load Control, and from a service provider perspective. He is currently providing services to a major airline Departure Control Systems provider in the United Kingdom, and also regularly delivers Load Control lectures and Weight and Balance Engineering courses.

Ron Bartsch BA, BSc, LLB, LLM, MPhil, Dip Ed. ATPL (AvLaw International Pty. Ltd., Australia) is Chairman of AvLaw International and currently a presiding member with the Commonwealth Administrative Appeals Tribunal (AAT). Ron is also a senior visiting fellow at the Australian National University and the University of New South Wales, and lectures in Australian and International Air Law. Ron was admitted as a barrister in 1993 and then took up a senior management position with the Australian Civil Aviation Safety Authority and then later was appointed as Head of Safety and Regulatory Compliance for Qantas Airways Limited and held this position until 2009.

Steve Buchanan (Qantas Airways, Australia) has worked in the airline industry for over twenty-six years with roles in Finance, Front line Airport Operations and is now managing an Integrated Operations Control Centre. A career highlight was having the opportunity to manage the off-airport check-in with two other colleagues at the Sydney Olympics and Paralympics in the year 2000, processing over 11,000 athletes and officials. This also led to his assisting at the Beijing and London Olympics where Qantas brought home the Australian Athletes on specially chartered aircraft.

Charles Cunningham (Southwest Airlines, USA) has been in aviation for over thirty years, the entirety of that time with Southwest Airlines. He became more involved in operational recovery in 1993 as an Aircraft Dispatcher. For the past seventeen years he has served as a Flight Dispatch Superintendent, which at Southwest is the group that makes day-to-day decisions regarding the network, irregular operations and operational recovery. He has been involved in several high profile projects at Southwest, including being part of the International Flag Certification Team, enabling the airline to begin international service some five years ago. For the past three years, Charles has been on special assignment, working as part of a team developing a recovery optimization tool 'The Baker' which has been tremendously successful helping the airline manage IROPs.

Nicholas Donnison (Cathay Pacific Airways, Hong Kong) originates from Melbourne, Australia, and holds an Air Transportation Management qualification. After completing an internship in Flight Dispatch at Southwest Airlines in Dallas, Nicholas began a career with Cathay Pacific in cargo sales and operations. His career with Cathay Pacific has taken him from Melbourne to Singapore and Hong Kong in cargo operational roles, and Hong Kong and San Francisco in quality assurance roles. He is currently based in San Francisco, where he is an embedded representative of the Group Quality department, responsible for quality awareness, education, engagement and auditing of passenger and cargo operations within the United States, Canada and Mexico.

Patrick Fennell (Salam Air, Oman) is a native of Ireland and has been involved in the aviation industry since 1994. He has worked at almost a dozen carriers employing various business models, and currently heads up the Integrated Operations Control Centre at Salam Air. Prior to this he was Head of Operations at Asia's best-known LCC, Air Asia. He holds a Master's degree in Air Transport Management from Cranfield University in the UK.

Markus Franke PhD (Franke Aviation and Transportation Consulting, Germany) is an independent transportation consultant and senior aviation advisor, with a functional focus on strategy, organizational governance, and commercial functions (such as network management and pricing). He has twenty-one years of experience in top management consulting for major airlines, airports, private and state-owned investment companies, public authorities like national MoTs, and has track record in transport, logistics, and rail traffic. He has published widely, speaks at international conferences and lectures in Strategic Network Management at the International University of Bad Honnef (IUBH). Dr Franke holds a diploma in aerospace engineering (with distinction) and in economic sciences, and was awarded a doctorate by the RWTH Aachen University in Engineering (Hypersonic spacecraft propulsion systems, summa cum laude).

Matthew Franzi (Jetstar Airways, Australia) has fifteen years' experience in the aviation sector across Asia-Pacific, working in various fields including Flight Operations, Ground Operations, and Safety. Matt is currently the Head of Safety for Jetstar Airways, Australia. Matt has a Bachelor's degree in Business and Technology and a Master's degree in Aviation. He is also a part-time university lecturer in airline operations, and aviation safety and security management.

John Frearson   (Civil Aviation Safety Authority, Australia) began his career on the Fokker F27 with Trans Australia Airlines and went on to fly the DC-9, Boeing 727, Boeing 777 and Airbus A320 based variously in Australia, Europe and Asia. He has had roles in planning, standards, training, safety, audit and management with airlines and ICAO and now works for Australia's Civil Aviation Safety Authority (CASA). John holds a Bachelor of Economics degree from La Trobe University and a Master of Business Administration from the University of Melbourne.

Jamie Horswell   (Qantas Airways, Australia) has thirteen years' Cabin Crew experience and is currently an A380 customer service manager (CSM) for Qantas Airways. Complementing regular line flying as a trainer and a LOSA Safety Auditor, he completes audit flying across the Qantas fleets. Jamie holds vocational and higher qualifications in Management, Aircraft Operations and Safety/Human factors and was awarded a Master of Technology in Air Transportation Management in 2007. His previously-held posts include Manager Service Development and Performance, Manager of Qantas Centre of Service Excellence and Promotional Team and Developer Qantas 'Sommelier in the Sky' training programme. Prior to aviation, Jamie had a background in hotel management.

Christopher Jarvis   (Airbiz Aviation Strategies Pty Ltd, Australia) has over thirty years' experience in airport master planning, forecasting of aviation and airport landside activity, airport movement area planning and design, airport terminal planning, airport and aviation infrastructure planning and design, feasibility studies and project management. As well as his involvement with numerous airport planning and development projects in Australia and New Zealand, Chris has undertaken airport planning studies in the United Kingdom, the Pacific, Asia and the Middle East. Chris lectures in Airport Planning, Operation and Management, and is also a course tutor for Airport Planning modules at postgraduate level.

Gene Kim   (Southwest Airlines, USA) is the Senior Director of Flight Dispatch, Training and Standards within Network Operations Control (NOC) for Southwest Airlines. He has over twenty-six years of Dispatch experience, previously working at Korean Air, Polar Air Cargo, United Airlines, and AirTran Airways. Gene's experience includes domestic and international operations, instructing, and serving in various union and management positions throughout his aviation tenure.

Samuel Lucas   (Australian Representative to ICAO, Australia) is a lawyer by training, and has worked on a wide range of aviation issues in his career with the Australian Government Department of Infrastructure and Regional Development, including facilitation, aviation industry policy, safety regulatory policy, and the negotiation of bilateral air services agreements.

He has represented Australia at a number of ICAO forums, including the Council of ICAO, the Air Transport Regulation Panel, and the Facilitation Panel, which he chaired from 2012 to 2015.

Nathan Miller (Qantas Group, Australia) commenced his aviation career with general aviation flying instruction and charter. His airline career has included Impulse Airlines, Ansett Airlines, Qantas Airways, Jetstar Airways and QantasLink. Aircraft types operated include Be99 and Mu2 turboprops (and endorsed on the Dash 8-Q400 series), BAe146, Boeing 737 and 747-400, Airbus A320, A321 and A330 jets. He has operated aircraft in regional, mainline domestic, international, full-service and low-cost airlines. Nathan has held a variety of Flight and General Operations Management roles, including Manager Line Operations A320/A321 and Manager Flying Operations at Jetstar, Chief Pilot and EM Airline Operations at QantasLink.

Rik Movig (KLM Royal Dutch Airlines, Netherlands), after being a licensed riding instructor for several years, changed to an IT career within KLM. She became responsible for KLM input on international standardization platforms for Engineering and Maintenance and schedule development. Rik then changed to a career in baggage capacity analysis and simulation with KLM ground services in 2000. Since then, she has been closely involved in all developments of the baggage handling system of Schiphol Airport used by KLM, including development of robotic loading and unloading of baggage containers.

Mark Palmer (Thales, France) graduated with a degree in Computer Systems Engineering, and worked initially as a software engineer through a number of different projects in Australia before spending five years working on the flight management system of the Hawk Lead-in Fighter aircraft. Upon returning to Australia he joined Thales, working on Air Traffic Control solutions, including being the Technical Director for Asia Pacific for six years, guiding the introduction of advanced systems into main countries including Taiwan, Thailand, South Africa and Singapore. He currently holds the position of Innovation Director for ATM solutions worldwide, leading three Innovation labs in France, the USA and Australia. Based in Toulouse, France, he also leads the joint Avionics/ATM innovation group.

Gary Parker (Airline Revenue Management Training Group, Canada) has over twenty-six years in airline passenger marketing and revenue management, with over seventeen years' teaching and consulting at airlines, and rail and bus companies around the world. In his career at Air Canada, he participated in the development and successful implementation of a new fare family business. He analysed and evaluated market environments for the purpose of developing yield strategies, capturing incremental revenue opportunities and improving profitability. Gary was also responsible for leading innovation and project activities in passenger marketing.

Andrea Roberts (former Quality Manager Ground Handling, Munich Airport, Germany) was born in Munich where she joined the aviation industry in 1986, gaining hands-on experience in multiple sectors of the aviation industry including ticketing, sales, marketing and operations. Andrea worked for an international airline providing customer service and operational support; in 1990 she joined Munich Airport Corporation. Andrea worked as the first female Central Dispatcher at Ground Handling (GH) and later joined the Quality Management Team, responsible for all corrective and preventative actions and the implementation of a Safety Management System in GH. In 2007 she immigrated to Melbourne, Australia, and is the Quality and Safety Manager for a leading Flight Training Organization (FTO).

Alan Swann (Consultant (ret.), Australia) has enjoyed a forty-year career that has covered most of the areas of Aircraft Maintenance Management and Flight Operations Administration in a major Australian Airline. Experience at senior management level provided him with a unique insight into the demands of the aircraft maintenance function in a large organization as well as other segments of the aviation industry.

Rodney Williams (Virgin Australia, Australia) has over thirty years in commercial aviation, working for both major carriers in Australia – Qantas and Virgin Australia. Rod has held a number of management roles covering areas such as Frequent Flyer, Alliances, Network Development, Pricing and Inventory, Corporate Planning, Revenue Planning, Route Economics and Finance, including three years in the USA as Manager Market Planning The Americas. He holds a BCom (with Merit) from the University of Wollongong and an MCom from UNSW, is a member of CPA Australia and a Justice of the Peace.

Frank Zimmermann (Consultant, Australia) is the founder and application architect of AIRPORT Online and AIRLINE Online, economic and management simulations. The simulations allow participants to experience the complex world of aviation management in a realistic and challenging environment. Frank travels regularly and extensively (for research and pleasure), experiencing all travel classes, often speaking at universities and conferences around the world.

Foreword

Airlines have been flying passengers and freight between cities for over a century, but for all its glamour, the industry has developed very little in the way of profits for those who have invested in it.

There is much to like about the aviation industry – a mixture of exciting technology, skilled practitioners, customer service and international links.

But it is so easily buffeted by a myriad of forces, both internal and external. Fuel costs, currencies and travel markets can quickly change, often much more rapidly than airlines are able to adjust in response.

In the early days of the industry, most airlines were government owned and run. Some still are, but many have been privatized over the last four decades. As governments have relinquished airline ownership to private industries, they have become much less prescriptive about airlines' commercial agenda and route networks.

Bilateral aviation agreements are now much more liberal, and airlines are increasingly free to build route networks around commercial opportunity rather than government diktat.

In many of the early airlines, including some of the best known and most admired, carriers in the industry struggled to cope with the resulting increased competition. Iconic names from the post-war boom in commercial aviation are no more – Pan Am, TWA, Eastern and British Caledonian to name but a few. Others have only survived because they continue to be propped up by governments that are still committed to the idea of the national 'Flag Carrier'.

More recently the rise of the low-cost carriers has increased the pressure on the legacy airlines still further. The latter's short-haul networks in particular have been aggressively challenged by these newcomers with a simple business model and a relentless focus on costs.

The airlines that have survived and prospered have only done so by being agile and adaptive – by challenging the way things are done and embracing new ideas and game-changing technologies, and by chasing new markets. The winners have put the customer at the centre of their thinking rather than clinging to the production-centric mind-set of the past.

This book covers the important aspects of airlines' operations in considerable detail. It provides both a historical context and some very important pointers to the future in the core functions of an airline's operation.

The authors bring a thorough understanding of the aviation industry to their work. Successful airlines get the details right – and attention to the key detail runs through this book.

It reminds us what a complex and fascinating industry aviation has been and still is – and one that has transformed our lives in so many wonderful ways.

Rod Eddington, February 2017

Part I
Planning for products and customers

John M. C. King

In this opening part, the authors consider a number of elements which initially may be thought of as extraneous to the work of the practical manager involved with operations. However, closer analysis shows that each of the chapters provides either operational or strategic context for the activities that an airline undertakes in doing what it does – transporting passengers and cargo. This part provides the legal and regulatory framework in which aviation operations are conducted. While domestic interstate[1] aviation in Australia is regulated only in terms of safety, many readers of this book have experienced economic and policy regulation impacting on both their domestic and international operations. Thus, the focus is on the legislative controls which are placed on the operations of airlines, their contractors and suppliers, and the airports from which they operate. The other key providers of services to the airline industry are air navigation service providers or air traffic control systems. The pricing regulation of air navigation services is an important element in an airline cost structure, but is not directly linked to the day-to-day operations of the airline and the airport.

The product in the marketplace is sometimes seen differently by different participants in the air travel business. The perception of Michael O'Leary, the CEO of Ryanair, is that Ryanair provides transportation and only transportation, whereas Etihad is providing total luxury in its 'Residence' first class suites. Etihad's 'luxury in the sky' is seemingly incidental to the transport function which the airline and its aircraft provide. So the focus moves to the customer and consequently the market. While the customer is an individual, that customer constitutes part of the market. The passenger market for air transport has been considerably enlarged by the arrival and growth of the low-cost carrier.

There is also an examination of two business models and strategies: low-cost and hybrid carriers, as well as alliances and cross-alliance activity. While KLM was the early initiator of the sixth freedom hub, the Gulf State carriers – in partnership with the airports from which they operate and the government (which is the owner of both carrier and the airport) – have developed extensive networks and very large fleets. Alliances, both branded and unbranded, are considered and there is an extended discussion of low-cost carriers and their place in the market. The focus then changes to examining options for a carrier's network; in particular, there is consideration of the main drivers of network design, and the performance indicators for the measurement of the success of network design are shown. Each airline will have its own specific framework for designing its network and elements of this framework are identified, drawing attention to the trade-offs between long- and short-term objectives.

Consideration is also given to the customer points of contact: the travel agents, call centres, carriers' websites, and the airport experience. In this regard, issues of self-handling versus third-party handling are discussed. Overall attention is given to the interface between the passengers and the airline and, in particular, expert deliberation to pricing issues and revenue management. This part concludes with a comprehensive review of the airport infrastructure required, especially the terminal planning process, and shows how terminal design should meet the needs of its two primary users, the passengers and the airlines. There is also recognition of the relationships among meeters and greeters, farewellers and suppliers with the airport and its terminal. Finally, consideration is given to the importance of airport access, especially public transport.

Note

1 Some interstate routes in some states are regulated and some subsidized.

1 Regulatory framework

Ron Bartsch

The beginning of aviation

It is no revelation that aviation and regulation are intrinsically linked. It is generally recognized that aviation is the most strictly and extensively regulated industry.[1] Managing change in the context of a highly technological and rapidly changing industry has, since the advent of aircraft, been the most challenging role of aviation regulators. Since its beginning, aviation has been subject to stringent legal and regulatory control. Regulations pertaining to flights in balloons and airships had been developed and promulgated in the eighteenth century. It all began in France in the 1780s with Joseph-Michel and Jacques-Étienne Montgolfier, sons of a wealthy paper-maker of Annonay. The brothers noticed that bags, when held above an open fire, grew lighter and lifted into the air. Joseph and Jacques discovered that hot air did not leak through paper. They experimented with balloons made of paper, and manufactured larger balloons capable of lifting considerable weight.

At the time, it was widely believed that altitude sickness would restrict manned ascents to within close proximity of the earth's surface. To test this hypothesis, the Montgolfier brothers, on 19 September 1783 in Versailles, put a sheep, a duck and a rooster in a basket attached to a hot air balloon. They named the aircraft the Aérostat Réveillon. The flight, in front of Louis XVI and Marie Antoinette, lasted just eight minutes, covered two miles and reached an altitude of approximately 1,500 feet before crashing to the ground. The flight proved that life was sustainable in the atmosphere well above the surface of the earth with the three farmyard 'passengers' surviving the ordeal. The first manned flight took place two months later from the Château de la Muette in Paris on 21 November 1783.[2] Before a crowd of 100,000 spectators, in a paper-lined silk balloon designed by the Montgolfier brothers, scientist Jean-François Pilâtre de Rozier and fellow aviator the Marquis d'Arlandes soared over Paris belching out black smoke and, on descent, nearly catching fire. It was from these beginnings that structures such as the 'Zeppelin' airships later developed, eventually leading to the Wright Brothers' historic flight in a powered fixed-wing aircraft in 1903.

The first aviation regulation

In 1784, the year following the first manned balloon flight, over 1,500 balloon flights were recorded in France, and it was clear with the rapid development in aviation activities that regulations were needed. The Paris police passed regulations on 23 April 1784 requiring flight permits for all future balloon operations. In 1819, the Chief of Police of the Seine introduced regulations requiring all balloon operations be equipped with a parachute. While earlier legislation focused more on addressing issues relating to aircraft impacting the ground, this rule appears to have been the first to promote safety on board an aircraft. Following the introduction of the airship to America in the early 1900s, the Chief Justice of the Supreme Court of Connecticut, Professor Simeon Baldwin, in 1909 wrote a treatise entitled: 'Will airships change our laws?' The publication highlighted the ramifications of airship operations upon the legal framework. Professor Baldwin raised the issue of whether airships should have the right to fly over people's property. His view was that government regulation of airships was necessary because there was no line of authority in customary or common law to settle such disputes. Considering the extent and complexity of litigation in this area today, Baldwin displayed a remarkable degree of wisdom and foresight.

Governments throughout the world were quick to respond to the increase in aviation operations and by 1911 two of the most powerful nations, Britain and the USA, had both passed domestic aviation laws to regulate and control aviation activities. Brewing political tensions in Europe, some of which were aggravated by balloon operations infringing the airspace of adjacent states, led to even greater restrictions being imposed. As a consequence of World War I, aircraft design and technology progressed at an astonishing rate. By the end of the war, the aeroplane had developed from a flimsy single-engine biplane to large, multi-engine, alloy construction transporters. Aircraft were now capable of flying significantly increased payloads higher and further than ever before and at previously unimaginable speeds. The number of aircraft also increased dramatically. To provide context to this astonishing rate of aviation development, consider the following: at the beginning of the war in 1914 Great Britain possessed only twelve military aeroplanes; by the war's end in November 1918 there were 22,000 aeroplanes. Civil airliners were waiting in the wings to play an important role in the advancement of world trade and commerce.

Although the commercial potential of this now vastly improved means of transportation was universally realized by states, it was more specifically the demonstrated capacity of aviation as a weapon that prompted governments to act to control this potentially destructive new technology. Immediately following the end of the war in Europe, and only six months after the commencement of the first regular international passenger air service, twenty-seven states signed the Convention Relating to the Regulation of Aerial Navigation in Paris on 13 October 1919. The Paris Convention (as it became known) heralded the beginning of international air law in confirming, virtually at the dawn of airline operations, the desire of governments throughout the world to systematically control aviation.

Although the First World War brought about a realization of the importance of aviation and its potential danger to nation states and their citizens, it was another seven decades until that 'potential' was fully realized.

Aviation is a form of transportation, and not surprisingly requires a unique form of regulation. It is the freedom and agility by which air transport operations can readily transcend previously restrictive geographic and political boundaries, that differentiates flying from other modes of transport. To harness this freedom, aviation regulation provides the requisite authority, responsibility and sanctions. The regulation of aviation is as fundamental and important to the industry as civil order is to modern society. Just as the acceptance of the notion of freedom of the high seas enabled maritime activities to change the world, so too has an application of this principle to international airspace, for aviation activities changed the world. It is almost impossible to imagine a world without commercial international air transportation and it is equally impossible to imagine the world of aviation without regulation. The challenges for the law to accommodate new forms of aircraft continue. The introduction of unmanned aircraft systems or remotely piloted aircraft systems (RPAS) into civil aviation has been described as being as significant to this industry sector as the advent of the jet engine. One commentator goes even further and suggests that the RPAS is arguably the greatest innovation in commercial aviation since the Wright Brothers' Flyer. With the rapid emergence of drones in the civil aviation sector, unique issues arise that challenge existing assumptions and regulatory models.[3]

Globalization of aviation

There has been a developing trend of globalization in many areas of the law. The adoption by many countries of international conventions has had a unifying influence on the regulation of certain technologies. Nowhere has this effect been more evident than with the development of aviation law. Since the mid 1990s, airlines throughout the world began establishing strategic alliances with each other. The **one**world, Star and other alliances have demonstrated the advantages and commercial benefits that can be derived from 'codesharing' and other arrangements. The work of international organizations, such as the International Air Transport Association (IATA), has also played a vital role in promoting and facilitating international cooperation and the globalization of the industry. For instance, since 2003, IATA Operational Surveillance Audits (IOSA) have provided a universally accepted system of auditing standards and practices between participating airlines. Regulatory authorities in the United States, Canada and Australia have supported this initiative. Modern technology has had an ongoing globalizing effect on the aviation industry. For example, Airservices Australia was instrumental in the development of the global Future Air Navigation System (FANS) that utilizes satellite technology to provide a more efficient air traffic system. Further, the International Civil Aviation Organization (ICAO) approval process for the assessment of Reduced Vertical Separation Minimums (RVSM) operations has consistent, globally accepted standards.

International air conventions

Today, the Convention on International Civil Aviation (Chicago Convention 1944), which updated and replaced the Paris Convention 1919, has been ratified by more than 190 sovereign states. These countries have agreed to be bound by the technical and operational standards developed by ICAO and detailed in the nineteen Annexes.

What is aviation law?

Throughout the world there has been considerable debate in relation to the formation of a universally agreed definition for the terms 'air law', 'aeronautical law' and 'aviation law'. Sometimes the terms are even used interchangeably. With respect to the terms 'air law' or the 'law of the air', if they were to apply to the literal or common meaning of the word 'air' as the medium or the atmosphere, then this would include all the law associated with the use of the air, including radio and satellite transmissions. In the main, *air law*, as it applies to aviation, has a far narrower interpretation and is generally considered to be 'the law governing the aeronautical uses of the air space'.[4] Air law is predominantly the concern of specialist lawyers. Consistent with the above definition, air law has received widespread acceptance and usage even though the actual term is somewhat of a misnomer. As Milde states:

> It is safe to conclude that the term *air law* from its inception was confined only to the legal regulation of social relations generated by the aeronautical uses of the airspace. The term *aeronautical law* would be more precise but a century of common use of the term *air law* should be respected and any terminological doubts, disputes or preferences are of no practical relevance.[5]

An alternate definition of air law, and one which has received considerable support, is 'that body of rules governing the use of airspace and its benefits for aviation, the general public and the nations of the world'.[6] The second definition significantly expands the scope of activities to which air law applies; not that there is anything fundamentally irreconcilable with the first definition. However, to deviate so substantially from the subject matter of the first definition potentially creates confusion and ambiguity as to its meaning and usage. Thus, throughout this chapter, air law will be considered as originally defined as 'that branch of law governing the aeronautical uses of airspace'.

Aviation law is a broader term than air (aeronautical) law and has been defined as 'that branch of law that comprises rules and practices which have been created, modified or developed to apply to aviation activities'.[7] Aviation law is to air law what maritime law is to the law of the sea. To assist with the clarity of expression and reduce the potential for problems arising in the application of these terms, the above definitions will respectively apply to the terms *air law* and *aviation law*.

Aviation law therefore encompasses the regulation of the business aspects of airlines and general aviation activities. Consequently, aspects of insurance law, commercial law and competition law all form part of aviation law. Security and environmental regulations applicable to aviation activities are also within the scope of aviation law. Also included within the domain of aviation law is the regulatory oversight of aviation activities by government agencies. Aviation law is not separate from other divisions of law such as the law of contract or the law of negligence. The fact that there are relatively few reported cases on aviation has tended to obscure and mask the identification of this branch of law.

International law is that body of legal rules that applies between sovereign states and such entities that have been granted international personality. Within the aviation community, the concept of international personality extends to organizations including ICAO, which is a specialized agency of the United Nations, both of which are key players in international law. International conventions (e.g., the Chicago Convention 1944 with regard to ICAO) detail and confer international personality upon organizations. As there is no sovereign international authority with the power to enforce decisions or even compel individual states to follow rules, international law has often been considered as not being a 'true law'. In aviation, however, because of the extensive and important role of international institutions such as ICAO and IATA, and the proliferation of honoured bilateral air service agreements between nations, including the almost universal ratification of international conventions concerning international civil aviation, the existence of an international air law would be difficult to deny. The branch of international air law that determines the rules between contracting states and other international personalities is known as 'public international air law'. The Paris Convention 1919 and the Chicago Convention 1944 are the charters of public international air law. This law contrasts with the law relating to private disputes in which one of the parties may be of another state. This is the realm of 'private international air law' or conflict of laws.

International air law is essentially a combination of both public and private international air law. It has been suggested that its principal purpose is to provide a system of regulation for international civil aviation and to eliminate conflicts or inconsistencies in domestic air law. Convention law is the major source of international air law, and it is constituted by multilateral and bilateral agreements between sovereign states. To provide a further insight into the application and importance of both public and private international air law to the aviation industry, three major international conventions will be examined; but first it is important to highlight the importance of the concept of sovereignty as it applies to airspace.

National sovereignty

In international aviation, the concept of sovereignty is the cornerstone upon which air law is founded. At the Paris Convention 1919, twenty-six Allied and Associated nations had to decide whether this new mode of transport was to follow the predominantly unregulated nature of international maritime operations, or whether governments would choose to regulate this new technology. It was the First World War that had brought about the realization of both the importance of aviation and its potential danger to states and their citizens by threatening their sovereignty. It was, therefore, not surprising that the first Article of the Paris Convention 1919 stated:

> The High Contracting Parties recognise that every Power has complete and exclusive sovereignty over the air space above its territory.

This proclamation addressed the debate of whether airspace was 'free', as it is with the high seas, or whether it was part of the subjacent state or territory. The decision to follow the latter path was almost unanimous. While the Paris Convention 1919 clearly asserted that exclusive or absolute sovereignty extends to the airspace above the territory of the state, issues were raised as to what constitutes the vertical and horizontal territorial limits of each state. With respect to vertical limits, customary law, based on an ancient Roman principle, had long recognized that absolute sovereignty of the state over its territorial airspace extended to an unlimited height. The Roman principle was based on an old maxim, *cujus est solum ejus usque ad coelum*, translated to mean 'whose is the soil, his is also that which is up to the sky'.

Although international treaties have since modified this position in asserting that '[no] national appropriation by claim of sovereignty' can prevent overflight rights of satellites in outer space (space beyond the navigable airspace), no precise definition of outer space is provided. The Treaty on Principles Governing the Activities of States in the Exploration and Use of Outer Space, including the Moon and Other Celestial Bodies (1967) does not provide a precise definition of outer space either. Once again, with respect to horizontal or lateral limits of sovereignty, international treaties have clarified the situation. Article 2 of the Chicago Convention 1944 states:

For the purposes of this Convention the territory of a state shall be deemed to be the land areas and the territorial waters adjacent thereto under the sovereignty, suzerainty, protection or mandate of such state.

The United Nations Convention on the Law of the Sea defines the limits to which sovereignty of the coastal state may apply to the airspace above the territorial waters or sea.[8] It is important to realize that the Paris Convention 1919 did not create the principle of exclusive air sovereignty but rather recognized it. Article 1 was drafted such that it was 'declaratory of pre-existing customary international law'.[9] Furthermore, the principle extends to all nations, irrespective of whether a particular state has signed or ratified the convention.

Subsequent conventions in Madrid in 1926 and Havana in 1928 achieved little by way of advancement in international air law. Significantly, however, the Havana (Pan-American) Convention 1928 was the first multilateral convention which challenged the principle of absolute sovereignty and was signed by the United States, Mexico and fourteen South American states. The principle of absolute sovereignty was again challenged with the Chicago Convention 1944, but ultimately the status quo prevailed. The Chicago Convention 1944 recognized and confirmed the principle that every state has complete and exclusive sovereignty over the airspace above its territory. The territory of a state for the purposes of the Chicago Convention 1944 was deemed the land areas and the territorial waters adjacent to them under the sovereignty, suzerainty, protection or mandate of the state. The question of the vertical extent of the airspace above a state's territory remains undetermined. However, the view that right in airspace extends to a height without any limit has been firmly rejected. Apart from the right of overflight by satellites in outer space, the concept of sovereignty remains the basis upon which both the structure and proliferation of bilateral air service agreements continue. This chapter now examines the most important international treaty in aviation, the Chicago Convention 1944.

Chicago Convention 1944

As in the aftermath of the First World War, the enhanced positive contribution of aviation during times of peace was again realized following the improved performance and capabilities of aircraft during the Second World War. By the end of the Second World War, advances in aircraft design and technology had culminated in the development of the first jet engine. Following preliminary discussions initiated by the British Government in early 1944, the US called for an international conference in Chicago in November 1944. It was the intention of the US and Allied nations to establish post-war civil aviation arrangements and institutions and, in particular, the US sought to promote the freedom of international exchange by removing the restrictions to international air travel imposed by absolute air sovereignty. The conference was attended by most of the established nations of the world, including Britain, the US and Australia. The general aims of the conference, in terms of promoting international air transportation, were:

- economic – including the promotion of freedom of airspace to nations and airlines; procedures for determining airfares, frequencies, schedules and capacities; arrangements for simplifying customs procedures and standardizing visas and other documentation
- technical – these were concerned with establishing international standards with respect to a variety of technical standards, including the licensing of pilots and mechanics, registering and certifying the airworthiness of aircraft, and the planning and development of navigational aids.

The resulting Chicago Convention, which was signed on 7 December 1944, only applies to civil aircraft and does not apply to state aircraft. However, Annex 13 of the Convention implies that states are expected to apply their provisions domestically. Annex 17 of the Convention was amended following the events of 11 September 2001 (9/11) to 'require' states to implement certain security standards domestically, except where it is impracticable to do so.

Freedoms of the air

As with the Paris Convention 1919, the Chicago Convention 1944 restated and reinforced the principle of absolute air sovereignty. Consequently, air transit and traffic rights between contracting states required specific agreement. The US advocated complete freedom of the air for commercial air transportation, while Britain, supported by Australia and New Zealand, proposed varying degrees of international regulation. A Canadian proposal for freedoms of the air was documented as the International Air Transport Agreement. Only twenty states signed the agreement at Chicago, including the US, but not all subsequently ratified it. Only five freedoms were discussed at Chicago. There are three other freedoms which, although not officially recognized by the Chicago Convention 1944 or granted in bilateral air service agreements, are referred to and taken into account in bilateral air service agreements.

Although nearly all the delegates at Chicago agreed that some degree of regulatory control was desirable, and indeed necessary for a cooperative development of international civil aviation, there was no general consensus apart from agreement on the first two freedoms. It was hoped that the other freedoms might be settled on a multilateral basis, but that was not practicable as the more powerful nations stood to gain more through negotiating bilateral arrangements. As the free market approach was not acceptable and multilateral approaches were not practicable, the only other way to secure international air travel consensus was by way of individual bilateral air service agreements that were negotiated between two national governments. Although there was not universal agreement as to which rights would be agreed in a multilateral treaty, there was consensus as to how such rights should be defined. The freedoms of the air can be explained as follows.

- First freedom of the air: the right or privilege, in respect of scheduled international air services, granted by one state to another state or states to fly across its territory without landing.
- Second freedom of the air: the right or privilege, in respect of scheduled international air services, granted by one state to another state or states to land in their territory for non-traffic purposes.
- Third freedom of the air: the right or privilege, in respect of scheduled international air services, granted by one state to another state to put down, in the territory of the first state, traffic coming from the home state of the carrier.
- Fourth freedom of the air: the right or privilege, in respect of scheduled international air services, granted by one state to another state to take on, in the territory of the first state, traffic destined for the home state of the carrier.
- Fifth freedom of the air: the right or privilege, in respect of scheduled international air services, granted by one state to another state to put down and take on, in the territory of the first state, traffic coming from or destined to a third state.

It should be noted that ICAO refers to all freedoms beyond the Fifth freedom as 'so-called' freedoms. The reason for this is that only the first five freedoms have been officially recognized as such by way of international treaties resulting from the Convention. The remaining 'so-called' freedoms can be described as follows:

- Sixth freedom of the air: the right or privilege, in respect of scheduled international air services, to transport, via the home state of the carrier, traffic moving between two other states. This freedom, unlike the first five, is not incorporated as such into any widely recognized air service agreements such as the 'Five Freedoms Agreement'.
- Seventh freedom of the air: the right or privilege, in respect of scheduled international air services, granted by one state to another state; whereby, the service need not connect to or be an extension of any service to or from the home state of the carrier.
- Eighth freedom of the air: the right or privilege, in respect of scheduled international air services, of transporting cabotage traffic between two points in the territory of the granting state on a service which originates or terminates in the home country of the foreign carrier or (in connection with the Seventh freedom of the air) outside the territory of the granting state.
- Ninth freedom of the air: the right or privilege of transporting cabotage traffic of the granting state on a service performed entirely within the territory of the granting state (also known as the 'stand-alone' cabotage).

Under the Chicago Convention 1944, all scheduled international air services (that either pass through airspace of more than one state, carry passengers, mail or cargo or service two or more destinations in accordance with a published timetable) must acquire prior permission before flying into or over foreign territories. To fill the gap with regard to scheduled international air services, most states, including Australia, Britain and the US, signed the International Air Services Transit (Two Freedoms) Agreement (Transit Agreement). This agreement has proven to be extremely effective in terms of simplifying overflight rights and being practical when diplomatic tensions arise between contracting states. Although in practice ICAO is authorized to resolve disputes arising from the Transit Agreement, this power is rarely invoked.

It is at the contracting state's discretion whether to adhere to the Transit Agreement. Bilateral agreements can, and usually do, include terms exchanging these two freedoms. This is an alternate arrangement for overflight rights where one or both states are not party to the multilateral agreement. The Transit Agreement does not specifically require contracting states to obtain a permit prior to exercising transit or non-traffic stopovers. In practice, irrespective of how overflight rights have been established, the filing of flight plans for operational purposes is usually all that is required to provide the requisite safety, technical and security information.

International Civil Aviation Organization (ICAO)

The most important contribution of the Chicago Convention 1944 was the agreement over technical matters and the groundwork which led to the establishment of ICAO. ICAO is without doubt the most important international organization in the area of public international air law. Article 44 of the Chicago Convention 1944 describes the purpose of ICAO:

> To develop the principles and techniques of international air navigation and foster the planning and development of international air transport so as to insure the safe and orderly growth of international civil aviation throughout the world.

On 6 June 1945, the required twenty-sixth state, including each of the twenty states elected to the ICAO Council, had accepted the Interim Agreement on International Civil Aviation. The 'Provisional' ICAO or PICAO came into effect as planned within six months of the signing of the Chicago Convention 1944. It was agreed by member states that PICAO would remain in operation until the permanent forum, ICAO, came into force within the three-year limit prescribed in the convention. ICAO provides the structure for the achievement of international cooperation and coordination in civil aviation. Through a variety of mechanisms, ICAO works to uphold the principles underlying the Chicago Convention 1944. It develops and adopts internationally agreed standards and procedures for the regulation of civil aviation, coordinates the provision of air navigation facilities on a regional and worldwide basis, collates and publishes information on international civil aviation, and acts as the medium by which aviation law develops at an international level.

Apart from technical matters, ICAO has also been instrumental in providing the organizational structure for the determination of less contentious economic arrangements. ICAO has addressed matters such as customs procedures and visa requirements, and also assumed responsibility for collecting statistical data for international civil aviation, including information on safety-related issues, most notably incident and accident statistics. The international specifications for civil aviation appear in nineteen Annexes to the Chicago Convention 1944. Each Annex addresses a particular subject. The specifications are divided into two categories, namely, Standards and Recommended Practices, although they are collectively, and most commonly, referred to as 'SARPs'. Today, the 190 signatories of the Chicago Convention 1944 are obliged to comply with the extensive and comprehensive technical, safety, operational, security and environmental provisions as set out in the SARPs. In the next part of this chapter, we move into the area of private international air law and, in particular, to carriage by air. This aspect of commercial aviation law was not considered at the Chicago Convention and has developed into a separate, distinct branch of aviation law.

Carriage by air

International carriage by air is predominantly governed by international conventions. These international conventions were established as a result of the development in the air transport industry and were aimed at addressing conflict of law problems commonly associated with international carriage.

Warsaw Convention 1929

The first true instrument of private international air law was the Convention for the Unification of Certain Rules Relating to International Carriage by Air (Warsaw Convention 1929). It adopted a uniform set of rules governing international carriage by air, and deals with the rights of passengers and owners or consignors of cargo and provides for internationally accepted limits on a carrier's liability for death, injury or damage. Prior to the establishment of the Warsaw system, there were no uniform rules of law concerning international carriage by air. The problems inherent in international air travel often relate to matters concerning conflicts of law. The rights of passengers and owners of cargo, most of which had been previously stated in the contract of carriage, would vary from country to country and in accordance with each country's domestic law. Similarly, the liabilities of the carriers would vary enormously. The Warsaw Convention 1929 represented the first uniform international effort to implement universal laws relating to international air carriage, especially in respect of carriers' liability. The implementation of internationally accepted limits on a carrier's liability for death, injury or damage was also a driving force which ultimately led to the Warsaw Convention of 1929. At that time airlines were predominantly state-owned and particularly supportive of the introduction of known limits on liability. Arguments advanced in favour of liability limits included:

- protection of a developing and financially vulnerable aviation industry
- distribution of potentially large risks
- practicality of carriers being able to fully insure against liabilities
- standardized and readily quantifiable damages awards
- allowing passengers to take out their own insurance policies
- reducing litigation against airlines and facilitating settlement of disputes.

The objectives of the Warsaw Convention 1929 were achieved for approximately two decades after implementation, but its effectiveness and support have been gradually eroded. In an attempt to retain its effectiveness, the Warsaw Convention 1929 was updated several times by way of amendments. As a consequence of the US (and other countries) not having adopted all of the subsequent amendments to the Warsaw Convention 1929, a non-uniform international system of liability of carriers governing international air carriage emerged. Moreover, the terminology and language used in the Warsaw

Convention 1929 (and amending protocols) had become outdated, and was the source of much ambiguity and dispute. It is important to realize that the Warsaw Convention 1929 only applies to international carriage. There is case law on this topic but it is not necessary to review it in this overview chapter.

Montreal Convention 1999

The development of various international conventions relevant to international air carriage, in the context of a maturing commercial aviation industry, gave rise to a complex system of international treaties, many of which have now become unwieldy and outdated. Although the Montreal Convention 1999 consolidates the many amendments to the Warsaw Convention 1929, it is an entirely new treaty that unifies and replaces the system of liability established by the Warsaw Convention 1929 and its subsequent amendments. Prior to the introduction of the Montreal Convention 1999, compensation limits remained generally low, in line with the early philosophies aimed at supporting a fledgling air transport industry. The industry, despite present-day challenges, has developed significantly in respect of its commercial stability and relative safety standards. Commercial arrangements such as interline, codeshares and airline alliance agreements and the complex nature of international trade have led to practices never envisaged by the drafters of earlier conventions, such as electronic documentation in place of traditional paper tickets and air waybills (AWBs).

The Montreal Convention 1999 establishes an alternative carriage by air regime for determining the liability of air carriers for injury or death of a passenger, loss of or damage to luggage or cargo and damage caused by, or delay in, the transport of passengers, luggage or cargo which occurs during the course of international carriage. Overall, the Montreal Convention 1999 has sought to address the problems that developed in the Warsaw system by substantially raising carriers' liability limits, presenting the liability framework in a single consistent convention and updating the language and terminology used. The Montreal Convention 1999 – also referred to by its abbreviation 'MC99' – distinguishes between international and domestic carriage. The convention applies to international carriage only. The convention lists five guiding principles agreed by its contracting parties as a preamble to its substantive provisions. Specifically, the Montreal Convention 1999:

- recognizes the significant contribution of the Warsaw Convention 1929 (as amended) to the harmonization of private international air law
- recognizes the need to modernize and consolidate the Warsaw Convention 1929 (as amended)
- recognizes the importance of ensuring protection of consumer interests in international air transport and the need for equitable compensation based upon the principle of restitution
- reaffirms the desirability of the orderly development of international air operations and the smooth flow of passengers, baggage and cargo in accordance with the Chicago Convention 1944

- promotes collective state action for further harmonization and codification of certain rules governing international air carriage through a new convention as the most adequate means of balancing interests.

Interesting issues have arisen throughout the ratification and implementation process of the Montreal Convention 1999. Legislation in operation in the European Union (EU) has taken a broad interpretation of the provisions of the convention. EC Regulation 261/2004, in particular, has attracted much attention. Argued to be overly-focused on 'passenger protection', the regulation imposes obligations on carriers to assist passengers in the event of delay, including those situations where the events giving rise to a delay are beyond the control of the carrier, such as adverse weather conditions or air traffic disruptions. This regulation proved to be particularly controversial because it has the potential to affect foreign, non-European carriers, and also since it appears to contravene those provisions of the Montreal Convention 1999 which provide carriers with a defence in circumstances where delay is beyond their control. Further such issues will probably continue to arise as additional implementing legislation is introduced by various state parties, who are likely to look to the example set by the EU as a point of guidance and comparison – most notably the 'Passenger Bill of Rights' enacted by the State of New York in the US and later overturned by the US Courts.

Differences between the Warsaw and Montreal Conventions

It is important to note that carriage under the Warsaw system does not cease to be legally binding because of the entry into force of the Montreal Convention 1999. The Warsaw Convention 1929 still applies to round trips departing from a state which is not a signatory to the Montreal Convention 1999 and to one-way flights between two states where either has adhered to the Montreal Convention 1999. The convention applies to all international air carriage in which the country of departure and the country of destination have both adopted it. The Montreal Convention 1999 establishes a new two-tiered scheme to govern passenger compensation. The first tier, which operates up to 100,000 Special Drawing Rights (SDRs), imposes strict liability upon the carrier. SDRs are an international monetary reserve currency created by the International Monetary Fund. They have the advantage of not being subject to national currency exchange fluctuations as was the case when French Francs were the basis of the Warsaw System.

The carrier's liability under the first tier can only be reduced by the demonstrated contributory negligence of the passenger. Liability under the second tier is unlimited if damages are proven in excess of 100,000 SDR, but can be avoided by the carrier proving that the damage was not caused by its negligence or was caused solely by the negligence or other wrongful act or omission of a third party. The Montreal Convention 1999 only applies if the parties agree to its application to transportation between two locations (the destination may be changed during the flight or the flight may be a round trip). This rule excludes pilot training and test flights. Although carriage occurs in these examples, it does not occur pursuant to a contract of carriage. Therefore, the Montreal Convention is excluded by the absence of a contract and not by the absence of carriage. It follows that carriage does not need to be defined according to the parties' subjective intentions. As at 2016 over 130 states have adopted the Montreal Convention, and accordingly the importance and application of the Warsaw Convention 1929 was significantly reduced.

As the Montreal Convention 1999 applies to international carriage only, it is imperative, in the first instance, to determine whether or not a particular flight is domestic or international.[10] International carriage under the convention includes baggage (luggage) and cargo. In the case of cargo, Article 4 of the convention requires that every carrier of cargo has the right to require the consignor to generate an air consignment note, called an 'air waybill'. Every consignor has the right to require the carrier to accept this document. The question arises as to whether the convention provides an exclusive right of action in respect of claims arising from international air transportation.[11]

International harmonization

The extent to which there has been an adoption of international treaties such as the Chicago Convention 1944 and the Montreal Convention 1999 is unique to aviation. The Montreal Convention 1999 not only influences all aviation activities: that is, international, domestic and, to an increasing degree, military, but to a large and increasing extent, dictates all operational, technical, safety and security standards within the industry. The study of international air law is important; not just to attain a more complete picture of aviation in its international environment, but rather to provide a clear understanding of the legal basis upon which all aviation law is founded. As an industry, what makes aviation unique can be explained in terms of both its development and the way in which it is regulated. These two aspects of aviation, although quite distinct, are in fact highly interrelated and, to a large extent, explain why there is a greater degree of international harmonization of aviation legislation than with any other industry. From the outset, aviation activities have been subject to strict regulatory control.

It is worth mentioning that the trend of international harmonization, towards universal conformity of aviation standards, is not only increasing but is doing so at an ever-increasing rate. The catalyst for this was the First World War and the trend has continued to be fuelled by subsequent major worldwide events including the Second World War, international terrorism, government economic rationalization, airline strategic alliances, pandemics and epidemics, customer loyalty (frequent-flyer) programmes, codesharing, global reservation systems, highly dynamic oil prices, the proliferation of low-cost carriers, internet bookings, the global financial crisis of 2007–2008, and increased government liberalization towards more and more 'open skies' policies. New aerospace technologies, such as the challenges arising with the integration of unmanned aircraft into civilian airspace, likewise have a universal harmonizing effect.[12] Quite unlike any other mode of transportation, aviation activities are not restricted by political and geographical boundaries. The 'internationalization' of aviation activities and the legal processes will persist until international harmonization is absolute.

Notes

1 Milde, M. 2008. *International Air Law and ICAO*, Eleven International Publishing, Montreal, Canada.
2 For a more detailed account of the development of aviation regulations see Bartsch, R. 2012. *International Aviation Law,* Ashgate Publishing, London. pp. 14–23.
3 For a detailed account of the development of regulations for unmanned aircraft see Bartsch, R. 2017. *Drones in Society*, Routledge, United Kingdom.
4 Milde, M. 2008. *International Air Law and ICAO*, Eleven International Publishing, Montreal, Canada.
5 Op. cit.
6 Diederiks-Verschoor, I.H. Philepina. 2012. *An Introduction to Air Law,* Kluwer Law International, The Netherlands.
7 Bartsch, R. 2012. *International Aviation Law,* Ashgate Publishing, London.
8 United Nations Convention on the Law of the Sea (UNCLOS), 1982.
9 Haanappel, P. 1998. 'The Transformation of Sovereignty in the Air', in Cheng, C-J. (ed.), *The Use of Air and Outer Space: Co-operation and Competition,* Martinus Nijhoff Publishers, The Netherlands.
10 The leading authority on this issue is *Stratis v Eastern Airlines Limited* 682 F.2d 406 (2d Cir. 1982).
11 This question was discussed in the context of the Warsaw Convention 1929 in *Sidhu v British Airways* (Scotland) [1997] AC 430.
12 See Chapter 3, Bartsch, R. 2012. *International Aviation Law,* Ashgate Publishing, London.

2 Market, product, and customer

Rodney Williams

The market

There are multiple markets in which an airline can choose to operate, but the primary question in choosing the markets in which to operate is 'Can a reasonable financial return be expected from participation in that market, or does that participation enhance the overall financial performance of other activities within the airline?'. The first decision is in which network environment the carrier will operate – domestic, international or a combination of both. The carrier may have a phased strategy – for example, choosing to start domestic operations, then once firmly established, expanding into international services. Once decided, each of these networks can be further divided into three broad markets – passenger, freight, and servicing, with each having a number of sub-segments.

Passenger market

The passenger market can be split broadly on the basis of purpose of travel – business or leisure. The most lucrative segment has always been the business traveller; specifically, the loyalty of the frequent business traveller which is a prized possession almost regardless of the class of travel. For an airline that chooses to participate in the business traveller sub-segment, then almost the entire product offering of the airline is tailored to meet the demands of this sub-market, whether that be the aircraft type selected, the physical on-board product (cabins and catering), schedule frequency and reach, fare structure and distribution, ground product (priority check-in, lounges, valet), or partner connections (loyalty programmes, codeshares, global alliances).

Freight market

The freight market can be split into several subcategories, such as mail, excess and unaccompanied baggage, express courier, perishables, live cargo (such as racehorses and seafood) and general cargo. Unlike the passenger market (which is normally a round trip, in which the customer returns to their home city after each trip), freight is generally a one-way product – that is to say, the product, for example live seafood, is time sensitive and travels from source to the dinner table; never returning to its source. As such, freight loads are generally highly directional, resulting in high load factors on some segments with corresponding low load factors on the return service, as empty containers are returned to be reused for the next shipment. In many aspects, the freight market has a significantly different structure to the passenger market, with several carriers opting to sub-lease the cargo hold capacity of their aircraft fleet (after allowing for passenger baggage space requirements) to specialist cargo and logistic operators who undertake the sales, warehousing and airport ground operations of loading and unloading the freight.

Servicing market

The servicing market, while comparatively small, can often be lucrative, either as standalone business units or as a means of smoothing out peaks and troughs within the airline's own business. Activities within this segment include engineering and maintenance, catering operations, ground handling services, warehousing, crew training (both technical and cabin), travel and tour sales and services, and leasing and chartering of aircraft. For example, an airline acquires a B787 flight simulator to train its technical crew, but it may only be used for fourteen hours each day. The remaining ten hours per day, after undertaking necessary maintenance and cleaning, can be sold to other airlines or individuals for training, using their own training teams or those of the simulator owner.

Each of these markets provides a source of revenue (along with complexity in structure and costs) that an airline can access, and the mix of revenues varies greatly depending on the structure of the airline. Devising a good mix of revenues from varying market segments can assist in reducing the impacts of external shocks and general economic fluctuations. For example, if freight revenue forms a significant proportion of a carrier's business, then the financial impacts of, say, a SARS (Severe Acute Respiratory Syndrome) outbreak may be reduced. Freight revenue would probably be less affected by such an outbreak, while passenger revenue would almost certainly dip. In general, however, most airlines operate primarily in the passenger market, deriving more than eighty-five per cent of revenue from passenger operations, with freight and servicing activities providing additional sources of revenue.

Market segmentation

In order to communicate with and engage customers effectively, the airline must first be able to identify them clearly. Market segmentation is a process whereby the customer base can be divided into smaller, defined groupings, which often have unique characteristics. In the passenger market, a number of further sub-markets (or segments) can be identified as follows:

- purpose of trip – business, holiday, visiting friends and relatives (VFR), education

- profile of traveller – age, income category, occupation, nationality
- characteristics of trip – domestic or international, short- or long-haul, duration (day, week, month, weekend).

Through market research and data analysis, subcategories of passengers can be identified and defined by combining a number of these characteristics – for example, Australian residents of Chinese background managing business from Australia requiring frequent short trips to north Asia. Once these subgroupings have been identified, then the marketing mix – Price, Product, Place and Promotion – can be tailored to meet their needs and wants. The airline can also monitor each segment better once its characteristics have been identified. Trends can be followed more easily and lucrative segments can be grown at the expense of lower margin segments. The identification of the frequent traveller segment led to the development of loyalty schemes in the 1980s which were designed to retain these passengers within the airline grouping.

Product differentiation and service

Fundamentally, commercial airlines have a limited choice of aircraft, which are supplied predominantly from just two companies, Airbus or Boeing, although Embraer and Bombardier have fleet offerings in the 70- to 140-seat market. Cabin layout, while varied, is also limited, and between carriers (in particular full-service carriers), there is a continuous race as to which carrier can introduce the next advancement in seating, inflight entertainment (IFE), catering, lounges, or on-board service offering in order to atract the lucrative business traveller. A major problem is that all of these changes/advancements require considerable capital investment, while concurrently their lifecycle (the time interval between each refurbishment) is reducing. A fundamental dilemma is presented then that the money invested in a product and its improvement sometimes cannot be justified on financial grounds. However, to stay relevant, carriers must modernize in order to keep passengers returning and hopefully prevent them shifting to competitors. While price can be used as a weapon to counter any customer-perceived shortfall in product offering, this will only be effective in the short term, for as time goes by, the product differences will become too great. Two programmes – Frequent-flyer (or Loyalty) and Alliances – have been developed and deployed by carriers to aid in attraction and retention of passengers. Alliances will be considered more fully in Chapter 3.

Loyalty programmes

Frequent-flyer programmes were initially launched in the USA in the early 1980s by American Airlines (AA) in order to protect its market share during deregulation. The programmes are now a fundamental element of most airline marketing tools and an essential benefit for frequent travellers. Initially, programme points were only earned as a result of flying, with the number of points earned dependent on distance travelled, value of the airfare purchased, class of travel (First, Business, Economy), or a combination of these elements. The very frequent travellers soon accumulated more points than they could use. To retain these loyal travellers, the airlines then introduced 'status tiers' based on flights taken and distance travelled. As travellers moved up the tiers (Silver, Gold, Platinum), services offered and value-added benefits were enhanced. Status tier benefits soon became as important to frequent traveller as the points themselves, if not more so, as status tier benefits permitted access to lounges, priority services and personalized recognition by the airline's staff. High status tier members are really the 'frequent flyers' and generally represent less than seven per cent of the membership of an airline's programme. However, most members of an airline's frequent-flyer programme are non-flyers or low-frequency travellers.

The lure of air travel is, however, sufficient to encourage large sections of the general public to become members of these schemes, with many people often having active membership in two or more airline programmes simultaneously. Some carriers require air travel to be undertaken, say, every three years in order to retain points and/or miles. As a result, programmes have changed their names from frequent-flyer to loyalty programmes, designed to maintain loyalty to the airline brand while making everyday purchases of products and services including groceries, online shopping, car rentals, hotel stays, restaurant dining, insurance, real estate or petrol. Points are earned on every transaction, and often twice, if paid for with a credit card that is aligned with the programme. Loyalty programmes are now very powerful marketing tools, maintaining allegiances while also creating substantial cash flows to airlines. Programmes continue to grow their membership and expand into new areas of the economy, directing loyalty to one brand and its partners.

Codesharing

The rate of growth within commercial aviation, particularly since deregulation in the USA, combined with the introduction of aircraft such as the Boeing 747, has provided the opportunity to travel the globe safely and cheaply. No single airline has the ability to cover the entire globe, despite the travelling public's desire to access all corners of the earth, whether for business or leisure. The need to cater to the demands of their own passenger base led carriers into new areas of cooperation. The late 1980s saw rapid growth in codeshare services. All airlines operate services using a unique IATA-approved designator. For example, Lufthansa has LH, Qantas – QF, Japan Airlines – JL. To this designator, the airline's flight number is added in order to get a unique service code; for example, LH123, QF64, JL507. Codesharing allows one carrier – the operating carrier – to accept the code of another carrier – the marketing carrier – thus creating two 'flights' on a single aircraft. For example, Qantas does not fly the domestic sector Tokyo to Sapporo. Assuming Qantas has the bilateral traffic rights to do so, then Qantas could enter into an agreement with Japan Airlines and codeshare on this sector. The actual flight would be operated by Japan Airline's Flight JL456, together with Qantas's marketing code of QF5678. Both carriers could then sell the same service under two flight numbers. The series of flight numbers used emanates from the way in which carriers group their flight numbers in range bandings such as 1–300, 301–700, 1000–3500, 5000–5400, 9000–9999, in order to readily identify their operations such as (in no specific order) domestic, international, codeshare, charter, training, and disruption management flights.

Types of codeshares

Codeshares fall broadly into two types: 'freesale' codeshares and 'hardblock' codeshares. In a freesale codeshare situation, the marketing carrier is able to sell any number of seats on the operating carrier's flight. The price is either at a negotiated level or at an agreed discount from published fares. When the codeshare is a hardblock, the marketing carrier agrees to buy from the operating carrier a specific number of seats at an agreed price, and to pay the operating carrier for all of the seats (i.e. the block) irrespective of the number of seats sold. The contract for seat purchase may include clauses which allow 'clawback' by the operating carrier, hand-back by the marketing carrier, or even allow the marketing carrier to buy more seats. The commitment to such a block of seats by the marketing carrier is 'pro-price' competition, as it must sell as many seats as possible in order to profit on the route.

There have been growing concerns about the anticompetitive impacts of codesharing particularly where there is only one operator and where there is little or no scope for third carrier competition on a route. An absence of Fifth or Sixth freedom competition is a barrier to the competitive nature of codesharing. In 2016, Australia's International Air Services Commission (IASC) made a decision which prevented Qantas from codesharing as marketing carrier with Air Niugini as operating carrier on the Cairns–Port Moresby–Cairns (CNS–POM–CNS) route. The IASC, however, approved codesharing on the Brisbane–Port Moresby route where there are three operators (QF, PX and VA) and where the type of codeshare sought was a freesale; that is, that there was no hardblock purchase of seats by the marketing carrier. Hardblocks are generally perceived as operating in a more competitive way, as the marketing carrier is incentivized to sell as many seats as possible in the block it has purchased from the operating carrier. The pressure to sell seats results in price competition. In freesale codeshares, there is limited opportunity for price competition, as the marketing carrier only pays the operating carrier for the seats it actually sells.

There is also a widely held view that codeshares act as a deterrent to the entry of third carriers on a route, especially when the dominant carriers codeshare on each other's services. This was true in the proposed CNS–POM example above. In the United States, the US Department of Justice has intervened in the approval of the sale of Virgin America to Alaskan Airlines to prevent Alaskan codesharing with American Airlines on routes which were previously operated by Virgin America, and on which Alaskan and Virgin were competitors to American. To have done otherwise was seen as reducing the competitive environment. In

Europe, the European Union has also restricted some codeshares which were perceived to prevent or inhibit competition in the market.

Codesharing allows an airline to create what is called a 'virtual network', offering its passengers a greatly enhanced network by utilizing the actual network of another carrier. Benefits such as frequent-flyer programmes and lounge access, for example, can be extended by the marketing carrier to its passengers on the marketing flight number. The effect of this is to maintain the loyalty of its own passengers who actually travel on another carrier. The operating carrier will charge for the seats, with the marketing carrier then adding these 'costs of loyalty' plus a reasonable profit margin, in order to determine the price at which to sell the marketing seats. Codesharing has proven to be an extremely efficient way of quickly expanding an airline's network without the need for the heavy capital investment in new fleet and ground infrastructure. The proliferation of codeshares means that today many airlines offer more flights and destinations via codeshare than with their own aircraft.

Alliances

In less than a decade since the rapid growth of codeshare services, the world's first global alliance, Star, was formed by five carriers in May 1997. Soon after, on 1 February 1999, **one**world was established, followed quickly, in June 2000, by SkyTeam. Since then, competition between many airlines has sustainably transformed into competition between alliances. Of course, joint operations between a limited number of carriers were in existence in the late 1940s and 1950s, but these were closer to today's antitrust immunized joint ventures. All three global alliances have a similar structure – carriers based in the USA and Europe form the core of the alliances, adding carriers with similar service and standards from other geographic areas such as Asia, Latin America, Africa, the Middle East and Australasia. The aim is to cover as wide an area as possible, align products and services, networks, and so forth, in order to provide 'seamless' global coverage to all member-carrier passengers as if they were travelling on their own home country's airline.

The cost of this alignment can often be high when initial links are established. For example, IT standardization can be a major expenditure in joining an alliance. The need to maintain certain mandatory alliance product offerings may also restrict a carrier from modifying its own unique product for its customer base. Additionally, as carriers become members of a global alliance, cooperation with other carriers may significantly reduce or even stop, such as, for example, domestic interline passenger feed and its associated revenue flows. The target market for all three global alliances is the business traveller, the most lucrative passenger market in the airline business. Specifically, for an airline, the loyalty of the frequent business traveller is prized, almost regardless of class of travel, and that continues to apply when it comes to global alliances. For those airlines with small domestic customer bases, global alliances are heavily targeted to the international frequent traveller, as it is this market segment that offers the highest return to airlines on their alliance investment and for whom alliances can offer the most benefit. Understanding this target market helps explain the types of benefits alliances deliver and why some travellers will receive little benefit at all from global alliances.

Whilst revenue benefits flow almost immediately on joining an alliance, cost benefits achieved through collaboration have still to be fully achieved despite alliances now having been around for twenty years. Why? Because perceived 'brand values' of carriers often hinder the potential cost savings available through joint procurement and simplification. So, from the basic objective of delivering global travel as easy and seamless as if on one airline, there are four key propositions that global alliances generally offer the traveller:

- global access – via codeshare and schedule harmonization (i.e. a better spread of schedule choice and routings across the day or week)
- seamless travel – via coordinated schedules, simplified pricing, interline electronic ticketing, through-check of baggage and seating, terminal co-location, one point of service contact (i.e. one alliance member can service the needs of another member's passenger, even if the passenger isn't travelling with that carrier)
- recognition – via frequent-flyer programmes (points and status), lounge access and priority handling and boarding
- value – via lower fares, simplified round-the-world fares and regional air passes, and discounts to corporate clients.

There are obviously clear benefits for the frequent traveller in global alliances. To illustrate where these benefits provide real value to an alliance member's passengers, take the case of Air New Zealand. Table 2.1 shows that the Star Alliance offers Air New Zealand's passengers global access to benefits they could only get on Air New Zealand's limited services before joining the alliance.

	AIR NEW ZEALAND	✈
Lounge access	20 international lounges	Over 1,100 lounges
Frequent-flyer status and recognition	1 airline	28 airlines
Status miles	1 airline	28 airlines
Earn and redemption airpoints	1 airline	28 airlines
Priority check-in	30 international airports/ 1 airline 30 international destinations	More than 1300 airports
Additional baggage allowance	1 airline 30 international destinations	28 airlines / More than 1300 airports

Table 2.1 Air New Zealand and STAR alliance access

Source: www.airnewzealand.co.nz/; www.staralliance.com/

Pricing

Pricing is a crucial element in airline management. In general terms, until the late 1990s, airfare pricing was controlled by governments and industry bodies. However, today pricing has become one of the key drivers of business, and in many market segments it is generally quite volatile. There are two basic factors that determine the level of price in a market place – supply and demand. A fundamental characteristic of demand theory is that as price falls, demand for the product will rise and vice versa. Hence, there is an inverse relationship between price and quantity demanded. Economists call this relationship the law of demand. Basically, price is an obstacle to people travelling more often – lower the fare and in general, more people will be willing to travel. Pricing, combined with several other product and service features, can generate demand. But pricing is the key mechanism whereby the demand for air services is matched with the supply. The business imperative of an airline is to sell the capacity it has placed in the market place at the prices it sets that will return an acceptable profit. Apart from price, other major determinants of demand are the total market size for that particular segment, the price competitors are offering, the preference of passengers, the passengers' ability to pay, alternative transport options, and passengers' expectations of future prices – both increases and decreases.

Most airlines will normally have a clear profit objective, taking into account return of shareholder funds and return on capital invested, but there may be other corporate objectives, sometimes driven – in the case of state owned airlines – by national objectives. These other objectives may impinge on pricing policy, and may include expansion into new routes and new markets, rapid growth, or the attainment of a particular size of operation. Many airlines want to be large and cover as many points on the globe as possible. There may be cost advantages to growth and size, but ultimately the purpose of growth should be to maximize profit. A further role of pricing is that it should, in theory, be a guide to new investment. Where demand (the number of consumers who are prepared to pay the price (including a reasonable profit) of the services they consume) exceeds supply, then producers have a clear indication that if they can supply more at the same or a lower price, demand should grow, and profits be generated. Conversely, if total sales do not generate sufficient revenue to cover the full costs of services offered, rational businesses would not invest in expansion. If pricing is to be used as a guide to further investment, the prices charged should reflect the full cost of production, plus a reasonable profit.

Inherent instability of airline tariffs

Airline profitability depends on the interplay of three variables – unit costs, unit revenues (also known as yields) and the load factors (both passenger and freight) achieved. Managers must juggle all three variables to produce a profitable combination which is sustainable over time. This is a very dynamic and interactive process, made more difficult by the pricing instability inherent in the airline industry. While the aviation industry in the main is a fixed cost business, short-term marginal costs are close to zero. That is to say, the marginal cost of carrying an extra passenger on a flight which is due to depart in sixty minutes is no more than the cost of additional airport passenger taxes, reservation costs, a meal and a few kilograms of fuel. The problem is that even when operating with high year-round load factors of eighty per cent or more, there will still be a significant number of empty seats. Or to put it another way, up to twenty per cent of seats on average are empty – about thirty-five empty seats on a B737, or ninety empty seats on an A380, for each and every flight every day!

The product that airlines offer – a seat or a volume of cargo capacity – is extremely perishable. Seats or cargo capacity cannot be stored to be sold later. If they aren't sold at the time of departure (i.e. at the time of production) the opportunity to gain revenue on those seats is lost forever. An airline committed to operating its published schedule for a particular season (or a tour operator committed to a series of charter flights) understands that its short-term total costs are effectively fixed and therefore it makes business sense to try to maximize short-term revenues. Having sold as much capacity as possible at normal fares, the airline is tempted to sell any remaining empty seats at discounted prices, provided the fare covers the very low marginal cost of carrying the additional passengers. The problem is how to prevent 'slippage' or diversion of traffic by passengers who are prepared to book early and pay the applicable fares, into buying *lower* fares. If slippage does occur, the total revenue generated may fall as passengers may be encouraged to wait, knowing that the fare will become cheaper. Another issue is whether this 'last minute' traffic comes from other services on the same city pair operated by the carrier, from other destinations operated by the same carrier, or from competitor services. Alternatively, the market may have grown as a result of the lower pricing. Answers to these questions are difficult to provide and measure. The way in which the airline industry prices its product – both passenger and freight – has evolved into an extremely complex process. Chapter 5 addresses general pricing issues in more detail as well as yield management.

Structure of passenger fares

The price a consumer pays for an airline seat has evolved over time, such that today, an airline ticket is probably the most segmented product a consumer can buy. There are literally millions of prices in the market today with dozens of different prices per city pair. It is an interesting situation given that the basic product – transportation of a passenger from one city to another – is the same for everyone on the aircraft no matter what price they paid, a point that generates a lot of criticism. Despite the criticism, the pricing of air transportation has evolved to the point where it is today, because it benefits both the airlines and the passengers. In earlier days of air travel there was only one price, the full Economy fare set by the government or industry body, and the consumer could buy that fare at any time up until departure. As new cabins were introduced, a

First class fare was added, but there continued to be only two alternative prices available in the market place, a First class fare or an Economy class fare, both of which could be bought up to twelve months from departure or even at the airport on the day. Airlines competed on service, reputation, schedule and network, but not on price.

With the introduction of larger jet aircraft in the 1970s, alternative cheaper pricing was introduced on certain international routes in the form of advanced purchase or APEX fares. These fares carried certain restrictions in that they required the advance purchase of a round-trip ticket and set minimum and maximum lengths of stay at the destination point, but they were sold at significant discounts to the full fare previously on offer. Shortly after, often following deregulation, these types of fares spread to domestic markets and thus the practice of fare differentiation was born. With it came an explosion of different fare types on the same routes, as airlines fought to grow travel demand, divert business travelling by rail and road to aviation, and gain a larger share of the total market – a practice that is now common throughout most of the world.

Fare differentiation generated the need for more sophisticated revenue and inventory management systems to enable airlines to maximize the demand for the differently priced products. Revenue Management is now an essential tool for any competitive airline, and is discussed more fully in Chapter 5. Although today there are still fully flexible full fares available in all cabins (First, Business, Premium Economy and Economy) there is a plethora of differentiated fares, mainly but not only, in the Economy cabin, aimed at a wide range of different market segments. These are the majority of airfares sold today.

An overview of market demand for air travel in any market will show that there are varying levels of demand by direction, by month, by day of the week, and by time of day. Hence there is a need to stimulate demand at certain periods and today, price is the main driver of such stimulation. The way airfares are designed is actually in the reverse order typically used in the segmentation process. Normally the product is designed with characteristics that are favourable to different market segments. Using the motor industry for example, the base model car has no 'options' included and is therefore priced at the lowest level. 'Options' such as air conditioning, a sunroof, entertainment systems, etc., are added in order to make the car more desirable to various customer segments, with the price of the car including options being higher than the base model.

Airfares, on the other hand, have as their base a product that has all the options (flexibility, refunds, changeability, among others) built in and priced at the highest level. From this 'base', a range of other products at lower prices are offered, which have a number of restrictions (i.e. fewer options) 'added' to them to make them less desirable and therefore cheaper. These restrictions are put in place to discourage consumers who are willing to pay the full fare from buying the cheaper fare. At the same time, they can encourage consumers who cannot pay the highest fares to travel by air instead of by some other form of transportation (road, rail, sea) or who may consider air travel beyond their means. Hence, these restrictions divide the market into two broad passenger

	High fares	Low fares
Passenger type	Business traveller	Leisure traveller
Cabin	First / Business / Economy	Economy
Restrictions	Nil or few	Multiple
Time of travel	Weekday, early morning / late afternoon	Weekends, Saturday nights, Sunday mornings, midday on week days, public holidays
Season	School holidays, Lunar New Year, Christmas, major events	Mid-winter, wet season, cyclone season
Routing	Non-stop	Multi-stop

Table 2.2 Fare restrictions categorized by factor

segments – business and leisure. Airlines target these segments by creating products that appeal to them sufficiently to encourage them to travel, but also discourage those *willing* to pay a higher fare from purchasing lower fares. These restrictions apply to a wide range of different factors as shown in Table 2.2.

In moving from conceptual responsibility to real-time practice, airline pricing becomes quite complex. The pricing process is heavily dependent on automation as a result of having many different fare levels published which then have to be changed as an airline responds to competitors' changes and initiatives. Having set the airfare that will be charged for a particular market segment, the airline then publishes that airfare in the marketplace. The fare, with all its restrictions, will be communicated to a distribution company, which in turn broadcasts the information to all participating airline computer reservation systems (CRS) and global distribution systems (GDS) like Sabre, Amadeus, Travelport, etc. These companies then load their systems with the updated information to facilitate automated itinerary pricing for travel agents or travel websites.

Over 500 airlines participate in this fare filing process via the Airline Tariff Publishing Company (ATPCO), which is jointly owned and funded by a number of airlines. ATPCO serves as an electronic clearinghouse for fare information and changes. Year round, ATPCO accepts thousands of fare changes per hour, consolidates and processes the changes, then transmits and displays these changes to all carriers every four to six hours. At any point in time, because carriers collectively serve tens of thousands of origin and destination (O and D) market-pairs with each O and D having multiple fares often in several cabins, the total fare inventory managed by ATPCO is in the millions of individual fares. Any single airline's share of ATPCO's database may amount to several hundred thousand fares, with carriers charged a small fee each time they list or update a fare.

In deregulated domestic markets like Australia, airlines are able to set their own fare levels according to 'what the market will bear' or in other words, at market levels. In other domestic environments, the government may set the airfare prices for all airlines. Australia also does not require international fares to be filed as there is total deregulation of both international and domestic fares. However, some countries, such as Japan, Russia, and many African countries, either set fares or require filing. With the growth of Global Alliances (Star, oneworld and SkyTeam), alliance fare products have further simplified 'Round the World' (RTW) fare offerings, with these products now accounting for the bulk of RTW fare purchases due to their comprehensiveness, global coverage, minimum rules and restrictions, and ease of sale.

Unpublished fares

While all the fares described above are made public, either via CRS and GDS, or on carriers' websites, there is another broad group of fares that are not public (often for competitive reasons) which are described as unpublished fares. These fares are provided directly to corporate clients, individual travel agencies or travel agency groupings, and sometimes to individuals who will ticket directly with the airline. Airlines are extremely sensitive about the level of discount they offer any corporate client or volume producer for fear of having to extend these discounts to other clients or channels. Therefore, these fares will not be available to the general public or be quoted in CRS or GDS, and neither will they be quoted on the passenger's ticket. Instead, the passenger ticket will display the so-called published fares.

Price economics

In deregulated markets like Australia, Europe and the USA, the need to attract or maintain market share has led to price wars that continue to change the industry. The behaviour of the airline industry as a whole highlights the tendency to both produce excess capacity (too many seats or too many frequencies), and to price its product often well below the fully allocated cost. Several factors cause this (apart from management decisions), such as the 'lumpiness' of adding extra frequencies or starting new routes as a result of having the aircraft available to operate them. The demand for high frequency to serve the business market can also produce excess capacity at certain times of the day and week, which is often sold by lowering prices to levels that fail to cover full costs. In times of economic strength, well-managed airlines generally generate acceptable profits, but in a downward cycle, the aircraft and number of seats offered are still in the marketplace, and this produces extreme pressures on the airlines to cover their costs and remain profitable. The result is often heavy price discounting.

The airline industry is very capital-intensive, requiring high levels of investment in operating equipment and facilities. In addition, fuel and labour costs constitute a significant percentage (generally over fifty peer cent) of an airline's total costs. To cover high fixed costs, airlines are often desperate to produce any revenue possible, and in environments where there is a revenue shortfall, variable pricing strategies are used to boost contributions. It is better to discount a seat to levels below full cost to earn some contribution to fixed costs rather than let the seat go empty. An airline has the flexibility to reduce prices to deeply discounted levels in order to attract additional consumers. As a result, the price of a ticket bears no relation to the cost of its production, but reflects the nature of market conditions, including competition.

Accordingly, deep discounts, which are almost always matched by the competition, and/or waiving of ticketing rules and other fare-reducing behaviour, encourage consumers to hold unrealistic expectations of what a ticket should cost and conditions them to expect lower prices nearer the date of departure. This strategy may be rational for airlines individually, but as an industry it is irrational, as it is ultimately unprofitable, requiring the airlines to raise load factors to uneconomical levels just to break even. Further, this creates fare erosion in the market place that restricts the carrier's ability to increase revenue to cover rising costs. As a result, we see the majority of airlines focused on costs reduction to allow themselves the flexibility to compete on price. In driving costs down to increase volume or share or contribution, airlines have created a downward spiral that has forced them to lower costs to enable them to match the ever-low fares that they themselves introduced.

In the end, airlines that are unable to lower costs any further and continue to sell a disproportionately high number of seats lower than cost, go bankrupt. We have seen many examples of this dynamic in the last twenty years, and in a deregulated market context there are likely to be more failures and/or consolidation as government control over airlines relaxes around the world. A fundamental component of the deeply competitive pricing environment many airlines operate in, is the ability to 'revenue manage' the different elements of demand described above and to maximize the ability to capture the high yield business traveller market and minimize the reliance on the low yield leisure market. The development of global alliances in the late 1990s was driven by the need of full-service carriers to lock in the business traveller market. The requirement to effectively 'revenue manage' these different elements led to the development of Revenue Management, the process of combining price with inventory (seats) to maximize revenue. Or as Sabre's CEO once said, revenue management is 'selling the right seat, to the right customer, at the right price, at the right time to maximize system revenues and profitability'.

3 Business strategy and airline models for operating managers

John M. C. King

Introduction

Aviation has been significantly impacted by both technology and changes in public policy. Indeed, the confluence of the two as represented by the immense growth in computing power that occurred in the 1970s and 1980s and the rapid deregulation of the economic aspect of the airline industry that occurred at the same time resulted in the arcane but powerful technique called 'yield management': a management technique which enables airlines to maximize each departure load at the optimum price. Since 1970, air transport has increased sixfold; even faster than the global economy which has grown more than four times. While RPK growth and GDP have not been identical in each year since 2000, from 2007 to 2014 the two indicators ran together with air transport growth, then exceeding GDP growth in 2015. The distance flown has also increased, passenger kilometres performed have increased ninefold, and cargo carriage twelve times. The two forces driving this expansion are inflation-adjusted airfares, which have reduced by half, and larger aircraft with more efficient engines, which have enabled unit costs to stay low. Whilst profits increased significantly in 2015/16, in the forty-five-year period from 1970, profits have been scarce and the industry has not been uniformly and consistently profitable. As fuel prices continue to rise, airline profits will fall; for example, 2017 was forecast to produce lower results than 2016.

Indeed, in 2015 airlines were recording record profits, largely but not exclusively driven by significantly lower fuel prices and a strong market. Whilst on a regional basis, there have been variations in growth overall, travel has been strong. In 2015 the airline industry earned a global aggregate profit of approximately $US35 billion. For 2016 IATA (International Air Transport Association) was forecasting an aggregate profit of approximately $US709 billion, with a margin of 5.6 per cent (profit on revenues). In terms of passengers carried, the aggregate earnings represent $10.40 per passenger. The aggregate profit figure is important as it represents, for only the second time in the history of the industry, that earnings on invested capital have surpassed the cost of capital (9.8 per cent and 6.8 per cent respectively). The airline business may be starting to look like a normal business. The principal drivers of airline profitability are described below.

- Oil prices – IATA based its 2016 forecast on the Brent price averaging US$45 a barrel or $8 a barrel lower than the 2015 average. Fuel price hedging has not given all carriers equal and immediate benefits because of the variations in timing and scope of hedging contracts.
- The global economy – weak economic conditions continue, with global GDP expanding by only 2.3 per cent in 2016 (the lowest growth rate since 2008). Consumer discretionary spending is fairly strong but business has cut travel, both frequency and class of travel.
- Passenger demand – growth in demand by passengers was expected to be 6.2 per cent, twenty per cent less than the 7.5 per cent for 2015. However, capacity was forecast to grow even faster at 6.8 per cent whilst load factors were expected to remain high, driven by a reduction in yields (7 per cent). Unit costs are impacted significantly by oil prices but were forecast to fall by 7.7 per cent.
- Cargo demand – cargo only had a two per cent growth in demand. Much of the market for air cargo is met by efficient wide-body passenger aircraft such as the B777-300 and the pure air cargo business is flat. Cargo yields were forecast to fall by eight per cent. Both IATA, the scheduled carrier trade association, and ICAO (International Civil Aviation Organization), a UN specialized agency dealing prominently with aviation safety and related matters but also involved in the economic liberalization that has progressed into the twenty-first century, have forecast continuing growth.

Business practice

This chapter deals primarily with two elements of contemporary aviation business practice that are most likely to impact upon the operating airline manager: alliances and the low-cost carrier (LCC) phenomenon. Another key aspect of contemporary airline practice has been yield management. As noted above, it arose from the fortuitous confluence of an increase in computing power and economic deregulation. Thus, airlines were able to set fares on a trip basis by forecasting traffic in both service and fare classes. The practical operating manager, whilst able to contribute to local marketplace fares, will not be involved in the forecasting processes. International carriers tend to set fares on a seasonal basis and stimulate demand on the basis of 'early birds', i.e. pre-booking well before travel and short-term specials. Domestic carriers with high frequency short-haul operations, on direct routes, are much more likely to use rapid and frequent fare changes. Chapter 5 discusses this further.

The current chapter will focus on areas that are of more immediate concern to the operating manager: the business practices that surround the functionality of alliances and low-cost carriers. The competitive advantage of the LCC will also be briefly explored. The first part, though, considers alliances and codeshares. Emphasis will be given to formal alliances but the ability of carriers who are not members to enter into a 'small a' alliance with an alliance member will be observed as well. Etihad's re-establishment of the lightly branded alliance based on equity investment will also be considered. Etihad uses the branding 'Etihad Partners' and has, of course, avoided the membership of Global alliances, unlike its geographic neighbour, Qatar Airways, which has joined **one**world. As will be seen, the largest Gulf State carrier, Emirates, has a strong bilateral alliance, with antitrust immunity, with **one**world carrier, Qantas. The future of alliances is often discussed but until airlines can find superior ways to enhance revenues through selective partnering on a broad basis without breaking antitrust regulations, there remains a positive outlook for branded alliances.

The Global Alliances

Whilst the airlines have endeavoured to optimize the relationships that membership of a Global Alliance allows, such membership does not exclude commercial relationships, even amounting to joint operations, with other airlines who may not be in any alliance, or with carriers from other alliances. As well as the Global Alliances – Star, **one**world and SkyTeam, and Etihad's 'Etihad Partners'–there are some regionally based alliances. These currently exist in

Table 3.1 Global alliance members (as at 2016)

Star

ADRIA	Avianca	
AEGEAN	Brussels Airlines	Shenzhen Airlines
Air Canada	Copa Airlines	Singapore Airlines
Air China	Croatia Airlines	South African Airways
Air India	EgyptAir	SWISS
Air New Zealand	Ethiopian Airlines	TAP Portugal
ANA	LOT Polish Airlines	THAI
Asiana Airlines	Lufthansa	Turkish Airlines
Austrian	SAS	United

one**world**

airberlin	Iberia	Qantas
American Airlines	Japan Airlines	Qatar Airways
British Airways	LAN	Royal Jordanian
Cathay Pacific Airways	Malaysia Airlines	S7 Airlines
Finnair	TAM	SriLankan Airlines

SkyTeam

Aeroflot	China Eastern	Korean Air
Aerolineas Argentinas	China Southern	MEA
Aero Mexico	Czech Airlines	Saudi
Air Europa	Delta	TAROM
Air France	Garuda Indonesia	Vietnam Airlines
Alitalia	Kenya Airways	Xiamen Air
China Airlines	KLM	

Source: Airline and alliance websites

Africa, Latin America and around the Indian Ocean, but are limited as to their scope and effectiveness. The following description of the three Global Alliances will establish the framework for understanding both the alliances themselves and commercial practices outside of the alliances. See Table 3.1 for members of the three Global Alliances.

Membership may change but the Global Alliance websites provide up-to-date lists. Star is both the largest of the Global Alliances and has the greatest geographic reach. **one**world, unable to match Star's numbers in both geographic reach and carriers, positions itself as the alliance of quality carriers having Cathay Pacific, Qantas and British Airways among its membership. The largest **one**world member is of course American Airlines, and whilst its international services may meet **one**world quality standards, its domestic services are more akin to LCC standards, particularly in economy or coach class.

Table 3.2 shows the relative size of the three Global Alliances and Emirates Airlines. It is of course necessary to recognize that there are other alliances but in general, they are geographically specific, even if multilateral. Bilateral alliances may be route or partially network specific, as is the Emirates/Qantas bilateral alliance.

One of the most interesting alliances outside the alliances above is that developed by the Gulf carrier Etihad, which has taken equity stakes in eight airlines including Virgin Australia and Alitalia, and thus constituted its own equity-based alliance. It was, in 2016, exploring a joint venture with Tui to create an additional pan-European carrier to be based in Vienna.

Table 3.2 Relative sizes of the three Global Alliances and Emirates Airlines (as at 2015)

	Star	oneworld	SkyTeam	Emirates
Membership	28	15	20	–
Total revenues (US$ billions)	179.05	141.40	144.38	22.5
Daily departures	18,500+	14,313	17,343	500+
Countries served	192	154	177	29
Airports served	1,330	1,011	10,562	144
RPK billions	1,364.83	1,134.35	?	235 million
Annual passengers (millions)	641.10	512.6	665	49.3 million
Employees	432,603	?	481,691	56,000
Fleet	4,657	3,414	3,946 + 1,580 in related carriers	93 A380 148 B777

Source: Alliance websites/Emirates website

Table 3.3 Etihad's investment-based alliances (as at 2016)

Carrier	Country of designation	Etihad % of equity	No. of points codeshared	Global Alliance
Alitalia	Italy	49.1	36	SkyTeam
airberlin	Germany	29.2	39	**one**world
ETIHAD Regional	Switzerland	33.3	4	NIL
JET AIRWAYS	India	24.0	140	NIL
NIKI	Austria	indirect – via airberlin	4	**one**world associate
air seychelles	Seychelles	40	6	NIL
AirSERBIA	Serbia	49	22	NIL
Virgin Australia	Australia	25.1	41	NIL

Table 3.3 lists the carriers in Etihad Partners, their country of designation, the percentage of equity held by Etihad, the number of points served on a codeshare basis and Global Alliance participation. Further, Table 3.4 shows that whilst Etihad serves 350 destinations, the total served by Etihad and all of its investee carriers is a further 272 and that non-equity codeshare partners contribute a further 539 destinations on a codeshare basis. This is a strong demonstration of the way in which even a lightly branded alliance when combined with extensive codeshare, extends the reach of a carrier.

Unlike SWISSAIR, which branded its equity-based alliance as the Qualifier Alliance, Etihad has not brought its airlines into a rigorously branded structure but has labelled it 'Etihad Partners'. Etihad Partners, has, unlike the Global Alliances, no central management unit but is coordinated from within. Etihad has been content to allow its partners to enter into a series of bilateral alliances. At the same time two of its investee carriers – Air Berlin and Alitalia – maintain membership of different Global Alliances. Air Berlin is a member of **one**world and Alitalia is a member of SkyTeam. What Etihad plans to do in the future in terms of coordination of its carriers to form a more effective, even if only marginally, branded alliance is unclear. Etihad has developed not only Etihad Partners (in which one of its investee carriers, Virgin Australia, does not

Table 3.4 Destinations served by Etihad/Etihad partners (as at 2016)

Etihad	350
Etihad Partners and Virgin Australia	272
Non-equity codeshare partners	539

Table 3.5 Etihad non-equity codeshare partners (as at 2016)

Carrier	Country of Designation	Global Alliance	Points served on codeshare
Aegean Airlines	Greece	Nil	12
Aer Lingus	Ireland	Nil	25
Aerolineas Argentinas	Argentina	SkyTeam	13
Air Baltic	Latvia	Nil	9
Air Canada	Canada	Star	7
Air Europa	Spain	Nil	15
Air France	France	SkyTeam	9
Air Malta	Malta	Nil	5
Air New Zealand	New Zealand	Star	9
American Airlines	USA	**one**world	100+ domestic 3 international
ANA	Japan	Star	9
Asiana Airlines	Korea	Star	10
Bangkok Airways	Thailand	Nil	15 domestic 1 international
Belavia	Belarus	Nil	2
Brussels Airlines	Belgium	Star	11
Czech Airlines	Czech Republic	SkyTeam	4
Flybe.com	UK	Nil	30
Flynas	Saudi Arabia	Nil	2
Garuda Indonesia	Indonesia	SkyTeam	14
GOL	Brazil	Nil	19
Hong Kong Airlines	Hong Kong SAR	Nil	3
Jet Blue	USA	Nil	39
Kenya Airways	Kenya	SkyTeam	9
KLM	Netherlands	SkyTeam	23
Korean Air	Korea	SkyTeam	10
Malaysia Airlines	Malaysia	**one**world	16
MEA	Lebanon	SkyTeam	2
NIKI	Austria	**one**world affiliate	4
Philippine Airlines	Philippines	Nil	20

Carrier	Country of Designation	Global Alliance	Points served on codeshare
PIA	Pakistan	Nil	5
Royal Air Maroc	Morocco	Nil	4
S7 Airlines	Russia	**one**world	14
SAS	Denmark, Sweden, Norway	Star	19
SNCF	France	Train system	20
South African Airways	South Africa	Star	16
Sri Lankan	Sri Lanka	**one**world	7
TAP Portugal	Portugal	Star	18
Turkish Airlines	Turkey	Star	2
Vietnam Airlines	Vietnam	SkyTeam	6

participate), but also a very broad range of codeshare partners who are members of the three Global Alliances; eight are members of Star, six are members of **one**world and nine are members of SkyTeam. Table 3.5 identifies the non-equity codeshare partner, their country of designation, their Global Alliance (if any) and the number of points served on a codeshare basis.

The sustainability of alliances

With the growth of cross-alliance partnership usually involving codeshares, but in the case of Air New Zealand and Cathay Pacific Airways, a joint service, many have asked if the Global Alliance is sustainable. Certainly, the Global Alliances have done little in terms of bringing significant cost savings to their members. Indeed, membership has usually created additional costs, particularly in the form of IT standardization. However, anecdotal evidence suggests that carriers have benefited from enhanced revenue flows. The special pro-rate agreements (SPAs) that are negotiated between the members have directed traffic, wherever possible, within the alliance. Carriers have, however, negotiated joint ventures outside of an alliance; e.g., Qantas and Emirates is a very broad joint operation, and at the margin the SPA between Air France (SkyTeam) and Cathay Pacific (**one**world) allows Air France to direct some of its France–Australia traffic via Hong Kong. As noted earlier, Cathay Pacific has a joint operation on the Auckland, New Zealand route with both carriers in competitive alliances. Another example is the Qantas codeshare relationship with China Southern Airways to Guangzhou and points beyond, including Urumqi and Xiamin among others. China Southern is in SkyTeam but Qantas is in **one**world. Global

Alliances will persist whilst traffic and revenue enhancements can be enjoyed, and if the direct costs are lower than the benefits.

For the practising airline manager at the operational level, alliances, joint operations and codeshares all create practical issues. Passengers can become confused by flight information displays (FIDS) with multiple carrier flight numbers. Passengers often do not understand the difference between the operating carrier and marketing carriers and can try to check-in at the wrong place, or worse in the case of multi-terminal airports, at the wrong terminal! It is possible that there will be issues with handling agents when some flights are joint-ventured or codeshared and others are not at terminals that have multiple handling agents (including, by some carriers, self-handling).

Regulatory authorities require airlines and their agents to advise the passenger as to who is the operating carrier and who is the marketing carrier. But passengers, inevitably it seems, do not read the fine print or if they do, do not understand it. This lack of understanding is exacerbated by frequent-flyer programme membership where there is a lack of consistency about codeshare recognition and award of frequent-flyer points. An example is that BMI Regional flies the route (inter alia) FRA–BRS (Frankfurt–Bristol) and vice versa. BMI acts as operating carrier and codeshares the flight with Lufthansa as marketing carrier. So, as well as the flight carrying the BMI (BM) code and flight number, it carries a Lufthansa (LH) code and flight number, but Lufthansa does not give miles/points for travel on the flight irrespective of which code and flight is used for ticketing. Although this type of query can seldom be resolved at an airport, operating managers need to have a sufficient understanding of the codeshare alliances and frequent-flyer programmes to know how to advise the passenger to best deal with the problem.

The LCC

The LCC is a phenomenon of the twenty-first century, and whilst LCCs initially developed in the post-deregulation period (which occurred in different parts of the world at different times), the most rapid growth, including the development of long-haul (but not multi-stage) flights has been in the post-2000 period. The success of easyJet and Ryanair in Europe has been a twenty-first century event. LCCs have changed. Some such as Ryanair have stayed (largely) true to the original model of point-to-point flights, with minimal service ('we provide transportation only' – Michael O'Leary), one type of aircraft, and very low, indirect costs. In 2016, however, Ryanair announced that it was trialling 'assisted connectivity', i.e. emulating full-service carriers (FSCs) in the way they provide connecting flights, through ticketing and boarding passes, and transferred baggage. Whilst the outcome at this time is unknown, there is no doubt that LCCs and FSCs are converging. Other carriers have morphed into hybrid carriers. Air Berlin is an example: it has the characteristics of a full-service carrier (alliance membership of **one**world) and of LCCs, though its subsidiary NIKI, (named after its founder, Niki Lauder) is closer to the LCC model. Another example is British Airways, which is now charging for food on short-haul European services.

Aer Lingus, a long-established FSC (and now part of IAG, along with British Airways, Iberia and Vueling), operates as an LCC (minimal service and even charging for water) on short-haul routes. In Australia, Virgin, initially established under the name Virgin Blue as an LCC, has evolved since the 2001 demise of Ansett, into an FSC with a full suite of domestic routes and a limited number of 'own metal' international routes, both medium haul (SYD–DPS) and long haul (SYD–LAX). In addition, it has been a contract charter operator for the resource sector. The 2016 scheduled fleet of Virgin is a complex one with aircraft ranging from B777-300ER (of which it has five) to ATR72s. In 2016 Virgin announced both an alliance with Hainan Airways, and future operation of routes to Hong Kong and mainland China, as well as a fleet simplification programme.

The benchmark LCC is Southwest, the Texas-based initiator of the LCC product in the USA. However, it too has evolved, by responding to both need and opportunity. Co-founder and now retired CEO Herb Kelleher has a saying (among many), that 'to rest on your laurels was to get a thorn on your butt'. The Kelleher/Southwest style was to provide friendly on-board service (peanuts delivered with a joke), high aircraft utilization, low fares and high load factors. The first flight of Southwest was in 1971. On day one, the airline had a fleet of four aircraft but forty-five years later, it was carrying in excess of 135 million passengers: twenty per cent of the whole US market. It has made profits for forty-five consecutive years and has delivered an average annual return (AAR) of 17.5 per cent, compared to the US share market as a whole which has returned eleven per cent since Southwest listed on the New York Stock Exchange (NYSE) in 1977.

Southwest is, however, in the process of reinventing itself: it appears to be reaching the limits of growth as an LCC and is moving towards a hybrid model. In October 2015, it commenced international service into Latin America from a new international terminal at Dallas's 'in town' Love Field, its initial and continuing home base. The international operations are, in part, Southwest's response to the decline in growth in its traditional short-haul point-to-point services. The second strategic response is to grow long-haul domestic business travel: to invade the space of the FSCs United, Delta and American. Southwest is searching for universal appeal to sustain growth; short-haul leisure travel is no longer sustaining the growth that Southwest needs to retain its twenty per cent plus market share. The challenge is immense. In the USA, as elsewhere, FSCs are on aggressive cost reduction campaigns. Traditional and umbrella type mergers have resulted in larger networks and lower unit costs, which, together with merged frequent-flyer programmes, have a strong resonance with business travellers.

Southwest has the lowest cost per seat mile of the four largest US carriers (9 US cents per available seat mile). The next most efficient is Delta at almost 12.5 cents per ASM. The challenge is not so much reduction of costs but enhancement of revenues. How can an LCC do that without increasing its cost base, at a time when the FSCs are reducing their cost base? Short-haul carriers have a lower daily utilization of aircraft than do medium- and long-haul carriers. However, Southwest works its fleet hard, achieving nine hours' flight time per day per aircraft. A significant part of the reason for this is the very nature of the Southwest point-to-point operation. Hubs provide significant connectivity for passengers but high levels of non-productive time for aircraft and crews because of uneven spoke lengths radiating from hubs. The five-year strategic goals of Southwest are to increase the percentage of business travellers on board from thirty-five per cent to forty per cent. US FSCs operate on the basis of a fifty-fifty split of leisure/business travellers. Simultaneously Southwest plans to increase seat load factors to ninety per cent.

These are significant challenges: business travellers are used to perks – lounges and frequent-flyer programmes, among other things. One of the techniques to achieve this goal is to access the airports that business travellers use but, in the past, Southwest had avoided because of cost and congestion issues. However, it has commenced operations at Newark, NJ, an airport much favoured by the Wall Street community of business travellers. Reagan National in Washington DC and La Guardia (New York) have also become Southwest points, along with Boston (Logan). Whilst falling short of full-scale hubbing, Southwest does promote limited connectivity. Winning the loyalty of business travellers is not easy. Virgin Australia has also faced this challenge, and Southwest, when accessing further hubs such as Atlanta (the hub of Delta), has a yield which is said to be fifteen per cent below that which it has in other major cities. Price is not the only determinant of carrier choice by business travellers. The carrier does however have two weapons in its strategic armoury which are not used by other LCCs: the Southwest baggage policy and its fare flexibility. There are no charges for changing tickets nor for checking luggage up to two pieces. In comparison, both Ryanair and easyJet in Europe charge high fees for both ticket changes and luggage check.

Southwest has a frequent-flyer programme based on dollars spent rather than distance travelled. This approach, being one of rewarding the most valuable frequent travellers, is being adopted by FSCs though often in a hybrid distance/value form. The future of Southwest, whilst absolutely positive, may be different from its past. For example, the introduction of a business class cabin (US domestic first class) will limit fleet interchangeability unless introduced on the whole fleet, but many routes would not sustain even a very small business class cabin whilst some routes, especially those out of La Guardia, Reagan National and Newark, have the potential to sustain large cabins. In Asia Pacific, LCCs operating on medium-haul routes with wide-body aircraft have a premium cabin, but LCCs generally do not offer a premium cabin on domestic short-haul services.

LCCs and costs

LCCS have at their heart the notion of cost reduction. There is always value in being, in terms of the business segment in which a firm operates, the lowest cost operator. The ongoing rise of Ryanair in the European airline sector is testament to that proposition. In air transport the cost allocation between passenger and air cargo, when cargo is carried on a scheduled passenger service, is an ongoing debate in most carriers. However, as LCCs seldom carry air cargo it is not a significant issue, but is critical to understanding costs. An airline seeking to be an FSC will have a higher cost structure than an airline which seeks the LCC space. The FSC must achieve a higher revenue for a given load factor in order to support its costs. LCC costs must be lower than FSC costs in order to provide lower fares to passengers.

The middle ground (the hybrid carrier) is a difficult but not impossible place to be. The problem is that its costs are higher than the LCC because of its aspirations to match or at least approach FSCs service standards, but it seldom has the revenue yield of the FSC. There is, however, one outstanding example of a successful hybrid. Jet Blue in the US has reportedly higher service levels than most US FSCs and operates from a mainstream airport (New York JFK) as its initial and principal base and at the same time, in many regards, acts as an LCC. One of the economic characteristics of an airline is that on any given flight there is little difference between average total cost and the passenger load factor or yield needed to meet the cost. The margins are slim and airlines are very sensitive to market changes. A terrorist event or a significant financial market event will have a heavy impact on an airline (if the event is localized, then it is route profitability that will suffer). An interesting example is the withdrawal of many low-cost and other carriers from Sharm-el-Sheik in Egypt following the collapse of the market after the downing of the Russian-operated A321 by an explosion, purportedly caused by a terrorist bomb.

Differentiation

How is an LCC differentiated from an FSC? Table 3.6 shows a comparison of LCCs and FSCs.

From the airline and airline manager's viewpoint, the critical difference is the way FSCs operate a hub-based network with connecting flights within a time bank whereas LCCs operate a large number of specific routes (often on a seasonal basis) from small bases without regard to carrier-enabled connectivity. If connectivity is achieved, it is done so by the passenger with minimal or no facilitation by the airline. Baggage will not be through-checked and another check-in may be necessary if the passenger has not checked in on-line. The point-to-point operation of LCCs facilitates the higher aircraft utilization rates that LCCs achieve as compared with hub-focused FSCs. As most of the spokes from an airline hub are not of the same length, the FSC will have downtime

Table 3.6 Comparison of low-cost carriers and full-service carriers

Low-cost carrier	Full-service carrier
Simple brand	Complex brand
Low fare	Service classes and fare classes
Online and call centre bookings	Network complexity
Simpler fare structure	Multiple products
Focus on secondary airports and multiple bases	Predominantly third party intermediaries
	Complex fare structure
High aircraft utilization	Hubs at major airports
No or little interlining	Lower utilization
Offer is basic transportation, all else is ancillary	Interlining, possible bilateral and multilateral alliances, and complex,
Short-haul focus	integrated products
Some sectors medium haul	Short-haul, long-haul, and possible
Common fleet	multi-sector routes
	Complex fleet, route type specific

on some aircraft. As timely feed into the hub is essential, the aircraft may have to have long turnaround time at the end of short spokes. The use of labour is not optimal either, as there are gaps between the hub time banks when few, if any, flights operate. Not all FSCs operate hubs: in Australia the geographic and demographic features mitigate against US-style hubs, and whilst Australian carriers have connecting flights, the routes are largely linear. Of course, even with the multiple base, multiple route system that LCCs operate (at least in Europe) there may be different approaches. Ryanair tends to operate more thin routes whereas easyJet tends to give emphasis to few routes but with a greater density of operation.

Competitive advantage

Cost reduction does not, of itself, provide competitive advantages. Competitive advantage is, in essence, perceived by the consumer who sees competing products. Does Qantas at $100.00 a sector have competitive disadvantage against Jetstar at $90.00? The consumer will decide: an assessment will be made about the value of snacks, status credits and frequent-flyer mileage, amongst other things. The consumer is unlikely to be aware or even consider the cost base. If the cost leader in an industry exceeds average price, then it is likely to be highly profitable. It is notable that Jetstar is able to sell some of its fares at or above the lowest fares offered by its FSC parent airline Qantas. Jetstar ought to be profitable with its lower cost base and ability to earn at or near the level of an FSC. An important question is the sustainability of carriers' low-cost strategies: there have been a very large number of failures of LCCs, usually through inability to effectively realize the cost strategy coupled with a lack of competitive advantage.

Conclusion

This chapter has dealt with two business practices that carriers use as part of twenty-first century aviation and that will impact upon or at least closely relate to the work of the operating manager. Global Alliances were considered as were cross-alliance arrangements and codeshares. The nature of LCCs was also described: they are different from FSCs, and airlines and airports need to remain alert to those differences, as they impact upon day-to-day management.

4 Network design strategies

Markus Franke

Introduction

Networks are a core production factor of airlines, accounting for the majority of all revenues and costs generated in the course of airborne transportation. The interdependency of involved resources, varying across different business models, leads to a highly complex mathematical and operational optimization problem. Since there is no fully integrated mathematical solution for this problem so far, airlines apply a sequence of stepwise-designed paradigms and planning algorithms to ensure appropriate fleet structures, attractive route patterns, competitive service levels, and efficient airport operations. Quite frequently, network scenarios will be compared and refined until the network contribution appears to be optimal.

Since there is no single ideal network design, the scenario evaluation needs to take into account the specifics of each airline, such as regulatory framework, home market, or shareholder structure. Trade-offs between short-term and long-term objectives have to be carefully managed. Besides pure profit, satisfied travellers, attractive jobs, and ecological sustainability may be on the agenda of shareholders and managers. Considerable regulation, as well as structural overcapacity in the markets, reduce the leeway in this exercise, and impose an additional burden on airline managers.

This chapter provides an overview of the main drivers relevant to sound network design, and examines the performance indicators suited to measure successful design and operations. Furthermore, it illustrates selected interlinkages between major drivers, and introduces common methodologies to solve the inherent trade-offs.

Value of network design for airlines

To offer their air transport service to clients, airlines need to define a certain number of flights on specific routes they intend to operate, hopefully meeting demand for airborne mobility. The entirety of these flights and routes, complemented by the assets and resources required to physically deliver the offered services, is usually referred to as a 'network'. Networks are well known across many industrial as well as private sectors, including more recently, the most prominent occurrence of social media networks. What are the characteristics of airline networks? There are many viable definitions, but the constituting element of all transportation, including airline networks, is the interlinkage between core resources. Consequently, these resources cannot be planned separately, but need to be planned in conjunction with adjacent resources, which results in complexity.

For instance, an aircraft's daily itinerary ('rotation') may significantly differ from the respective rotation of a crew licensed to operate the aircraft, due to different operational limitations (e.g. maximum duty times of crew members). Nonetheless, it needs to be ensured that an appropriate crew is available on each segment of the aircraft's rotation ('leg'). This kind of correlation is valid for all other resources as well, including, for example, ground handling staff, or aircraft maintenance capabilities. The larger an airline's network, the more complex the calculation will be. Possible combinations of resources will grow exponentially with size. The most complex case occurs if an airline decides to operate a 'hub and spoke' network, that is, to cumulate demand flows at one or more central airport(s). In this case, incoming flights to some extent 'feed' outgoing flights, enabling clients to reach more destinations worldwide by transferring at this hub. Through the 'feeding' approach, hub and spoke networks feature an even higher level of resource interlinkage, and thus, planning complexity (for details see 'Morphology', below).

In an ideal world, the described complexity would not bother any airline manager, since there would be a mathematical model delivering the perfect combination of all relevant resources at each point in time. Unfortunately, there is no such model, and even if it were available, current information technology is not advanced enough to compute the required solutions quickly enough. The latter shortcomings may change, but the first aspect may not: there is no such thing as a mathematically sharp, optimum solution for a specific network problem. Every airline operates its network in a specific environment (e.g. regulatory framework, labour laws, home market, or shareholders), and pursues its very specific set of objectives. The maximum profit may not be achievable with a given fleet, or a scenario that may be favourable in the short run may endanger the airline's strategic objectives. Instead, airline managers usually deploy partial or sequential solutions, slicing the problem into manageable portions. There are optimization algorithms, for example, for fleets, network design, rotational planning, crew planning, and hub operations. These solutions still imply massive complexities. However, it is easier to handle such complexities in a stepwise approach (for details see 'Facets of network design', below).

Irrespective of the specific network model or calculation approach, the particular value of network design and planning lies in the fact that networks account for the vast majority of revenues and costs an airline may have. Further, network planning is the only function of an airline that combines the revenue *and* cost perspective of air transport. Network contribution schemes are the core of an airline's profitability calculation (for details see 'Measurement of successful network design', below).

Morphology: different planning paradigms for different types of network

As stated previously, the optimum design and operations of an airline network depend strongly on the type of network operated, with respect to the business model chosen by this airline. There are three major types of network found in practice (with a variety of sub-types and variations):

- hub and spoke network (passenger and air cargo)
- point-to-point networks (passenger and air cargo)
- gateway networks (express cargo).

Hub and spoke network

In a hub and spoke network, the number of economically viable destinations is boosted by accumulating demand in one or more central airports, and feeding/de-feeding flights that would otherwise have too little demand for a decent service quality (i.e. frequency of flights per day/per week). This effect is particularly beneficial for long-haul intercontinental destinations, which often could not be offered in a commercially viable way on a point-to-point basis. The hub and spoke model is usually chosen by traditional full-service carriers, and has the benefit of covering almost every possible revenue stream available to that respective carrier. Furthermore, the number of services needed to cover a certain number of destinations is as low as it can be: n destinations can be connected by n flights using a hub.

This upside, of course, comes at a cost. As stated earlier, hub and spoke networks establish an even higher complexity than point-to-point networks, since the interlinkage of resources is significantly stronger. For instance, outbound flights need to wait for a variety of inbound flights to collect all envisaged transfer passengers to leverage the feeder effect. This causes a relatively poor productivity of aircraft, plus operational risks: if one or more feeder flights are late, the outbound flight will automatically be delayed as well (subject to operational discretion).

This effect becomes even more noticeable if a hub and spoke carrier structures its inbound and outbound hub flights in a special format called 'banks'. That means the airline compresses flights into one or more peaks to increase the probability that an inbound passenger can reach as many outbound flights as possible ('connectivity'). A peaked hub structure with clear, distinct banks usually entails good hub performance in terms of connectivity and fleet productivity, provided that the chosen bank structure reflects the operational framework and scale of the respective hub well. Nonetheless, operational peaks are a challenge for asset and resource utilization, and they increase the risk of operational instability. The inherent trade-offs need to be managed efficiently to ensure an overall good result (for details see 'Network and hub structure', below).

Point-to-point network

A point-to-point (P2P) network is usually deployed by low-cost carriers (LCCs). It is the simplest way to form a network, although not the leanest one. As opposed to the hub and spoke network, which is suited to connect *n* destinations with *n* flights (via a hub), the P2P network requires (n – 1) × n/2 flights. On the other hand, the interdependency of resources is much less than in the hub and spoke model, resulting in significantly lower complexity. In its purest version, each aircraft commutes between just two destinations in a 'ping-pong-like' manner, minimizing the interlinkage between different routes. Furthermore, LCCs usually try to avoid operating hubs, so there is no transfer of passengers, and no waiting of outbound flights for feeder services. This ensures maximum aircraft productivity compared with hub and spoke operations. In addition, the inherent operational instability of hubs is non-existent as P2P networks are structurally robust.

In the recent past, however, the boundaries between the above-mentioned business models have been blurred, leading to hybrid network patterns. Hub and spoke carriers have always offered P2P services on selected routes with high business traveller share. Due to the ongoing success of LCCs, and declining yields (revenue per seat), full-service airlines have recently been forced to adopt more and more elements of low-cost business, or even to found low-cost subsidiaries to defend continental traffic shares. On the other hand, the rapid growth of LCCs slowed down in the same time span, forcing them to unleash new business opportunities, especially in the business travel segment. To attract these clients, though, LCCs need to abandon certain rules of lean operations, and raise their service levels.

In essence, the maturing aviation industry experiences a convergence of business models, also leading to an assimilation of network designs. The latest evidence of this trend is the emergence of low-cost long-haul business models, introduced both by LCCs such as Norwegian, and full-service carriers such as Lufthansa (with Eurowings), or Singapore Airlines (with Scoot). Long-haul services usually cannot exist without at least some feeder traffic, so long-haul LCC models need to invent low-cost hub operations.

The ongoing streamlining and commoditization driven by hybrid business models has also absorbed two other traditional airline segments: the charter business (mainly P2P), and regional networks (P2P and hub feed). The former is nowadays mainly covered by LCCs (short- and mid-haul, but also long-haul routes – see above), while the latter have mostly lost their commercial viability. In the past, some secondary but high-yield connections justified sub-networks operated by regional jets or even turboprop aircraft (often outsourced to local partner airlines), and the additional revenue potential (from regional feed) or higher yield (from regional P2P) overcompensated for the unfavourable unity cost position of smaller aircraft. Due to overall yield decline and cost pressure in the industry, mostly driven by the expansion of the LCC model, this regional sub-network model has almost been pushed out of the market.

Gateway network

The gateway network model is the typical operational model of global express delivery companies ('Integrators') such as FedEx, UPS, or DHL. It is based on regional/continental networks with a very high density for time-definite parcel delivery, connected on a global level through long-haul flights between gateway hubs. As opposed to passenger or air cargo carriers, Integrators do not primarily sell empty capacity, but a certain quality level, which makes the high-density regional networks indispensable. For all mentioned air traffic network types, there is a common phenomenon: in comparison with other industries, whose business models basically consist of sales-oriented and operational processes, airlines feature a third pillar–network design and planning. Combining the revenue and cost perspective of business, this pillar acts like a transmission belt, at least for hub and spoke airlines. Market data are extracted from business intelligence, transformed into network scenarios suited to achieve financial goals, then translated into sales budgets and operational schedules. These plans will then be physically performed to realize the envisaged profits. This paradigm is illustrated in Figure 4.1.

For other business models, network design and planning is still a crucial function. However, this is not as much a core activity as for hub and spoke carriers. For LCCs, network design is much less complex than for hub and spoke carriers due to the dominance of P2P traffic. In this case, lean operations are of the essence, so that the business model of LCCs is mostly driven by operational management. Global gateway-based networks of Integrators are mainly driven by the quality levels promised to the clients. As long as clients pay for the envisaged quality level, seamless capacity and speedy operations are of the essence, rather

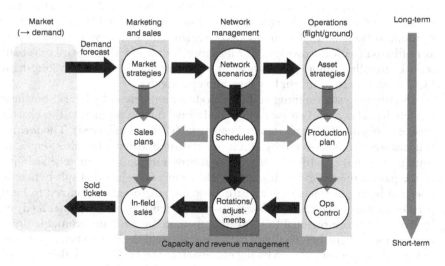

Figure 4.1 Transmission belt function of network design and planning at airlines[1]

than highly-utilized capacities or lean production. Consequently, this business model is dominated by commercial planning, determining products, quality levels, and appropriate prices. Network and Operations are *cost centres*, aiming at delivering the required quality at minimum cost.

Measurement of successful network design: main key performance indicators

Irrespective of the concrete business model, route networks represent a huge proportion of an airline's revenues, as well as causing a major share of the operational costs. Consequently, *network* performance indicators are *airline* performance indicators. The most common approach to measuring and comparing network performance is to count the passengers paying for their tickets on certain routes, and multiply that by the distance they were flown on that route. The result is called 'Revenue Passenger Kilometre' (RPK), and stands for the total demand, i.e. revenue potential raised on a single route, or aggregated across all routes in a network. Likewise, if the seats *available* on a certain route are multiplied by the flown kilometres, the result aggregated across all routes represents the total capacity supply produced in a network. This indicator is called 'Available Seat Kilometre' (ASK).

If the demand indicator (RPK) is divided by the supply indicator (ASK), the result can be interpreted as the average utilization of flown capacity across a given network, and is called 'Seat Load Factor' (SLF). On a certain route, however, it is sufficient to divide the number of paying passengers by the number of seats to receive the concrete SLF. A good load factor obviously indicates a good utilization of the very expensive resources – aircraft and crews.

The second performance indicator monitored by airlines is the so-called 'yield', which is the revenue per seat, per passenger, per flight, etc. High yields (per seat) are expected to sum up to economically successful flights, and finally to a profitable network, provided the costs are under control. Profitability is often measured in relative terms, i.e. as the difference between yield and unit cost. Similar to the measurement of demand and supply volume in a network as mentioned above, the yield is often defined as 'Revenue per Available Seat Kilometre' (RASK), while unit cost is calculated as 'Cost per Available Seat Kilometre' (CASK). The profit of a certain flight, as well as that of a bundle of flights or even an entire network, obviously springs from the difference between the respective RASK and CASK figures.

The third performance indicator takes into account that even if a flight is fully booked (with an SLF of 100 per cent), this is not yet sufficient to ensure that the capital locked in the aircraft pays off. This may be the case if an aircraft has a limited daily operations time (counted in 'Block-hours'), and stands idly on the ground for some, or much, of the day. Since passengers only pay for travel time in the air, unproductive times on the ground endanger the profit of an airline, since many of the costs associated with merely owning (not even flying!) an aircraft continue to occur even if it stands still.

This time-related productivity of an aircraft, called 'Block hours per day', is driven by a variety of different parameters. First, aircraft used for long-haul flights achieve an excellent productivity much easier than one deployed on shorter (continental and domestic) routes, since the flown stage is much longer. This is both in absolute terms and relative to unproductive times such as taxiing, or waiting for feeder flights with transfer passengers. The latter aspect hints at another major driver: that aircraft productivity is dependent on the chosen business model. While traditional network carriers operate hubs to connect their people to more destinations worldwide, LCCs up to now have avoided the complexity of hubs, and do not support their customers in connecting flights. As a result, LCCs do not have to make their aircraft wait in hubs for feeder flights, which ensures that aircraft can depart again as soon as they have been serviced and filled with new passengers. In this case, only the Minimum Turnaround Time (MTT) of the respective airport, plus the size of the aircraft determine the unproductive time on the ground.

To make managing an airline network even more complex, the three key performance indicators (KPIs) mentioned above are partly interlinked. As an example, it is very difficult to achieve both a high seat load factor and a high yield per seat, unless the respective market is underserved and short of supply. In practice, it gets more and more difficult to fill an aircraft beyond an SLF of some ninety per cent. In most cases (except in a high-demand market with limited supply), the last few seats will only sell at discounted rates. If clients understand this pattern, the down-selling effect impacts many of the seats, not only the last few, resulting in the paradox effect that an aircraft with a ninety-five per cent load factor may contribute less total revenue than the same aircraft on the same route on the same day with only ninety-two per cent load factor. This is the reason why airlines very often intentionally leave the last few seats empty, as selling them would deteriorate, not improve, the result of the flight. There are other important drivers of network profit such as aircraft type and size, frequency of services, or hub patterns (for network carriers). However, these drivers are at the same time network design and planning parameters. Thus, they will be discussed in the next chapter. A good overview of airline economics and management can be achieved by reading Doganis.[2]

Facets of network design and planning

An airline network is constituted by the combination of routes and the resources required to physically transport passengers and/or cargo on these routes. The complexity of designing and planning a network is determined first of all by its sheer size. As more destinations are included, more routes need to be flown, and more resources (aircraft, crews, etc.) are required. The number of viable scenarios to combine these resources grows disproportionately, if not exponentially, with the number of routes and resources involved. This effect is greater for hub and spoke networks than for P2P networks, since a hub establishes transfer opportunities, and thus additional options to connect destinations with given resources. Put simply, a P2P network with ten destinations can easily be designed and planned in an Excel spreadsheet, while a hub and spoke network with, say, 100 destinations worldwide requires a variety of sophisticated optimization models, as well as significant computing power.

In an ideal world, there would be a fully integrated optimization model, capable of designing an efficient and profitable network for a given set of destinations and environmental parameters such as hub location, fleet structure, or regulatory regime. Furthermore, this model would be suited to planning and steering the involved resources at all instances, from strategic scenarios all the way to operational allocation of resources. However, this ideal model does not exist, at least not yet. Instead, airlines deploy a series of sequential optimization steps, unravelling the mathematical problem to a level where a subset of the problem can be handled by state-of-the-art algorithms and computers. There are two dimensions of unravelling: by type of resource and by timeline.

Unravelling by type of resource

In designing their network, airlines usually determine their resources: first those which have the highest asset value, or are at least flexibly available. For instance, selecting a hub locks up considerable capital (such as infrastructure) and cannot be revised quickly. Then, aircraft type and deployment patterns will be selected, since aircraft absorb enormous investments (if not purchased, then leased with considerable lease rates). All other resources/assets are determined in the order of either declining capital lock, or of increased flexibility, such as crews, maintenance capacities, and ground handling staff. This sequence is no more than a heuristic, but it is pragmatic and delivers reasonably efficient network designs.

Unravelling along the timeline

In a complex environment such as the aviation industry, things tend to change, and often don't go as planned. Airlines consequently apply a planning sequence with at least three steps:

- long-term strategic planning (three to ten years prior to a certain flight event)
- mid-term market planning and scheduling (six months to three years prior to a flight event)
- short-term operational planning and resource steering (last few weeks prior to a flight event).

In the past ten years, this ideal sequence has been somewhat blurred, since the threshold between mid- and short-term capacity allocation is difficult to define in practice. Furthermore, airline demand has become even more short-term and seasonal, to which airlines have responded by increasing the number of annual schedule cycles from three or four (e.g. summer, winter, holiday season) to ten or more schedule periods per year. Thus, most airlines have merged mid-term and short-term planning into one function, and focus more on the continuous interplay between market planning (taking into account expected demand) and rotation planning (taking into account efficient deployment of supply). A very comprehensive view on aviation network structures and state-of-the-art planning methodologies is, for instance, provided by Goedeking.[3]

Network and market coverage

The primary goal of designing an air transport network is to capture as much demand for air travel as possible in a profitable way. Demand occurs between city pairs, i.e. between origins and destinations. Origins and destinations represent local markets, featuring specific customer segments and buying behaviours. The vital question for every airline is *how many* and *which* local markets should be covered by the network. A large number increases the theoretical revenue potential and fosters scale effects. On the other hand, it increases the number of routes to be offered, as well as the risk of ending up with unprofitable routes. This effect is also dependent on the respective business model. While LCCs can opt for a 'cherry picking' approach, and select only the obviously profitable routes, network carriers have to deal with profitable and less profitable routes, since their network patterns are highly complex and interdependent, due to the hub rationale. They tend to cross-subsidize feeder flights with trunk routes, as well as (less profitable) connecting flights with (usually profitable) local demand, without exactly knowing how big the cross-subsidization is.

Having said that, it becomes obvious that network carriers are facing a challenging dilemma, which is that in order to participate in as many traffic flows as possible, they establish a hub. To run the hub efficiently, they need a good utilization, i.e. a large number of connections. To make that system attractive for both local and connecting travellers, they need to offer a broad range of destinations to all originating passengers, otherwise they will use a competing hub or direct flights. This need for size and market coverage is referred to as the '360° model', meaning that an airline operating a hub needs to achieve a more or less comprehensive coverage of major markets within its reach.

The result is, as stated above, a risky mix of profitable and less profitable routes. Furthermore, a dominant share of resources, as well as of management capacities, is usually absorbed by the least profitable connections facilitated in a certain hub, for example, domestic or intra-continental connections. This leaves little room for manoeuver for the really profitable, long-haul connections. However, understanding this effect means being able to fix it (for details see 'Network and hub structure', below).

In the past, some airlines were forced to downscale their hubs, e.g. Lufthansa in Munich. Compromising on the 360° approach bears the risk of entering a downward spiral, where reduced market coverage results in a diminishing attractiveness, which then dilutes demand and finally competitiveness in terms of scale and utilization. However, real-life examples prove that this can be handled, and that a consolidated hub can be more sustainable than an oversized one. This will also be elaborated below. Besides operating a hub, another very powerful means of increasing market coverage is partnering with other airlines, either on a bilateral level (e.g. interlining, codesharing, or joint venture), or through joining an alliance such as Star, **one**world, or SkyTeam.

Network and fleet structure

The most important resources needed to operate an aviation network are aircraft, slots, and crews. In addition, ground handling and aircraft maintenance capacities are required. Aircraft lock up huge amounts of capital (if owned), so that establishing the right fleet structure is absolutely success-critical for an airline. Once again, the 'right' fleet structure is highly dependent on the chosen business model. For LCCs, which operate P2P networks mainly on a continental or domestic level, it is feasible to operate one or two (narrow-body) aircraft types only.

This commonality of fleet improves the economics of a network, since it keeps the complexity of maintenance and crew assignment as small as it can be. Network carriers, on the other hand, cannot avoid operating a more heterogeneous fleet, since they have to cover long-haul as well as short-haul routes, and connect small feeder markets to large trunk routes. They need to continuously evaluate the trade-off between commonality of fleet, and a larger number of aircraft types suited to accommodate the specifics of different markets (in terms of range and capacity). In general, the basic rule of thumb is that an airline should always deploy the largest aircraft it can fill in a certain market, since unit costs (CASK) show a digressive tendency with growing aircraft capacity. However, there are at least two limitations to that rule.

- A larger aircraft may, in general, have better unit cost (and thus, incremental profit) than a smaller one. However, this does not mean that the largest available aircraft ensures the highest *total profit* on a certain route. Depending on market as well as aircraft characteristics, it may happen that the gap (profit) between the curve of accumulated yield and the total cost of available aircraft is not larger for the maximum number of passengers and the largest aircraft, than it is for a smaller aircraft type with a smaller number of passengers. For most airline managers, this rationale is severely counterintuitive, since they were trained in the paradigm of unit cost and scale effects. The above-mentioned exception to the rule would mean that the airline would, on purpose, leave some of the potential passengers on the ground with part of the theoretical revenue potential untapped.
- In certain highly competitive markets, it may be wiser to cover the available number of passengers with smaller aircraft and, in return, with a higher number of services per day/week ('frequency'), compared to the scenario with the largest available plane for that route.

The latter aspect is closely linked to the so-called 'S-curve effect'. This empirical effect states that if a carrier enters a market with limited capacity (available seats × frequency), it will, first of all, have a niche position. Any frequency extension from that low level will not be fully 'rewarded' in the beginning by the passengers, since their perception is blurred by the more comprehensive offering of incumbents on this route. Thus, an *increase* in frequency share will only create a *disproportionately lower increase* in passenger share, and vice versa – a carrier holding a stronger position in that market and offering a significant number of seats and frequencies will benefit from the opposite effect in the supercritical area of the S-curve. Thus, a *further increase* of an already strong frequency share will entail a *disproportionately higher increase* in passenger share, until finally the saturation area is reached. The S-curve phenomenon is illustrated in Figure 4.2.

The conclusion from this phenomenon is that if an airline is a niche player on a certain route, and does not intend to leave the niche, it can deploy the largest aircraft type it can fill in this market, and minimize its unit cost. On the other hand, a carrier with a strong position may decide to compromise on aircraft size and unit cost, and instead invest in greater frequency, in order to fully extract the dominance effect on the revenue side. Deprosse *et al.*, for instance, provide a very helpful overview on network planning methodologies from the practitioner's perspective.[4]

Network and human resources

Besides aircraft, human resources are an indispensable element of aviation networks, especially crews (cockpit and cabin crews) and ground handling staff (for aircraft, passenger, and baggage handling). The interplay between aircraft and crew is quite complex, since operating an aircraft has fewer restrictions than deploying crews. Crew members need to have the right licence to work on a certain aircraft type, plus their working hours are restricted by law and by contracts. Consequently, the round trips of crew members ('rotations') are

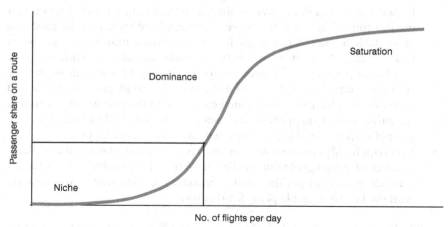

Figure 4.2 S-curve effect[5]

different from round trips of aircraft. Planning the round trips for the crews is a challenging task, since the schedules must not only ensure a seamless staffing of the aircraft, but also observe legal restrictions and personal availabilities and preferences of crew members (see Chapter 9 for details of crew planning).

This challenge is usually mastered with a two-step approach: first, the round trips of aircraft are coupled to potential round trips of crews with the required licences to operate that aircraft type ('pairing'), until all aircraft are perfectly staffed throughout their entire operational schedule. Pairing is usually performed two to three months prior to a scheduled flight, and does not yet include individual names of crew members, or tail numbers of aircraft. This is added in a second step ('rostering'), when the paired rotations are translated into concrete working plans for individual crew members and aircraft, commonly one month in advance. On the current day, unexpected irregularities related to the crew (e.g. illness) need to be handled at short notice, usually by the airline's Operations Control Centre (see Chapters 22 and 23 for details).

Network and hub structure

Network carriers operate hubs to accumulate demand in one spot, and leverage that scale effect to offer more routes, capture more revenue potentials, and deploy larger aircraft than carriers with a focus on P2P services. As mentioned earlier, the downside of this business model is the massively increased interdependency of resources, resulting in complex operations and less productive resources. Furthermore, operational stability is more critical than in P2P networks. A hub is first and foremost a means of production, *then* a local market. Its success will be defined as the ability to capture as many traffic flows (and thus, revenue potentials) as possible, at minimum cost. On a more detailed level, its major KPIs are *connectivity* (its ability to connect inbound and outbound passengers in a convenient way), *productivity* (first of aircraft, then of all other involved resources), operational stability, and profitability of offered connections.

Since aviation is a scale business, the dominant success factor of a hub is its mere size and economic potential, determined by the strength of its catchment (i.e. number of people living close to the hub), and the wealth and mobility level of potential air travellers within this catchment. In addition, the balance between local demand and connecting traffic is crucial. As mentioned earlier, direct services often generate higher ticket fares than transfer connections, so carriers tend to cross-subsidize transfer traffic with local traffic, as well as feeder traffic with long-haul services.

To achieve good connectivity, hub airlines have developed the paradigm of compressing their inbound and outbound flights into peaks, increasing the probability that an inbound passenger can reach an appropriate outbound flight to his or her final destination without too much waiting time. The higher the number of qualified 'hits' (potential outbound flights reachable for an inbound flight within a predefined waiting time), the higher is the share of the theoretical traffic that the respective carrier can cover by accumulating demand in their hub.

The peaks in this wavy schedule pattern are referred to as 'banks'. Hub carriers optimize the number of banks, as well as the detailed shape and structure of the banks, on a continuous base. Initially, after the invention of bank structures for hubs forty years ago, there was a trend towards large numbers of banks at major airports–up to eight inbound and eight outbound banks. Large bank numbers in theory boost both connectivity (as long as passengers care about waiting times during transfer) *and* productivity. However, the pendulum swung back at the beginning of the last decade, since airline managers realized that going for the maximum number of banks comes at the price of massive downsides:

- The wavy structure of the hub schedule with many peaks entails peaks in the utilization of airport resources (e.g. ground handling staff, terminal space, baggage transfer systems etc.) as well, resulting in buffer capacities to be built up for peak demand, and thus very poor productivity of these resources.
- Likewise, strong schedule peaks overload the airspace as well, resulting, for example, in holding patterns for inbound aircraft, and thus delays and a deterioration of aircraft productivity.
- A high number of banks fosters short connecting times between inbound and outbound flights, close to the Minimum Connecting Time (MCT) operationally determined for a certain airport. This sounds favourable at first glance, since it reduces idle time for both aircraft and passengers. However, short connecting times bring the risk of missed connections if anything goes wrong with one of the flights involved, plus inconvenience for passengers who can barely make the connection in a very large airport with long walking distances to cover. Thus, short connecting times may result in operational instability and inconvenience for clients, which is counterproductive for hub airlines.
- Banks designed for short-haul connections have different efficiency requirements from connections for long-haul traffic, and combining them in a very dense hub pattern may result in compromises, thus hampering the efficiency of both connection types.
- Designing their hub and bank structure, hub carriers often try to take a strategic perspective, for example, by optimizing the banks for expected future growth. This is risky, since growth may not occur as planned. The hub pattern may then be oversized, spreading the existing demand too thinly across the banks. If banks are not filled with a minimum number of flights and passengers, they become under-critical, which means that every incremental bank dilutes connectivity instead of boosting it as in the theoretical case. In this case, rightsizing the hub and compressing the banks is the only way to regain a commercially and operationally sustainable structure (see Franke for comparison).[6]

Consequently, most airlines have, in the meantime, abandoned the ideal hub paradigm ('de-hubbing', 'de-peaking'), and established hybrid approaches which are suited to attenuate the above-mentioned downsides of peaky hub patterns. At very large hubs (with more than 40 million passengers per annum), hub carriers have condensed their banks into some four mega-banks (e.g. Frankfurt), or completely switched to a continuous connecting mode ('random hubbing', e.g. at London Heathrow or Istanbul Atatürk).

However, home carriers in mid-sized hubs (say 10–40 million passengers per annum) do not own enough volume to deploy continuous hubbing, so they still have to find the right bank structure to ensure profitable and stable operations. Besides the major drivers such as overall demand and transfer share, the ideal number and shape of banks depends on a variety of local drivers specific for that airport, such as opening hours, geographical position relative to key markets, or minimum connecting time. Franke[7] demonstrates that most mid-sized airports have a theoretical sweet spot in terms of bank number between five and seven banks (inbound and outbound); the ideal number being determined in a first step by overall traffic volume and transfer share of the home carrier at that airport (see Figure 4.3). This heuristic, based on a simplified driver model, as well as on a benchmark across various European airports, may then be adjusted taking the specific drivers of the respective airport into account, resulting in a recommendable bank number somewhat below or above the initial estimate.

If the ideal number of banks has been determined for both the primary drivers (traffic volume, transfer share) and the specific local drivers, the next level of

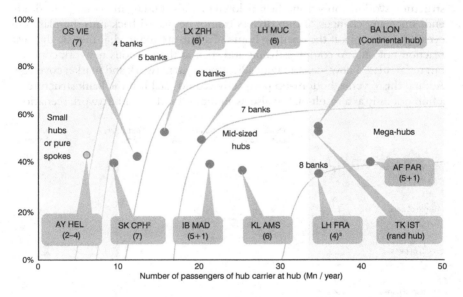

Figure 4.3 Heuristic calculation ('meta-model') of recommendable number of banks for mid-sized airports[8]

Notes:
1   Number of actually operated banks
2   Local passenger share estimated
3   Overlapping megabanks

optimization can be achieved by fine-tuning the shape and relative position of the banks (see Figure 4.4). For instance, in an ideal setting, a certain outbound bank should start no earlier than the last flight from the respective inbound bank has landed, because an overlap between inbound and outbound flight dilutes the theoretically attainable number of hits between those two banks. In practice, it may nevertheless be appropriate to establish some overlap, since that measure increases the quality of connections (such as average connecting time), as well as the productivity of fleet and ground handling resources (since the peak effect is smoothed).

Another finding from the above-mentioned study[9] is that the strategic value and fit of designing hub structures can be improved if a new perspective is added. The traditional way of planning network and hub structures is a one-way road: the strategy of an airline is translated into fleet and network scenarios, which will then be translated into a market schedule and rotational patterns. In this paradigm, the hub and bank structure is perceived as the ultimate result of the fleet and network concept, standing at the very end of planning. However, this approach may lead to local optima, if not to inefficient results, since the impact of levers on the hub level may be as large as on the fleet or network level. Thus, a bank structure perceived as the natural outcome of a fleet and network concept may massively underestimate the interplay between strategy, demand, fleet, network, and hub structure. Working only from the top down may also end up in a conceptual dead-end, since any changes of hub drivers cannot be played back into the planning cycle. For example, if the opening hours of a hub are reduced, it may be the best reaction not only to compress banks and stick to the previous network concept, but to calculate a new scenario with adjustments to network and market coverage. Adding this reverse, bottom-up perspective could establish the bank structure of a hub not only as a result of, but also as an input for, fleet and network scenarios.

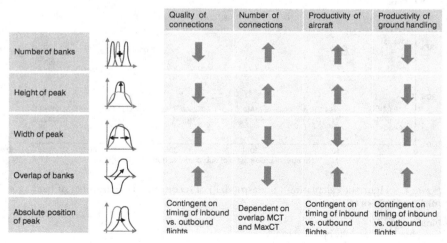

Figure 4.4 Impact of shape and relative position of banks on key performance indicators of a hub[10]

Network and regulatory aspects

Despite four decades of ongoing deregulation, air traffic is still a massively regulated business. Consequently, network design and operation are not only driven by economic factors and physical resources, but by legal or regulatory restrictions. There are at least five major regulatory drivers:

- Traffic rights: throughout history, transportation of passengers and goods has been highly regulated, since transport has always been a source of wealth and thus power. Today, air traffic rights are mostly negotiated on a bilateral level between countries, building on an entrenched system of freedom rights established for deep sea and inland water transport many centuries ago. Freedom rights start with Level One (overflight right for a foreign country) and culminate with Level Eight (some authors even define a Ninth Freedom) called *cabotage*, being the right to freely transport passengers and/or cargo *within* a foreign country. Some political federations such as the European Union have designed multilateral agreements for their members, treating every member like a home carrier in that federation.
- Slots: due to limited capacities both in airspace and at airports, airlines need to apply for slots for take-off, flight, and landing. Flight slots are assigned on a case-by-case basis by the respective air navigation service provider, while airport slots are granted on application by the International Air Transport Association, IATA. Officially, slots are granted biannually at IATA slot conferences and cannot be traded among airlines. Informally, there is a grey zone, since slots at very popular and congested airports such as London Heathrow are tremendously valuable. In the past, airlines have happened to acquire other airlines mainly to get hold of their attractive slot portfolio. (See Deprosse for details regarding slot management.)[11]
- Opening hours of airports (and night curfew): in densely populated regions, noise emission of incoming and outgoing aircraft is perceived as a major nuisance for people living in the vicinity of airports. Thus, many municipalities restrict aircraft movements throughout the night to protect the health of their citizens. Usually, departures and landings are not allowed during the night (during 'curfew', typically 2300–0600), or at least are limited.
- Operating hours of crews: while aircraft can be operated as long as it takes to reach a destination within their flight range (provided that their maintenance requirements are fulfilled), crew members are much more restricted time-wise, in order to protect their health, and avoid fatal mistakes due to fatigue. Both duty times and flight times are limited per day, per month, and per year. However, many airlines have labour agreements with their crews which contain limitations even stricter than the legal ones.
- Flights standards, safety and security requirements: there is a variety of legal standards defined to ensure utmost safety and security standards (in Europe for instance EU 965/2012 for flight standards and Airline Operations Control Centre (AOCC) management, or European Aviation Safety Agency

Continuing Airworthiness Management Organisation (EASA CAMO) Part M for maintenance compliance).

Conclusion

Impact of network design on commercial and operational levers of an airline

This chapter has provided an overview, from both an academic and practical perspective, on success factors, building blocks, methodologies, and metrics of state-of-the-art aviation network design. Network operations account for the vast majority of airline revenues and cost, since they generate the core product of airlines, and at the same time absorb most of the assets and resources an airline has. Thus, designing an attractive network and operating it efficiently is the most important step towards running an airline profitably.

However, networks tend to be complex as a consequence of many interdependent resources. LCCs fight hard to keep their networks much simpler than their full-service competitors, which usually operate a hub. But even for LCCs, designing and operating the network is far from simple, as soon as they own more than a handful of aircraft. Furthermore, competition is fierce, with major changes every couple of days, and aviation is still a highly regulated industry with a plethora of restrictions and legal requirements. To make it even worse, aircraft capacity is skyrocketing in most regions of the world, while airport and airspace capacity are rather scarce.

Consequently, designing and scheduling an efficient aviation network requires advanced analytical and operational research (OR) capabilities, abundant market and traffic flow data, and lots of experience. At this point in time, there is no such thing as a fully integrated network planning model capable of digesting all framework parameters, and designing the ideal network for this environment in a single step. Instead, even state-of-the-art planning paradigms deployed by market leaders consist of stepwise and iterative optimization loops for network schedules, aircraft rotations, crew rotations, hub bank structures, etc. On the other hand, the more that interdependencies between network resources are taken into account, the more efficient and robust the resulting network scenarios and schedules will be.

It needs to be borne in mind that there is not a single 'correct' network design, but more and less efficient concepts for a given set of external and internal framework parameters. For instance, with a certain existing fleet, a night curfew in the airline's hub, and specific labour agreements, one carrier may end up with a significantly different network design from its neighbouring carrier with similar size, but with different fleet, no curfew, and different labour agreements. Yet both designs may be perfectly reasonable and suited to their respective economic environments. In the future, the business models of network carriers and LCCs will further converge, resulting in new and more hybrid network design patterns (e.g. LCCs may feed network carriers' hubs). Furthermore, rapidly increasing computing speed and analytical capabilities may bring new and more efficient network design algorithms.

Notes

1 Franke, Dr Markus (FATC): Lecture on 'Strategic Network Management', International University of Bad Honnef (IUBH), Düsseldorf, 2015/16
2 Doganis, Rigas: *Flying Off Course: Airline Economics and Marketing*. 4th Edition, Routledge, London, 2009
3 Goedeking, Dr Philipp (Avinomics): *Networks in Aviation: Strategies and Structures*. Springer Verlag, Berlin, 2010
4 Deprosse, Harald and Händel, Michael: 'Network Planning and Slot Management' (Deutsche Lufthansa AG), in Wald, Andreas; Fay, Christoph; Gleich, Ronald (editors); *Introduction to Aviation Management*, Lit-Verlag, Berlin, 2010 (pp. 211–227)
5 Franke, Dr Markus (FATC): Lecture on 'Strategic Network Management', International University of Bad Honnef (IUBH), Düsseldorf, 2015/16
6 Franke, Dr Markus (FATC): 'Airline Hub Optimization – Screening Bank Structures to Boost Hub Performance', G.A.R.S. Workshop prior to European Aviation Conference, Amsterdam, 5 November, 2014
7 Op. cit.
8 Op. cit.
9 Op. cit.
10 Op. cit.
11 Op. cit.

5 Customer points of contact

Gary Parker

Introduction

Within the past few years, airline carriers have come to realize that there are abundant opportunities to engage with travellers at touch points throughout the travel-planning and booking process to engender additional brand loyalty and generate incremental revenue via ancillary services. There can be up to eight essential stages of the overall travel experience:

- inspiration
- planning
- booking
- purchase
- pre-trip
- departure
- in-flight
- post-trip.

Many airlines are taking steps to transform their brand images and operations from mere providers of a commodity product (seats on a plane) or means to an end (a transporter of passengers from A to B) into entities providing timely and alluring travel services throughout the customer experience.

Points of contact

Consider the different ways customers may interact with an airline. The following contact points are adapted from the Managing Customers Tutorial at KnowThis.com, having been modified slightly to suit the airline context.

- In person – Customers seek in-person assistance at travel agencies or ticket counters, and corporate customers from airline salespeople who visit them at their place of business.
- Telephone – Customers seeking to make purchases or have a problem solved may find it more convenient to do so through phone contact. Many airlines have a dedicated call centre handling incoming customer inquiries.

- Internet – The fastest growing contact point is the internet. The use of the internet for purchasing (e-commerce) has exploded and is now the key area where customers research, shop and look for assistance.
- Kiosks – A kiosk is a standalone, interactive computer, usually equipped with a touchscreen that offers customers several service options. Kiosks are now widely used for airline check-in, boarding passes and baggage tags.
- In-person product and service support – Some in-person assistance is not principally intended to assist with selling but is designed to offer support once a purchase is made. Such services are often handled by passenger service agents and flight attendants.

At each step of the customer's journey, there is an exchange of information between the traveller and the airline. The reservation system records each interaction with the traveller, allowing real-time delivery of sales and service through the journey. See Figure 5.1.

Interaction opportunities

One of the biggest challenges for airlines with the introduction of branded products and ancillary services is the need to ensure consistency in the sales process across all channels and customer points of contact. Each contact point with the customer must communicate the value of the product and address three components:

- core product
- ancillary services
- delivery process.

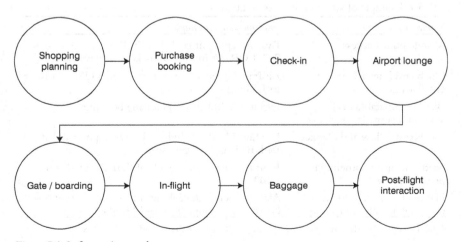

Figure 5.1 Information exchange

Core product

A 'product' is a defined and consistent 'bundle of services'. The ancillary elements facilitate and enhance the core service offering. In the case of airlines, the core service is transporting the passenger from A to B. The ancillary service elements differentiate the full-service carrier from the low-cost carrier (LCC). And these ancillary services don't merely involve the airlines' own optional services such as checked bags, lounge passes and on-board meals – they can also include the sales of hotel rooms, car rentals, ground transportation, and a bevy of other services before and after the actual flight.

Ancillary services

Adding ancillary elements or increasing the level of performance should be done in ways that enhance the value of the core product and enable the service provider to charge a higher price. Those ancillary services are revenue opportunities that appear throughout the 'revenue production pipeline' (interconnected departments and their sequential activities). An audit of the revenue pipeline could indicate whether a carrier's guidelines with respect to fare flexibility or excess baggage fees are working. Front-line staff should be aware of the impact of waiving fees and how they can cause leakage in the revenue stream. Unless everyone working at a carrier is committed to effective merchandizing, and departmental strategies are aligned, the potential increase in revenue may be undermined. Ancillary services can be broadly classified as follows:

- Air extras are ancillary services consumed by a passenger on board the flight. Examples of air extras are in-flight entertainment, headsets, internet service, prepaid seat selection, baggage service, meals, etc. See Table 5.1.

Table 5.1 Example of air extra services and fees

Service provided	Implementation example
Mobile phone access	Ryanair: approximately 0.5 EUR for text messages, 2–3 EUR per minute to make or receive calls
On-board internet and/or email access	AirTran: laptop access starting at 5.95 USD for up to 1.5 hours
Blanket, inflatable neck support, eyeshade and socks	Jetstar: 5 USD also sold during booking
On-board pillow and blanket	JetBlue: 7 USD includes 5 USD coupon valid at Bed, Bath and Beyond store
Seatback entertainment, video programming	Frontier: view 24 channels of 'DIRECTV' for 6 USD
Handheld entertainment device, video programming	Alaska: reserve 'digEplayer' in advance or rent on-board, prices range from 6–12 USD

Note: The amounts shown are as of 2009 and are shown for their relative value only

Source: Airline websites reviewed August 2009

- Travel extras are travel-related ancillary services consumed by a passenger either before or after the flight. Examples of travel extras are airport parking, baggage forwarding services from home to the airport, ground transportation to/from airport, lounge access, etc. See Table 5.2.

- Ticket transaction fees can apply under several scenarios:
  - to pass on a merchant fee imposed by a particular credit card to the consumer
  - an airline may recoup the costs associated with airport or call centre ticketing versus those of website ticketing. See Table 5.3.

Airlines exempt high revenue passengers from normal ticketing fees via fare basis, ticket designator or account code. These additional fees do not appear on the airline ticket, but on a new passenger receipt, which totals the airfare and fees.

Table 5.2 Example of travel extra services and fees

Service provided	Implementation example
Kerbside check-in with skycap	US Airways: 2 USD per page, paid at the airport
Airport check-in at a staffed counter	Ryanair: 43 EUR fee if arriving at airport without a pre-printed boarding card
One-time airport lounge access	United: 39 USD per guest
Priority boarding	Wizz Air: Early boarding at gate – 4 EUR or boarding via bus 2.50 EUR (double when paid at the airport) per passenger, one way (varies by airport of departure)
Priority boarding and check-in	easyJet: Early boarding and priority check-in 11.25 EUR per passenger, one way
Priority boarding, check-in, fast track security screening, lounge access, and premium meal	Jet2.com: Jet2Plus is offered on select routes for 35 EUR per person per sector
Seat assignment in forward rows	Vueling: Seat Optimum feature ahead of exit rows 5 EUR per seat, one way
Seat assignment in rear rows	Vueling: Seat Basic feature behind exit rows 3 EUR per seat, one way
Empty seat between two seats	Vueling: Duo seat feature for 25 EUR per seat, one way
Seat assignment in exit row	Qantas: 80 AUD short haul, 160 AUD long haul per seat, one way

Note: The amounts shown are as of 2009 and are shown for their relative value only

Source: Airline websites reviewed August 2009

Table 5.3 Example of ticket transaction fees

Service provided	Implementation example
Online booking	Allegiant: 14 USD per passenger in itinerary (no charge applies when booked at the airport)
Receive itinerary via mobile phone	Wizz Air: 1 EUR per itinerary sent
Online payment with a credit card	easyJet: Payment by Visa, MasterCard, Diners Club, or American Express will incur a fee of 2.5% of the total transaction value, with a minimum charge of 5.50 EUR, whichever is greater
Online payment with a debit card	Wizz Air: Payment by Solo or Maestro will incur a fee of 3 EUR, per passenger each way
Protection from booking change fees	Allegiant: 7.50 USD per passenger each way (proprietary product – not trip insurance)
Fare lock before purchase	Clickair: 2 EUR for a 24-hour hold and 5 EUR to guarantee the fare for 72 hours

Note: The amounts shown are as of 2009 and are shown for their relative value only

Source: Airline websites reviewed August 2009

Delivery processes

The third component in designing a service concept concerns the processes used to deliver both the core product and each of the ancillary services. The design of the delivery must consider:

- the delivery method (e.g., in person, telephone, internet, kiosk)
- the nature of the customer's role in the process (active or passive)
- the delivery duration (immediate or ongoing)
- the prescribed level and style of service to be delivered (branded fares and ancillary service).

Defining ancillary service pricing methods

Branded fares and fare families utilize product bundling. These pricing methods encourage consumers to buy a higher fare by including a package of defined amenities. Branded fares are similar to fare families with two major distinctions. First, each fare type is always offered on a flight, unless the flight is sold out. For example, American Airlines always offers the lowest priced *Choice* fare on a flight, regardless of whether the flight has low or peak booking activity. The revenue management function will increase this fare as determined by consumer demand. Second, the price difference between fare products is fixed and usually promoted as a product attribute. This method represents an improvement of the fare family approach. Branded fares apply retail psychology by assigning a simple price point to a better bundle of amenities.

À la carte pricing

À la carte is at the opposite end of the spectrum from methods that bundle amenities using distinct price points. Allowing consumers to click and choose their way through the booking process is a favourite practice among LCCs and a growing number of traditional airlines. It's one of the easier implementation choices because it merely adds optional extras to a carrier's existing fare structure. À la carte pricing clarifies the value of services for the consumer. This allows them to pick and choose services and features based upon the desire to maximize convenience or minimize price.

À la carte features

The list continues to grow, but the following are typical activities:

- on-board sales of food and beverages
- checking of baggage and excess baggage
- assigned seats or better seats such as exit rows
- branded insurance programmes managed by the carrier (e.g., Air Canada's 'On my Way' programme)
- call centre support for reservations
- fees charged for purchases made with credit or debit cards
- priority check-in and screening
- VIP lounge access
- early boarding benefits
- on-board entertainment systems
- wireless internet access
- ground transportation upon arrival.

Commission-based products

Ancillary revenue activities include commissions earned by passenger carriers on the sale of hotel accommodations, car rentals and travel insurance, and other travel items such as tours and transfers. The commission-based category primarily involves the carrier's website, but it can include the sale of duty-free and consumer products, and fees for internet access on-board.

Loyalty programmes

The loyalty category largely consists of the sale of miles or points to programme partners such as hotel chains and car rental companies, co-branded credit cards, online malls, retailers, and communication services. Checked baggage and frequent-flyer programmes represent the largest sources of airline ancillary revenue. Income from a loyalty programme largely depends on the size of the carrier's co-branded card portfolio. Some airlines have the advantage of operating in markets that offer abundant credit card potential.

Channels of distribution

The respective roles of the major carriers, global distribution systems (GDSs), traditional travel agents, and the consumer have changed and continue to evolve. The internet has had a tremendous impact on carrier product distribution, particularly in parts of the world where it has entered into mainstream use. New online travel agencies and other full service and specialty travel websites have entered the online travel market and put pressure on everyone to adapt quickly and develop new business models and technologies. This section of the chapter will look at each of the different distribution elements in the rapidly changing context provided by the internet.

The air travel customer is the final element in the traditional distribution channel. Although obviously an important element in initiating the travel request and finally purchasing the carrier ticket, before the internet the customer was relatively inactive and also unaware of much of the detail involved. The internet provided direct and inexpensive access to consumers who were ready to take control and assume a larger and more active role in the process. Combined with other carrier factors such as rising distribution costs and system bias, a receptive and eager consumer population was key in driving the development and adoption of the internet-based travel industry. The travel industry was one of the first to go online. As will be seen below, the internet provided customers with the resources to research and book their trip online. Early online reservation functions were limited to bookings and payment transactions requiring customers to reserve flights well in advance of their departure to receive tickets in time for departure. With the introduction of electronic tickets, or e-tickets, lead time and costs have been reduced.

Consider the case where a customer purchases an e-ticket directly from a carrier's branded website. In addition to bypassing the costs of the traditional intermediaries such as travel agents and GDSs, the carrier needs fewer internal reservation agents to answer questions or make telephone reservations when customers book online. The situation is similar to the late 1970s when carriers reduced costs by outsourcing the labour-intensive process of researching and booking travel to external travel agents. Now the customers are doing this work and lowering the carrier's costs once again. At the same time though, customers have access to competitors' websites and fares, both locally and internationally.

Carrier websites

Most carriers now have branded websites where they can sell directly to the consumer (business to consumer – B2C) using their own software, and avoid paying GDS fees and travel agents' commissions on bookings. In countries where internet penetration has been slower, carriers often use their sites to reach travel agents and corporate travel departments (business to business – B2B) rather than individual consumers.

Most major carriers have a competitive advantage through user-friendly websites that provide comprehensive information and transparent pricing. This approach increases consumer trust and confidence. In addition to customer reservations and e-tickets, such carrier websites offer seat selection, merchandise, reward points, and discounted departures that are unavailable elsewhere. Customers can also provide a personal profile and sign up for email services that alert them to promotions tailored to their interests. Providing additional travel products for sale online, such as accommodation or transportation package deals and departure insurance, is another strategy to increase revenues and attract and retain customers. The new distribution channel that the internet provides has helped existing LCCs to reach more customers and new LCCs to enter the industry. Initially, to keep their distribution costs down, LCCs were not interested in paying the GDS fees.

Other travel websites

There is a broad range of full service and specialty consumer travel websites. There are the 'new' online travel agencies, such as Travelocity and Expedia, which quickly took advantage of the internet to create their businesses. Traditional 'bricks and mortar' travel agencies, such as Carson Wagonlit Group (CWT), or Amex (American Express Travel Services Group), have adapted and now offer their services online. Some of these online travel sites were developed in collaboration with existing GDS companies (Travelocity by Sabre) but many other independent sites also provide customers with direct GDS access. CWT and Amex have both developed new user interfaces that enable customers to use GDS services at a lower cost. There are also auction or bidding sites, such as Priceline.com, where customers can submit bids for deep discount air travel. Of course, other travel service providers in the hospitality, ground travel and leisure business have created their own websites. There are also many destination sites, usually run by tourism associations, that provide information about a country or city, ground transportation, accommodation, sightseeing, dining and local cultural events.

It is increasingly difficult to divide the different types of travel websites into categories. As they evolve, and in part due to competitive pressures, many sites have expanded the range of features and services they provide so there is often considerable overlap between them. In addition to carrier tickets and hotel reservations, online travel agencies provide travel tips and destination information. GDS companies are expanding product offerings to include transaction processing and information management services. Mergers are also a factor that is blurring the distinctions between the different types of distribution elements. Today a number of large travel conglomerates own multiple online travel agencies, a GDS or two, and perhaps a range of other online travel service providers. At the time of writing, the Travelport Group included the Galileo and Worldspan GDSs and the Orbitz internet site. GDS Sabre owns Travelocity, Lastminute.com, and a long list of other consumer-oriented internet travel sites. Sabre also operates a major carrier consultancy service and sells different carrier operations and management products and services.

New Distribution Capability

New Distribution Capability (NDC) is a travel industry-supported programme launched by IATA (the International Air Transport Association) for the development and adoption of a new XML-based data transmission standard to replace the legacy system languages and their limitations. The NDC Standard will enhance communications between airlines and travel agents. It will facilitate a more efficient airline distribution system, thereby benefitting airlines, agents, GDSs, IT providers and travel start-ups. Structured around seven distribution-related functions, the NDC Standard provides the opportunity to address the end-to-end airline distribution process, for example, shopping, booking, etc., and to deliver enhanced customer experiences. NDC will enable the travel industry to transform the way air products are retailed to corporations, leisure, and business travellers, by addressing the industry's limitations with the current legacy systems. These consist of a lack of product differentiation and long time-to-market, minimal display format and content, and finally, a non-transparent shopping experience.

Worldwide perspective

It is important to consider the role of GDSs and travel agencies outside of North America and Europe, particularly in countries where the internet has not entered mainstream use. For example, reliance on GDSs and travel agencies in the Asia-Pacific region remains strong. Lack of penetration of the internet and credit card use is one factor. However, established business practices and relationships, and cultural differences each play an important role. Asia is complex and diverse. Access to certain regions and business environments can only be achieved through the GDS. At the time of writing there were three large GDSs operating in Asia: Abacus, Amadeus and Galileo. China also has a GDS called TravelSky that operates in their highly-regulated market. International carriers who are capitalizing on internet distribution at home cannot hope to penetrate the huge Indonesian and Chinese travel markets opening up to the world without using travel agents and GDSs. Of course, GDSs are also an important international distribution channel for the national and 'local' Asian carriers, which have a huge domestic market but need the GDS network to get foreign bookings.

The five steps to success in ancillary service revenues (methodology)

1 Defining ancillary revenue brand

Every carrier would benefit from an intensive effort to define their brand. Airlines are especially guilty of not creating brand awareness among customers. Few management teams have adequately defined the carrier's brand, and almost none has defined a brand for ancillary service revenue activities.

2 Equipping managers with resources

The desire to grow ancillary service revenue usually begins with a senior executive seeking ways to boost the bottom line through à la carte elements or commission-based products. Sometimes a team is formed to evaluate the opportunity and perhaps a leader is assigned. Choosing leadership and having executive sponsorship for the ancillary service revenue role is a key consideration. The person chosen for the task will face scrutiny because of the disruptive nature of à la carte pricing and unbundling. What was once provided free-of-charge must now be sold. That can create challenges for marketing, pricing, public affairs, cabin services, airport operations, catering, and finance. The development of a business plan provides ancillary service revenue professionals compelling evidence of the organization's dedication to the new initiative.

3 Creating consumer clarity

Consumers, media, and politicians expect clarity. For these groups, clarity also contributes to greater integrity, especially regarding the mysterious and suspect art of ancillary service revenue. Clarity is based upon the visibility provided to à la carte fees and the ethics of how sales are accomplished. Visibility is the more easily accomplished of the two. But surprisingly, few carriers adequately disclose à la carte fees. Perhaps the lack of transparency is a symptom of greater problems such as a confused ancillary service revenue strategy or the lack of a systematic approach to à la carte pricing. In the rush to implement ancillary service revenue initiatives, many carriers create a patchwork of poorly defined products that fail to achieve their full potential.

4 Integrating the selling message

Airlines that sell a higher percentage of travel online enjoy greater direct access to customers and greater sales flexibility. The ancillary service revenue movement was born in Europe and early converts, such as Ryanair and easyJet, implemented services that could easily be sold via company websites. Most LCCs could not care less about global distribution systems. So the message is to sell by being persistent, not obnoxious. This means:

- placing commission-based products on the home page based upon alignment with the brand and revenue potential
- focusing in-path on the à la carte features provided by the airline, such as baggage, seat assignment, lounge access, early boarding, and pre-purchased meals
- giving placement priority to the big three: hotel, car rental, and insurance
- selling airline seats remains the greatest profit generator, so customers aren't lost
- sending follow-up emails to provide more service and sell more products.

5 Engaging employees as supporters

The five steps are designed to culminate with employees. There is truly one rule for this step, and that is to engage employees early and often during the design process. This is especially crucial for labour-represented employee groups. Support for ancillary revenue activities begins at the top with communication from the CEO that emphasizes the importance of ancillary revenue. The ultimate objective is to create a company of sales-oriented employees to support the ancillary revenue movement, can be achieved by creating a sales-oriented culture. This means:

- engaging labour groups early in the process
- stressing the economic importance of ancillary revenue
- sharing the results of testing and consumer surveys
- soliciting feedback in the design of airport and on-board processes
- equipping employees to become sales-oriented through training
- communicating financial results on a regular basis
- providing incentives to boost sales activity.

The beauty of the five steps is the simplicity of the message and the applicability to other projects. Brand, resources, clarity, selling and employees are words that should be integrated into every new project and programme.

The customer experience

To differentiate, gain market share, optimize profitability and create long-term loyalty, a carrier must properly invest in and execute its unique customer-experience strategy. Investment in strategy execution and organizational readiness through talent and technology has proven lucrative in many industries, and the airline industry will be no different. Because many other service-providing industries have made the first investments in the customer experience, customers are now more informed about what's possible and have, therefore, come to expect more from their airline experience.

Bibliography

Anon. 2014. *Your Global Guide to Alternative Payments*, Second Edition, Worldpay.com, February.

Anon. 2016. *Customer Contact Points*. From Managing Customers Tutorial. KnowThis. com. Accessed June 16, 2016 from http://www.knowthis.com/managing-customers/customer-contact-points.

ATPCO. 2010. *Optional Services and Branded Fares*, Brochure. www.atpco.net. Revised November 2016.

Bacon, T. 2014. Rethinking the organisation of revenue management: Time for a fresh look, Travel Industry News & Conferences, *EyeforTravel*, January.

Birdsong, E. 2016. *The Evolution of the Customer Experience. Why customer-centric airlines will lead the market*. White paper, Sabre Airline Solutions, February.

IATA – *New Distribution Capability*. www.iata.org/whatwedo/airline-distribution/ndc/ Pages/default.aspx. Accessed 26 June 2017.

Karvir, A. 2014. Smart Travel Analytics North America 2014, Knowledge is Power: Lesson in Analytics from Expedia's 'Fail-Fast' Culture. *Expedia*, January.

Lees, E. 2016. *A Better Way to Manage Airports: Passenger Analytics*. Insights from ICF International, White paper, ICF International.

Lovelock, C. and Wirtz, J. 2011. *Services Marketing, People, Technology, Strategy*. Seventh Edition, Pearson Education, Harlow.

Mourier, J-F. 2013. The Future of a Revenue Manager 2.0 – Part Human, Part Computer, All Profits. *Hotel News Resource*.

Parker, G. 2015. *Merchandising, Ancillary Revenue, Fare Families, Branded Fares and "a-la-carte" Pricing*. Airline Revenue Management Training Group, October.

Parker, G. 2015. *Practical Revenue Management for Passenger Transportation*. Airline Revenue Management Training Group, October.

Peppers, D. and Rogers, M. 2014. *What Kind of Customer Experience Are You Capable of Delivering? And Explaining Customer Centricity with a Diagram*. Don Peppers, Founding Partner, Peppers & Rogers Group at TeleTech, January.

Pomeroy, B. and Hornick, S. 2009. Plugging the leaks, "The revenue side of the profitability equation holds large but often hidden benefits for virtually every carrier". *Airline Business Report*, February.

Sabre. 2011. *Branded Fares in Availability, Quick Reference*. Sabre Travel Network.

Sorenson, J. 2009. *The Guide to Ancillary Revenue and a la Carte Pricing*. Edited by Eric Lucas. IdeaWorks Company.

Sorenson, J. 2011. *Ancillary Revenue Report Series for 2011, Billions of Dollars in Baggage Fees Travel the Globe*. Edited by Eric Lucas. IdeaWorks Company.

Sorenson, J. 2012. *Ancillary Revenue Report Series for 2012, It's a Constant Challenge to Keep Corporate Travelers from the Candy Store of à la Carte Goodies*. Edited by Eric Lucas. IdeaWorks Company.

Sorenson, J. 2013. *Choice and Creativity: Carriers Build Ancillary Revenue by Empowering a Consumer's Right to Choose*. Edited by Eric Lucas. IdeaWorks Company.

Sorenson, J. 2013. *The 2013 CarTrawler Yearbook of Ancillary Revenue*. Edited by Eric Lucas. IdeaWorks Company.

Taneja, N. K. 2013. *The Passenger has gone Digital and Mobile, Accessing and Connecting through Information and Technology*. Ashgate, Aldershot.

Vinod, B. and Moore, K. 2009. Promoting branded fare families and ancillary services: Merchandising and its impacts on the travel value chain. *Journal of Revenue and Pricing Management*, Vol. 8, Issue 2, pp. 174–186.

6 Airport infrastructure

Christopher Jarvis

Introduction

This chapter discusses landside, terminal and airside facilities and processes that affect the passenger experience as they pass through an airport. The discussion focuses on facilities and processes associated with landside access, the passenger terminal used by passengers travelling in scheduled commercial aircraft, and airside turnaround of passenger aircraft.

Landside access

As a major airport handles a large number of passengers and freight, it generates very large volumes of surface traffic. It is therefore not sufficient for the airport operator to consider the problem of getting to and from the airport as a concern solely for urban or regional transportation authorities. The airport itself has a vital interest in ensuring that easy access to the airport is provided, with a minimum of congestion.

In order to provide convenient access for a wide range of the travelling public, employees at the airport and for servicing/delivery activities, good road access and increasingly rail connections are provided. Some airports situated at coastal or estuarine locations may have water (ferry) access.

People who make trips to the airport comprise:

- airline passengers (e.g., originating and destination)
- employees at the airport (e.g., airline and other businesses located at the airport)
- visitors (e.g., greeters, farewellers, sightseers)
- suppliers and contractors (e.g., delivery personnel, construction).

Airline transit and transfer passengers make no use of land transport. The level of traffic attracted to a particular land access mode is dictated by relative factors of cost, comfort and convenience.

Road

Road access to airports often comprises the main, and in many instances the only, surface transport link to/from the catchment of an airport. Where possible, each type of traffic (e.g., passengers, freight, staff, deliveries) should be separated at entry into the airport. Peak traffic times at the various airport activity centres may occur at different times of day, and this can be taken into account when road requirements are determined. For example, staff at aircraft maintenance facilities are most likely to start and finish at a different time from passenger terminal staff, who in turn would tend to arrive and depart prior to and after the peak passenger flows. In order to maintain secure airport access, it is desirable to provide a main road link as well as a secondary link. Road widths (numbers of lanes) provided must be designed such that they can accommodate the required peak period traffic volumes, with external roads designed to cater for both airport-generated and general traffic volumes using the road network. As the catchment for an airport is likely to be spread over a wide geographical region, with only a proportion of traffic having its origin and destination in the dominant central business district, the airport access roads must have easy linkage into the regional road network.

Rail

Rail links to/from an airport can transport a significant proportion of passengers, staff and visitors, thus reducing the demand for road travel. Rail transport can be provided as follows:

- dedicated (often high-speed) rail link to a major transport interchange in the main commercial centre
- linking into the city's suburban rail network – either heavy or light rail
- integrating the airport with high-speed rail services; this system extends the airport's catchment over a wide geographic area.

Water

Water-based surface access to/from airports is confined to airports located on an island or adjacent to suitable seas or estuaries (e.g., Maldives, Hong Kong).

Parking

Terminal kerb – conventional

A 'conventional' terminal kerb is located directly at the front of the passenger terminal. Normally, the terminal kerb has zones for departing and arriving passengers. Typically, parking at the terminal kerb is very short term and is free. In order to increase the available kerb length, sometimes dual kerbs are provided in the front of the terminal. At large airports where the departures level is above the arrivals level, a dual level road layout is usually provided with the departures kerb at the upper level and the arrivals kerb at the lower level.

Departures kerb

The departures kerb normally provides parking for the following vehicle types:

- private cars, for drop-off of departing passengers
- taxis, limousines
- transit buses, long-stay car park shuttles, hotel shuttles, staff shuttles, etc. at designated zones
- tourist coaches at the kerb or at separate docks adjacent to the terminal entrance.

Arrivals kerb

The arrivals kerb normally provides parking for the following vehicle types:

- private cars
- taxis at designated zones
- hire cars, transit buses, long-stay car park shuttles, hotel shuttles, etc. at designated zones
- tourist coaches either at the kerb or at separate docks adjacent to the terminal.

Terminal kerb – modern trends

The traditional pick-up/drop-off kerb, while offering good service levels to some airport users, creates vehicle–pedestrian conflicts at road crossings and encourages private car use of 'free' spaces close to the terminal. It also requires that the airport deploys traffic marshals to keep the forecourt moving during busy periods, as vehicles tussle for scarce free spaces. Furthermore, close access to the terminal front by private cars can expose the terminal to potential security threats.

Accordingly, current trends for the layout of passenger terminal landside interface with road transport is to replace the traditional kerb with a central pedestrian precinct connecting the terminal frontage to the main car parks or ground transport centre that incorporate dedicated pick-up and drop-off zones for public transport vehicles, thus removing pedestrian–vehicle conflicts in front of the terminal. Private cars are directed into the main car park or ground transport centre where a drop-off and pick-up kerb frontage may be provided in the vicinity of the pedestrian precinct.

Parking facilities

Private cars

Parking of private cars is most commonly provided as follows:

- short stay – located close to the terminal, usually in a multistorey car park at large airports

Figure 6.1a Heathrow Airport Terminal 5 and adjacent car park

Figure 6.1b Heathrow Airport Terminal 5 – landscaped zone between car park and terminal

- long stay – remote from the terminal, normally within a ground level area, with parking charged at cheaper rates than for short stay; shuttle buses typically transport passengers between the car park and terminal.

Taxis

After taxis have dropped their passenger at the departures kerb, they recirculate to a remote holding area, awaiting call-up to the arrivals kerb for passenger pick-up. A call-up system notifies when taxis are required at the pick-up taxi rank.

Hire cars, limousines, etc.

These vehicles normally have designated parking zones relatively close to the arrivals kerb. This allows drivers, who are at the airport to meet passengers by arrangement, to park for short periods and enter the terminal to meet their passengers.

Rental cars

Air travellers generate the majority of rental car business, so airport facilities for pick-up, drop-off and separate areas where cars can be valeted and serviced should be provided. Key considerations for car rental operations are as follows:

- Pick-up and drop-off. In Australia, most airports are able to offer high service quality with pick-up and drop-off being accommodated within the short-term car park, usually at ground floor level when the short-term car park is in a multistorey facility. In many countries, car rental pick-up and drop-off are undertaken at off-airport depots. In this case, each car rental company operates shuttle buses to transport their customers between their depots and the terminal arrivals and departures kerbs.
- Servicing and valet facilities. Usually car rental valet and servicing facilities are provided within commercial lease areas on the airport. Rental cars are returned to these facilities after drop-off and returned to the pick-up area for re-letting after they have been valeted and serviced. Where insufficient land is available within airport commercial lease areas, the car rental companies may undertake cleaning and servicing of their vehicles within their own facilities at an off-airport location.

Tourist coaches

Airports with a high proportion of inclusive tour groups require specific facilities to accommodate the large number of coaches required to transport the groups. Loading docks are often provided adjacent to the departures hall for set down and arrivals hall for pick-up. After set down, coaches are stored at a remote storage area from which they are called forward to the arrivals docks to pick up arriving passengers.

Staff

Staff requiring the use of car parking facilities may be employed by airlines, government agencies, terminal concessions or any of the other employee groups at an airport. Staff parking is either provided within the lease areas of each facility located on the airport or within a common parking area. Transport between a remote common car park and the main activity areas, particularly the terminal, may be provided by staff shuttle busses.

Servicing/loading docks

These provide parking and loading facilities for vehicles connected with delivering goods to and removing waste from passenger terminals. Access roads and docks should be provided at areas not normally accessible to the public.

Terminal design

This section reviews the planning of passenger terminal buildings, and how demand is met through the optimal provision of capacity. While the processes in place in passenger terminals are generally common worldwide, some differences associated with specific local and national regulations need to be accommodated.

Passenger demand

Passenger demand in periods of peak activity is the main driver of the size and layout of passenger terminal facilities. While airports are commonly classified based on the number of annual passenger movements, sizing of passenger terminal facilities is generally based on the demand over a busy hour. As demand varies across the day, week, seasons and the year, a passenger terminal will likely be operating below capacity at most times but must still provide the capacity to meet the demand during peak periods. In order to avoid designing a passenger terminal based on a single peak hour associated with a unique event, the industry has established some typical planning parameters which allow the airport to operate at or below capacity at most times but to still have sufficient capacity to meet demand during peak periods. An appropriate balance should be struck between the need to meet passenger demand without overproviding space and facilities because of infrequent traffic surge occurrences.

Typical planning busy hour design parameters include:

- Thirtieth Busiest Hour – the hourly rate above which only twenty-nine hours experience busier levels of traffic over a year
- Ninety-fifth Percentile Hour (or five per cent Busy Hour) – the hourly rate above which five per cent of the annual traffic is handled
- Average Day/Peak Month (ADPM) and Average Day Peak Hour (ADPH) – the peak hour of the average day in a peak month.

Level of service

In order to define the capacity of terminal facilities and to assess their suitability under various demand conditions, the concept of Level of Service (LoS) was developed. The concept of capacity in a passenger terminal can be subjective because of the complexity and interdependencies between processors and holding areas. The LoS concept is a way of ensuring that considerations of demand, processing rates and service quality are taken into account when defining airport service levels. The concept of LoS, as applied to airport terminal design, was originally developed by Transport Canada in the 1970s. In 1981, the first edition of the Guidelines for Airport Capacity/Demand Management, which contained a tabular presentation of LoS guidelines by airport processing area, was published and these were later incorporated into the International Air Transport Association's (IATA's) Airport Development Reference Manual.

The concept of level of service has been applied in various ways for the design of new facilities, the expansion and monitoring of existing facilities, and as a benchmark that determines whether the contractual obligations of airport owners, operators and/or third-party service providers are being met. It has also been highlighted that the importance of the previous airport LoS guidelines was perceived to be higher in correlation with other key quantitative (e.g., wait times, process rates) and qualitative (e.g., perceived service quality, information flow, way finding, walking distances) characteristics. These alternative key performance indicators are used in the industry but often not with the same consistency as LoS guidelines. Taking some of these considerations into account, the LoS references have been reviewed and refined in a way that now incorporates waiting-time aspects and perceived service quality in addition to the spatial requirements. The new LoS framework is now based on three levels: overdesign, optimum and suboptimum.

Terminal design and LoS should reflect the various characteristics and volume of passengers and baggage to be handled. They may also be used to determine contractual service levels. Managing terminal capacity and designing with LoS in mind are key requirements in the development of competitive airports. These factors have long-term financial and operational implications for passenger facilities. IATA now recommends that all new developments and terminal redesign projects balance LoS with cost and quality in order to achieve the best value terminal infrastructure possible.

Terminal types

The passenger terminal layout is generally based on a range of physical, environmental, operational and socio-economic factors. The runway system often dictates the location of the passenger terminal while the fleet mix during busy periods will often guide the shape of the terminal as planners attempt to make the best possible use of space for aircraft while providing an optimal experience to passengers. However, the characteristics of five basic terminal configuration concepts can generally be observed at most passenger terminals, whether as a clear depiction of the concept or as a hybrid. See Figure 6.2.

Terminal Type and Key Characteristics	Layout
Linear The linear concept can incorporate either a centralized or a semi-decentralized processing facility. Passenger processing activities occur in a central building. Passengers proceed to gate areas that are located along the length of long linear concourses. Mechanical devices can be installed to reduce walking time and distance but the associated costs are significant.	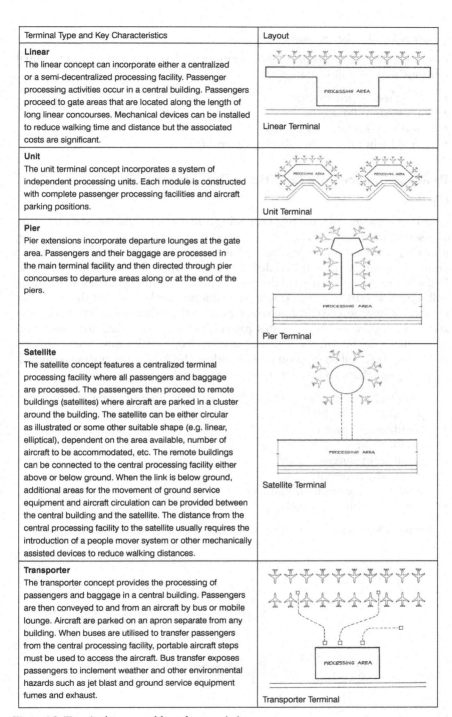Linear Terminal
Unit The unit terminal concept incorporates a system of independent processing units. Each module is constructed with complete passenger processing facilities and aircraft parking positions.	Unit Terminal
Pier Pier extensions incorporate departure lounges at the gate area. Passengers and their baggage are processed in the main terminal facility and then directed through pier concourses to departure areas along or at the end of the piers.	Pier Terminal
Satellite The satellite concept features a centralized terminal processing facility where all passengers and baggage are processed. The passengers then proceed to remote buildings (satellites) where aircraft are parked in a cluster around the building. The satellite can be either circular as illustrated or some other suitable shape (e.g. linear, elliptical), dependent on the area available, number of aircraft to be accommodated, etc. The remote buildings can be connected to the central processing facility either above or below ground. When the link is below ground, additional areas for the movement of ground service equipment and aircraft circulation can be provided between the central building and the satellite. The distance from the central processing facility to the satellite usually requires the introduction of a people mover system or other mechanically assisted devices to reduce walking distances.	Satellite Terminal
Transporter The transporter concept provides the processing of passengers and baggage in a central building. Passengers are then conveyed to and from an aircraft by bus or mobile lounge. Aircraft are parked on an apron separate from any building. When buses are utilised to transfer passengers from the central processing facility, portable aircraft steps must be used to access the aircraft. Bus transfer exposes passengers to inclement weather and other environmental hazards such as jet blast and ground service equipment fumes and exhaust.	Transporter Terminal

Figure 6.2 Terminal types and key characteristics

Terminal layout – key principles

Key principles to be incorporated in planning the layout of a passenger terminal must include the following:

- straight-line processing
- self-evident flows
- clear way-finding and signage
- good flight information display systems (FIDS).

Passenger processing facilities – Departures flow

Check-in

Check-in is traditionally the first processing function encountered when entering a passenger terminal. However, modern check-in processing is increasingly being undertaken using new technologies that permit passengers to check-in either online from a desktop or mobile device or at the airport from a self-service kiosk. In the future, it can be expected that the use of new technology check-in methods will replace at least to a large extent conventional check-in within the passenger terminal. Conventional check-in counters allow the airlines to receive passengers and their baggage and to check that passengers have appropriate documentation (particularly for international flights) and to assign their seats. Some airports with a dedicated rail connection provide airline check-in at the city rail terminus. Conventional check-in counters incorporate the following equipment:

- computer equipment to allow the agent to identify and confirm the passenger for the flight
- boarding pass printers
- bag tag printers
- document printers
- telephone/intercom
- storage for the required stationery
- baggage weigh scales and read out.

Figure 6.3 presents a typical configuration for check-in counters.

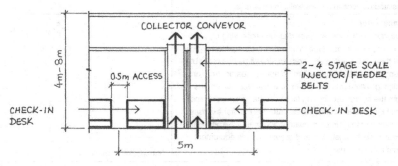

Figure 6.3 Typical conventional check-in counters configuration

Conventional check-in counters are typically provided in groups with sufficient numbers of counters to accommodate at least one flight. Typical check-in counter layouts and dimensional spacings are illustrated in Figure 6.4.

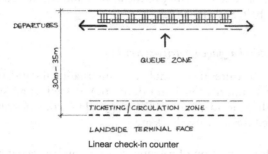

Linear check-in counter

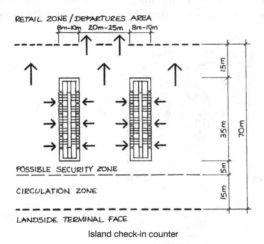

Island check-in counter

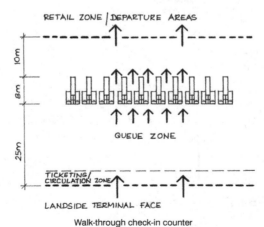

Walk-through check-in counter

Figure 6.4 Check-in counter configurations and layout

Self-service check-in and bag tag is becoming increasingly common, with passengers depositing their bags onto the baggage conveyor system at a bag drop position. Where remote check-in is used and the passenger has checked bags, bag tags must be obtained on entry to the airport and the tagged bags deposited on the bag drop belt. See Figure 6.5.

Passenger and cabin baggage security screening

Security check procedures that comply with international standards are required for all passengers (international and domestic) as well as all staff and others who pass from the landside zones of the terminal into the security sterile zones. Facilities required for security check are:

- X-ray unit for inspection of passengers' carry-on baggage items
- magnetometer unit to detect metallic objects carried by passengers

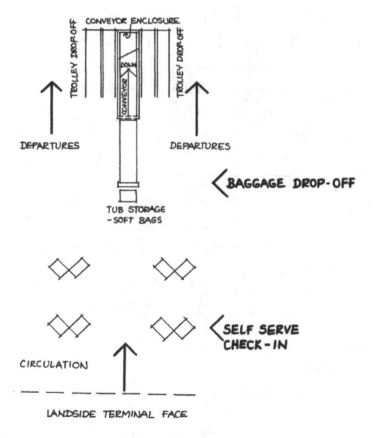

Figure 6.5 Typical self-check-in kiosks with baggage drop

- search benches for additional manual search of baggage items, if required
- random trace element screening
- interview room/search room adjacent to security check point
- adequate space for queuing, repacking checked bags and circulation.

The number of units required will depend on the peak passenger flow and the average processing time per passenger and visitor. See Figure 6.6.

Outwards immigration (international passengers)

Many countries (including Australia and New Zealand) require the checking of the documentation of all international passengers on departure from the country. Issues to be checked for departing passengers include:

- custody of minors (to ensure that any minors are not subject to court-applied custody requirements)
- taxation issues
- prevention of criminals from leaving the country.

Sufficient counters must be provided to process passengers and adequate space must be provided for queues, both in accordance with the level of service criteria adopted (average processing time per passenger and maximum waiting time in a queue). Interview rooms should be provided adjacent to the counters to allow private interview of passengers by immigration personnel, should this be necessary. Outwards immigration may be provided prior to or following the security check process. See Figure 6.7.

Smart technologies and bio recognition of passengers that automate and speed up the outwards immigration process are being increasingly adopted worldwide, resulting in reconfiguration of immigration facilities with the provision of self-check facilities and less conventional counters.

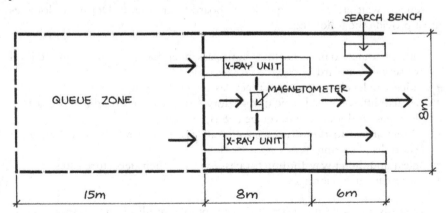

Figure 6.6 Typical passenger and hand baggage security check facilities layout

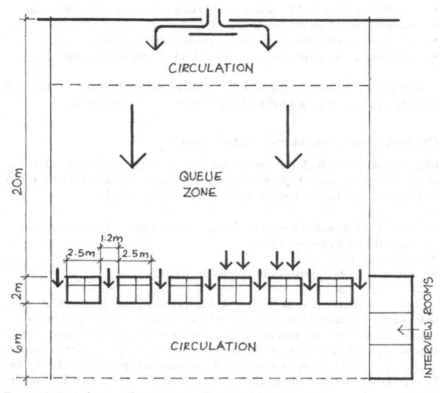

Figure 6.7 Typical outwards immigration facilities layout

Departure lounge and boarding reconciliation

Departure lounges are areas within the terminal, close to the gates, where passengers wait prior to being called to board their aircraft. Departure lounges must provide the following:

- adequate area to meet the busy hour passenger demand at the required level of service standard
- adequate levels of seating to meet passenger demand
- availability of retail (including duty-free near international departure lounges) and food and beverage (F&B) facilities
- direct access to the boarding zones at each gate from the gate lounge or centralized seating area
- clear and direct way-finding for passengers to their departure gates
- access to airline lounges.

Typically, in modern airports, the concept of centralized or common lounge facilities is preferred as this makes the full range of retail and F&B facilities easily available to the maximum number of passengers. Seating is arranged around the retail facilities but with clear views to aircraft parked at the gates. Good and clear flight information display systems should be provided throughout the lounge so that passengers are constantly advised of the status of their flight and when it is boarding. Seating areas in common departure lounges can be cross-utilized by passengers boarding aircraft at different gates, making more economical use of seats and space. The layout of a departure lounge will vary dependent on whether it is to be used by international or domestic passengers and the particular configuration of each terminal.

Airline lounges

Airline lounges are provided as a waiting area for the airline's club members and premium passengers. These lounges are equipped to a high standard and usually provide premium facilities including:

* check-in (domestic only)
* comfortable lounge seats
* complimentary catering and bar
* business centre
* meeting/conference facilities
* toilets and shower facilities.

   Separate airline lounges are typically provided for first class and VIP passengers and for business class/airline club members who pay an annual subscription. No specific layouts are applicable for airline lounges, as the layout will be dependent on the space available and the particular airline's requirements. However, consideration of the business model for the lounge (e.g., pay-per-use, paid membership, class of service, etc.) will be important to determine the occupancy of the airline lounge. Access into the airline lounges should expose passengers using these facilities to as wide a range of retail outlets (and duty-free) as possible, because, once in the lounges, these passengers are unlikely to return to the retail outlets. Joint ventures with high-end retailers to supply pop-up shops immediately beside lounge entrances or within lounges could be a way to increase retail exposure without necessitating moving lounges in established airports.

Passenger processing facilities – Arrivals flow

Inwards immigration (international passengers)

Passport/document controls are required for all arriving international passengers. This is undertaken at the Inwards Immigration control or the Primary Line, which is usually the first process encountered by passengers on arrival in a country. In recent years, speeding up of this process has occurred with the introduction of advance passenger information (pre-clearance), whereby information on passengers is transferred electronically to the authorities at the arrival airport at the time of check-in. Passenger recognition technology in conjunction with self-check immigration kiosks is further speeding up this process. It is expected that in the future most immigration processing will be undertaken using self-check facilities. Usually, the government agencies that are concerned with passengers arriving in a country (e.g., health, immigration, customs, quarantine) use one official on behalf of all agencies to make initial checks on passengers. In Australia, Australian Customs Service personnel staff the inwards immigration counters. Conventional counter and queue requirements, with adjacent interview/inspection rooms, are similar to those required for Outwards Immigration.

Baggage claim

Checked baggage is transported from the baggage breakdown zone by conveyor into the baggage claim hall, where it is presented for reclaim on baggage reclaim units. The baggage claim hall must provide adequate space for:

- the baggage reclaim units
- storage of baggage trolleys
- the number of people requiring to reclaim their bags plus trolleys
- baggage services
- circulation.

While international arriving passengers will first need to clear inwards immigration, domestic arriving passengers will proceed directly to the baggage reclaim area. The type of baggage claim units selected for a particular terminal will be dependent on the layout of the terminal, the peak period arrivals passenger flow and the number of flights to be accommodated simultaneously on each unit. Baggage claim units can be one of two basic types as shown in Figure 6.8.

Customs check (international passengers)

This process is more accurately described as Secondary Customs Check or Customs Baggage Examination. In most countries, there has been a trend to reduce the degree of customs inspection of terminating passengers' baggage. Where this is implemented, only a proportion of passengers are selected for baggage inspection. Thus, two basic flows are introduced for Secondary Customs Checks as follows:

- green channel for those passengers who do not have goods to declare to customs officials
- red channel for passengers with goods declared at the primary inspection line or for passengers selected by customs officials whose baggage they wish to inspect.

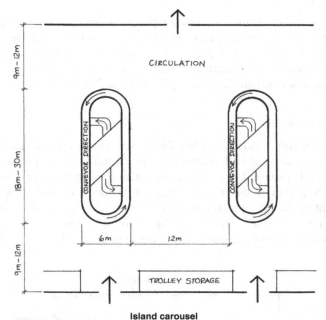

Island carousel
Fed by transport conveyors located either above or below the reclaim unit.
Claim units usually have inclined presentation surfaces.

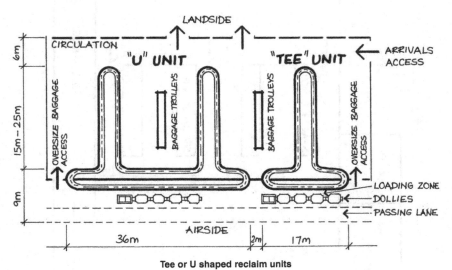

Tee or U shaped reclaim units
Bag presentation units are usually flatbed.

Figure 6.8 Baggage claim units

Where a green/red channel separation is provided, the ability to divert passengers from the green to the red channel is required. Inspection benches are required to undertake secondary customs inspection. In addition, adjacent interview/search rooms are required for conducting more detailed inspection. A typical secondary customs inspection red/green layout is illustrated in Figure 6.9.

Quarantine check

Quarantine officials in Australia, New Zealand, and some other countries that are free of diseases that might affect their agricultural industries and native flora and fauna inspect checked and carry-on baggage of all arriving passengers to safeguard against the importation of plants, foodstuff, timber products and other items that might result in the introduction of such diseases. This has resulted in a further inspection process separate from Secondary Customs Check where checked and carry-on baggage of arriving international passengers can be subject to X-ray and/

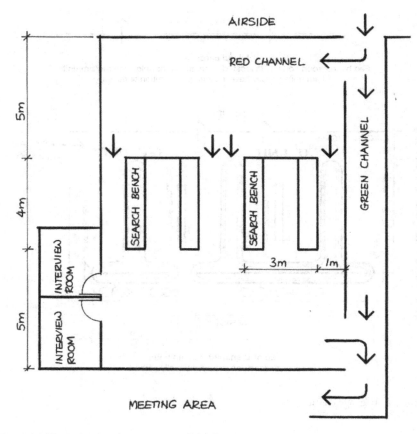

Figure 6.9 Typical secondary customs check layout

or physical inspection. This process is mandatory for most passengers, regardless of whether they are proceeding through the green or red channel.

Thus, space must be provided for:

- X-ray units
- inspection benches
- queuing
- interview rooms
- circulation.

Arrivals hall – international

International arriving passengers, after clearing all incoming procedures, pass from the secure area into the non-secure arrivals hall. The arrivals hall is where passengers are united with their meeters/greeters and from where they leave the terminal to continue their journey by ground transport. The international arrivals hall must provide sufficient space for the following:

- meeters (with allowance of an appropriate dwell time prior to arrival of their passengers)
- passengers
- arrival concessions (e.g., car rental, banks/money exchange, hotel services, tourism information, ground transport, food and beverage)
- transfer check-in to domestic flights
- circulation.

Arrivals hall – domestic

The domestic arrivals hall and baggage claim are usually co-located. Space within the domestic arrivals hall must be sufficient for:

- the baggage reclaim units
- storage of baggage trolleys
- the number of people requiring to reclaim their bags plus trolleys
- meeters of arriving passengers (with allowance for an appropriate dwell time for meeters who arrive prior to the arrival or their passenger)
- arrival concessions (e.g., car rental, banks, hotel services, food and beverage)
- baggage services
- circulation.

Checked baggage handling

Baggage handling represents the second most important function within an airline terminal after the processes for ensuring the smooth passage of passengers. In principle, departing passengers and their baggage are separated as soon as possible in the processing sequence, and arriving passengers are reunited with their baggage as late as possible. After checked baggage has been received from passengers at check-in, it is transported to the baggage make-up area. The baggage handling system must be able to sort large numbers of bags into their required flights quickly and accurately, and have a high degree of performance reliability.

Hold-stow baggage screening

Two basic systems to screen hold-stow baggage are available, as follows.

- Screening prior to check-in. In this system, passengers must have their checked baggage X-rayed and/or physically inspected by security staff, and obtain security clearance, prior to check-in. Where this system is used, usually only passengers are permitted to enter the terminal and baggage is screened immediately after entry into the terminal.
- Downstream screening. Methods of screening hold-stowage baggage after check-in are to incorporate in-line X-ray facilities in the baggage handling system (BHS) or to take bags from the BHS for checking and then to reintroduce them into the BHS after checking is completed.

Recently completed and currently planned new airports and terminals have either incorporated or are incorporating in-line X-ray facilities to permit 100 per cent hold-stow baggage screening. Separate X-ray screening is required for oversized baggage items.

Baggage make-up

Baggage make-up consists of either a manual or automated system. Principal features of each system are as follows:

- Manual systems can either involve a straight belt delivery, or a recirculating loop.
  - ○ Straight belt delivery systems usually feed onto a flat roller bed from which bags are loaded onto dollies or into containers. This system is used at smaller airports or where relatively low volumes of traffic are handled. They are the cheapest to install and operate. See Figure 6.10.
  - ○ Recirculating loop systems present bags for manually loading onto dollies or into containers from a recirculating belt on which bags are fed from the transporter conveyors above. The length of recirculating loop make-up belt required is determined by the number and types of aircraft to be loaded in the peak period. Containers and/or dollies are assembled around the loop for loading. When containers or trolleys are filled, they are removed from the belt and replaced with empty dollies/ trolleys for further loading. See Figure 6.11.

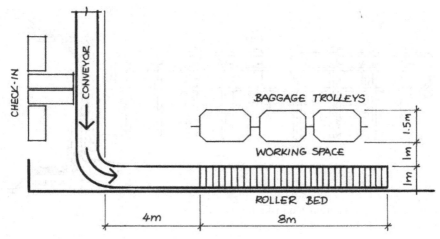

Figure 6.10 Typical straight belt make-up layout

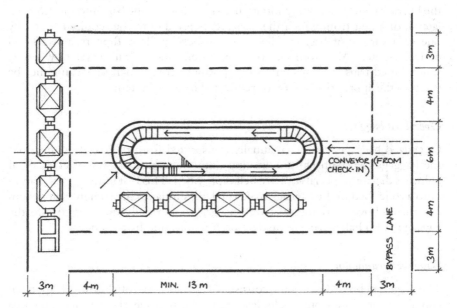

Figure 6.11 Typical recirculation make-up layout

- An automated baggage sortation system incorporates a barcode scanner that identifies each bag being transported on the main conveyor that delivers it to a designated lateral (a dead-end conveyor from which bags are manually loaded into containers or on to dollies for transport to aircraft). Automated systems are essential at major airports in order to handle the large volumes of bags involved and multiple destinations. See Figure 6.12.

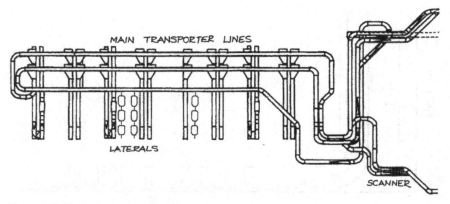

Figure 6.12 Typical automated make-up layout

After bags have been identified by the barcode scanner, they are transported to the lateral on either a tilt tray sortation system that tips the bag onto the required lateral, or a belt from which the bags are diverted onto the required lateral by one of a variety of baggage diverters (pushers, pullers, flippers, powerfaced deflectors, etc.). All automated sortation systems incorporate a system whereby unidentified bags are transported to a position from which they can either be taken to the appropriate lateral or reinserted into the system.

Oversized baggage

Oversized baggage is either manually transported from the check-in area into the baggage make-up hall for loading onto containers or onto aircraft, or, if volumes dictate, a special oversize belt is provided. This belt normally discharges onto a roller bed in the baggage make-up hall, similar to the straight belt system described above. Arriving oversized baggage is normally transported into the baggage claim hall at a designated point, for collection by passengers.

Baggage breakdown

The baggage breakdown area consists of an area for off-loading bags from containers or dollies onto belts leading to the baggage claim units. The area must allow sufficient space for container dollies and baggage dollies to pass those positioned at the offloading points for the breakdown belts.

Support facilities

As well as areas within a terminal necessary to accommodate the passenger processing requirements, additional areas are needed to accommodate a range of ancillary or support facilities. These facilities include:

- retail
- circulation
- police
- offices
- toilets
- plant rooms.

The floor area required for support facilities can often be some fifty per cent of the total floor area of a terminal. Key issues relating to each of the support facilities are outlined below.

Retail

The provision of a wide range of retail outlets in airport passenger terminals has expanded rapidly in recent years and is now expected by the travelling public. Many airports have created retail as a major feature, which is used in marketing the airport. Airports with a wide range of retail facilities have become destinations in their own right, with passengers, where possible, arranging their itineraries to transit through the airport in order to avail themselves of the shopping. Airports and airlines view retail as a valuable source of revenue to the airport. This allows aviation charges (landing charges, use of terminal gates, aircraft parking charges, etc.) to be kept lower than if there were no retail. Factors that affect the amount of retail that an airport can successfully sustain include:

- layout of the terminal
- mix and types of retail provided
- whether the terminal handles domestic or international passengers
- socioeconomic mix of passengers using the terminal
- passengers' propensity to spend at the shops
- airport's policy with respect to prices compared with downtown prices.

Ultimately, determining the amount of retail floor space an airport can profitably sustain requires a detailed understanding and analysis of the many factors involved at a particular airport. Retail offering in an airport terminal typically comprises a mix of the following types. These retail outlets are spread throughout the airside or landside areas of the terminal and in both arrivals and departures areas, as appropriate:

- food and beverage (F&B)
- duty-free (principally in international terminals)
- speciality retail
- currency exchange
- hotel reservations
- car rental.

Determining the appropriate mix of retail within an airport requires detailed analysis of the types of passengers (e.g., age, sex, nationality, business/holiday) and their spending patterns. There are three principal design parameters to be considered in the planning and design of airport retail areas as follows:

- footfall – a measure of how many passengers go past a store, with the target being to achieve as close to 100 per cent as possible
- sight density – the proportion and mix of retail outlets that a passenger can see at a time
- dwell time – the amount of time a passenger spends in a retail precinct (as opposed to the time spent in the airport generally).

Circulation

Areas for circulation are spaces allocated for this purpose within all functional areas as well as connecting corridors and other areas that provide links between the main functional areas. Sizing corridors and passageways should take account of parameters such as the level of service standard to be provided and the rate of flow. The effective width of a passageway is that available for passenger flow – i.e. not impacted by obstructions, counterflow and edge effects; all of which provide an impediment to clear flow. The floor area in a terminal required for circulation purposes varies widely depending on the terminal configuration adopted at an airport and the particular layout of the terminal.

Police

Typically, a police presence is maintained at a large airport. A dedicated facility is, therefore, required to accommodate the police presence. The size and particular requirements will vary from airport to airport.

Offices

Offices are required to accommodate a wide range of occupants. The number of offices and the amount of space within a terminal dedicated to offices will vary from airport to airport depending on the requirements of the airport, airlines and others who require such office space. In general, office space within a terminal building is relatively expensive and often offices are provided in a more cost effective manner in a dedicated office building separate, and often linked to the terminal.

Toilets

Toilets are required throughout the terminal to accommodate the forecast demand (passengers, visitors, staff). The number of toilets and their location will be determined based on the terminal layout and local building regulation requirements for provision of toilets.

Plant rooms

Plant rooms are required to accommodate all services required in the terminal building. The range of plant items include:

- power sub-stations
- air conditioning
- heating
- telephone/communications
- fire control systems.

There are no particular area requirements to be allocated for plant rooms in a terminal building. Much of the plant facility may possibly be located on the terminal roof.

Airside facilities

Airside facilities include runways, taxiways, aprons and all support facilities required to provide a safe and efficient service to passengers and airlines. Only airside elements that directly affect the passenger experience are discussed in this section.

Aircraft boarding/deplaning

The most direct interface of the passenger with airside is for aircraft boarding and deplaning. This process will differ based on the airport facilities and airline operations.

Ground loading/unloading

Where passengers arrive or depart on an aircraft that requires them to walk across the apron, designated walkways should be provided on the apron to ensure their safety. If multiple aircraft stands are to be accessed from the terminal, a covered walkway may be provided, with openings at intervals opposite the aircraft stands to allow passengers to access the aircraft. In order to provide protection to passengers walking across an apron, as well as facilitating keeping passengers from walking over a wide area of the apron, a weatherproof flexible corridor system can be installed. Such a system 'concertinas' for storage and is pulled out using a small ground tug to link the terminal or gate with the bottom of the aircraft stairs. A typical system is marketed as 'Commute-a-Walk'. A system often used to guide departing passengers to the correct aircraft is to paint coloured lines, with a different coloured line leading to each gate. Thus, airline staff at the terminal departure gate can advise passengers to follow a particular coloured line which will take them to the correct aircraft.

Bussing

Bussing is used to transport passengers between the terminal and aircraft parked on remote stands. Mobile stairs or stairs built into the aircraft are required to allow passengers to board/deplane the aircraft. Designated zones are required at ground level in the terminal to:

- accommodate passengers waiting to board a bus prior to travelling to the aircraft; often a purpose-built bussing lounge is provided in the terminal for passengers waiting to board aircraft via a bus
- for arriving passengers to enter the terminal and proceed to baggage claim (domestic passengers) or inwards immigration, etc. (international passengers).

Mobile lounge

An alternative to bussing is purpose-built mobile lounges whereby passengers are transported between the terminal and aircraft in a lounge that is raised to the aircraft door on a scissor lift mechanism. Mobile lounges prevent exposure of passengers to weather when boarding/deplaning aircraft and provide a safe environment as passengers do not need to cross open apron areas.

Aerobridges

Aerobridges or aircraft passenger boarding bridges (airbridges) provide a link from an elevated terminal departure/arrival door to the aircraft boarding door, enabling passengers to walk between the two, protected from atmospheric conditions, aircraft engine blast and blown dust. The aerobridge provides a simple, convenient and controlled method for passenger boarding and deplaning. The floor of tunnel sections should not exceed the maximum gradient allowed by the relevant applicable codes. Aerobridges may be connected directly to the terminal, or a fixed link may be provided between the terminal and the aerobridge. Fixed links should be provided across airside roads where these are provided at the head of stand in order to provide a fixed known clearance from the airside road to the underside of the fixed link structure, thus eliminating the safety issue of variable clearances if the adjustable aerobridge tunnel spanned the road.

Ground services

Ground power

Ground power supply at 400 Hz, as required by aircraft systems, is provided either by individual converter units located at each gate, by a centralized unit with distribution to aircraft at the gates, or by a mobile generator. Where individual converter units are provided, these are typically mounted on the aerobridge, with mains supply provided from the terminal building. As can be expected, larger aircraft types require greater power supply, with the amount dependent on the on-board systems that remain operating on the aircraft during its turnaround. Electrical cable, for connecting to the aircraft inlet socket from individual converter units or a centralized system, is normally stored in a container mounted on the aerobridge. When a mobile generator is used, electrical cable connects this to the aircraft inlet socket. Ground power is connected to the aircraft as soon as it has docked at the gate and disconnected when the aircraft auxiliary power unit (APU) has been started prior to engine start and departure.

Preconditioned air

Preconditioned air supplies cooled air to the aircraft to ventilate the cabin while it is docked and the APU is shut down. As with ground power, preconditioned air units are commonly mounted on the aerobridge with air hoses connected to inlet points on the aircraft, or from mobile units.

Potable water

Potable water supply to aircraft can be provided from a hose mounted on the aerobridge pedestal or from a fixed outlet on the apron, with supply obtained from the mains system. Alternatively, potable water can be delivered to aircraft by tanker vehicles.

Lavatory service

Aircraft toilet waste is collected from waste disposal points on the underside of aircraft in lavatory service vehicles. Waste is disposed of at a discharge point into the sewerage system serving the airport.

Catering and cabin servicing

Aircraft catering and cabin servicing is undertaken during the turnaround of aircraft at the gate. Full-service airlines require comprehensive catering, comprising pre-prepared food as well as drink provisions and supply of consumables for use on the aircraft. Low-cost carrier aircraft are typically supplied with packaged food and drinks for sale on the aircraft. Dedicated vehicles are used to supply catering and cabin servicing and for removal of cabin waste. These vehicles have scissor lift mechanisms that permit access by the main body of the vehicle to the aircraft service door. Cabin waste is usually destroyed/incinerated at an on-airport facility or transported to a controlled off-airport disposal area.

Aircraft fuelling

The aircraft refuelling system used at an airport is dependent on the number and types of aircraft and the volume of fuel required to be supplied. Alternative fuelling systems applicable to modern airliners are:

- fuel tanker – suitable for fuelling both piston and turbine engine aircraft but typically used when relatively low fuel volumes are required
- under-pavement or joint user hydrant installation (JUHI) – suitable for use at large airports where large volumes of fuel are supplied; the system requires a mobile fuel dispenser vehicle to transfer fuel from the under-pavement hydrant to the aircraft fuel intake point.

De-icing

De-icing of aircraft prior to departure/take-off is not common in Australia, but is routinely required in areas where severe winter temperatures are common, such as North America, Europe and northern Asia. Normally de/anti-icing treatment of departing aircraft is undertaken using mobile equipment that sprays de/anti-icing fluid over the main control surfaces of aircraft just prior to them taxiing for take-off. Fixed installation de/anti-icing equipment is sometimes provided at large airports with high volumes of traffic. Other de/anti-icing methods using alternative technologies, e.g., infrared, are becoming increasingly used at major North American airports. However, spraying fluid from mobile equipment remains the most widely used method to de-ice aircraft.

De/anti-icing is undertaken either at the aircraft stands, or at a designated remote area, or at aprons along the taxiway leading to the runway meant for take-off. Suitable drainage for collection and safe disposal of de/anti-icing fluids must be provided to prevent ground water contamination. Although it is common to apply de/anti-icing fluid at the aircraft gate, there are significant drawbacks of applying the fluid at this location such as slippery conditions for ground handling staff and manoeuvring of ground service equipment, and the need for 'vacuum' sweepers to collect excess de/anti-icing fluid that lies on the apron surface. The excess de/anti-icing fluid running from an aeroplane de/anti-icing operation poses the risk of contaminating ground water and affects pavement friction characteristics. Where de/anti-icing activities are carried out, the surface drainage system should be designed to collect the run-off separately, preventing it mixing with the normal surface run-off.

Conclusion

As discussed in this chapter, a wide range of facilities and processes are required to facilitate passenger movement though a modern terminal including interface with ground transport and aircraft. This chapter has focused on those facilities and processes that directly affect the passenger experience as they pass through a terminal.

Further support facilities that do not directly influence the passenger experience and so are not discussed in this chapter are required to permit smooth operation of a passenger terminal and to accommodate efficient ground transport and aircraft handling. Such additional facilities are provided on a case by case basis dependant on the type of traffic, passenger profile, specific requirements of the airport owner/operator and requirements of the regulatory authorities in the country in which the terminal is located.

Part II
Planning for operations

Yi Gao

For any business that wants to survive and to sustain its place in the competitive marketplace, planning in advance is the key. The airline industry is by no means an exception to this rule, considering the extremely complex and challenging regulatory, technical, operational, and business environment surrounding airlines. Factors that could possibly affect the operation of an airline include external and internal, expected and unexpected ones. How an airline prepares itself for these factors largely determines the fate of the company amongst fierce competition.

Even from the early days of commercial aviation, the aviation industry understood quite well that airspace was not as wide open as it appeared, especially in the terminal area where aircraft took off and landed, as well as along the routes connecting major hubs. Aircraft must operate in a collaborative manner so that air traffic can grow in an orderly and safe manner. After all, it was the need for safety as well as efficiency that led to the creation of the Air Traffic Control (ATC) system in the 1920s, which the aviation industry has been using ever since. Besides providing real-time ATC services to crew to maintain necessary safety separation between aircraft, a modern ATC also makes sophisticated optimizations at strategic and technical levels to further improve operational efficiency.

If ATC is considered as an external environment to airline operations, then workforce planning and scheduling would definitely be internal factors for airlines. Of all the positions that need to be planned and scheduled by an airline, flight crew presents unique challenges due to the extremely complex regulatory and operational constraints. With major airlines nowadays operating hundreds of aircraft and employing thousands of pilots, crew planning and scheduling has created such complex mathematical problems that they can only be solved with advanced computer algorithms. On the other hand, due to the scale of the problem, tiny improvements in planning could be translated into huge savings, which provides the incentive for the vast number of studies on this particular problem.

Another internal factor that affects the service delivery of an airline is its maintenance program. If the planning and scheduling of workforce is about 'liveware', then the planning of maintenance would be hardware-centred.

Similar to other aspects of airline operations, maintenance planning is an operational issue, and, at the same time, a business issue. While an airline needs to consider and prepare for scheduled and unscheduled maintenance in order to ensure the airworthiness of its fleet, it must also decide between in-house and out-sourced maintenance in order to maximize its business profit – but not at the cost of safety.

With modern jet engines and other associated technologies becoming increasingly reliable, twin-engine jets started to dominate long-distance trans-oceanic operations, replacing aircraft having three or more engines in the 1980s. Regulators of major nations started to introduce changes to their respective aviation regulations in order to embrace such technical advances. The concept of ETOPS (Extended Twin Engine Operations), more frequently referred to now as EDTO (Extended Diversion Time Operations), was introduced during this period. In the past three decades of ETOPS (or EDTO), in effect the aviation industry has witnessed a dramatic improvement in terms of fuel and time saving, fleet upgrades, and carbon emission reductions.

7 Operational environment

Stephen Angus

Introduction

This chapter describes how Air Traffic Control (ATC) strategically, pre-tactically and in real time (day of operation) delivers service to the airlines. The Air Traffic Operation, also referred to as Air Traffic Management (ATM) or Air Traffic Services (ATS), is an operational service network that supports all aviation users including airline operations. ATC organizations are globally referred to as Air Navigation Services Providers (ANSPs). The two primary objectives of ATC are safety and efficiency. ATC provides two fundamental safety services to airlines: aircraft separation and terrain clearance. Efficiency services support airline on-time performance, the most effective flight trajectory, while achieving the most efficient fuel burn to minimize cost and emissions.

ATC operations and service standards and procedures are based on the Standards and Recommended Practices (SARPs) promulgated by the International Civil Aviation Organization (ICAO). There are a variety of guidance documents but the main ones are:

- Annex 2 – Rules of the Air
- Annex 11 – Air Traffic Services
- Procedures for Air Navigation Services – Air Traffic Management (PANS-ATM, Doc 4444).

ICAO Annex 11 states the following objectives with regard to ATC:

The objectives of the air traffic services shall be to:

a. prevent collisions between aircraft
b. prevent collisions between aircraft on the manoeuvring area and obstructions on that area
c. expedite and maintain an orderly flow of air traffic
d. provide advice and information useful for the safe and efficient conduct of flights
e. notify appropriate organizations regarding aircraft in need of search and rescue aid, and assist such organizations as required.[1]

ATC meets these ICAO obligations by delivering services that rely on three key aviation concepts:

- communication
- navigation
- surveillance.

For each of these three parameters, commonly referred to as Communication, Navigation, and Surveillance (CNS) ATM, there are ICAO-stipulated performance requirements which, when combined, determine what spacing (separation standard) ATC can provide between each aircraft. These performance requirements relate to attributes such as CNS signal latency, reliability and availability, and are the building blocks of the means by which ATC assures safety of the airline operation. The corollary of this is that the higher the CNS compliance is, the smaller the separation standard that ATC can provide between aircraft, which then determines how many aircraft can operate in any given airspace or along a route. This influences the level of efficiency that can be achieved. When the available separation standard is as little as five nautical miles horizontally this means that more aircraft can access their preferred altitude. The size of the separation standard both in the vertical and horizontal plane is a key determinant of the capacity of that airspace. In essence the air traffic controller's ability to deliver the most efficient flight trajectory, while limited by many other factors, will be heavily influenced by how far apart each aircraft must be kept from all other aircraft. The types of technology that can be used to achieve CNS ATM vary from ANSP to ANSP, but can be summarized as follows.

Communication

There will typically be a mix of direct voice technology such as Very High Frequency (VHF), High Frequency (HF), and data link communications commonly referred to as Controller Pilot Data Link Communication (CPDLC). CPDLC is used extensively in regions of the world where direct voice communications are limited, unreliable or unavailable. The latency and reliability of HF, for example, means that the separation standards applied between aircraft by ATC must be greater than in circumstances where VHF can be used as the primary means of communication. Latency is a determinant of how long it would take for ATC to be able to contact the aircraft with instructions to ensure separation or to avoid a safety incident occurring.

Navigation

There will typically be a mix of ground-based and satellite navigation systems. Ground-based navigation infrastructure is being rapidly replaced by Global Navigation Satellite System (GNSS) operations due to satellite reliability, availability and relative cost. Global Positioning System (GPS)-based navigation both en route and for instrument arrivals is quickly superseding traditional navigation systems and is now in many circumstances the accepted primary means of navigation.

Surveillance

Similar to communications and navigation there is a range of surveillance technologies, which, for the moment, are ground based and range in sophistication from traditional radar to satellite-based surveillance. Augmented space-based surveillance systems are revolutionizing aviation safety and efficiency due to the accuracy and reliability of the systems. Most countries in the world provide some level of ATC service, and the level of CNS capability within each country will determine the level of sophistication of each country's ATC service. The ATC service will be influenced by factors such as the level of risk, the volume and complexity of operations, and the quality and availability of CNS infrastructure and airline demand. Even before the ATC service starts to consider the scheduling intentions of each airline, the country's regulator and ANSP will have completed design work for the airspace in which the airline will operate. Some of the design parameters or infrastructure design requirements include:

* airspace organization such as air routes
* facilities and services
* airborne capabilities.

ICAO stipulates various classes of airspace in which airlines may operate, and the way that the airspace is organized will be determined by its class. Often referred to as alphabet airspace, the ICAO classes range from Class A through to Class G. Simply put, airspace design reflects the standard of service and the route structure, with Class A providing the most sophisticated ATC services for aircraft suitably equipped, through to Class G which is commonly referred to as uncontrolled airspace. ATC provides limited or no services in Class G. The class of airspace will define the types of operations that can occur, such as, Visual Flight Rules (VFR) or Instrument Flight Rules (IFR), as well as the level and quality of CNS equipment that must be fitted. Typically, the volume, complexity and nature of operations will influence route structure designs. Wherever possible, routes are separated from adjacent air routes, and racetrack patterns are used for busy city pairs to 'design out' opposite direction operations. In a sense this creates the first layer of separation assurance between aircraft before ATC begins to tactically manage operations.

The key to efficiency and safety is the available CNS infrastructure. As described earlier, the quality and reliability of these technologies will determine what separation spacing can be applied, which ultimately is a constraint on how efficient the operation can be with regard to the number of aircraft that can occupy preferred altitudes and routes within a volume of airspace. The combination of CNS capabilities and equipment on the ground and in aircraft determines the separation standard distances that ATC can use. For example, in terminal airspace the separation standard is usually three nautical miles horizontally.

If the ANSP can provide a blend of Automatic Dependent Surveillance – Broadcast (ADS-B) with traditional radar and has aircraft operating with Required Navigation Performance (RNP) capability, then it is possible to provide a five nautical mile separation in the cruise phase of flight as well as during climb/descent. In terms of an extreme example where these high integrity technologies and performance capabilities are not available, the horizontal separation between aircraft may be as much as ten minutes. This can be the case in some oceanic and remote area operations. Given that aircraft in cruise may be operating at speeds reaching ten miles a minute, this equates to a required ATC distance between aircraft of up to 100 nautical miles. This certainly increases inefficiency, as aircraft will be constrained in terms of accessing their preferred flight trajectory. Fortunately, this is occurring less and less as most ANSPs and modern airlines are equipped to permit reduced separation between aircraft.

Strategic ATC Traffic Management

ATC starts to integrate airline flight intentions between twelve and six months in advance of the actual day of operation. While airline intentions at this stage will not provide an accurate picture of the day of operation, it enables the ATC system to start to understand what the broader flight intentions will be across the network. It is important that ATC planning, which at this stage is focused on efficiency, is starting to understand the seasonal impacts of flight scheduling and how the many airlines are likely to operate. This is a complex process as ATC starts to integrate a diverse range of airline intentions from international, national and regional carriers into one operational picture. Key issues such as airport curfews, the likely seasonal weather, known operational constraints such as facility repairs or upgrades, and military operations will start to form a picture of how ATC should plan the delivery of services. At this stage of planning, ATC will be looking at schedule management schemes which then allocate strategic landing slots based on the known capacity of the aerodrome. Tactical issues are not considered at this early stage. This is an evolving picture and will continue to be refined leading up to the real-time service delivery.

Depending on the sophistication of the ANSP operation they will employ a range of Traffic Management Initiatives (TMIs). These will be discussed further, below. The dominant theme in modern ATC and airline operations is Collaborative Decision-Making (CDM). CDM improves air traffic management by sharing information and data between airport operators, airline operators, military operations, ground handlers and ATC. The goal is to allow all users to be aware of the network demand, capacity and constraints and have a shared understanding of the needs of the users and service providers. The desired effect is a more knowledgeable and participative aviation community that enhances safety, and optimizes airspace capacity and services to reduce cost and emissions and deliver optimum on-time performance. The effectiveness of CDM is highly dependent on commitment of all participants and requires all users to adjust their plans and procedures where they are no longer compatible with the broader goals of the CDM group. ANSPs play an important role of facilitating access to the data and information that delivers CDM benefits.

Pre-tactical planning

As a general rule the pre-tactical period of ATC planning is in the range from the day prior, up to two hours before the flight. In the hours leading up to the day of operation the ANSP is looking at the main variables that will affect the capacity and sequencing of airline operations to all major destinations. Airlines' schedules are being reviewed and ATC network operations will be assessing weather forecasts, anticipated wind strengths and directions that will determine duty runways, and infrastructure limitations such as the availability of navigation aids, and any airport works, such as taxiway or runway works, which will constrain acceptance rates. Maximum runway capacity or rates are a combination of arrivals and departures and are calculated for all aerodromes. The calculated maximum rate will be a function of the number of available runways, the terrain, available precision approach navigation aids, and the layout and active runway occupancy and taxi distance times. The various factors are assembled to predict duty runways and what acceptance rates can be managed. ANSPs will be conducting network user teleconferences to gather all relevant information so that the most efficient national network picture and schedule can be built and delivered. These calls continue regularly and their frequency will be adjusted depending on the stability or variability of the day of operation circumstances in the network. Rapidly changing weather patterns or significant adjustments in airline schedules may necessitate more frequent calls to share information and fine-tune the network plan. Various commercial technologies and tools will be utilized by ATC, to incorporate all the various data inputs to create a national traffic network picture.

Typically, airlines that operate regularly are required to provide flight-scheduling data into this central database. This is usually submitted via a web client. Where demand is predicted to exceed capacity, TMIs such as Ground Delay Programs (GDPs) are prepared to smooth arrival sequencing and reduce airborne delays for each controlled airport. GDPs are specific to an airport and require cooperation by all users to be fully effective. The centralized GDP program equitably distributes a ground delay to those flights that are predicted to receive an airborne delay if they were to depart at their scheduled time. The program notifies the affected airline operators, typically via a web-based interface, advising them of their assigned slot and associated Calculated Take Off Time (CTOT).

This centralized traffic management procedure is the first stage in seeking to ensure the most predictable flight can occur with the minimum of delay. The GDP recognizes that, where possible, delay is most effectively absorbed on the ground, as this is less costly to the airline. This has the added safety benefit of minimizing airborne congestion for ATC and the pilot by reducing complexity and workload, particularly in the high-demand arrival phase of flight. GDPs are relatively tactical and can be adjusted or terminated where demand ceases to exceed capacity. GDPs are heavily dependent on compliance, and business rules may vary from ANSP to ANSP. Non-compliance is often managed tactically on the day of operation.

Flights which intentionally do not comply with their assigned ground delay (or CTOT) will often have to absorb any remaining delay airborne, as priority of sequencing of arriving aircraft is given to those that comply. Some ANSPs will require an airline that misses its slot (or CTOT) to apply for a new one, which will further delay the departure. This ensures fairness to airlines that do comply. Additionally, post-operation compliance reports are prepared which compare CTOT with Actual Take Off Times (ATOT) and are communicated to the relevant operators and the airport for improvement action. Operational Air Traffic Controllers do not monitor or adjust taxi times or airways clearances to achieve the calculated CTOT. It is the responsibility of the pilot to achieve this time and to communicate this to ATC when there is a compatibility issue between ATC intention and the GDP. The weather specialists will be constantly updating forecasts so that the network plan can be fine-tuned, and military ATC specialists will also be providing regular updates on military exercises that may impact on airline operations.

Real time (day of operation)

By now ATC is supporting the day's airline operations at a tactical level and ATC planning is inside the two-hour period of the scheduled flight. The pre-tactical traffic management or network plan will have been shared with airline operations based on available arrival slots, and the information provided by ATC regarding acceptance rates. A range of variables will be managed tactically by operational ATCs who are providing the service directly to each aircraft. This will influence the efficiency of the day's operation. These variables will include:

- changes in actual weather, particularly prevailing winds at airports that will determine duty runways and acceptance rates; other significant weather events that may impact on network capacity, and cruise speeds which will affect arrival sequences
- facilities, which cover a myriad of equipment and infrastructure such as any navigation aids that may become unserviceable; availability changes will be documented and available to airlines through Aeronautical Information notification services such as Notices to Airmen (NOTAMs)
- military exercises and active restricted airspace which influence available air routes and track miles
- itinerant flights
- emergencies, which have priority.

The ability to provide the most efficient and safe service in real time becomes a tactical service provided by ATC, and the variables described above are the ultimate determining factors for delivering efficiency for airlines. The planned GDPs will be operating as calculated during the lead up to the actual operation. In the event of an unplanned or unforeseen event, which creates an imbalance between demand and capacity, a Ground Stop (GS) program may be necessary. This is rare, but at times necessary when airspace capacity will exceed the point where workload and safety are potentially compromised, or where there is no likelihood of landing within the predicted flight time of the scheduled operation.

Once airborne, ATC works to avoid any impact on the climb profile such as speed restrictions or intermediate level stops as the aircraft climbs to its preferred or available cruise altitude. There are a range of en-route and arrival TMIs, usually technology supported, which can be used by ATC. They vary in sophistication and are often designed around specific city pairs. These applications integrate planned intentions with known flight trajectory information and weather to calculate the most efficient sequence to the destination aerodrome. These systems are displayed at the ATC workstation, and ATC use speed and vectoring instructions to the aircraft to achieve the calculated sequence.

ANSPs have varied levels of sophistication in achieving the most efficient and safe arrival sequence. A range of short- and medium-range flow management tools is used. The more sophisticated operations utilize technology that calculates many operational variables to design the en-route and arrival sequence. ATC uses speed adjustments and in some cases vectoring, to establish this sequence well in advance of the aircraft commencing descent. The objective is to create a seamless and uninterrupted flight trajectory to the landing. This is important for fuel savings and on-time performance but importantly it provides more predictability into congested and often complex terminal environments. This improves safety as it reduces the need for ATC to tactically manage the flight. In less sophisticated operations, ATC uses flow management that is calculated by the operational Air Traffic Controller based on their qualifications, experience and knowledge of the operating environment, to create the most efficient and safe arrival sequence. When congestion results in demand exceeding capacity close to an aerodrome, ATC may need to use traffic holding procedures to achieve the required landing sequence and to ensure safety. While undesirable, it is at times necessary.

Most arrival environments have route designs to achieve segregation between arriving and departing aircraft. This reduces the need for tactical intervention by ATC. The design typically involves Standard Instrument Departures (SIDs) and Standard Terminal Arrival Routes (STARs) which have inbuilt altitude requirements to create vertical separation between the two aircraft at crossover points. The design of these flight paths is always a balance between the ideal capacity, complexity and constraints such as terrain, number of runways and the availability of instrument approaches. This balance is focused on efficiency while ensuring the highest standards in safety. The altitude requirement on a SID or STAR also assists in ensuring aircraft remain inside controlled airspace and ensure terrain clearance. Wherever possible, the STAR is linked directly to the most accurate instrument approach and ideally the aircraft operates without the need for tactical ATC intervention.

Incorporating international airline flights into pre-tactical traffic management strategies remains a challenge for ATC. Technologies today generally do not operate successfully across ANSP boundaries or between different countries' Flight Information Regions (FIRs). There are some limited operations where CDM data is shared between countries to create a longer-term traffic management plan for the day of operation. This level of cooperation is still in its infancy compared with domestic in-country traffic management planning. In some parts of the world international flights have many hours of endurance and operate through the airspace of many ANSPs. Because of this, the predictability of their arrival time cannot be calculated with any accuracy until the airline is operating in the ANSP airspace of the final destination aerodrome, or is within a few hours' flight time of the airline's destination. ATC must integrate these operations tactically into the domestic network schedule once the international flight intentions are more predictable. GDPs are of limited value for international flights that have departed from a foreign airport unless they are from parts of the world where ANSP-to-ANSP cooperation exists and the flight duration is relatively short, so that there is a reasonable predictability in calculating landing times.

Integration of military operations and airline access to active military airspace varies in sophistication depending on the technology and operational communication capability between the civil and military operations. There are certainly times when military operations are not compatible with airline operations, and in some circumstances ATC will be required to ensure airline operations remain clear of military restricted airspace. Flexible Use of Airspace (FUA) is the common term used to describe the cooperation between civil and military operations where access to military restricted airspace can be facilitated. Most military operators are responsive to civilian needs and recognize the efficiencies that can be achieved when access can be provided. Track shortening is often the desired outcome for airlines where access can be facilitated. Military ATC also works hard to activate restricted airspace only when operationally required. Cooperation between civilian and military ATC has matured significantly and there is a common understanding of competing needs and a shared objective to balance these needs as much as possible. The advent of centralized air traffic planning in the form of ATC operations centres, similar to airline operations centres, where military liaison staff are co-located, has advanced the utilization of FUAs dramatically in recent years.

General Aviation (GA) operations are generally, by their nature, quite segregated from airline operations. In most cases GA charters operate from separate aerodromes. This minimizes the impact on airline operations and allows GA operations to be conducted with minimal delays and interruption. Where GA operations do operate in the same airspace as airlines, they are generally treated with the same level of priority based on the GA aircraft's performance and capability and the intentions of the flight. In most circumstances this will be in and around aerodromes, as most GA operations do not operate at the same altitudes as airlines during the cruise phase of flight. GA operators are required to be equipped with appropriate communication and navigation equipment defined by the class of airspace so that ATC can process them in the same way as airlines. They will receive ATC instructions on altitude, position and speed, in the same way as an airline operation to fit into the arrival or departure sequence.

Helicopters, like GA, typically operate from locations that are separate to major city aerodromes where airlines generally operate. When a helicopter does intend to operate in the same airspace as airline operations, they are managed by ATC in exactly the same way as GA. Helicopter manoeuvrability can assist with positioning the flight to minimize disruption and impact on both the helicopter and other users such as airlines.

How operations are changing

The aviation industry is far from static with regard to emerging and disruptive technologies. One significant entrant is the rapid growth of Remotely Piloted Aircraft System (RPAS) platforms. This is changing the way ATC operates to integrate airline operations with these new market entrants. RPAS growth is unprecedented, with the majority of RPAS operations occurring outside controlled aircraft and often by enthusiast operators. The RPAS platforms are often less than two kilograms in weight and with limited endurance and range. The weight category is popular as they are relatively cheap to buy and operate and have less onerous regulatory obligations. ATC is now faced with an evolving safety and efficiency challenge to integrate these new platforms. RPAS platforms vary in sophistication and do not fit neatly into existing regulatory frameworks. Because of this, regulators are dealing with this in a number of ways including establishment of rules for operations and education for operators. ATC manage RPAS operations in three broad operating models: the equipment level of the RPAS, the location and height of intended operations, and the class of airspace that determines ATC service obligations. The three models are:

- segregated operations – RPAS platforms are shielded from other operations by designating specific airspace for their use including such classifications as Danger or Restricted areas
- coordinated operations – these operations require interaction with ATC and typically occur within the proximity of a controlled aerodrome, usually three nautical miles, and for operations above 400 feet above the ground
- integrated operations – this typically involves RPAS platforms with equipment levels and capability highly reflective of conventional piloted aircraft, and their operations can be integrated into traditional operations by ATC.

The operating concept for RPAS platforms where ATC provides a service is broken up into Fly Zones as follows:

* No Fly – ATC approval is very unlikely as the complexity is too high
* Apply to Fly – prior ATC approval is sought so that compatibility can be assessed
* Advise and Fly – RPAS operations advise ATC but explicit approval is not required.

By far the most challenging airspace for integration is the airspace surrounding an airport, and one of the significant issues for regulators, airlines and ATC is that many RPAS owners and operators are not familiar with aviation or the critical safety environment in which aviation operates. The ease of access and relatively low cost of a platform means that the traditional methods of licensing and approving operators are limited. Point of sale education is one way to try to address this. Modern Safety Management Systems (SMSs) include incident reporting that helps inform regulators and ANSPs of close proximity events between traditional flight operations and RPAS platforms. The quality and level of reporting relies on pilots seeing the RPAS platform, and that makes the statistical accuracy and quantity of close proximity incident reports very uncertain. Regardless, reporting is an important way of understanding actual operating circumstances and trends and the information can assist operators, regulators and ANSPs to refine procedures and practices to harmonize operations as safely and efficiently as possible.

Conclusion

ATC is an important service that supports airline operations. The combination of front-line ATC and strategic and pre-tactical air traffic flow management procedures work to deliver the most efficient and safe day of operation service to airlines. The operating network is a complex mix of operating variables so the service is both challenging and rewarding for Air Traffic Controllers as they strive to provide the most efficient and safe service while responding to the unpredictable nature of the aviation environment. Future ATC services will evolve and improve rapidly as new collaborative technologies and techniques are introduced. ANSPs will pursue broader and more extensive CDM services that extend further into more effective strategic planning and scheduling. CDM practices will progressively extend further from airports and across ANSP borders to deliver more predictable flight trajectories leading to more efficient and cost-effective and environmentally responsible operations.

Glossary of acronyms and abbreviations

ADS-B   Automatic Dependent Surveillance – Broadcast
ANSP   Air Navigation Services Provider

ATC	Air Traffic Control
ATM	Air Traffic Management
ATOT	Actual Take Off Time
ATS	Air Traffic Services
CDM	Collaborative Decision-Making
CNS	Communication, Navigation, and Surveillance
CPDLC	Controller Pilot Data Link Communication
CTOT	Calculated Take Off Time
FIR	Flight Information Region
FUA	Flexible Use of Airspace
GA	General Aviation
GDP	Ground Delay Program
GNSS	Global Navigation Satellite System
GPS	Global Positioning System
GS	Ground Stop
HF	High Frequency
ICAO	International Civil Aviation Organization
IFR	Instrument Flight Rules
NOTAM	Notices to Airmen
PANS-ATM	Procedures for Air Navigation Services – Air Traffic Management
RNP	Required Navigation Performance
RPAS	Remotely Piloted Aircraft System
SARP	Standards and Recommended Practices
SID	Standard Instrument Departure
SMS	Safety Management Systems
STAR	Standard Terminal Arrival Route
TMI	Traffic Management Initiatives
VFR	Visual Flight Rules
VHF	Very High Frequency

Note

1 Annex 11 to the Convention on International Civil Aviation, Air Traffic Services, 2.2 Objectives of the air traffic services, Thirteenth Edition July 2001.

8 Operational planning and control

Steve Buchanan

Introduction

Each airline around the world has, in one form or another, an Operations Control Centre (OCC). This department looks at the everyday movements and activities of the airline and coordinates the Operations, Crewing, Maintenance and Flight Dispatch functions, which are the core operations in running the schedule integrity of the airline. As an airline evolves and survives in the cutthroat environment of the airline business there are many influencing factors that are driving not only efficiency but also customer expectations, such that the old model of an OCC is starting to be superseded. In the twenty-first century, airlines are turning to a model called the Integrated Operations Centre (IOC). In some airlines, this may be termed a Network Operations Centre (NOC).

The concept of an IOC

An IOC structure is used extensively by all the premium airlines around the world. There are a few differences between them, but the general concept is consistent. The IOC is an *integrated* model whereby key decision-making departments are co-located in the one room, and importantly, processes are integrated between the departments to bring together collaborative and dynamic decision-making processes. With these elements in mind, a key step next is to provide consistency in decision outcomes and reliability of day of operations service to the airline customers.

Structuring the IOC

Co-location is the first step in the reorganizational process, and to achieve an optimum structure a thorough understanding is needed of the departments that should form the core of the IOC. The more traditional OCC tended to consist of controllers who liaised with two or three other key stakeholders in order to manage disruptions or to manage the schedule integrity of the airline. In contrast, the IOC concept invites participation from many more departments which are likely to be crucial to the decision-making process in terms of realizing greater clarity of communications, faster provision of information, and direct input into problem-solving. The objective of this collaboration is to gain a synergy that enables the IOC to handle a wide range of complex scenarios or disruptions.

With current and envisaged technology, the IOC does not need to be located anywhere specific (such as an airport or downtown), as long as they have the right technology (such as communications, flight display and analytics tools), and the right people. Other than Operations (termed *movements* or *rerouters* in some airlines), Technical (Pilot) and Flight Attendant Crewing departments, Maintenance and Flight Dispatch, other departments that can make a valuable contribution and thus have largely been co-located within the IOC structure include the following:

- Meteorology
- Security
- Load Control
- Air Cargo Planning
- Catering Centre
- Operations Performance
- IT Support
- Commercial Operations
- Customer Advocate
- Social Media.

Once this structure has been identified (essentially from the list above but taking into account others that may from time to time warrant inclusion), there will be not only an excellent range of skilled resources and valuable information to feed the decision makers, but a platform from which the IOC can optimize its activities.

IOC layout

The physical layout of the IOC room is a crucial consideration when setting up an IOC. The interactions of the key areas, especially in a disruption, are vital in the collaborative decision-making approach. Being able to conduct clear, face-to-face conversations between specific individuals while managing a complex disruption is crucial, and leads to superior outcomes as the teams are working together and not in isolation.

The right people

Team fit is also a consideration for a great IOC. There are many times when an individual could imagine him- or herself in a five-star restaurant with a head chef barking orders to the sous chefs. An IOC could be considered in that same mould, except there are no head chefs barking orders; rather, subject matter experts of each area going about their business of running the airline and collaborating with each other. The key is the concept of *integration,* and the way in which the players all work in teams.

Operational planning

Planning is a critical function in the way an IOC operates. Planning tends to be overlooked but in a similar vein to our everyday functions such as shopping or budgeting for the family home, incomplete or incorrect planning increases pressure on the day of operation, leading to more instances of delays or other disruptive actions with commensurate customer dissatisfaction. Planning within the IOC starts with the Maintenance function to ensure that the maintenance of aircraft and the monitoring of aircraft flying hours are performed most diligently. In addition, ensuring the allocation of the right aircraft (in terms of capacity and performance) on the right route is critical both for commercial and operational reasons (we will look at this later in this section).

Planning for maintenance

Planning occurs approximately thirty days out from the day of operation, taking into account the range of maintenance check services (e.g., Check 'A's to Check 'D's) that are planned, along with the numerous maintenance work tasks associated with these (Chapter 10 discusses this in detail). Coupled with the ongoing maintenance issues that any aircraft accumulate during the course of their flying, the planned ground time to undergo scheduled maintenance along with the time needed for rectifying such unserviceabilities may increase the pressure on the current operation. This creates a balancing act between Maintenance Planning and the Operations Control areas of the IOC, as to whether an aircraft will be available in time for its scheduled service.

This maintenance planning function ensures the alignment of aircraft commitments with scheduled maintenance work such as, for example, wheel washes or avionic repairs to in-flight entertainment equipment (IFE). A maintenance planner will receive a 'wish list' from the Maintenance Watch area, with advice as to where each aircraft (registration or tail number) needs to complete its flying commitments, such that work on the aircraft can be allocated to various maintenance bases given the available expertise at each particular base. For example, repairs to avionics may be carried out primarily in Port A due to the number of skilled avionics staff, while repairs to thrust reversers may need to be carried out in Port B. With this in mind, the planner now goes about aligning the aircraft to complete their flying patterns at the particular bases. (Note that as international aircraft tend not to have schedules contained within calendar days necessarily, the way in which work tasks for them are planned may be quite different from domestic environments.)

The best of planning is always subject to change, and in the airline business, the many changes and disruptions that occur during the day of operation may not satisfy the desired plan for any number of reasons (see Chapter 22 for a detailed account). Should it be the case that an aircraft cannot meet the planned maintenance commitment in a specific port, the planner then has to weave his or her magic and try to negotiate another aircraft to replace it, so as not to waste the workforce organized. If warranted, this may also include considering options that will get the originally planned aircraft to its rightful port at the end of the day, even if delays are incurred deliberately.

Planning for payload

The other planning function of 'right aircraft – right route' has to take into account any payload-limited flights. Certain airlines are faced with payload limitations on particular operations such as very long-haul flights, or if a flight is expecting to encounter bad weather en route. Another reason may be variations in airline fleet complexity. Airlines may choose to limit the maximum thrust ratings of engines on some of their aircraft, for example, to extend engine life. For a very long-range operation, this reduced engine take-off setting may necessitate a reduced payload, in particular given that the aircraft will probably require a lot of fuel (see later chapters of this book for further explanations). Should this limitation result in offloading of payload, the way in which customers are handled is extremely important, as alluded to in the following scenario.

> Many years ago, an aircraft prepared to depart on a long-range with a full load of passengers in extreme heat. The Captain calculated his figures for take-off and found that the aircraft was 2,000 kilograms (kg) over the maximum take-off weight (MTOW). He alerted the ground staff that payload (this may consist of passengers, baggage and air cargo) needed to be taken off in order for the aircraft to take off safely. With only fifteen minutes to go to departure, the ground staff were faced with having to find exactly 'what' 2,000 kg to offload. This could either consist of cargo or passengers. Ground staff then liaised with Load Control to determine what could be offloaded. As the scenario unfolded, it was apparent that there was no cargo being carried, so passengers and bags then had to come off the aircraft. The over-weight situation equated to twenty passengers and bags having to be offloaded, but the difficult decision was then identifying whom these passengers would be. Remember that timing was critical as the aircraft was due to depart in fifteen minutes, and because of the long flight time, crew hours needed to be factored in. Further, the ability to operate the flight direct (i.e., without diverting via another port for fuel) was important operationally as the aircraft needed to be in the next port to operate its subsequent sector. Ground staff had some difficulty as no passengers volunteered to be offloaded. Of course, this was not a good look in terms of airline brand, and certainly not good for an on-time performance. So, negotiations commenced to ascertain what incentives could be offered to get twenty passengers off that flight.

In terms of being prepared for events like this, airlines look at bringing these sorts of problems from an operational window to the planning window. By managing them in the planning window, problems such as the one that evolved above, or ones that can have been foreseen, are dealt with well ahead of the actual time of departure. In most cases if passenger offloads need to be processed, passengers can be offered alternatives such as uplift on alternative flights and/ or inducements (such as upgrades, accommodation and spending money). In a scenario such as the one above, the Customer team could recommend the twenty passengers who need to be offloaded as those who had very low or no frequent flyer tier status as a measure. Normally, air cargo could also be offloaded provided that alerts to cargo owners advising of this could be sent in a far more timely manner rather than with a last-minute phone call. This would help to promote the brand and retain any future business, because the airline has then turned the situation to a proactive one.

Operational control – the day of operation

The day of operation consists of three key factors – Schedule integrity, Disruptions and Delays. The IOC is the overseer of the schedule and not only is it looking at individual ports and their operations but gauging any effect that a delay or disruption may be having on the rest of the network for that day and possibly up to five days beyond. Considerations that could disrupt an airline network include weather, mechanical, industrial, the need to manage slot times, and resourcing issues such as airport ground staff or ATC. (See Chapter 22 for further details.)

Controlled or uncontrolled delays

Delays can be either controlled or uncontrolled, as shown in the two scenarios below.

Scenario 1

A passenger had become disorientated at the airport and been waiting at the wrong gate for his flight. By the time he realized this, the flight was delayed while a search was made for the seemingly missing passenger, and then further delayed while his baggage was offloaded for security reasons. This caused the aircraft to miss its slot time at the destination and as a result, twenty passengers misconnected with their onward flight such that they either could be accommodated overnight (airline expense) or transferred to another airline (lost revenue) to continue their journey that night. Controlled or uncontrolled?

Scenario 2

Thunderstorms at an airport shut down all activity on the tarmac for approximately sixty minutes, such that ground staff were not able to attend aircraft to unload or load bags. Aircraft then became considerably delayed with a 'knock-on' (or downline) effect for the rest of the night, resulting in potential curfew breaks. Controlled or uncontrolled?

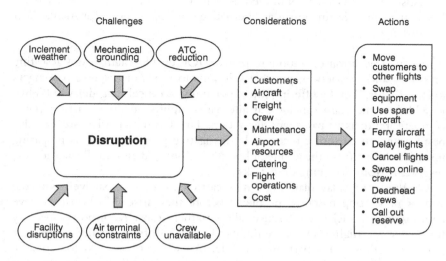

Figure 8.1 Decision-making model

The above examples show that there are situations that can be controlled and some that cannot. The question that may then be asked is 'What are the advantages of an IOC in this situation?'. A key purpose of the IOC is to manage disruptions and then devise and initiate a recovery plan. Figure 8.1 presents a decision-making model that provides a stepped approach to this.

Devising possible solutions

Each situation calls for a tailored approach. But some ideas that might be considered in the decision-making process could be along the following lines.

- Could two flights be consolidated? So instead of two narrow-bodied aircraft taking up two slots, could the flights be combined as one wide-bodied aircraft, thereby lessening the use of crews and using the resulting spare departure slot for minimizing a delay to another aircraft?
- Is it possible to 'triangulate' the routing of aircraft so instead of two aircraft being used, with one operating Port A to Port B and back, and the other operating Port A to Port C and back, could one aircraft just fly Port A to Port B to Port C and back to Port A, provided the combined loads of passengers did not exceed the aircraft capacity on any stage? This would have the effect again of reducing the number of aircraft used with the now 'spare' aircraft available to meet demand from other disrupted flights, and additional crew now available.
- Could passengers be offered alternative modes of transport to get to their final destination? In the case of short distances such as CBR–SYD in

Australia or LHR–MAN in the UK, is it possible and feasible to 'bus' them to their final destination as an alternative to a lengthy delay for such a short distance?

Having a *commercial* operations team in the IOC enables them to look at seating inventory and a variety of possible solutions to move or disperse passengers to later flights, thereby offering the opportunity to cancel long-delayed flights. In addition, the team can look at alternative uplifts on other carriers (even competitors) to assist passenger disruption. The 'Customer Advocate' can also be proactive in customer recovery by instigating processes such as preparing insurance letters from the airline or booking accommodation to alleviate airport resourcing from managing these tasks.

On the current day, planning can be carried out more proactively with the aim of preventing potential problems before they arise. Most airlines have communication such as conference calls with their respective airports especially for 'first wave' flights. These are flights that are the first departures from each port and if they can depart on schedule, this will set a pattern for on-time departures for the subsequent second and third waves of flights. This two-way communication is vital, as it not only provides the airport staff with current situational awareness of the status of the network (having heard directly from the IOC), but the IOC can also hear what constraints the airport may be facing, so that solutions can be identified ahead of time. So again, a collaborative approach is beneficial to managing any foreseeable disruptions. Previously the Operations Control Team would not have had the right stakeholders in the room to manage disruptions and delays, but now the team can be better informed and decisions can be made more dynamically.

Reviewing the operation

A key element to measuring performance in an IOC is reviewing the operations of the previous day or specific period. Reviewing disruptions or delays can lead to business improvements and future approaches to minimizing them. As mentioned earlier, the airline business is changing quite rapidly and one key focus of retaining business and securing repeat business is that of On-Time Performance (OTP). OTP provides key metrics which measure, for example, departure and arrival performance. To track and measure these parameters, departments within the airline examine certain processes and use sophisticated technology. To assist the process, all delays are 'coded' (given a category) to identify accountable departments that would then investigate causes and in doing so may look, for example, for frequencies of occurrence or adverse trends. An example is provided in the scenario below.

An aircraft was parked on Gate 25 for the first flight of the day as this was where it arrived the previous night. Each morning, gate staff experienced delays of 5, 7 or 10 minutes on this flight due to the late arrival at the gate by the Frequent Flyer lounge members. The Frequent Flyer lounge is situated at Gate 4, some distance away. By coding delays and observing patterns such as this, it was possible to identify the reason for the delays and recommend possible actions to mitigate them. Options included towing the aircraft in the morning to Gate 4, thereby tying up tug resources each day, or planning the aircraft that was to operate the first wave flight next morning, to arrive into Gate 4 as the last arrival of the night. Hence Frequent Flyers were then able to arrive at the gate in time with no delays incurred.

This is a simple example of having the data as evidence in the review process that by merely having better bay planning, delays can be avoided. Reviews can also examine processes and procedures so that there is continual business improvement. By having all the stakeholders in the single room of the IOC 'mini tabletop', exercises can be conducted to improve the way disruptions are handled and test any processes prior to the event occurring.

Commercial versus operational input

Within the IOC there are many operational areas such as Operations Control, Crew Scheduling, Flight Dispatch, Load Control and Maintenance Watch which work together to ensure aircraft are flying safely and on time. However, as noted at the start of the chapter, the old model of the Operations Control Centre is being superseded. Hence, there is a drive to ensure that the passenger or customer is considered as a key part of the decision-making process for solving a disruption. This is a critical consideration, especially with competition between airlines as fierce as it is. So, there is great emphasis not only on the product alone, but recognition of the importance of frequent flyer loyalty and on-time performance. Both are valued very highly by customers and factored into their decision as to choice of airline. By including a Commercial team within the IOC, there is assurance that when a disruption recovery is being handled, the customer is well and truly at the forefront of the recovery action. This inadvertently pushes the Operations Team into searching for other alternative measures to satisfy customer needs. It also injects a Commercial flavour into the IOC such that the Commercial arm of the airline which initiated a sale can realize the consideration given to the customer throughout the journey, and especially the consideration given to customers in the event of disruptions.

Technology and sharing of information

This is evolving at such a great pace that the IOC needs to keep evolving as well. In terms of new technologies, many airlines are looking at slot optimization programs to assist with on-time performance and also aid the recovery of delays by ensuring that the best available slot is obtained. This is managed now by particular departments, but with the aid of newer technology this process is being streamlined and slot management is becoming more dynamic. In saying this, there is also a call for better crew optimization and better disruption recovery tools to ensure that the Operations Team is able to find solutions more quickly and more cost effectively. By sharing this information in the IOC between Commercial and Operations teams, airlines will be better informed and better equipped to tackle the myriad of issues and hurdles they are presented with. Technology is enabling payload restricted flights to be scrutinized in greater detail, providing faster and more accurate data that helps to minimize disruption to the customer. Airlines are steering away from technology-centric companies to broader platforms which encompass inventory, load planning, slot optimization, and more, as a suite of tools that can be fully integrated. In the past, these pieces of software would not 'talk to each other', making problem-solving very inefficient and lengthy.

Conclusion

Airline Operations Control Centres are evolving to meet the demands of cost, efficiency and customer expectations. The new world of IOCs ensures collaboration not only within the IOC, but with external stakeholders such as airports, other departments and senior executives to achieve the best outcomes. The IOC of the future will not only use the knowledge of the subject matter experts in the IOC but harness the rapid advances in technology and be better informed to improve the decision-making process. The key is integration of all parts of the IOC and the sharing of the knowledge to ensure that there is constant development.

9 Crew planning

Patrick Fennell

Introduction

The Crew Planning department of an airline is tasked with producing and maintaining the duty rosters for the company's pilots and flight attendants. At its most basic, crew planning involves the creation of a timetable that allocates a crew member to a specific duty. This may be a flight, a series of flights, or another assignment such as a standby, training, or ground duties, and these activities collectively form a duty roster. However, the actual process is considerably more complex than this and requires numerous checks, balances, variables, and constraints, to be taken into account before the overall plan can be deemed complete, legal, and most importantly, safe.

In order to make the various tasks more manageable, airlines typically divide their crew planning functions into two distinct stages: the strategic stage where the planning takes place, and the tactical stage where the day-to-day management of the plan is carried out. The size and complexity of an airline's Crew Planning department is proportional to the size of the carrier, and a small operator with just a handful of aircraft and a small number of crew may combine the various crew planning functions into a single role carried out by just one or two people. In contrast, a large networked carrier can have dozens of staff in the Crew Planning department, working around the clock in support of producing and managing the various stages of the rostering lifecycle for thousands of crew members. Carriers such as these may have hundreds of aircraft of varying types, spread out over a number of bases, and across multiple time zones. Before delving deeper into the crew planning process, it is important first to explore the rules and regulations, also known as 'flight and duty time limitations', that govern crews' working hours, as these largely dictate how their schedules are planned.

Flight and duty time limitations

Every country that is a signatory to the ICAO (International Civil Aviation Organization) mandates will have in place a set of regulations governing the amount of time that flight crews, including flight attendants, can be on duty. The regulations are primarily time-based and prescribe daily, monthly, and annual limits on the accrual of crews' duty hours; this is further subdivided into flight time and duty time, which are dealt with in more detail later. In addition to regulations on duty time, limits on the minimum amount of rest and days free from duty that must be provided to crews are also dealt with.

This rule set is often called a 'scheme' and every airline registered with the regulatory authority of a particular country will apply the respective flight time limitations scheme (FTLS) to the scheduling of their crews. Rather than 'reinvent the wheel', some countries have found that the regulations of another suit their needs and have therefore chosen to adopt them,[1] while others have chosen to create their own FTLSs with varying local allowances and restrictions. As the variances between rule sets are numerous, it is beyond the scope of this text to explore their many nuances, however, suffice it to say they all have one prime objective in common 'to ensure that crew members are adequately rested at the beginning of each flying duty period, and whilst flying, be sufficiently free from fatigue so that they can operate to a satisfactory level of efficiency and safety in all normal and abnormal situations'.[2]

Before going into further detail, it is important to elaborate on some of the most common definitions which form the basis of a typical FTLS.

- Duty: Any time a crew member is required to undertake activity on behalf of the airline is considered as duty time. This includes flying, dead-heading, admin duty, standby,[3] training, etc.
- Duty period: Calculated from the moment a crew member reports for duty and ends once they are free from all work-related activities.
- Flight time: Calculated from the moment the aircraft moves under its own power for the purpose of flight until it comes to a full stop and the engines are shut down; essentially off-blocks to on-blocks time.
- Flight duty period (FDP): Calculated from the moment that a crew member signs on for duty and reports for a flight, and ends once the aircraft comes to rest with engines powered down at the end of the last sector.[4] The duration of FDP depends on the number of sectors to be operated and the time of day the crew is required to report.
- Acclimatized: A crew member is considered to be acclimatized when their body clock is synchronized with the time zone in which they currently reside. This occurs after they have spent a prescribed minimum amount of time[5] in that zone.
- Circadian rhythm: The body's internal clock that determines and regulates periods of wakefulness and sleep. The rhythm fluctuates throughout the day with some variance from person to person.
- Window of circadian low (WOCL): A period of time when the physiological effects of being sleepy are at their highest. There are two main periods where this is experienced – a primary period said to be between 02:00–05:59, and a secondary one between 15:00–17:00. During these periods the desire for sleep is said to be at its highest, together with a commensurate drop in performance, as well as other negative attributes associated with feeling tired.

- Rest: This is a period of time allotted either side of a duty that gives the crew the opportunity to avail themselves of sufficient sleep before undertaking their next duty. The rest required is a predefined minimum value according to the regulations of the state but may be longer depending on the length of the previous duty operated. For example, some states mandate a minimum of twelve hours' rest. However, if the preceding duty has been in excess of this, say fourteen hours, then the rest required must also be at least as long, i.e. fourteen hours or more must be given. See Figure 9.1.

There are circumstances where the rest required may be reduced, but this is only to be used in exceptional cases and typically requires the regulator to be officially notified afterwards. Figure 9.2 is an overview of the various elements that make up a typical single sector duty, followed by a period of rest.

To aid in the calculation of FDP, the regulations generally contain a quick reference chart – see Figure 9.3. This is an example of the one in use by the UK's Civil Aviation Authority (CAA) and shows the maximum FDP available for an 'acclimatized' crew.[6] The maximum FDP permitted is determined by locating the intersection of the starting time of the duty and the number of sectors to be flown. The WOCL is one of two primary considerations when calculating the available FDP; the other being the number of sectors that the crew must operate. Note how the FDP varies based on the time that duty starts and how duties commenced in the primary WOCL (02:00–05:59) offer the shortest FDP. Note also how regardless of duty start time, the available FDP decreases as the number of sectors increases. The critical nature of take-off and landing and the demands placed on the crew during these phases of flight have

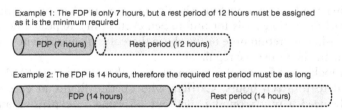

Figure 9.1 Required rest

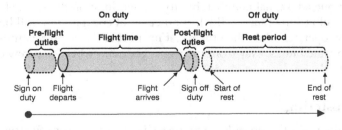

Figure 9.2 Duty periods

Local time of start	No. of sectors							
	1	2	3	4	5	6	7	8+
06:00–07:59	13	12¼	11½	10¾	10	9½	9	9
08:00–12:59	14	13¼	12½	11¾	11	10½	10	9½
13:00–17:59	13	12¼	11½	10¾	10	9½	9	9
18:00–21:59	12	11¼	10½	9¾	9	9	9	9
22:00–05:59	11	10¼	9½	9	9	9	9	9

Figure 9.3 FDP hours

been recognized in the FDP table and consequently the duration that crew may be on duty is reduced incrementally as the number of sectors (take-offs and landings) increases.

In the bold, it can be seen how a crew signing on for duty between the hours of 08:00–12:59 can operate four sectors provided they are not on duty for more than eleven and three-quarter hours. As more sectors are added the available FDP decreases and if the crew is to carry out the same four sectors during the primary WOCL, they must complete it generally within nine hours FDP.

There are circumstances where the FDP may be extended beyond what is prescribed in the regulations.[7] This is commonly called 'discretion' and allows crews who have experienced unforeseen delays to their flights to go beyond the limits of the FDP in order to complete their *planned* duty.[8] This is only done once all crew members have been consulted and are in agreement that they are fit and free from fatigue in order to continue. On completing the duty, the captain must make a report on the circumstances that led to discretionary time being used. Discretion time should never be used to overcome known operational restrictions; it is for unforeseen events only. Repeated occurrences of crews using discretion time or the abuse thereof is likely to invite scrutiny of the airline by the respective regulator.

From looking at Figure 9.3, it can be seen that the longest FDP available is limited to fourteen hours. Carriers who operate flights in excess of this obviously need a way around it without resorting to expensive and time-consuming intermediate stops. They achieve this by carrying additional crew members on board. For smaller increases in FDP a crew may be 'augmented' with just one additional member, but for longer duration flights, such as those classed as ultra-long range (ULR), another set of cockpit crew will be carried. One crew operates while the others rest in suitable on-board accommodation, usually private bunks away from the passenger cabin where the crew can sleep undisturbed.

Crew rostering

The production of a monthly[9] crew roster is one of the core functions of the Crew Planning department and consists primarily of the following elements:

- flight duties
- reserve duties (home and airport)
- ground duties (administrative work, medical check)
- training (simulator, ground school)
- rest periods
- days off (mandatory and requested)
- annual leave.

Before the process of constructing the roster can commence, however, a number of complex parameters must be established. Many of these must take place months or even years in advance, while others happen concurrently in the month prior to the roster being released. Figure 9.4 is an overview of the various stages in the crew planning lifecycle, from the long term, such as deciding what aircraft to operate, to the short term, where managing the day-to-day crew schedule happens.

The steps of course will vary from airline to airline but the goal does not – to produce an efficient, robust crew schedule that maximizes productivity while minimizing costs. This must be done while maintaining a quality of life for the crew member, and managing the potentially deadly issues of tiredness and fatigue.

Commercial scheduling

Commercial scheduling[10] is the process of planning the destinations, timings, and frequencies to be flown by the airline. The commercial schedule has the largest impact on the crew plan and determines how many crew will be needed by the airline in order to meet the demands of the future flying program. It also determines the type and number of aircraft to be operated, and from this, the fleet utilization can be estimated. Any new destinations that are planned will require a separate assessment for operational suitability and this may result in additional training requirements that must be factored in. Commercial scheduling typically undergoes two major iterations per year: the summer and winter schedules.[11] For example (in the northern hemisphere):

- summer: March 28 – October 28
- winter: October 29 – March 27.

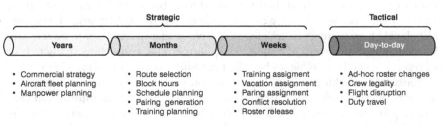

Figure 9.4 Overview of crew-planning stages

Outside these periods the commercial scheduling department is usually restrained from making any significant capacity adjustments without consulting those responsible for workforce and crew planning. Short-notice capacity adjustments can and do occur but they can also be disruptive to the rostering process and detrimental to roster stability if they require unexpected increases in aircraft utilization or workforce resources. An additional requirement at this stage of the planning is to have precise flight and block times. These are typically calculated on a seasonal basis and take the changing wind patterns and varying taxi-times at airports into account. Inaccurate block times, especially when the actual time is longer than that planned, can result in crews exceeding their FDP. This can cause consistent pairing breakages.

Workforce planning

Increasing cost discipline, largely driven by high energy prices and intense competition, has resulted in carriers seeking to optimize how they deploy their assets and resources. This has inevitably led airlines to focus not just on the utilization of their aircraft, but also on that of their crews, as the two are inextricably linked and have a potentially large impact on the cost structure of the business. The cost of labour is a significant contributor to an airline's operational overheads and, at the time of writing, represents thirty-three per cent of overall costs,[12] exceeding that of fuel at fourteen per cent.[13]

Once the draft commercial schedule is released, those involved in workforce planning will have a basis for estimating the optimum crew resources required. The final output is a breakdown by the various ranks of pilot (Captain, First Officer, Second Officer), and Flight Attendant (Purser, Senior/Junior Flight Attendants). Simply calculating the number of personnel required is not enough however, and additional factors such as attrition, upcoming promotions, and planning for retirements must be taken into account.

This exercise also includes estimating the number of reserve crew that will be needed to cover irregularities on the day of operation. Forecasting reserve crew demand is not a straightforward task as the reasons that drive the utilization, or 'call-up', of reserve crew are varied, such as short-notice crew sickness, bad weather, and aircraft technical delays, etc. Airlines may also bulk up their reserve coverage based on known times of need; for example, in tandem with a peak bank of departures, early in the morning, during busy travel periods, or during times of the year where the weather is known to be problematic. They must also decide how many crew to keep in reserve at an airport, ready to be activated immediately in the event of a sudden requirement, as well as how many to keep in reserve at their domicile, to be called up when more notice is available.

Once the workforce plan has been completed, it is compared with the quantity of crew currently available. Any required increases in numbers of crew will require one of several actions to be taken. Either the commercial benefits warrant the hiring and training of additional crew, or the schedule may need to be readjusted to fit the limited number of crew available. This can often be the case when insufficient time prohibits the recruitment of additional crew, particularly with regard to pilots, due to the lead-in time required and expense involved to select and train them.

There are also further restrictions, in addition to the legal ones, that must be considered. Many airlines have strong labour unions to contend with, which may impose additional limits on the number of hours that crew may fly, and this also increases the number of crew required.

Furthermore, in order to provide a certain level of customer service, airlines will often roster flight attendants with specific language skills on the respective route. For example, it wouldn't be helpful on a flight to or from Tokyo if none of the crew spoke Japanese!

The larger low-cost carriers (LCCs), in particular, have excelled at fine-tuning their workforce requirements and can refine their numbers of crew-sets per aircraft down to two decimal places.[14] An example is 5.15 crew-sets per aircraft, with a crew-set defined as two pilots plus the required number of flight attendants commensurate with the aircraft configuration. These airlines will operate with the minimum number of crew required, as opposed to their full-service counterparts who typically have additional crew on board to assist with service delivery, particularly in the premium cabins.

Pairing generation

A pairing is a sequence of flight segments, or sectors, connected to form a flight duty that starts and ends in the same crew base. It can span one day or several days, depending on the operation, and may or may not include one or more layovers. The creation of pairings is a critical step in the rostering process, as inefficient pairings can lead to a waste of resources such as aircraft spending excess time on the ground, or crews having unnecessarily long transits between flights, which reduces their productivity.

Figure 9.5 is a basic short-haul flight pairing showing four sectors for a Heathrow (LHR)-based crew. It commences with a roundtrip from London to Paris (CDG), followed by another round trip from London to Brussels (BRU). One crew would operate this pairing and spend minimum time on the ground in both CDG and BRU, then return to base at the end of their duty.

Figure 9.6 shows a simplified long-haul pairing for an LHR-based crew on a flight to Miami (MIA). It can be seen from the space between the flights that the crew will spend a given amount of time in MIA in order to take their legal rest, also known as a layover, before undertaking another flight. In this example a fresh crew would already be in MIA waiting to operate the return flight back to LHR.

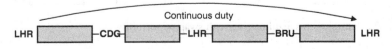

Figure 9.5 Sample short-haul pairing

Figure 9.6 Sample long-haul pairing

A typical crew roster is constructed of many such pairings arranged together and interspersed with non-flying assignments, days off, training, etc. The task of creating crew pairings has been the subject of much discussion and academic study in the field of Operations Research (OR).[15] The optimization of pairings has been treated as an interesting problem that can be solved with the use of advanced algorithms and various branches of applied mathematics. The aim of this is to find a result, as close to optimum as possible, which yields full coverage of the flying program with the smallest number of pairings and crew, at the lowest cost. In addition to this, schedule robustness that maximizes the opportunities for aircraft swaps is a highly desirable feature. This is achieved by facilitating the meeting of aircraft, ideally at the base or hub that allows the aircraft to be swapped. See Figure 9.7.

Smaller operators and those carriers that do not run according to a predefined schedule will neither need, nor be able to fully benefit from, optimized pairings in the same way that large complex scheduled carriers will. One well-known US-based business jet operator gives their crews rosters primarily consisting of standby duties on a fixed rotation of seven days on and six days off. These are quite dynamic schedules and the days spent on standby are regularly subject to multiple duty changes on the day.

In this regard, again the LCCs have led the way in terms of utilization of both aircraft and personnel due to their use of highly optimized pairings that minimize the use of layovers and time spent on the ground in order to maximize productivity. They also avoid the need to augment their crew by making sure that the pairing complies with the standard FDP allowances. Crews who work at these types of operators will often come close to, or even achieve, their maximum allowable flying hours per month and year. Many of the large software vendors who specialize in crew planning systems have realized the potential for OR to augment their systems and now offer this functionality to carry out the optimization task.

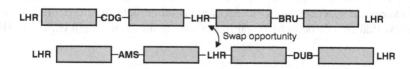

Figure 9.7 Sample short-haul pairing with swap opportunity

Training planning

Training planning involves the assignment of training in order for new crew to become qualified and for existing crew to maintain currency on their various qualifications. Training falls into two main categories:

- Initial training. When new crew members are hired, they will be required to undergo a variety of training such as ground school, flight simulator, safety and emergency procedures, etc. This leads to the crew members receiving their initial qualification. For example, a pilot who has never flown an Airbus A320 will undergo initial training comprising ground school, instruction in the simulator, and time in the actual aircraft. This results in the granting of a type-rating on that type of aircraft.
- Recurrent training. At predefined intervals in the future, this same crew member will undergo refresher training to renew the validity, or currency, of that qualification. All of these training events have an expiry, typically from the date the initial training was carried out, to a point in the future. Depending on the type of training or course, a period of six, twelve, or twenty-four months may elapse before the crew member is required to undergo recurrent training for that qualification.

In order to facilitate a measure of flexibility for the operator, it is allowed for certain training to be postponed or preponed, usually by up to a month, often called a 'grace' month. This allows a measure of flexibility when rostering crews and helps to avoid a situation where a large number of crew will fall due for training in the same period which renders them unavailable for duty, and may have a commercial impact on the operation. Airlines that operate aircraft from the same 'family' may also train their crews in order to cross-utilize them and it is not uncommon at some airlines to have an A320 pilot also rated on an A330. There is even greater flexibility to be gained from cross-functional flight attendants who, once trained on the safety aspects of the individual aircraft, can operate on multiple types without significant additional expense to the airline.

Leave planning

As with training, ground duties and days off, time spent on annual leave is considered as being non-productive from an operational perspective and must therefore be planned in advance in order to ensure sufficient crew are available to operate the flying program. There are a variety of leave planning methods in use by airlines and the size of the airline largely dictates how the process is managed. Small operators often choose to manage this manually by accepting leave requests from individual crew members and then seeing where it fits into the overall roster. Larger operators typically use software systems that can be configured to offer leave slots that can be bid for on a first come, first served basis, or a past success basis, or can be assigned based on seniority. Peak travel periods, when the airline is expected to be operating at full capacity, are typically embargoed or will have reduced leave slots available, to ensure the availability of maximum workforce resources.

Pairing assignment

The assignment of pairings to an individual crew member is the last major stage of roster production and typically takes place in the month preceding the release of the roster. The process is carried out separately between pilots and flight attendants due to the differences in work rules for both.

There are three main methods in use at airlines around the world to accomplish this.

- Line bidding. The line bidding system is considered outmoded and was most commonly used at mainline carriers in the United States where its use is now in decline. It consists of pre-constructed duty rosters, or 'bid lines', that are released to the crew for review. They can be thought of as month-long tours of duty made up of various flights and days off which the crew members then bid for in order of personal preference. The bid is awarded based on seniority, and if a crew member is outbid by someone more senior then they may be awarded their second or third choice, and so on. It has the advantage of allowing crews to know in advance what their schedule will look like if their bid is successful but is an inefficient process that is also unpopular with those towards the bottom of the seniority scale.
- Preferential Bidding System (PBS). The PBS system has largely taken over at airlines that formerly used line bidding and is seen as more efficient in terms of workforce planning and crew utilization. It retains crew seniority as the basis for awarding a bid but differs in terms of what the crew bid for. Instead of pre-constructed lines, it allows crews to bid for, or avoid, certain types of duties. A crew member may have a preference for layovers in certain cities but may want to avoid them in others, or perhaps request weekends or specific days off. It is seen as a more equitable method of constructing rosters, especially for those lower down the seniority scale who typically see greater bid satisfaction compared with line bidding. Other benefits are reportedly lower rates of sick days as crews have an opportunity to fly the trips they have selected for themselves.
- Fair assignment. As the name implies, the aim of this method is the equitable distribution of workload across all active crew members irrespective of seniority, rank, or experience. It is a popular method of rostering particularly among LCCs. The criteria for pairing assignment are generally governed by various work rules and the application of the local flight and duty time regulations. The fair assignment method also offers a degree of flexibility for airlines that wish to introduce elements of PBS into their rostering. For example, an airline may allow crew to bid for certain days off or make other requests. A common feature of fair assignment is a fixed pattern

work rule which stipulates a fixed number of days on duty, followed by a fixed number of days off duty; e.g., five days of flight duty followed by three days off (5/3). Crews that are following a fixed pattern may benefit from a relatively predictable schedule and while the individual trips may not be known until the roster is published, a reasonable estimation can be made as to when days off are likely to fall, several months in advance. One well-known UK-based LCC operates a rotating fixed pattern of '5/3–5/4'.[16]

Regardless of the method used, a final stage of conflict resolution will be required before the roster can be published. This is the result of the inevitability that clashes will occur between the assignment of flying duties and other components such as mandatory training, days off, annual leave, or other events. Once the crew roster has been completed it is released to the crew member on a monthly basis, also known as 'publishing'. This typically takes place seven to ten days before the expiry of the current month's roster. At the point of being published, the responsibility for day-to-day tactical management passes to crew control and the process of creating the next roster begins.

Crew control

Despite the precise planning and care taken in producing the monthly rosters, the reality on the day – once operations are live – is often quite different. Deviations from the script will always occur and by the time the end of the month is reached, the roster will have undergone countless adjustments to cater for unforeseen events, to the extent that it won't resemble its original form as first published. This happens for a variety of operational reasons and crews may be delayed or stranded out of base due to an aircraft technical problem or bad weather, or their flight(s) may even be cancelled. In addition to this, crew may inevitably fall sick or have other personal issues that render them unavailable for duty at short notice.

To deal with these issues as they occur, airlines have personnel to manage the tactical, day-to-day events, often called Crew Control or Crew Scheduling, whose primary role is to ensure that flights are fully crewed, and to maintain the operational integrity of the flying program. Their duties include, but are by no means limited to, monitoring crew legality, handling sick calls, calling up reserve crew, providing advice and guidance to the Operations Control team during periods of schedule disruption, plus handling a myriad of other unforeseen upsets. In addition to this, Crew Control will often support crew members by assisting them with trip trades and duty swaps. Some airlines also involve them in the crew logistics, which requires the booking of dead-head flights (where crews sit in passenger seats on the flight), hotels, and arrangement of visas.

Larger airlines often further subdivide the workload of their Crew Control into two operational windows. One is a tactical day-to-day function that works in a limited timeframe, commonly a 48- to 72-hour operational window from the current day of operation. This is then supported by a more strategic second

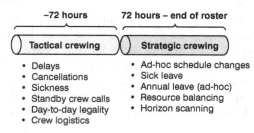

Figure 9.8 Division of Crew Control role

layer that looks out ahead of that 'close-in' period until the end of the roster. This allows the tactical team to focus only on immediate or imminent issues while the second team deals with things outside of the operational window that are less time-sensitive. Figure 9.8 presents this division in Crew Control tasks.

Crew Control can also carry out resource balancing by looking ahead for potential limitations in crew availability, looming crew legality issues, adjusting standby coverage, and helping to further stabilize the roster. This horizon scanning for problems also paves the way for a smoother execution on the day of operation. In addition to the crew control function, many airlines that consistently have large numbers of crew in training will have dedicated Training Coordinators who function in a similar capacity to Crew Controllers except that their role is primarily to manage upsets to the crew training plan. This is a supporting role that ensures training resources are not wasted due to unnecessary idle periods, especially expensive simulator slots and valuable instructor time.

IT systems

The deployment of technology has greatly enhanced the ability of Crew Planning departments to gain maximum efficiency and handle ever-increasing workloads and complexity. Before the advent of computers, crew planning was an even more complex task carried out entirely on paper. These methods, which involved reams of printed rosters, 'white-out', stickers and highlighter pens, would appear crude by today's standards and many a seasoned crew planner may look back on those days and wonder how they did it. Nowadays, most airlines use sophisticated software systems to carry out the optimization, planning, and day-to-day tracking of crew duties. It would be quite labour intensive and take an inordinate amount of time for humans to manage this through manual processes or to create a roster for thousands of crew members if unaided by such software.

In the planning stage, airlines can avail themselves of powerful optimizers and automation that are programmed to take into account the myriad of limitations such as fleet types, airport slots, crew qualifications and the FTLS and then automatically assign the various duties to crew members. In addition to this, crew labour contracts and union rules impose further restrictions and introduce even more complexity. These systems help reduce planners' workloads, increased utilization of crew and aircraft, and drive cost efficiency. For the management of day-to-day operations, modern crewing systems alert the controller to impending rule violations, give advanced notice on expiry of qualifications, and provide warnings to prevent the assignment of an incompatible crew member to an illegal duty. The more advanced ones even help during schedule disruption by presenting solutions to crew controllers, which saves valuable time.

The recent deployment of crew-facing applications allows crew members to trip-trade, bid for annual leave and duties, as well as interact with their own schedules in a way never before possible. This can be done right from their own personal devices and offers a reduction in workload for the crew controllers and an increase in crew satisfaction. These systems afford a measure of protection to the airline and the crew member. However, the onus remains with the crew member to ensure that they are legal and fit for duty.

Fatigue

The continuous advancement of technology has allowed for ever greater aircraft endurance, and non-stop flights in excess of fifteen hours are commonplace at many of the world's carriers. In addition to this, crews criss-cross multiple time-zones, fly through the night, and are often awake while everyone else is asleep. Terms such as 'red eye' and 'back of the clock' are colloquial references to flights that operate in these night-time periods when crews are commonly exposed to the fatiguing aspects of flying. A study carried out by Australia's Transport Safety Bureau found a correlation between 'back of clock' operations and an impaired neurobehavioural performance, and high levels of subjective fatigue.[17]

ULR flights, in particular, present a challenge, where crews face the issue of maintaining an adequate level of alertness while on duty for twenty hours or more. In one study, which looked at the relationship between time spent on duty, fatigue, and aircraft accidents, evidence was found to suggest that 'there is a discernible pattern of increased probability of an accident the greater the hours of duty time for commercial aircraft pilots in the United States', and, 'the empirical analysis points to increased risk of accidents with increased duty time and cumulative duty time'.[18] Further studies by airlines involved in ULR operations noted that although adding a fourth pilot allowed crews to maintain better alertness than an additional night's rest, crews attempting to get some in-flight rest were at risk of being disturbed by turbulence. The study went on to note that sleep taken in flight was less efficient than sleep taken at home and consisted of the lighter rather than deeper stages of sleep.[19] One of the earliest references to fatigue in relation to aviation was recorded in the Chicago Convention of 1944 (ICAO Annex 6), which recognized that pilot fatigue poses a risk to the safety of flight operations. Since then, numerous regulatory bodies and safety agencies have acknowledged this risk and its role in aircraft accidents.

But what is fatigue and how does it differ from tiredness? ICAO defines fatigue as a 'physiological state of reduced mental or physical performance capability resulting from sleep loss, circadian phase, or physical/mental workload, that can impair a crew member's level of alertness and ability to safely operate an aircraft or related duties'.[20,21] It is important to recognize that fatigue is distinctly different from tiredness, which is seen as a more transient state that can usually be overcome with a period of rest consisting of an adequate amount of sleep. Fatigue, on the other hand, is the accumulation of bouts of transient tiredness that are not fully recuperated from. These then build up and manifest into a potentially debilitating state. In extreme cases this can lead to a state known as chronic fatigue syndrome which results in severe physical as well as mental impairment.

The traditional means of managing fatigue in aircrews had been to follow the FTLS, but it has been recognized that this alone is insufficient and the inducement of fatigue is not solely related to loss of sleep but also affected by physical exertion as well as by mental, social, and financial stressors. As a result of this, the need to manage fatigue was identified and from this the concept of Fatigue Risk Management Systems (FRMS) arose. FRMS is a data-driven means of continuously monitoring and managing fatigue-related safety risks, based upon scientific principles and knowledge, as well as operational experience, which aims to ensure relevant personnel perform at adequate levels of alertness.[22] The ICAO guidelines prescribe a three-stage approach where risks are i) identified, ii) assessed, and iii) mitigated against. At airlines where FRMS is deployed, potentially fatiguing elements of crew schedules are identified and corresponding countermeasures are incorporated into the crews' rosters to mitigate against them. Some examples of how an FRMS would reduce the impact of potentially fatigue-inducing elements on an individual crew member are as follows:

- reduce the allocation of flights that commence in the WOCL
- minimize the allocation of flights that are known to be delay-prone; i.e. requiring crews to enter into discretion
- balance the rostering of flights according to airfield classification; e.g., Category C Airports[23]
- minimize the excessive rostering of multi-sector days[24]
- minimize the allocation of duties that are preceded by minimum rest
- minimize the disturbances to circadian rhythms by maintaining consistency in duty start times; i.e. avoiding assignment of alternating day/night duties.

As part of the continuous process of improving the FRMS, crews are encouraged to report potentially fatigue-inducing hazards so they can be reviewed by the relevant department responsible for managing the program, thereby enhancing the program on an ongoing basis.

Notes

1 An example of this is Saudi Arabia where the United States FAA rules are in use.
2 UK CAA CAP371 – The Avoidance of Fatigue In Aircrews. http://publicapps.caa. co.uk/docs/33/CAP371.PDF. Accessed 27 June 2017.
3 Whether standby duty is considered as 'duty time' or not depends on the duration of the elapsed standby time, and whether spent at home or at the airport. Consult

the respective national regulations as to whether or not time spent on standby is to be considered as duty time.

4   Some regulators include post-flight duties in the FDP calculation.

5   The amount of time varies between regulators, and some stipulate that a minimum number of local nights is achieved as opposed to basing the calculation solely on hours.

6   A non-acclimatized crew has stricter criteria.

7   This is typically a two-hour maximum extension, for a non-augmented crew, to the time stated in the FDP table.

8   Activating discretion is usually only permitted in order to either return to base or to complete a previously planned duty. Discretion cannot be used to allow crews to undertake an unplanned flight.

9   The concept of a monthly roster is the industry standard. However, depending on the type of operation, the period may be shorter.

10   This primarily applies to scheduled passenger operations and it is acknowledged that many cargo, charter, and business jet operators do not operate according to a fixed schedule.

11   These dates are not fixed and there are slight variations from year to year.

12   For US carriers.

13   A4A Quarterly Passenger Airline Cost Index: U.S. Passenger Airlines, 2016, http://www.eglobaltravelmedia.com.au/a4a-quarterly-passenger-airline-cost-index-u-s-passenger-airlines-5/ accessed 27/09/16

14   The use of contract crew is becoming more common, particularly at European-based LCCs. Many of these crews are employed on fixed-term contracts that are usually timed to expire at the end of peak periods. This allows the airlines the flexibility to reduce capacity when needed and lay off crews without the added worry of dealing with labour unions.

15   Operations Research is the application of advanced analytical techniques to provide implementable solutions to complex business problems.

16   Five days of early duties, followed by three days off, and five days of late duties followed by four days off.

17   Thomas, M. J. W.; Petrilli, R. M.; Roach, G. D. 2007. The Impacts of Australian Transcontinental 'Back of Clock' Operations on Sleep and Performance in Commercial Aviation Flight Crew. ATSB. Canberra.

18   Goode, J. H. 2003. Are pilots at risk of accidents due to fatigue? Journal of Safety Research.

19   Anon. 2005. Lessons From the Dawn of Ultra-long Range Flight. Flight Safety Digest.

20   IATA; ICAO; IFALPA. 2011. Fatigue Risk Management Systems: Implementation Guide for Operators. ICAO, Montreal. www.icao.int/safety/fatiguemanagement/FRMS%20Tools/FRMS%20Implementation%20Guide%20for%20Operators%20July%202011.pdf accessed 27 June 2017.

21   US FAA defines fatigue as – 'a physiological state in which there is a decreased capacity to perform cognitive tasks and an increased variability in performance as a function of time on task'. Fatigue is also associated with tiredness, weakness, lack of energy, lethargy, depression, lack of motivation, and sleepiness.

22   IATA; ICAO; IFALPA. 2011. Fatigue Risk Management Systems: Implementation Guide for Operators. ICAO, Montreal. https://www.icao.int/safety/fatigue management/FRMS%20Tools/FRMS%20Implementation%20Guide%20for%20Operators%20July%202011.pdf accessed 27 June 2017.

23   This can be addressed in the pairing generation stage and ideally two Cat-C airports should not be placed in the same pairing.

24   It is not uncommon for crews at some of the US-based commuter airlines to operate six to eight, or more sectors in one duty day, take minimum rest, and then do it all over again.

10 Maintenance planning

Alan Swann

Introduction

This chapter considers the various maintenance aspects that affect the planning and execution of the airline's operation. This includes activities such as planning for and accommodating scheduled and unscheduled small maintenance functions that are carried out on the line, through to scheduled heavy maintenance functions that may take an aircraft out of service for a period in excess of one month. Included in this mix is the ad hoc need for a maintenance function as a result of an extreme event such as a lightning strike, turbulence, heavy landing, mandatory aircraft weighing, and ground accidents.

Maintenance Organization

The Maintenance Organization consists of two organizations that are separated from each other. The two organizations with whom the airline's Operations Control Centre – more commonly, Integrated Operations Centre (IOC)–will interface are:

- The Continuing Airworthiness Management Organization (CAMO) (or similar title) which is the group that designs and approves the maintenance system as well as any deviations from the maintenance system. This group also plans the maintenance, manages maintenance contracts and provides technical support, usually in the form of data, to the Maintenance and Repair Organization (MRO), through liaison with the aircraft manufacturer.
- The MRO which has the physical capability to carry out work on the aircraft in order to implement the aircraft Maintenance System. This capability will consist of the hangar facilities, any necessary tooling, skilled workers and spare parts to carry out the work.

An airline may subcontract both of these elements to outside organizations but it is not uncommon for an airline to have the complete capability of the CAMO and MRO within its organization, although separated in accordance with regulations. While the above summarizes the Australian system, other countries, under different regulators, have similar systems. Collectively the function is sometimes referred to as Engineering and Maintenance (E&M).

Maintenance

For the efficient operation of an airline fleet, a certain level of reliability is required. The airline decides what level of reliability is necessary to maintain and improve its market. Apart from providing serviceable aircraft for on-time departures for the operation, the goal of the Maintenance Program and the E&M Organization is to:

* ensure inherent safety and reliability levels that are built into the design of the aircraft
* restore safety and reliability to inherent levels when deterioration has occurred
* obtain information for the optimization of the Maintenance Program to accommodate changes in the equipment brought about by experience
* obtain information which is fed back to the manufacturer for future design improvements for those areas where the inherent reliability has not been met
* accomplish the above at minimum cost to the airline.[1]

Maintenance Program

A Maintenance Program is a complicated set of processes and instructions aimed at restoring reliability of the aircraft as it deteriorates due to 'wear and tear' or exposure to its environment. The output of the program will be either detailed instructions to rectify a fault (i.e. unscheduled maintenance), or detailed instructions for scheduled maintenance to prevent a fault from occurring. The genesis of the Maintenance Program design is at the aircraft-type design and certification stage, where principles and disciplines learnt over a long time are applied to assemble individual 'maintenance functions' or tasks to accomplish the goals above, specifically for the aircraft type. The process is long, disciplined and detailed, and results in a document identified as the Maintenance Planning Document (MPD), or equivalent term, which is provided to the airline. This document contains all the maintenance functions (tasks) and the intervals (time) in which the tasks have to be performed, to ensure safety and reliability of the aircraft during operation.

The MPD originates from the Maintenance Review Board (MRB) which is convened by the aircraft manufacturer/designer. Organizations having an input into the MPD result are the manufacturer, design organization(s), airworthiness authority of the country of origin and a committee of end-user airlines. The purchasing airline has a certain amount of freedom to implement this document to suit its operational environment. However, the maintenance functions must be performed, with few exceptions, within the compliance interval identified in the MPD. There are many aspects of an operation that will distinguish one airline from any others. Some of the differentiators are:

- route type (long or short)
- route structure (location of maintenance facilities and bases)
- utilization (high or low, long haul or short haul, or a mix)
- check system – block or phased (there is a choice)
- airport environments (dusty, sandy, salt, humid, high altitude, hot, cold)
- hangar/workshops (available and location)
- maintenance (contracted out or completed in-house)
- distance to overseas maintenance contractor
- licensing system for mechanics
- Extended Diversion Time Operations (EDTO) requirements. (EDTO has been previously known as EROPS – Extended Range Operations, or ETOPS – Extended Operations.)

System of maintenance

The above differentiators will impact the choice of maintenance system to be adopted. Individual maintenance functions in the MPD are packaged together to produce a 'Check'. The smallest Check, an 'A' Check, consists of tasks that have a short compliance; typically, 400 flying hours. This Check usually requires minimal workforce, is of short duration, and can be performed overnight. Maintenance functions with longer compliance intervals are added to subsequent 'A' Checks, potentially making each of the 'A' Checks different.

For example, a particular lubrication task may have a compliance interval of 900 flying hours. That being the case, the task will need to be actioned at the 'A2' or second 'A' Check, which will be scheduled or *called* before 800 flying hours. Obviously, the third 'A' Check (at 1,200 flying hours) would be too late, resulting in an overrun of the MPD interval for that task. It also shows that sometimes maintenance credit is sacrificed for maintenance convenience. This simple example demonstrates that approximately 100 hours will be sacrificed because the task has been chosen to be completed at the 800 flying hour point rather than the 900 flying hour point, which is less convenient. Maintenance functions of longer compliance, typically 4,000 flying hours, are added to every tenth 'A' Check to make a 'C' Check, which is of a longer duration requiring the aircraft to be taken out of service for typically one week. Table 10.1 is representative of a maintenance system for a twin-engine jetliner. It shows Check intervals in flying hours, approximate man-hours and most importantly, indicative Check duration.

- Maintenance function intervals on different systems, structures, components, inspections can either be counted in terms of flying hours, cycles or calendar periods. (See below.)
- The maintenance functions have to be packaged in a form that is convenient to the airline's operation in relation to work methods/rules and available facilities and tooling; i.e. 'A' Checks at 400 flying hours and 'C' Checks at 4,000 flying hour intervals, etc.

Table 10.1 Aircraft maintenance check structure (representative)

Check description	Task elements	Interval between largest Check elements	Check type	Indicative manhours
A Check	a	400 flight hours	Minor	40
B Check	b	Not applicable	Minor	n/a
1C Check	1c	4,000 flight hours	Major	6 days
2C Check	2c + 1c	8,000 flight hours	Major	11 days
3C Check	3c +1c	12,000 flight hours	Major	7 days
4C Check	4c+2c+1c	16,000 flight hours	Major	19 days
5C Check	5c +1c	20,000 flight hours	Major	7 days
6C Check	6c+1c+2c+1c	24,000 flight hours	Major	15 days
7C Check	7c+ 1c	28,000 flight hours	Major	7 days
D Check	d+4c+2c+1c	32,000 flight hours	Major	29 days

- The maintenance functions must be packaged to minimize aircraft downtime.
- Subsequent 'C' Checks, i.e. '2C', '3C', '4C' etc. are inclusive of the lower Checks. For example, a '4C' Check consists of the 16,000 flying hours tasks of the '4C' Check and the 8,000 flying hours tasks of the '2C' Check as well as the 4,000 flying hours tasks of the 'C' Check and the 400 flying hours tasks of the 'A' Check.
- After the 'D' Check in this extended example, the process starts again at the 'A' Check, which is then due after 32,400 flying hours.
- For convenience, the '1C' Check may be *phased* and completed in small parts at the same time as the 'A' Checks. That is, the 'C' Check is divided into ten or more parts and each part is completed at the 'A' Check or during an overnight maintenance event. This can result in the six-day *block* layup being eliminated, as the work has already been done overnight in stages. This method typically suits a short-haul domestic operator and results in releasing an aircraft from what would have otherwise been a six-day layup. A long-haul operator is more suited to the *block* system as depicted in Table 10.1.
- Maintenance work must be budgeted for in terms of the number of spare aircraft required to support the flying, as well as the workforce required to do the work, and of course cost. Maintenance typically can account for approximately fifteen to twenty per cent of the airline's costs (depending on what is counted).
- For maintenance purposes, aircraft utilization must be tracked in terms of flying hours, cycles and calendar time.

Maintenance and deterioration

Deterioration of some components, systems and structure is determined by the hours flown. Many parts of the airframe 'flex', 'wear' and 'fret' as a function of the hours, minutes and seconds that the aircraft is flying. Examples include a generator rotating for the flight duration, or stressing of the wing structure. Examples of deterioration due to cycles include the gas turbine engine, where the greatest temperature on the blades and vanes that produce the work/thrust occurs at engine start, and to a lesser degree at shutdown. The landing gear is another example where the greatest stress is on landing. Hence, these components, as well as others, accumulate deterioration 'time' as cyclic wear. Deterioration of other parts of the structure and some components occurs all of the time even though the aircraft may not be currently utilized. This deterioration is usually due to corrosion or deterioration or loss/deterioration of some fluid, grease, protective oil/inhibitor etc. The maintenance functions on these items are determined by calendar date. As an example, restoring the corrosion prevention material would be based on a calendar compliance date, regardless of the aircraft's utilization.

Maintenance planning

Aircraft utilization is tracked by a computer system which is fed data direct from the aircraft by the Aircraft Communications, Addressing and Reporting System (ACARS). Utilization is accumulated in flight hours, cycles and calendar time. To calculate the maintenance for the coming year, the Maintenance Planners will work on the average utilization rate. Given that a major maintenance Check consists of many 'Maintenance Functions' (tasks) that can be decremented from the new or overhauled condition by hours, cycles or date, it follows that the compliance date for the Check can drift over the calendar. That is, while the 'due date' of the Check of a particular aircraft tail number can be predicted from its utilization, there are events that may necessitate the check being 'called' earlier than originally planned. Consider the impact on the calculation of Check 'due date' of two scenarios:

- One group of fleet units is a domestic carrier with an average stage length of, say, one flight hour with, hypothetically, eight flights per day. For every flight hour, there will be accumulated one cycle and for every eight flying hours, one day will be counted.
- The other group of fleet units is a long-haul carrier with an average stage length of eight flight hours and, hypothetically, one and a half stages per 24-hour period. For every cycle, there will be eight flying hours and for every day counted the aircraft will accumulate twelve hours and one and a half cycles.

The purpose of these examples is to demonstrate that determining exactly when the next major Check falls due is problematical and depends on the operation. In the first example, engine and landing gear deterioration is higher than the second group for the same number of flight hours, while the flight hours of the second group accumulate much faster in relation to the cyclic wear. The difficulty is to determine exactly *when* on the calendar the aircraft will be driven into the next maintenance function. Flight hours, cycles and calendar periods have to be managed by monitoring utilization on a daily basis. The difference between the two scenarios can also have a marked difference on cost per flying hour or cost per cycle. Both are well-used methods of benchmarking one operator against another.

A major maintenance Check is a big event, and capacity and spare parts for it has to be planned well in advance. In some cases, where the maintenance is performed by a third-party MRO, a 'slot' will have to be reserved. The MRO is in business to provide this service to other operators too, so the calculation of what date the aircraft is to be inducted into the maintenance facility is critical. Due to the competing priorities of other customers of the MRO, there is often little scope for a change of date. Should the MRO be located overseas, there will be the attendant penalty of relocation time with an international flight necessary at the start and end of the planned maintenance turn time. This addition to the contracted turn time must be considered in the spare aircraft budget.

Having indicated that the maintenance due date will be a result of the flying accumulated in terms of flying hours, cycles and calendar time, it will be seen that the nominal Check due date will move around due to the flying pattern of the aircraft within the operation. Along with the maintenance functions in the MPD there are other maintenance items that may drive the aircraft into maintenance. Some of these items are less easy to determine and consist of maintenance inspections, rectifications, and modifications that result from manufacturers' Service Bulletins (SBs), Airworthiness Directives (ADs) and even modifications that are a requirement of the airline for some operational reason.

ADs, for example, will usually come with a non-negotiable compliance, which will typically be in terms of flight hours, cycles or calendar time. Some of these maintenance functions are of a magnitude to require significant access within the aircraft in order to carry out the inspection, to the extent that they are only possible on a major layup. In addition to the required action, such as an inspection, consideration will need to be given to rectification if indeed the inspection uncovers a problem. This rectification may be extended over several days, with the potential that the delivery date may need to be renegotiated. As a result of this disruption, aircraft which, in turn, are planned to be inducted for maintenance, may be impacted. The implication of a new maintenance function such as an AD advancing the compliance date of the Check can be significant, and possibly result in disrupting the maintenance program by advancing the Check compliance date ahead of an aircraft that was initially programmed in front of it.

For that reason (and others), a program is built with some insurance, in that aircraft are programmed for their major Checks well before they could be grounded – declared as 'Aircraft On Ground' or AOG, due to running out of hours, cycles or calendar days. This deliberate process is commonly known as a 'buffer' and is an essential ingredient in the plan, designed to prevent an 'AOG due Maintenance' situation. On the other hand, a buffer is wasted maintenance credit. That is, it is maintenance credit that has been paid for and, as a result of being brought forward, is lost. So, careful planning is necessary to reduce the buffer to as low a level as possible while maintaining the insurance aspect of preventing 'AOG due Maintenance' events.

Maintenance Planning departments have ways of manipulating the plan which usually result in a call to the IOC with a request for a certain tail number on, perhaps, a 'lazy pattern' (series of flights) such as to conserve flying hours and/or cycles. Alternatively, the request may be for a long-haul pattern to conserve the aircraft's cycles versus its flying hours. Once the aircraft has been removed from the operation for a maintenance Check, the real issue for the IOC is the time that the replacement aircraft is returned in a serviceable condition. Usually for a domestic carrier the changeover is at the end of the day, where the aircraft next to be inducted into the hangar is taken off flying as a 'spare' while the overhauled aircraft is being towed back to the flight line.

The issue for the Maintenance Department is one of *turn time* to meet the operations schedule. Aside from that there is much pressure put on this aspect, as the loss of a fleet unit to maintenance usually has to be subsidized by a spare aircraft. The Network Scheduling Department would determine that x number of serviceable aircraft are required to fly the schedule. The Maintenance Department then must ascertain the maintenance downtime necessary for the fleet by adding up the downtime in 'A', 'C' and 'D' Checks for each aircraft to be maintained in that particular year's flying. In the budget year, for example, if the aircraft fleet required twenty-one '2C' Checks, fourteen '3C' Checks, fourteen '4C' Checks, eight '6C' Checks, and three 'D' Checks, then the total out-of-action time is equivalent to two years or two aircraft. It follows that extra *spare* fleet units will be required to fund the maintenance of the serviceable fleet units. Apart from the need for sufficient aircraft to fly the operation, the preparation of the budget has equal emphasis on calculating the workforce, spare parts and facilities required to complete the budgeted maintenance for the coming year. As a result, there is considerable science and attention to the planning of both the Heavy Maintenance layup to minimize turn time and the overall Fleet Maintenance Plan to ensure that there is no AOG event awaiting maintenance.

The operation

The operation is supported by a Line Maintenance organization and a centralized planning group. The Line Maintenance group will be represented at many of the schedule destinations or ports, either by licensed airline or contract mechanics who are responsible for receipt and despatch of the aircraft as well as any rectification or servicing that becomes necessary. These ports may have limited tooling and spare parts but have the ability to call on resources to assist in solving problems that occur. A centralized Maintenance Control group can provide data and logistics to expedite spare parts or data to a base where there is a problem. The centralized Maintenance Control group is also responsible for planning and organizing logistics for the Check and any deferred rectification, which will usually occur at a base where the aircraft overnights. In most cases an 'A' Check will need to be performed at a hangar. This will result in some time being expended in relocating (by towing) the aircraft to the maintenance facility. The facility may be located some kilometres away from the terminal and quite possibly the tow may have to cross active runways and avoid the conflicting traffic associated with such an operation. In most airports, this will mean a tow of from twenty minutes to possibly two hours, so this aspect has to be considered with respect to the availability of aircraft, since to get the aircraft ready for flight it will have to be relocated back to the terminal with, perhaps, a similar cost in time. Aircraft arriving *on blocks* at the gate with a defect are met by the Line Maintenance Mechanic who will assess the defect and determine a way to make the aircraft serviceable for the next scheduled departure of that tail number. The Licensed Aircraft Maintenance Engineer (LAME) has a number of options:

- If equipped with the appropriate data, tools, spares, training and approval, the mechanic may be able to fix the problem in the scheduled turn time available.
- If the appropriate spares are not available or the rectification requires a visit to the hangar or another base, then the mechanic may access a system of deferring the defect and declaring the aircraft serviceable.
- Should there be no method to defer the defect, or rectify the service difficulty, the aircraft will remain unserviceable requiring a replacement aircraft for the flight or even a cancellation of the flight by the IOC, i.e. a disruption!

Aircraft serviceability

Further to the second point above, there are a number of levels of deferring the defect. The first level is available to the Licenced Mechanic (LAME) who may determine that the defective item or system is listed in the *Minimum Equipment List* (MEL), and then declaring serviceability with reference to the appropriate procedure. This means that the aircraft can be dispatched into service with certain components or systems inoperative. Certain items may also be missing from the aircraft. Usually these items are on the aircraft's exterior such as door seals, hinge covers, taxi lights, etc. If these items are permitted to be missing they will be identified in the *Configuration Deviation List* (CDL) or similarly named document.

Both MEL and CDL items are categorised as a 'Permissible Unserviceability', which if utilised, do not take the aircraft below the serviceability level for which it is certified. These items are listed in the Maintenance Manual and the Flight Operations Manual and can be used by the Licenced Mechanic (LAME) to certify the aircraft for flight so long as any special conditions listed in the manual are met. For example, unserviceability of a system may result in a speed restriction below a particular altitude, in which case there may be a possible impact on the schedule that the IOC would need to know about.

Defects that are not listed in the MEL or CDL may be assessed by the Technical Services Department of the Continuing Airworthiness Management Organisation CAMO; and in conjunction with the Fleet Type Duty Captain, an *Authority to Proceed* (ATP), or similar term, may be issued for a flight or period. This is the second level of deferring the unserviceability which may take the serviceability down to or below the certification level of the aircraft. Operational conditions or restrictions for this approval are likely to be imposed.

A special *Permit to Fly*, or similar term, is yet another level of this complicated system that may be available to the operator. This type of approval is less likely to be a commercial flight but could be used to relocate an aircraft with a defect for some justifiable reason that would have to be approved by the regulator. As with the other process there are likely to be some flight limitations which may impact on the operation of the aircraft. This type of approval is likely to take the serviceability level lower than that for which the aircraft was certified.

Terms and processes indicated above may vary between operators, manufacturers and regulators.

Reliability

Technical reliability, as distinct from despatch reliability, is a measure of the effectiveness of how well maintenance is being carried out on the airline's aircraft in order to make them available and airworthy for operations. The Reliability Monitoring Program (RMP) should provide timely technical information to the operator so that changes can be made to restore the reliability of the aircraft when it deteriorates, and to meet the maintenance objectives outlined at the start of this chapter. An RMP provides the feedback to the System of Maintenance that allows the beneficial lessons of service experience to be incorporated into the System. The processes involved in an RMP include data collection, data analysis, maintenance task revision and ensuring that reliability data is sent to the Original Equipment Manufacturer (OEM) and National Aviation Authority (NAA).

The reliability data collected includes determining rates of occurrences of in-flight defects, incidents, delays, unscheduled engine shutdowns, component removals, MEL usage, etc. The data are subsequently analysed and presented in trend form so that adverse trends can be addressed and corrective actions taken. For components, the Mean Time Between Removals (MTBR) and the Mean Time Between Failures (MTBF) are particularly useful data that support the condition monitoring processes specified as part of the design of the maintenance system for that aircraft type. Data analysis is the process of evaluating the data and recommending corrective actions where necessary on the way the aircraft, its systems and components are maintained. Changes in the MTBR of a particular component, for example, may trigger an investigation that ultimately results in a modification to the component to make it more reliable. Improvements in reliability of individual components potentially translate into improved on-time reliability of the fleet.

Extended Diversion Time Operations (EDTO)

The primary requirement for EDTO was to modify specific aircraft systems and components to meet a higher standard of reliability. This rule initially required twin-engine aircraft to operate within sixty minutes of a *suitable* airfield. EDTO is in fact an extension of the Reliability Program. EDTO specifies the requirements for a higher level of reliability than the level normally certified, that is appropriate to the intended operation. While a functioning Reliability Program is a demonstrable requirement in the approval of an operator's Maintenance system, the EDTO approval is specified for the operator and any particular tail number that is EDTO approved. An EDTO-approved aircraft will have the modification status for a variety of essential components specified. It is likely that an airline operating EDTO flights will have the whole of the fleet maintained to the required modification standard so that any tail number can operate an EDTO flight. However, this may not always be the case.

Proposed modifications are notified to operators by manufacturers' SBs in which some modifications are optional, but some are mandatory. Modifications necessary for EDTO approval will be mandatory and the airline must have a system to determine that the aircraft is so approved before operating such a flight. Additionally, some of the items approved in the MEL of a non-EDTO-approved aircraft may not be available to implement if the aircraft is approved for EDTO. To enable an airline to be approved for EDTO, the Regulator will require the airline to be able to demonstrate:

- past performance
- flight crew training and experience
- maintenance program specifically for EDTO
- aircraft certification status (modification status).

Specifically, the Maintenance Program must be sophisticated to a level over and above the normal certification level in the following areas:

- pre-departure service check
- oil consumption monitoring program
- Engine Condition Monitoring program (ECM) – this is a process that monitors a number of engine parameters in real time and produces a deterioration trend analysis
- Propulsion System Monitoring program
- Resolution of Discrepancies Program (Sophisticated Reliability Program)
- maintenance of multiple, similar systems (e.g., the same maintenance function cannot be conducted on both engines simultaneously)
- EDTO parts control program (the despatched aircraft must meet the modification status)
- Auxiliary Power Unit (APU) high altitude start program (the APU must be able to start in flight and supply electrical power)

- EDTO training (licensed mechanics must undergo special training)
- identify EDTO significant items (critical components must be able to be identified for EDTO specific modification status).[2]

The implications for operations is that unless a particular tail number conforms to all the maintenance requirements to meet the approval requirements for EDTO then the aircraft cannot be used on an EDTO flight. However, the aircraft can be used for 'normal' operations. Part of the process of the Pre-Departure Service Check will 'check off' the modification status of installed critical parts.

Finally

The preceding has covered some of the basics of Aircraft Maintenance as it applies to the operation of the airline. The Technical Services Department of the CAMO, in addition to deferring defects, designing changes through Permits to Fly and approval of the Maintenance Program, etc., is also involved in 'theoretical' engineering activities that support Flight Operations. These areas include Weight and Balance management (see Chapter 16), assessing and preparation of airport charts and also evaluation and choice of new purchases of aircraft for the fleet.

The E&M group that supports the airline, whether the various parts of it are located in-house or contracted out, must be capable of communicating with the many organizations within the airline. In all cases, it is the airline that carries the responsibility for the MRO (physical) or CAMO (theoretical) activity. Importance is therefore placed on quality control, quality assurance and risk management of both the internal activity and that which is contracted out.

Maintenance is conducted in a high-risk environment, so a great deal of emphasis is placed on safety, both of the workers and the passengers and aircraft. There are many systems and policies put in place to monitor and ensure safety. Regulators, and there are a few, as well as the travelling public, have high expectations for this aspect which is demonstrated through regulations and surveillance of operators.

Glossary of acronyms and abbreviations

ACARS Aircraft Communications, Addressing and Reporting System
AD   Airworthiness Directives
AOG   Aircraft On Ground
APU   Auxiliary Power Unit
ATP   Authority to Proceed
CAMO   Continuing Airworthiness Management Organization
CDL   Configuration Deviation List
E&M   Engineering and Maintenance
ECM   Engine Condition Monitoring

EDTO   Extended Diversion Time Operations
EROPS Extended Range Operations
ETOPS Extended Operations
IOC   Integrated Operations Centre
LAME   Licensed Aircraft Maintenance Engineer
MEL   Minimum Equipment List
MPD   Maintenance Planning Document
MRB   Maintenance Review Board
MRO   Maintenance and Repair Organization
MTBF   Mean Time Between Failures
MTBR   Mean Time Between Removals
NAA   National Aviation Authority
OEM   Original Equipment Manufacturer
RMP   Reliability Monitoring Program
SB   Service Bulletins

Notes

1 Kinnison, H. and Siddiqui, T. 2012 *Aviation Maintenance Management*. 2nd Ed. McGraw-Hill, New York
2 Kinnison, H. and Siddiqui, T. 2012 *Aviation Maintenance Management*. 2nd Ed. McGraw-Hill, New York=

11 Airside resource planning

Andrea Roberts

Introduction

This chapter focuses on the planning, preparation and provision of a diversity of equipment to execute the complex procedures during an aircraft turnaround. Receiving an aircraft upon arrival and preparing it for departure is a major task, which requires the completion of numerous overlapping processes planned and organized to fit seamlessly within the schedules of the airline. Depending on the level of service an airline is offering, there is a huge range of ramp (airside) services and activities that require careful planning. The planning stage begins prior to any flight scheduled at a particular airport. For each airport within the planned network, the aircraft operator must acquire all relevant information regarding the airport's infrastructure, facilities and resources available to be able to operate within their schedule from the port. The complexity of the procedures shows the importance of well-structured Airport Traffic Management and the cooperation between all involved stakeholders from strategic planning to completion by a ground handling service provider.

Airport Collaborative Decision-Making

To create a more efficient Airport Traffic Management system, the European Organisation for the Safety of Air Navigation (Eurocontrol) developed a project called A-CDM (Airport Collaborative Decision-Making). Eurocontrol states that it is '…an intergovernmental organization with 41 Member … States … committed to building, together with our partners, a Single European Sky that will deliver the air traffic management (ATM) performance required for the twenty-first century and beyond'.[1] The website provides the current list of members using A-CDM as follows. 'A-CDM is fully implemented in 22 airports across Europe, including: Barcelona, Berlin Schönefeld, Brussels, Copenhagen, Düsseldorf, Frankfurt, Geneva, Helsinki, London Gatwick, London Heathrow, Madrid, Milan Malpensa, Milan Linate, Munich, Paris CDG, Paris Orly, Oslo, Prague, Rome Fiumicino, Stuttgart, Venice, Zurich'.[2]

Airservices Australia describes the concept of the program as follows.

Airport Collaborative Decision Making (A-CDM) is a concept that aims to improving the operational efficiency at airports by reducing delay, improving the predictability of events during the progress of a flight, and optimizing the utilization of resources and infrastructure.

A-CDM is about partners (airlines and airports) working together to make their own decisions and how best to utilise accurate, high quality and reliable information to enable ... more efficient use of resources, and improve event punctuality and predictability.

Modelled on the Eurocontrol A-CDM concept, Airservices is seeking to establish an A-CDM service at four major airports across Australia, including Brisbane, Sydney, Melbourne and Perth.[3]

Furthermore, Airservices Australia outlines the planned improvements due to CDM in their fact sheet:

Collaborative Decision Making (CDM) will improve air traffic management by sharing information and data between airport operators, aircraft operators, ground handlers and air traffic control.

It allows all users, including airport operators, aircraft operators, ground handlers and air traffic control, to be aware of constraints, issues and needs of other users and service providers.

The overall effect of CDM is a more knowledgeable and participative aviation community that improves services and reduces costs for all users and providers. CDM can apply to all time frames of decisions, from long-range planning of schedules to the tactical decisions of ground delay programs.[4]

Airside resourcing

Bearing this in mind, airport operators must conduct short- and long-term analyses on forecasts taking into account traffic development and flight schedule data, investments, personnel requirement, and regulatory requirements amongst other factors to identify the required resources. There are multiple methodologies and techniques that an airport operator or airline can apply to prepare a long-term forecast.

The technique of choice will depend on the resources available to the forecaster and the complexity of analysis required, but, either way, the forecaster will be expected to support his predictions on a firm foundation of facts, historical trends, and socioeconomic analysis.[5]

The forecast and actual passenger and aircraft movements will contribute toward the allocation of appropriate parking positions. Other aspects of the operation to optimize aircraft parking and resources are:

- existing capacity of the airport
- personnel and equipment required during normal and peak hours
- available infrastructure including number of aircraft terminals and remote parking positions
- time allocations for short-, medium- or long-term turnaround
- time of travel for personnel and equipment
- sub-processes of external service providers such as catering, cleaning and pushback
- time for preparation and clearance of parking position
- disembarkation of passengers
- unloading and loading of baggage, cargo and mail
- transhipping of baggage, cargo and mail
- transhipping of passengers
- fuelling
- lavatory and fresh water
- crew shuttle
- boarding of passengers
- deviations based on special airline requirements (e.g., baggage identification on position)
- arrangements for existing and new slot times.

The International Air Transport Association (IATA) defines an airport slot-time (or 'slot') as '… a permission given by a coordinator for a planned operation to use the full range of airport infrastructure necessary to arrive or depart at a Level 3 airport on a specific date and time'.[6] IATA's definition of a Level 3 airport is an airport '… where capacity providers have not developed sufficient infrastructure, or where governments have imposed conditions that make it impossible to meet demand. A coordinator is appointed to allocate slots to airlines and other aircraft operators using or planning to use the airport as a means of managing the declared capacity'.[7]

Airline-specific gates and ramps

Some airlines use their own specific hardware at the gate and require special security measures at the airport. This enables the airline to follow their particular check-in, customs and security procedures and avoids delays by blocking less restricted flights to depart on time. International hub airports might have constant allocated stand-alone terminals, gates and aircraft parking positions for that reason. To ascertain which type of ramp services the airline will need to utilize, both airport operator and airline or aircraft operator must consider further factors as outlined below.

Type of operation

- domestic/international passenger transport
- freight and cargo only
- regional charter.

Type of aircraft

- narrow body
- wide body
- small aircraft
- heavy aircraft
- freighter.

The regulations applicable to a country or port

This could vary between jurisdictions such as US Federal Aviation Authority (FAA), European Aviation Safety Agency (EASA) and Australia's Civil Aviation Safety Authority (CASA), for example. Thus, the ground-servicing performed in one country might not be subject to the same compliance and safety standards as another aircraft operating elsewhere.

Ground handling procedures

In addition to the long-term forecast and analysis, further planning is required to optimize the activities. Most airports have developed standardized ground handling procedures, based on the factors above. Each airport has specific characteristics which will have to be considered when optimizing turnaround processes and their possible variations, as these can influence the turnaround processes. ICAO (International Civil Aviation Organization) Annex 14, Aerodromes Volume 1, provides international standards and recommendations for aerodrome designs and operations, including servicing of aircraft and ground markings such as aircraft stand marking and safety lines. Some of these are given here.[8]

- apron: a defined area, on a land aerodrome, intended to accommodate aircraft for purposes of loading or unloading passengers, mail or cargo, fuelling, parking or maintenance
- aircraft stand: a designated area on an apron intended to be used for parking an aircraft
- manoeuvring area: that part of an aerodrome to be used for the take-off, landing and taxiing of aircraft, excluding aprons
- movement area: that part of an aerodrome to be used for the take-off, landing and taxiing of aircraft, consisting of the manoeuvring area and the apron(s).

Planning for aircraft turnarounds

The turnaround time of aircraft has been defined by IATA's Airport Handling Manual (AHM) as the time period an aircraft occupies a stand or a gate at the airport.[9] The Technical University Dresden describes in their publication *Aircraft Turnaround Management*[10] the importance of planning of all processes involved and the applicable duration to optimize a turnaround (TA) as follows:

The TA is framed by two activities: The positioning and removal of the aircraft wheel chocks, respectively named as on and off block times. It is generally represented as a [series] of processes, from which a subgroup may run in parallel, and others [which] are required to run sequentially, e.g., due to legal or logistical requirements such as limited space around the aircraft, tool availability, or legal constraints such as to prohibit fueling with passengers on board... As this time is directly impacting the airport capacity, there is a vital interest in predicting exactly the Gate Occupancy Time (GOT). Therefore, the prediction of each process duration will become a central planning parameter for further optimization tasks.

The critical path (CP) within the TA is the connection of specific parallel and sequential TA-processes that limit the shortest TA-time, due to the dependencies among each other. The applicable CP depends on various factors, but can be isolated in general to [the following] TA sub-processes between onblock and offblock:

- Deboarding
- Unloading
- Fuelling
- Cleaning
- Catering
- Loading
- Boarding.[11]

Each of the turnaround sub-processes is further split into multiple work processes which will have to be identified in order to be able to develop standardized handling procedures. The aim of the overall analysis is to optimize turnarounds. Thus, transhipping of passengers, baggage, cargo and mail should also be reviewed, as should the current aircraft utilizations and the average turnaround times for domestic and international operations. Supplementary considerations should be the identification of so-called 'bottlenecks' or areas of congestion, due to the flow of passengers, aircraft, ground service equipment, security personnel, and border control and customs personnel.

Some older international airports might only provide one access point for international departures and arrivals. Departing passengers have to pass through security, then customs and border control. After these processes, the passenger flow travels through duty-free and on to the allocated gates. All international arriving passengers may have only one egress from the gate to customs and border control, then baggage claim and quarantine. This can lead to congestion in those areas, particularly when several large aircraft with high passenger loads are departing and/or arriving at the same time.

Some airports have considered these predicted areas of congestion during the development and design of their infrastructure, and developed a terminal which is split into several sections. With this set-up the airport operator can provide more adequate personnel, manning access and entry points in each section. This means that security screening, customs and border control, and baggage claim areas can be dedicated to several inbound or outbound aircraft stands and gates within their section, and the flow of passengers and baggage can be optimized.

Planning for gate optimization

In order to optimize the current airside capacity and the subsequent workflows, airport operators take the dimensions of aircraft stands and the use of aerobridges into account to accommodate a greater range of aircraft to be serviced at the gate. In order to maximize gate capacity, many airports around the world plan substantial flexibility into the design. The IATA Airport Development Reference Manual[12] shows one approach referred to as the Multi-Aircraft Ramp System (MARS). This refers to a modular approach that enables two narrow-body aircraft to operate independently within the same footprint area of a large aircraft such as a B747 or A380, utilizing the same two loading bridges to serve all three aircraft positions. So-called hub airports (central ports from where an airline schedules a hub and spoke network to other ports, for example Emirates' Dubai hub) will also have to consider the amount of direct feeder aircraft when allocating aircraft stands and gates, in order to achieve minimum connecting times (MCT).

Gate allocations depend not only on airlines and their respective preferred networks, but need also to take into account all airside activities to avoid congestion on the apron and taxiways. Based on their current infrastructure and capacity, airport operators conduct analyses to determine the required travel times from runway to taxiway and from taxiway to the allocated aircraft gates. Airlines may prefer to have a shorter distance to the runway to decrease their overall turnaround time, and allocation of the appropriate aircraft gate is also affected by towing and ground service equipment movements on the apron. According to Dorndorf *et al.*,[13] some objectives of flight gate scheduling for airside operations are to:

- reduce the number of aircraft towing procedures
- minimize the total walking distance for passengers
- minimize the deviation of the current schedule from a reference schedule
- minimize the number of un-gated (open) aircraft activities
- maximize the preferences of certain aircraft for particular gates.

Dorndorf *et al.* also suggest classes of constraints:

- One gate can process only one aircraft at a time.
- Service requirements and space restrictions with respect to adjacent gates must be fulfilled.
- Minimum ground time and minimum time between subsequent aircraft have to be assured.

Pesch *et al.*[14] examined the models and methods of flight gate allocations.

The gate assignment also affects other ground services. A good assignment may reduce the number of aircraft tows required and may lead to reduced setup times for several ground service activities on the ramp as well as in the terminal. The problem of finding a suitable gate assignment usually has to be addressed on three levels. Firstly, during the preparation of seasonal flight schedule revisions, the ability to accommodate the proposed flights must be examined. Secondly, given a current flight schedule, daily plans have to be prepared before the actual day of operation. Thirdly, on the day of operation, the gate schedule must be frequently altered to accommodate updates or disruptions in the flight schedule (reactive scheduling).

Planning for resources

Whether the airline/aircraft operator decides to develop their own ramp procedures and establish a base at an airport with personnel trained in ground handling, or whether they decide to enter into a Service Level Agreement (SLA) with a ground handling agent is an economic decision. Either way, to determine the amount of equipment and personnel required for each arrival and/or departure, the ramp service provider will have to conduct further analysis based on the expected daily flying operations plan. This plan must contain all relevant information such as aircraft operator, type of aircraft, type of operation and service provider, including planned variations. All the factors mentioned before are also the basis which determines the personnel and equipment required to provide full airside services, and ensure enough resources are available in case of an emergency or response to unplanned activities. As mentioned before, personnel and equipment resource planning are often dependent upon the long-term forecast and the daily flight schedules. The daily flight schedules take fluctuations and additional demand into account.

Case Study: Munich (MUC) Airport

At Munich Airport, the flight schedule is split into two seasons: summer and winter plans. As a starting point for determining required personnel, the ground handler reviews the daily flight plan. Based on this plan, flexibility in numbers of personnel are required in order to meet varying demands of activity: from numerous, simultaneous movements, to very few, with both extremes requiring a broad range of ground handling services. This results in work processes having a distinct peak structure. In order to convert the operations plan into work to be performed, standardized handling procedures are utilized for each possible type of aircraft, from which the respective personnel requirements can be determined. Deviations for individual airlines with special handling procedures or which have particular quality key performance indicators (KPIs), can also be considered when developing those procedural standards.

The required personnel numbers depend on type of service provided, qualification of personnel and time allocated for turnaround. Movement numbers, and therefore demand fluctuations, mean that maximum usage of personnel and equipment is likely to occur during the existing traffic peaks due to the additional dispatch of aircraft and more work-intensive ground equipment used with subsequently longer process duration. Other disruptions will have to be allowed for in the daily resource planning. Possible fluctuations and disruptions are:

- seasonal flight plans (the summer flight schedule includes usually more movements than the winter schedule)
- weekly fluctuations due to public holidays, school holidays, increased hub traffic, variation of high-density and low-density traffic on a weekly basis
- daily fluctuations due to aircraft arriving before the scheduled time of arrival (STA) or departing delayed, severe weather conditions, maintenance issues, additional flights due to diversion from other airports, breakdown of equipment and other operational factors.[15]

Ramp planning activity

The ramp activities start well before the aircraft arrives. Based on the daily operations plan, which includes possible variation to the long-term schedule, Ground Dispatch will allocate the appropriately trained crew within a specific timeframe to have the position fully set up upon arrival of the aircraft. In the case of providing ground service for a regional charter operation, most airlines will process airside related activities such as refuelling, embarking and disembarking of passengers, and loading and unloading of any cargo or mail themselves. Some regional airports provide a ramp service for passengers and baggage including air cargo.

At major international airports such as Melbourne Airport or Munich Airport, most ramp services are provided by a local ground handling agent in cooperation with the airport and the airline. Munich Airport's Ground Handling Agent *AeroGround Flughafen München GmbH*, a 100 per cent subsidiary of Flughafen München GmbH, states that the ground handling is ' ... understood to be all services relating to the aircraft at the airport, including loading goods and boarding people, preparing the papers and documents necessary for transport, and supplying operational materials and consumables to the aircraft'.[16]

International airports usually allocate the most appropriate parking position for the type of aircraft and service conducted. At some airports, airlines can apply to reserve a section of gates and the allocation is determined by the airline in cooperation with the airport operations. The allocation of the position also requires sufficient space to provide a staging area where ground support equipment can be provided prior to arrival of the aircraft. Once the short and/or long-term allocation of gates and parking positions is set, a ramp agent oversees the particular aircraft arrival and/or departure. Only a few major airlines have their own personnel for the entire operation. The Ramp Agent might be a representative from the aircraft operator or provided by the ground handling service provider, depending on the airline's preference or the SLA with the ground handler. The Ramp Agent's responsibility is to oversee the airside operation in cooperation with the gate, operations, load control, baggage and cargo, as well as any other services required to ensure a smooth, safe and efficient turnaround of the aircraft.

Notes

1   EUROCONTROL – European Organisation for the Safety of Air Navigation [website] 2017, Who we are, http://www.eurocontrol.int/articles/who-we-are, accessed 24 Jan. 2017

2   EUROCONTROL – European Organisation for the Safety of Air Navigation, Airport Collaborative Decision Making (A-CDM), [website] 2017, Implementation http://www.eurocontrol.int/articles/airport-collaborative-decision-making-cdm accessed 27 June 2017

3   Airservices, Airport Collaborative Decision Making, updated 11 July 2016 http://www.airservicesaustralia.com/projects/collaborative-decision-making-cdm/airport-collaborative-decision-making/, accessed 6 Feb. 2017

4   Airservices, Collaborative Decision Making, updated 11 July 2016, http://www.airservicesaustralia.com/wp-content/uploads/cdm_fact_sheet.pdf, accessed 6 Feb. 2017

5   Transportation Research Board of the National Academies. 2010. *ACRP Report 25, Airport Passenger Terminal Planning and Design, Volume 1: Guidebook*, p. 81. Washington DC: TRB

6   IATA 2017, Worldwide Slot Guidelines (WSG), WSG Edition 8, January 2017, p. 14, http://www.iata.org/policy/infrastructure/slots/Documents/wsg-8-english.pdf, accessed 6 Feb. 2017

7   IATA 2017, Worldwide Slot Guidelines (WSG), WSG Edition 8, January 2017, p. 14, http://www.iata.org/policy/infrastructure/slots/Documents/wsg-8-english.pdf, accessed 6 Feb. 2017

8   ICAO Annex 14 – Aerodromes, Volume I, Aerodrome Design and Operations, Definitions, pp. I-3 and I-6, [website], http://cockpitdata.com/Software/ICAO%20Annex%2014%20Volume%201, updated 5 Jan. 2014, 5th Edition, July 2009, accessed 5 Jan. 2017

9   IATA AHM as cited in B. Oreschko, M. Schultz, J. Elflein and H. Fricke. (2010). *Significant Turnaround Process Variations due to Airport Characteristics*, Air Transport and Operations Symposium (ATOS), Delft, http://www.ifl.tu-dresden.de/getfileok.php?p=publications/&f=2010_ATOS_Turnaround_Process_Variations_1.2_bo010410.pdf, accessed 6 Feb. 2017

10 TUD, http://www.ifl.tu-dresden.de/?dir=Research/Current_Projects/Airport_Operations/Turnaround_Management , [website] accessed 4 Feb. 2017

11 B. Oreschko, M. Schultz, J. Elflein and H. Fricke. (2010). *Significant Turnaround Process Variations due to Airport Characteristics*, Air Transport and Operations Symposium (ATOS), Delft, http://www.ifl.tu-dresden.de/getfileok.php?p=publications/&f=2010_ATOS_Turnaround_Process_Variations_1.2_bo010410.pdf, accessed 6 Feb. 2017

12 IATA ADRM as cited in Transportation Research Board of the National Academies. 2010. *ACRP Report 25, Airport Passenger Terminal Planning and Design, Volume 1: Guidebook*, p. 111. Washington DC: TRB.

13 U. Dorndorf, F. Jaehn, C. Lin, H. Ma and E. Pesch (2007) Disruption management in flight gate scheduling. *Statistica Neerlandica* Vol. 61, nr. 1, p. 92–114 https://www.wiwi.uni-augsburg.de/bwl/jaehn/Veroeffentlichungen/stan_361.pdf, accessed Feb. 17

14 E. Pesch, U. Dorndorf and F. Jaehn, Flight Gate Allocation: Models, Methods and Robust Solutions, pdf, [website] http://www.patatconference.org/patat2008/proceedings/Pesch-HB1.pdf , accessed Feb. 2017

15 H. Ehrenstrasser, AeroGround, Director Ramp Operations, Munich Airport, Interview 24 Jan 2017

16 AeroGround, Company, https://www.munich-airport.de/en/micro/aeroground/company/index.jsp, accessed 24 Jan. 2017

12 Facilitation

Immigration, customs, and quarantine

Samuel Lucas

Introduction

At its most elemental, aviation facilitation is about moving people and things across international borders. Aviation security and facilitation are often perceived as contrasting objectives; however as aviation's operating environment changes in the twenty-first century, both disciplines are evolving to prevent the movement of the undesirable, while making routine and unobjectionable movement easier, with technology playing an increasing role.

International framework

International Civil Aviation Organization (ICAO) mandate and activities

ICAO's standard-setting role in respect of safety and security is well understood. Less understood, however, is ICAO's role in setting standards and recommended practices in relation to facilitation. The Chicago Convention tasks ICAO with developing standards and recommended practices relating to 'customs and immigration procedures' as well as 'other such matters concerned with the safety, regularity and efficiency of air navigation as may from time to time appear appropriate'. This role is reflected in ICAO's Strategic Priorities, one of which is to 'Enhance global aviation security and facilitation', reflecting the need for ICAO's leadership in aviation security, facilitation and related border security matters.[1]

Annex 9

ICAO has adopted a number of Annexes to the Chicago Convention, detailing the Standards and Recommended Practices (SARPs) with which states must comply. Annex 9 relates to Facilitation; the first edition being adopted by the ICAO council on 25 March 1949. By 2015, twenty-five Amendments to the Annex had been adopted, and the fourteenth edition of Annex 9 became applicable on 25 February 2016. The chapters of Annex 9 cover a range of elements where standardization of approach is required globally, including the requirements for entry and departure of aircraft and their passengers and cargo, international airport facilities, and passport and visa requirements.

ICAO Facilitation Panel

Facilitation has been part of ICAO's work programme since the organization's earliest beginnings, with the First Session of the Facilitation Division held in Montreal in February 1946. Today, the Facilitation Panel usually meets every eighteen to twenty-four months, or as needed. The Panel has a broad membership of states representing (as is common practice with ICAO Panels) a broad geographic cross-section of the world. International organizations attend, officially, as observers. Given the importance of industry cooperation in facilitation matters, industry lobby groups such as the International Air Transport Association (IATA) and Airports Council International (ACI) are very active participants, notwithstanding their 'observer' status.

Passports and visas

Passport standards

The standardization of standards for passports internationally is one of the most significant achievements of ICAO's facilitation work. Standard 3.10 of Annex 9 obligates all states to issue their passports in a format that is machine-readable, and in the format specified by ICAO Doc 9303, which has also been adopted by the International Organization for Standardization.[2,3] Following ICAO's mandating of machine-readable passports in 2005, by the end of 2015 all passports in use in the world should be machine readable. The almost universal implementation of Machine Readable Travel Documents (MRTD) has greatly facilitated airline operations – airline check-in staff routinely 'swipe' the Machine Readable Zone (MRZ) on an MRTD in order to input the passenger's passport data into their computer systems, greatly speeding passenger check-in. ICAO's standardization work has seen Doc 9303 expand beyond passports to include machine-readable visas and identity cards, which are used by many government agencies around the world to produce standard, secure identity documents.

ePassports

In the twenty-first century, governments around the world are moving beyond the machine-readable passport to a new, more high-tech option: the ePassport. An ePassport (or in the language of Annex 9, an eMRTD) has a contactless circuit embedded in the passport, and is able to support biometric identification of the traveller. To secure ePassport data, and allow verification of ePassport data, the Public Key Directory (PKD) has been developed under ICAO's auspices.[4] The PKD allows governments to verify that a passport is genuine and has not been altered or copied by providing a global system of security certificates. The assurance of a document's validity is important for utilization of ePassports to support automated border processing, as a passport used at a kiosk or similar system may not be physically seen by a border control official. The use of contactless chip technology has, however, raised some public concerns about security and the risk of theft of personal information.[5]

Visa systems

A visa is an authorization or endorsement for entry into the state that has issued the visa. Visas must usually be obtained in advance of travelling, allowing the destination state a greater opportunity to consider the appropriateness of the individual for entry. The use of visas reflects the basic principle that states have the right to control who enters their territory and the terms and conditions applying to such entry. While desirable for many governments as a means of controlling entry, visa requirements can be cumbersome and often unpopular with travellers. Standard 3.22 of Annex 9 obligates states to establish 'simple and transparent application procedures for the issuance of entry visas to prospective visitors'.[6] The World Tourism Organization has been vocal in pressing for the removal of visas globally, releasing a periodic 'Visa Openness' report,[7] but they remain an integral part of many states' border control systems.

With advances in technology, the traditional visa label in a passport is beginning to be phased out. Australia's *Migration Act 1958* (Cwlth)[8] applies a 'universal visa system' requiring every non-Australian seeking to enter the country to hold a valid visa. To facilitate travel, the Australian Government has been at the forefront of introducing label-free visas, eVisas, and the Electronic Travel Authority (ETA). The Australian ETA[9] system has been in operation for a number of years, and other states have since implemented similar systems, including the USA with its Electronic System for Travel Authorization (ESTA)[10] and Canada's Electronic Travel Authorization (eTA).[11] These systems allow travellers to apply online for an approval prior to travel, which is then stored electronically and often verified by an airline via an Advance Passenger Information (API) system. Annex 9 includes obligations on states to offer visa-free entry to airline crew (Standard 3.67) and civil aviation inspectors (Recommended Practice 3.72). Visa-free entry is an area in which many states do not comply with their obligations under Annex 9. For example, with its universal visa system Australia does not offer visa-free entry, but rather provides alternative means as outlined in Australia's filed differences to Annex 9,[12] including the Crew Travel Authority.[13]

Leaving a state

Immigration controls

To ensure they know who is attempting to leave, and to allow them to prevent departure in certain circumstances, most states have some form of outward immigration control. Most frequently, this takes the form of an outwards passport control point at which the state's immigration authorities verify the identity of the passenger and record their departure. Some states, such as the USA, Canada and the UK, do not have outwards control points. Instead, they often require airlines to report to immigration authorities lists of passengers transported out of the state. Standard 3.17 of Annex 9 bars states from requiring exit visas from either their own nationals or visitors, although exit controls will be an increasing priority for many states in line with emerging trends on 'foreign fighters'.

VAT refunds

Many states with a Value Added Tax (VAT) or a Goods and Services Tax (GST) provide refunds of taxation for tourists or other travellers. The scope of these refund services varies by country, but is usually on goods purchased in-country, and sometimes extends to accommodation and other services. In Australia, the Tourist Refund Scheme (TRS) is administered by the Department of Immigration and Border Protection, and allows travellers departing Australia to obtain refunds of GST on goods that travellers take out of Australia, provided the goods were purchased within sixty days of departure.[14] The claim is made by the traveller in person at the TRS counter at an Australian international airport. The scheme is popular with tourists and the tourism industry, but its implementation can provide challenges for airport operators and airlines, if tourists seeking tax refunds remain in tax refund queues and delay the boarding of their flight. The Australian TRS is not available to passengers within thirty minutes of their flight's departure.

Entering a state

Immigration controls

Arriving passengers are usually greeted by an immigration control point, often referred to as 'the primary line'. Here, the passengers' eligibility to enter the country of destination is assessed by government officials. The agency involved can vary from state to state – for example, for many years in Australia, immigration checks were actually conducted by officers of the Australian Customs Service, on behalf of the Department of Immigration. Immigration controls traditionally involved an officer verifying a traveller's identity via a face-to-passport check, and then verifying that a passenger met the eligibility requirements for entry, which might include holding a visa, meeting the terms of their visa, and having sufficient resources to maintain themselves.

With the advent of modern MRTDs and computer systems, many immigration services now verify the validity of the travel document via electronic means such as the ICAO PKD, search INTERPOL lost and stolen travel documents databases, and use biometric identification such as fingerprinting or facial recognition. As passenger identification becomes more complex, the use of technological solutions to allow self-service is logical, and many countries are now using Automated Border Controls allowing eligible travellers to self-process through electronic 'gate' systems. States have deployed a variety of systems, including SmartGate used in Australia[15] and New Zealand,[16] and BorderXpress developed by Vancouver International Airport and used in a number of countries.[17]

Customs controls

In most international airports, following immigration, passengers proceed to the baggage reclaim hall to collect checked baggage. Having collected baggage, passengers usually proceed to a customs control point. While the focus of the immigration control point is to control the entry of people, the customs control point is focused on the entry of things, particularly restricted substances or goods. Different states have different priorities, but most customs checks target a broad range of contraband, including:

- preventing the smuggling of illicit drugs
- blocking the trade in restricted items or substances such as antiquities, ivory or diamonds
- enforcing import bans on items such as weapons
- ensuring the collection of required customs duties on dutiable items such as alcohol and tobacco.

Some states, particularly those with more conservative societies, also use customs controls to prevent the entry of socially undesirable material. The degree of intervention at customs control points varies globally, and Standard 3.50 of Annex 9 obligates states to apply a risk-management approach, such as the 'dual channel' or 'red channel/green channel' system. Some states intervene with the vast majority of passengers, asking questions, searching or X-raying baggage, or using sniffer dogs to seek to identify contraband substances. In contrast, some other states rely on self-declaration, with many passengers exiting via 'green' channels for passengers 'with nothing to declare'. Where states apply duties to the import of products such as alcohol and tobacco, they will usually allow a traveller to import a limited amount of that product free of duty – that is, 'duty-free'. For most passengers, duty-free allowances are the most significant element of the arriving customs control experience; allowances vary from state to state, and apply as a passenger crosses the border.

Quarantine controls

While immigration and customs controls are commonplace around the world, a smaller number of states also include quarantine or biosecurity controls at their border. Quarantine is aimed at preventing the entry of pests and diseases, and states that are geographically more isolated (for example, islands) tend to have stricter quarantine requirements, as they are usually free from a range of pests and diseases common in other places around the world. Australia and New Zealand have some of the most stringent quarantine requirements, as their geography and isolation have left them free of a range of pests and diseases; a competitive advantage for their agriculture sectors. Accordingly, travellers arriving in Australia and New Zealand are often subjected to increased levels of intervention to ensure that fruit, vegetables, meat items, wooden items, sea shells, dirty hiking boots, and the like do not inadvertently introduce new pests or diseases to the ecosystems.

Disinsection

As part of their quarantine or biosecurity controls, some states impose disinsection requirements on arriving aircraft to ensure that insects on-board do not introduce insect-borne diseases. Disinsection is more common in island states where isolation has left ecosystems free of diseases common elsewhere. Amongst others, Australia, New Zealand, Fiji and Italy require disinsection of all in-bound flights; France, the United Kingdom, and Indonesia require disinsection on some flights.[18] The practice of chemical disinsection, which can expose passengers to insecticides, attracts criticism.[19] In response to these concerns, Annex 9 imposes a number of limitations on states' disinsection options, with Standard 2.25 limiting states to using methods approved by the World Health Organization (WHO). WHO highlights that disinsection has a role in preventing the spread of diseases such as malaria, and notes that there is no evidence that approved insecticide sprays are harmful to humans.[20] While a range of measures can be used, the two most common methods are:

- residual disinsection, in which aircraft cabins are periodically sprayed with a long-lasting insecticide that kills insects that may fly into the cabin or holds at a later date
- on-arrival disinsection, in which arriving aircraft are sprayed with quick-acting insecticide before passengers and cargo are disembarked, to kill any insects present in the cabin or hold.

The Australian and New Zealand Governments work together to align disinsection requirements, and require all arriving aircraft to have a valid residual disinsection certificate, or to complete on-arrival disinsection after arrival, and disinsection status is part of the mandated pre-arrival report.[21] On-arrival disinsection involves a quarantine officer attending the aircraft on arrival at the gate to supervise spraying. All passengers are required to remain seated, cabin storage is opened, and the quarantine officer verifies that cabin crew have correctly sprayed the required insecticide quantity throughout the cabin. After waiting several minutes to allow the insecticides to work, and after the quarantine officer has cleared the flight, disembarkation can commence. On-arrival disinsection imposes additional time and cost for airlines, and is unpopular with passengers. Most airlines operating regularly to/from Australia and New Zealand elect to incur the expense involved in maintaining residual disinsection certification for their aircraft.

Health

The final element of government-imposed arrival regulation for arriving international passengers relates to human health. Standard 8.12 of Annex 9 also obligates states party to the Chicago Convention to comply with relevant provisions of the International Health Regulations (2005) of WHO (although most ICAO member states would also be members of the WHO and thereby required to comply with the IHR). In accordance with Standard 8.15 of Annex 9, most states require arriving aircraft to report any unwell passengers on board to authorities ahead of the aircraft's arrival. Pratique, or clearance that an arriving vessel or aircraft is free from diseases and able to disembark, is normally given automatically, unless unwell passengers have been reported. States do not usually intervene with arriving passengers to verify their health, aside from requiring vaccination certificates if passengers have travelled to particular geographic areas. However, states can and do impose health measures when WHO has made declarations as to the existence of a public health emergency of international concern. Such measures may include the withdrawal of automatic pratique, the deployment of a 'Public Health Passenger Locator Card' as recommended in Recommended Practice 8.15.1 and Appendix 13 of Annex 9, or a similar health declaration card, or the deployment of thermal scanners to identify arriving febrile passengers. Measures applied by states depend upon the situation and risks posed by a particular health issue.

Passenger data systems

(Dis)embarkation cards

The original form of 'passenger data' system is the traditional card filled out by passengers before their arrival – whether called a landing card, customs card, incoming passenger card, or disembarkation card. While Appendices 5 to 9 provide an international model card, in practice, states which require cards design their own; many states require multiple cards, covering different purposes (for example, customs and immigration cards). Standard 3.29 of Annex 9 requires governments to distribute cards to airlines free of charge, and airlines engage in complex logistics to ensure that each international flight has the right cards on board, usually for both the outbound and (return) inbound service.

Passenger Name Record (PNR) data

In the airline industry, large amounts of data about a passenger's booking are contained in the PNR. This information includes details on a passenger's journey, covering not only the passenger's identity and flight details, but details of changes to the booking, as well as payment information, and upon departure, details of seat assignment and baggage details. As technology has advanced, states' increasingly complex analytical systems are able to make use of this information to identify details or patterns that may indicate matters of interest to border agencies. Accordingly, some states require airlines to provide PNR data to their border agencies, ahead of passengers' arrival. ICAO has published guidance material on the PNR systems,[22] which includes the standardized 'PNRGOV' message format.

API systems

Advances in information and communication technology have made it possible for states to require the prior transmission of arriving passengers' details. API systems achieve this by requiring airlines to collect (or extract) whatever data elements are requested by states' border control agencies, and to transmit that data before the flight arrives, to be utilized by agencies when processing passengers upon their arrival.[23] Sometimes called 'legacy API' or 'batch API' to distinguish them from iAPI (Interactive Advance Passenger Information) systems, these systems allow agencies to check passengers against enforcement databases and alert lists, prior to passengers presenting at the immigration checkpoint. As part of a suite of actions initiated by the United Nations (UN) Security Council in 2015, ICAO is moving to further increase states' usage of API.

When a state imposes a requirement on airlines to provide API data, airlines bear an increased burden in adapting their operational computer systems to retrieve, collate, and transmit the required data. The development and introduction of API systems by individual states led to airlines needing to comply with a range of differing API systems. In response, a joint working group of IATA, the World Customs Organization (WCO) and ICAO developed joint Guidelines on Advance Passenger Information published in 2010. Standard 3.46 of Annex 9 requires states implementing an API system to do so using an established international format, in an attempt to restrain the proliferation of differing standards. The message format recommended in the WCO/IATA/ICAO Guidelines is the UN rules for Electronic Data Interchange for Administration, Commerce and Transport 'PAXLST' format, known as UN/EDIFACT PAXLST.[24]

iAPI systems

API provides a one-way flow of information from airlines to border control agencies. The next step beyond API is to move to an interactive process by which a state gives approval to embark passengers prior to their departure.[25,26] Such systems are known as Advance Passenger Processing (APP), or iAPI. The most common iAPI system is SITA's APP, used by Australia, South Africa, Bahrain, Kuwait and New Zealand. APP provides an interactive system in which airline check-in systems communicate in real time with the government's systems, to verify that a particular passenger holds the necessary visas or similar authorizations for travel, and has not been placed on a Movement Alert List or similar. The APP system then provides a 'red light/green light' or 'ok to board'/'not ok to board' response to the airline. Without an 'ok to board' message, the airline may not board that passenger for the flight; doing so will place the airline at risk of incurring penalties from the arriving state's border agencies.

When implemented successfully, iAPI provides a valuable addition to a state's border processes, as it effectively allows a state to refuse *travel* prior to departure, rather than merely refusing *entry* after a passenger has physically arrived.

Effective iAPI systems require a significant investment by the state. Reflecting this, Chapter 3 of Annex 9 requires states implementing iAPI systems to provide considerable support to the airline industry, including liaison officers, 24/7 contact centres to provide support, and backup systems and processes to deal with system interruptions. While integration and compliance with iAPI systems and their requirements impose additional complexity and cost on airlines, they also provide airlines with a greater degree of surety that the passengers they board and carry to their destinations will indeed be admitted, reducing the rate of refused admissions for which the airlines are liable.

Air cargo

Challenges

Air cargo presents a range of challenges for border facilitation. Cargo shipped by air is often high-value and time-sensitive, and delays either in loading or unloading in order to facilitate either security or border control inspection could undermine the commercial efficacy of air cargo. At the same time, the large quantities of cargo being shipped present a significant customs and quarantine risk for governments.

SAFE Framework

Building on supply chain security approaches, and seeking to introduce into the customs sphere the degree of industry–government collaboration necessary to improve both facilitation and border controls, the WCO introduced, in 2005, the SAFE Framework of Standards to secure and facilitate global trade. The SAFE Framework brings together a range of measures to improve both facilitation of cargo and application of border controls, including electronic manifests, standardized risk management approaches, frameworks for cooperation between customs agencies, 'single windows' for data provision, and strengthening the use of supply chain measures to ensure border control requirements are met. Regular engagement between ICAO and the WCO has seen Annex 9 amended to align with the SAFE Framework.

Supply chains and data flows

The movement of air cargo relies on the use of secure supply chains, and the flow of data in standardized reporting processes.[27] Secure supply chains see controls or inspections applied not at the airport (as is the case with passengers) but 'upstream' in the cargo's journey, with inspections taking place in the hands of a 'known consignor' or 'regulated agent'. This allows cargo to be consolidated and packed ready for shipping well in advance of arriving at the airport, with the trusted agent certifying to aviation security and border control agencies what is in a shipment, and that it can be safely and securely carried by air.

Prior to cargo travelling on a flight, the shipper delivers the cargo to a freight forwarder, which works with a customs agent, if they are not one themselves, to submit an export goods declaration to the state of origin's border control agency. The border control agency clears the shipment for departure in the form of a customs release, and the freight forwarder provides an air waybill to the airline that will carry the cargo, which is used to track the cargo throughout its journey by air. The airline or freight forwarder may submit advance cargo information to the border control agencies of the destination state, to alert them to the shipment and allow risk assessments prior to arrival of the goods, in much the same way as API is provided. These processes to prepare for departure usually take place before the cargo is accepted at the airport by the airline or its ground handlers. Accreditation of the supply chain process is required to satisfy agencies that the shipment remains under appropriate controls, and a Consignment Security Declaration is required to confirm the security of the shipment.

On the day of flight, the airline will send the flight's manifest and air waybills of all of the cargo to the destination border agencies. On arrival, the airline and/or the destination freight forwarder will submit to the destination border agencies an import cargo declaration, while the goods are transported by a customs agent or freight forwarder to secure storage until cleared. Once the destination border agencies are satisfied that the shipment can be imported, they will issue an import goods release authorizing delivery to the recipient of the shipment. Today, many of these processes have moved to electronic transmission, speeding the process and enabling faster movement of freight through the system. The 'single window' requirements of the SAFE Framework and Annex 9 seek to streamline data flows by channelling all of the information required by a state's border agencies through one contact point, avoiding the need to send different declarations to different recipients within one state.

Mail

International airmail operates within a framework administered by the Universal Postal Union (UPU). Under this system, the originating and receiving postal services take responsibility for screening and processing international mail before and after departure. Customs declarations attached to postal items are also moving online, with the UPU introducing new electronic message formats for the transmission of electronic customs documentation instead of paper-based systems. Within the international postal system, postal service providers interact with both airlines (providing assurances that mail has been screened appropriately) and customs agencies, which clear the mail for delivery to its end recipient.

Irregular operations

Inadmissible passengers

Inadmissible passengers can represent a significant cost to an airline. Standard 5.11 of Annex 9 provides that if a passenger seeks to enter a state, but is refused entry, then the airline which transported the passenger to the state is responsible for removing them. Annex 9 prescribes a range of procedures applying to the removal of inadmissible passengers, and to where they may be removed (for example, to the state from which they commenced their travel). For airlines, taking steps to identify passengers who may be found to be inadmissible is an important element of their own processes, with check-in staff verifying visa and document validity prior to check-in. Although Standard 5.14 of Annex 9 restricts states from imposing penalties on airlines for carrying improperly documented passengers, if the airline can demonstrate it has taken 'necessary precautions', airlines still face a potentially significant burden and most take visa verification quite seriously. iAPI systems greatly assist this process, and can reduce the rate of inadmissible passengers; however airlines' check-in staff still retain significant responsibilities for verifying that a passenger has valid travel documentation.

Delay/disruption

From time to time, the smooth flow of aircraft, passengers, baggage, and cargo, will be disrupted. Airlines devote considerable resources to preparing for and dealing with disruption. Considerations in managing delays or disruption are not purely operational. In some jurisdictions, governments regulate the actions by airlines in such cases. The USA requires all airlines serving destinations in the USA, and airports in the USA, to have a Tarmac Delay Contingency Plan in place.[28] This Plan must give passengers the option to leave an aircraft that has been delayed on the tarmac after a certain delay, and legislated notice requirements apply to flight delays. While some states, such as Australia and Singapore, leave airline customer service standards to be a commercial matter regulated by the contractual relationship between customer and service provider, others intervene in the relationship. The USA requires airlines to have in place a Customer Service Plan and also regulates various elements of the customer–airline relationship.[29] In the European Union, delays or disruption can give rise to prescribed service responses and/or compensation levels.[30]

Force majeure

Extreme weather events, such as cyclones, winter snow and ice storms, and dust storms, all impact aviation and restrict airlines' and airports' normal operations. At their most extreme, they can disrupt entire networks or regions. Volcanic activity can have global impacts, for example, in 2010 the eruption of Eyjafjallajökull in Iceland shut down most European and transatlantic air travel for over a week, and in 2011 the eruption of Puyehue-Cordón Caulle in Chile disrupted aviation right around the southern hemisphere. Aside from the operational challenges posed by these eruptions, which can cause serious safety concerns for airlines, such mass disruption events cause a range of facilitation problems for airlines and airports, as large numbers of passengers (and their baggage, as well as cargo) are stranded at airports or diverted en route. These passengers may not have the necessary visas, or may have expiring travel documents, or other factors that impact their ability to enter or remain in the state they find themselves in.

Chapter 3 of Annex 9 contains a number of provisions requiring or encouraging states to put in place measures to deal with this disruption, including allowing passengers to travel even if visas have expired, or even if passengers do not hold valid visas. They also allow passengers short-term entry to take accommodation rather than being stranded in the airside area of an airport. As many of these provisions are Recommended Practices rather than Standards, implementation is encouraged but not mandatory, and states' own domestic laws and regulations relating to entry and exit remain the primary control of passengers' movements in these situations.

Pandemics

The rapid growth in travel in the second half of the twentieth century has opened the door to the potential rapid spread of disease around the world. Standard 8.16 of Annex 9 requires all states to develop a national plan for dealing with an outbreak of a communicable disease posing a public health risk or public health emergency of international concern. Recent events have included an outbreak of Ebola virus disease (EVD or Ebola) in West Africa in 2014. In that event, countries with Ebola cases were requested by WHO and ICAO to introduce exit screening to reduce the chances of an Ebola-infected person leaving the country.[31] Many countries introduced some form of enhanced on-arrival screening for passengers in an attempt to identify and intercept Ebola cases. Australia has established plans in place for dealing with a pandemic such as influenza.[32] A range of scalable options are available, from the withdrawal of automatic pratique, to the deployment of Health Declaration Cards and temperature scanners at airports to seek to identify febrile or otherwise unwell passengers.

Current and future trends

Risk-based intervention and reductions in contact points

As passenger numbers increase, and global fiscal challenges limit governments' abilities to increase resourcing for border control agencies, there is an increasing trend to increase and improve border agencies' use of risk assessment, in line with Annex 9, to minimize intervention with low-risk passengers (and cargo) and better target intervention on higher-risk passengers (and cargo). As part of this, governments are increasingly seeking to reduce the number and extent of contact points in the processing chain.

Differentiated service provision

For many states, some form of differentiated service provision is an effective way of increasing the facilitation rate. Usually, these services involve expedited queuing, or marshalling, for identified premium customers, while retaining the same interaction with government officials. Customers may be identified on the basis of their class of travel (with first and/or business class passengers receiving expedited handling) or their frequent-flyer status, membership in a program by which they have previously undergone background checking or pre-clearance, such as the USA's Global Entry program,[33] or on the basis of fee for service, such as at Gatwick Airport.[34] While sometimes criticized as offering 'the rich' a better service,[35] such systems meet the twin desires of airlines and airports seeking to offer differentiated service for high value customers, and governments wanting to find ways to increase the facilitation rate. Frequent travellers, such as high-status frequent-flyer members, or frequent business travellers flying in business class, usually know customs requirements and processes better than inexperienced travellers, lessening the chance of inadvertent breaches, and as such they can often be processed more quickly and efficiently.

Integration of data: between countries, and between purposes

With states increasingly collecting and utilizing passenger data for border control, and some states introducing passenger data systems for aviation security, a greater degree of convergence between these two objectives is likely in the future, including states working together to share information. However, progress towards such integration has been slow, with data privacy a primary barrier. The European Union's data protection laws restrict the transfer of data out of the EU; these restrictions apply even if a non-EU airline is operating a flight between two non-EU member states, but uses a European-hosted computer system such as Amadeus.[36] To facilitate the transfer of data without breaching EU data protection laws, the EU has concluded treaty-level agreements governing the transfer and processing of PNR data with the USA, Canada and Australia. These agreements place limits on the purposes for which PNR data can be used, and on its transfer.

Exit controls

The phenomenon of 'foreign fighters' associated with the Islamic State in Iraq and the Levant (ISIL) and similar groups fighting in Syria, Yemen, and other conflict zones, has focused increased attention on states' exit controls. In many states, exit controls (whether in the form of an outwards control point in an airport, or an electronic-based reporting system) are used as a means of knowing who has left the state, rather than a means of actively preventing a departure. In 2014 the UN Security Council passed Resolution S/RES/2178 (2014) which obligates states to take measures to prevent the international flow of such terrorist fighters, including departure from their territory. The Resolution specifically references API as a means of detecting the entry into, transit through, or departure from their territory of potential 'foreign fighters', and urges its use. For states not used to preventing exit, particularly for their own citizens, the onus placed on them by

Resolution 2178 could prove challenging. Passenger data systems allowing quick and effective cross-matching of departing passengers against watch lists and alert lists, ideally ahead of their presentation at an outwards control point, will be an important tool for states in meeting this obligation.

Glossary of acronyms and abbreviations

ACI	Airports Council International
API	Advance Passenger Information
APP	Advance Passenger Processing
eMRTD	Electronic Machine Readable Travel Document
ESTA	Electronic System for Travel Authorization
ETA	Electronic Travel Authority
eTA	Electronic Travel Authorization
GST	Goods and Services Tax
iAPI	Interactive Advance Passenger Information
IATA	International Air Transport Association
ICAO	International Civil Aviation Organization
IHR	International Health Regulations
INTERPOL	International Police Organization
ISIL	Islamic State in Iraq and the Levant
MRTD	Machine Readable Travel Document
MRZ	Machine Readable Zone
PKD	Public Key Directory
PNR	Passenger Name Record
SARP	Standards and Recommended Practices
TRS	Tourist Refund Scheme
UPU	Universal Postal Union
VAT	Value Added Tax
WCO	World Customs Organization
WHO	World Health Organization

Notes

1 ICAO, *ICAO Strategic Objectives 2014–2016*, ICAO, viewed 27 December 2015, http://www.icao.int/about-icao/Pages/Strategic-Objectives.aspx
2 ICAO 2015, *ICAO Machine Readable Travel Documents (ICAO Doc 9303)*, seventh edition.
3 International Organization for Standardization (ISO) 2008, *ISO/IEC 7501-1:2008: Identification card – Machine Readable Travel Documents*, ISO.
4 ICAO, *ICAO Public Key Directory (PKD)*, ICAO, viewed 10 January 2016, http://www.icao.int/Security/mrtd/Pages/icaoPKD.aspx
5 Privacy Europe 2013, *How Secure is the electronic passport?*, Privacy Europe, viewed 10 January 2016, https://www.privacy-europe.com/blog/how-secure-is-the-electronic-passport/
6 ICAO 2015, *Annex 9 to the Convention on International Civil Aviation – Facilitation*, fourteenth edition.

7   World Tourism Organization 2014, *Visa Openness Report 2014*, UNWTO, http://cf.cdn.
    unwto.org/sites/all/files/docpdf/2014visaopennessreport2ndprintingonline.pdf
8   *Migration Act 1958* (Cwlth), Federal Register of Legislation, s.42, viewed 13 June
    2016, https://www.legislation.gov.au/Details/C2016C00297
9   DIBP, *Electronic Travel Authority (subclass 601)*, DIBP, viewed 16 January 2016, https://
    www.border.gov.au/Trav/Visa-1/601-
10 United States Customs and Border Protection (USCBP), *ESTA*, USCBP, viewed
    16 January 2016, https://esta.cbp.dhs.gov/esta
11 Citizenship and Immigration Canada (CIC), *Electronic Travel Authorization (eTA)*,
    CIC, viewed 16 January 2016, http://www.cic.gc.ca/english/visit/eta.asp
12 Airservices Australia (Airservices) 2017, *Aeronautical Information Package: Differences
    from ICAO Standards, Recommended Practices and Procedures H24/17*, viewed 27 June
    2017, https://www.airservicesaustralia.com/aip/current/sup/s17-h24.pdf
13 DIBP, *Crew Travel Authority (subclass 942)*, DIBP, viewed 16 January 2016, https://
    www.border.gov.au/Trav/Visa-1/942-
14 DIBP, *Tourist Refund Scheme*, DIBP, viewed 10 January 2016, https://www.border.gov.
    au/Trav/Ente/Tour
15 Department of Immigration and Border Protection (DIBP), *Arrivals SmartGate*,
    DIBP, viewed 24 January 2016, https://www.border.gov.au/Trav/Ente/Goin/Arrival/
    Smartgateor-ePassport
16 New Zealand Customs Service, *Smartgate*, New Zealand Customs Service, viewed
    13 June 2016, http://www.customs.govt.nz/features/smartgate/Pages/default.aspx
17 Vancouver Airport Authority 2016, *BorderXpress Self-Service Border Products*, Vancouver
    Airport Authority, viewed 13 June 2016, http://www.yvr.ca/en/business/self-service-
    border-products
18 United States Department of Transportation (USDOT) 2016, *Aircraft Disinsection
    Requirements*, USDOT, viewed 13 June 2016, https://www.transportation.gov/office-
    policy/aviation-policy/aircraft-disinsection-requirements
19 McGee, B. 2013, "Should fliers worry about pesticide spraying on planes?", *USA
    Today*, 13 May 2015, viewed 17 January 2016, http://www.usatoday.com/story/travel/
    columnist/mcgee/2015/05/13/disinsection-airplane-pesticide-spraying/27177835/
20 World Health Organization (WHO) 2016, *Aircraft Disinsection*, WHO, viewed 17
    January 2016, http://www.who.int/ith/mode_of_travel/aircraft_disinsection/en/
21 Department of Agriculture and Ministry for Primary Industries 2014, *Schedule of
    Aircraft Disinsection Procedures for Flights into Australia and New Zealand*, Version 4.1,
    viewed 27 June 2017, http://www.agriculture.gov.au/SiteCollectionDocuments/
    aqis/airvesselmilitary/airpoirts/operators/disinsection/aircraft-disinsection.pdf
22 ICAO 2010, *Guidelines on Passenger Name Record (PNR) Data (ICAO Doc 9944)*, first
    edition.
23 WCO/IATA/ICAO 2010, *Guidelines on Advance Passenger Information (API)*, WCO/
    IATA/ICAO, viewed 13 June 2016, http://www.iata.org/iata/passenger-data-toolkit/
    assets/doc_library/02-api/2010%20API%20Guidelines%20Final%20Version.
    ICAO.2011%20full%20x2.pdf
24 WCO/IATA/ICAO 2010, *Guidelines on Advance Passenger Information(API)*, WCO/
    IATA/ICAO, viewed 13 June 2016, http://www.iata.org/iata/passenger-data-toolkit/
    assets/doc_library/02-api/2010%20API%20Guidelines%20Final%20Version.
    ICAO.2011%20full%20x2.pdf
25 WCO/IATA/ICAO 2010, *Guidelines on Advance Passenger Information (API)*, WCO/
    IATA/ICAO, viewed 13 June 2016, http://www.iata.org/iata/passenger-data-toolkit/
    assets/doc_library/02-api/2010%20API%20Guidelines%20Final%20Version.
    ICAO.2011%20full%20x2.pdf
26 IATA/Control Authorities Working Group (CAWG) 2007, *iAPI Statement of
    Principles*, IATA/CAWG, viewed 13 June 2016, http://www.iata.org/iata/passenger-
    data-toolkit/assets/doc_library/03-interactive_api/iAPI%20SoP_%2017May07.pdf

27 WCO and ICAO, 2016, *Moving Air Cargo Globally* (second edition), viewed 27 June 2017, https://www.icao.int/Security/aircargo/Moving Air Cargo Globally/ICAO_WCO_Moving_Air_Cargo_en.pdf

28 USDOT 2016, *Flight Delays*, USDOT, viewed 13 June 2016, https://www.transportation.gov/airconsumer/flight-delays

29 USDOT 2016, *Aviation Consumer Protection*, USDOT, viewed 13 June 2016, https://www.transportation.gov/airconsumer

30 European Commission (EC) 2016, *Air Passenger Rights*, European Commission, viewed 13 June 2016, http://europa.eu/youreurope/citizens/travel/passenger-rights/air/index_en.htm

31 World Health Organization (WHO) 2014, *Travel and transport risk assessment: Interim Guidance for public health authorities and the transport sector*, WHO, viewed 13 June 2016, http://apps.who.int/iris/bitstream/10665/132168/1/WHO_EVD_Guidance_TravelTransportRisk_14.1_eng.pdf?ua=1&ua=1

32 Department of Health 2009, *FluBorderPlan: National Pandemic Influenza Airport Border Operations Plan*, Department of Health, viewed 13 June 2016, http://www.health.gov.au/internet/main/publishing.nsf/Content/7BB496A8142E8705CA257E35007F691A/$File/040208%20Fluborderplan%20strategic%20-%20final.pdf

33 USCBP, *Global Entry*, USCBP, viewed 24 January 2016, https://www.cbp.gov/travel/trusted-traveler-programs/global-entry

34 Gatwick Airport, *Premium Gatwick Passport Control*, Gatwick Airport, viewed 27 June 2017, http://www.gatwickairport.com/at-the-airport/flying-in/premium-passport-control/

35 Dick, T. 2015, 'The rich have different rules to you and me', *The Age*, 21 June 2015, viewed 24 January 2016, http://www.theage.com.au/comment/the-rich-have-different-rules-20150621-ghtibe.html

36 European Council 2016, *Regulating the use of PNR data*, European Council, viewed 24 January 2016, http://www.consilium.europa.eu/en/policies/fight-against-terrorism/passenger-name-record/

Part III
Operating the current day

Peter J. Bruce

One of the purposes in compiling this text was to piece together several different elements of an airline that contribute to providing a flight for passengers. Often these elements are seen separately and even personnel in industry have only a vague knowledge of their interaction with each other or the effect that one has on another. The first two parts in this text have alluded to the intricate planning required in terms of preparing an airline to offer its product range across a market or number of markets. To do this, the airline is characterized by a chosen business model that takes into account financial, economic and commercial objectives among others, but crucially needs to conduct its business within an international regulatory framework that provides for safe conduct of operations.

The meticulous and extensive operational planning that is invested by an airline is also vital in preparation for operating a set of flights to meet the expectations of stakeholders, i.e., anyone who is involved in any way with the conduct of these flights. Thus, the second part examined some of the key functional areas, such as Operations Control, Crewing, Maintenance, Airside Resources and Facilitation, which focus on the preparatory stages pertaining specifically to operating a flight. Having then set the scene, Part III draws the reader on a journey through the activities that take place on the operating day itself. For many, this is the 'sharp' end of the business – where the hive of activity under various conditions and at times intense pressure is highly challenging. For some, though, the operating day with its complexities and uncertainties is the most interesting and fulfilling part of airline life.

This part explains the processes that take place on a *normal* operating day. Opinions differ as to what *normal* really means in this business, as disruption to the scheduled patterns of flying in any airline is common for a variety of reasons and could be considered normal too! Disrupted operations are the focus of the final chapters of the book. This part provides an overview of the operating environment within which airlines operate – the Air Traffic System. The focus then moves to consider the key areas that work together on a daily basis to provide the services that support the flights. The ramp or apron is the most obvious area of intense activity, where many services such as loading and unloading of baggage and air cargo, water and waste, cabin service, fuelling and so forth take place. In addition, crews, maintenance and other ground personnel access the aircraft during the 'turn' (turnaround) time on the ramp.

As well as the high workloads on the ramp, many other activities such as load control, flight planning, dispatch and flight following are also taking place – behind the scenes, as it were. These emphasize the planning, correct loading and balancing of aircraft to ensure efficient handling on the ground, as well as processes to ensure safety in flight. The final chapters of this part give the reader detailed synopses of what happens on a typical flight, from the perspective of a Pilot, a Flight Attendant and a passenger.

13 Ramp operations

Matthew Franzi

Ramp operations and the importance of the ramp

Also known as the 'apron', the ramp is the area outside the airport terminal in which an aircraft is serviced as a function of its arrival or impending departure. Generally speaking, the ramp is a highly dynamic, variable and hazardous environment that requires the effective sequencing of a range of activities to ensure continued safe and efficient airline operations. As is often said in the industry, an aircraft doesn't make any money on the ground; therefore, the sooner it can get airborne the better for business. This adage is one of the founding principles for ramp operations, which if managed poorly not only impact an airline's financial viability but can place very expensive assets at risk and – more importantly – endanger the lives of passengers, crew and other airport personnel.

Despite the variable and hazard-rich environment of the ramp, technological advances in aircraft ground handling have, at best, been limited. Whether this is a function of limited regulation of ramp operations, restricted competition amongst service providers, cost management, a preferential focus towards developing flight operations and maintenance practices, or a factor of socioeconomics, is unclear. Arguably it is function of all of these and others. What is clear is the strategic opportunity for ground handling companies or airlines which handle their own aircraft to provide a sustainable competitive advantage through the provision of efficient, consistent and safe ramp operations. With ramp accidents costing the industry a reported US$10 billion per annum and an estimated 243,000 injuries per year,[1] improvements to practices will undoubtedly leave organizations in a much stronger position than their competitors. This excludes the obvious and far more operationally advantageous outcome of on-time and efficient turnarounds. This chapter will explore the various functions of ramp operations, including airport infrastructure requirements, and the processes and equipment required for aircraft arrival, servicing and departure, as well as the safety considerations for ramp operations including industry regulations and standards.

Functional elements of ramp operations

Airport infrastructure and aircraft parking

Airport infrastructure to support aircraft parking and servicing varies significantly; it is not merely a matter of providing a paved and appropriately line marked (painted) surface for the aircraft to taxi to and park. The first and immediate consideration is the aircraft type that is operated, with its size and weight being the primary restrictions. For example, consider the three aircraft types below: the SAAB 340B, the Airbus A320 and the Airbus A380.

Generally speaking, large international airports will be able to support commercial aircraft types of all sizes, although with the introduction of the A380 many were required to upgrade their infrastructure (runways, taxiways, parking bays) and facilities (terminals, aerobridges) to support it. However, secondary or domestic airports may not have parking bays wide or long enough to accommodate all aircraft types. Alternatively, an aircraft such as the A380 may consume two adjacent parking bays limiting the overall number of aircraft that can be serviced at any one time. Conversely, airport planners will be able to accommodate more than one SAAB 340B on the same parking bay. Aircraft weight is also a critical consideration for airport infrastructure and aircraft parking.

For all civilian airports that handle aircraft of more than 5,700kg, the International Civil Aviation Organization (ICAO) requires the airports to determine the strength of the pavement, known as its bearing strength.[2] The bearing strength of pavement relates to the overall weight the pavement can withstand without deformation, and is also a function of the materials used in its foundation or subgrade. Pavement strength is represented as a Pavement Classification Number (PCN) with all aircraft having a corresponding Aircraft Classification Number (ACN). An aircraft can operate to an airport provided its ACN is equal to or less

Table 13.1 Comparison of aircraft types

Aircraft	Seating	Length	Wingspan
SAAB 340B	34	20m	21m
Airbus A320	186	38m	36m
Airbus A380	470-544*	73m	80m

* based on 3 class configuration

Table 13.2 Comparison of aircraft weights

Aircraft	Maximum take-off weight
SAAB 340B	13,155kg
Airbus A320	77,000kg
Airbus A380	575,000kg

than the reported PCN. This plays a crucial role in infrastructure assessments for aircraft handling. Assuming an aircraft can operate to a particular airport, the first question relevant to ramp operations is how the aircraft will park. Will the aircraft be parked at the terminal or on a remote 'stand-off' bay? Does the airport have technology such as 'Nose in Guidance Systems' (NIGS)[3] to assist with accurate aircraft parking, or do ground personnel need to manually 'marshal' flight crew to the correct parking position using hand signals?

If at the terminal, will the aircraft be serviced by an aerobridge or will stairs be used with the passengers embarking and disembarking via the ramp area itself? Will multiple doors be used for passengers (e.g., forward and aft cabin doors)? For an airline, these are fundamental questions that define the airline's levels of service, operational efficiency (e.g., using two cabin doors for passengers to board or de-plane is faster than one), and ultimately cost. Airports will typically charge a premium for the use of aerobridges, which, with the rise of low-cost carriers (LCCs), has seen the transition to increasing usage of stand-off bays and push-up or mobile passenger stairs. Irrespective of the airport's design, layout and infrastructure, the key principle for airlines and ground handling agents alike is the need to tailor the operation to each location. As much as organizations endeavour to keep their practices and processes consistent, failure to adapt and mould their operation to the local environment will result in operational inefficiencies and ultimately a deterioration in the quality of the service.

Arriving aircraft

Parking bay layout and set-up

Prior to the arrival of any aircraft, ground personnel must ensure that the bay itself is ready to receive the aircraft. This consists of ensuring there are no vehicles or other ground service equipment (GSE) obstructing the aircraft's path. There are usually markings on the ground such as painted 'equipment limit lines' behind which all equipment has to be positioned until the aircraft has parked on the bay. Furthermore, ground personnel may perform a visual sweep of the parking bay surface to identify and remove any Foreign Object Debris (FOD) that may damage the aircraft on arrival or become a projectile due to an aircraft engine's jet blast or propeller wash. Ground personnel will also ensure any NIGS is set up correctly for the particular aircraft type and/or ensure a ground marshaller is present. To maximize the efficiency of the turnaround, ground personnel will pre-position as much of the necessary servicing equipment at the parking bay as possible. This could include:

- aircraft scissor-lift and belt loader(s)
- empty baggage barrows or dollies for arriving baggage and cargo
- the next flight's baggage and cargo containers or barrows
- passenger stair(s)
- ambulatory vehicle or a Passenger Assisted Lift device

- potable water servicing equipment
- aircraft waste servicing equipment
- refuelling truck
- catering vehicle(s)
- ground power unit(s)
- preconditioned air unit(s)
- air start unit
- pushback/tow vehicle.

Receipt

Aircraft receipt involves the process of the aircraft taxiing into an aircraft parking bay and coming to a complete stop, and the shutting down of the aircraft's engines. This process involves effective coordination and communication between the flight crew and personnel on the ground, and may involve verbal or visual communication techniques, or both. As mentioned previously, depending on the airport infrastructure, the flight crew may be guided to the correct parking position via automated visual guidance docking systems (VGDSs) or via a ground marshaller. When a ground marshaller is used, the International Air Transport Association (IATA) has established standard aircraft marshalling hand signals which are globally recognized and adopted. A marshaller will generally have some form of visually identifiable clothing to indicate they are the marshaller, and use some form of lighted batons or table-tennis-type bats for signalling to aircraft. It is important to note that whilst flight crew maintain the overall responsibility for aircraft safety, receipt personnel are critical in ensuring the safety of the operation and for other ground personnel not directly involved in that aircraft's servicing. Examples may include the detection of an aircraft fluid leak or fire, or the identification of an impending collision with another aircraft or vehicle/equipment.

Generally speaking, once an aircraft has come to a stop in its allocated space (usually identifiable via a painted stop line marked on the ground), receipt personnel will place wheel chocks at the relevant aircraft wheels and make contact with the flight crew. At this point the flight crew will shut down the aircraft engines and the receipt personnel will give clearance to the remainder of the ground handling personnel that servicing of the aircraft can safely commence. Airlines have a standard practice of using the aircraft's anti-collision beacon mounted externally (using one above and one below the fuselage) to indicate to ground personnel whether it is safe to approach the aircraft or not; if active, the aircraft is unsafe to approach; if extinguished, the aircraft is safe to approach.

Aircraft servicing

Overall turnaround coordination on the ramp

As other chapters of this book provide comprehensive details of aircraft loading, cargo and baggage management, this will not be further explored in detail.

However, it is particularly important to note that all of these processes and others are activities that necessitate strong and effective coordination on the ramp. Airlines employ a variety of methods to ensure ground servicing activities are coordinated, particularly on the ramp. Many airlines and ground handlers utilize a 'Turnaround Coordinator' who may be responsible for one or more flights at a time. Such a role generally provides the overarching direction and oversight of turnaround activities, and as defined by IATA, successful performance of the role will (a) enhance safety management of the turnaround process; (b) improve punctuality performance through adherence to a standard timing schedule; and (c) ensure continuing compliance with company procedures and processes.[4] This role generally coordinates all parties in the turnaround of an aircraft and includes oversight of both 'above wing' (i.e., passenger handling) and 'below wing' (i.e., ramp) activities. Importantly, this individual will coordinate the various contractors and organizations involved in the turnaround. For example, many full-service network airlines, and nearly all LCCs, utilize third-party catering organizations to service their aircraft, and another contractor supplies and handles fuelling activities. The turnaround coordinator is responsible for ensuring their timely and accurate provision of agreed services. Considering the fact that on any one turnaround there could be different organizations providing aircraft loading services, passenger handling, fuelling, de-icing, pushback services, catering, cleaning, security and aircraft maintenance activities, it is not surprising that at times airlines suffer from poor punctuality.

For ramp-specific oversight and coordination, airlines (again) use a variety of methods and/or roles. Generally speaking, the loading supervisor or load controller provides the leadership and coordination of aircraft loading related activities. This includes baggage and cargo onload/offload, passenger stairs positioning and any required potable water and aircraft waste servicing. Where ramp coordination is often challenged is with catering and cleaning services; as mentioned above it is common for these services to be provided by another organization, with its own frontline leadership and supervisory structure. Ramp coordination can be further hindered when additional ramp services are provided by different organizations, such as aircraft pushback/towing and dispatch (requiring ground–cockpit headset communication).

Globally, airlines combat the lack of clear delineation for ramp coordination through the use of a Precision Timing Schedule (PTS). The PTS provides a documented timeline, shared across all relevant ground handling parties, which provides a detailed breakdown of the specific activities that are to occur on a standard turnaround. Airlines generally develop multiple PTSs that outline more or less detail and roles dependent on the audience; for example, there will usually be a PTS that includes all flight and cabin crew activity as well as passenger handling, ramp servicing, catering and cleaning. In other cases, they may provide third-party organizations with a scaled back version of the PTS that relates to their activities only. There will also be several versions of the PTS depending on whether it is the aircraft's first flight of the day or if it is a turnaround at an airport that is not the base of the airline or aircraft (e.g., an outstation). Irrespective and most importantly, the PTS defines *when* specific activities are to occur and by whom. A PTS will usually also include the 'critical path', which highlights the mandatory activities that need to be completed before other activities can commence.

Passenger boarding/disembarkation (aerobridge/stairs)

As mentioned previously, airlines can adopt one of two methods for passenger boarding and disembarkation: via an aerobridge directly connected to the terminal or via the use of mobile passenger stairs. From a passenger perspective, aerobridges provide the most convenient solution. Aerobridges provide protection from adverse weather conditions as well as limiting their exposure to the relatively loud ambient noise of the ramp. For airlines, aerobridges also provide benefits in reducing the overall safety risk to passengers during embarkation and disembarkation. Heavy vehicular movements – and indeed aircraft movements – in the ramp environment require firm passenger marshalling and control to ensure their safety when transiting between the aircraft and terminal. This also has the potential to increase the overall resource requirements for handling the aircraft with a dedicated marshaller on the ramp for the duration of the passenger disembarkation/embarkation process. Furthermore, exposing passengers to inclement weather conditions such as rain and ice/snow introduces the risk of slips/trips/falls on the tarmac or motion of the mobile passenger stairs themselves. The use of aerobridges also limits the need for specialist equipment to support passengers with specific needs boarding aircraft, such as passengers with wheelchairs. Additionally, aerobridges are almost exclusively the property of the airport authority, and as such the costs and management of maintenance programs are the responsibility of the airport, not the airline.

The immediate downside of using aerobridges is usually the usage cost to the airlines, with airport authorities recovering costs and gaining some profit. Depending on the airline's service model, this may be immaterial or considered part of the ticket price for a premium service offering. However, as mentioned earlier, this 'luxury' is wherever possible avoided by true LCCs. To compound the challenge to the LCC approach that predominantly utilize single aisle, narrow-body aircraft such as the B737 and A320, aerobridges can only service a single cabin door on the aircraft, impeding the speed by which passengers can embark and disembark the aircraft. Some airports allow the utilization of an aerobridge on the forward cabin door and mobile stairs on the rear cabin door (with those passengers traversing the ramp to the terminal). However, this is not common, particularly at international airports. Given that many LCCs target 30- (or even 25-) minute turnaround times, the utilization of two cabin doors for boarding is a matter of necessity. To counteract the cost and limitations of aerobridge usage, airlines can seek to utilize parking bays that require mobile passenger stairs (motorized or manual), acknowledging that the acquisition of these assets also comes at a price; ranging between $20,000 USD for a manual push-up set of stairs to beyond $200,000 USD for motorized passenger stairs with a canopy. These bays may be immediately adjacent to terminal facilities whereby passengers are able to walk directly to/from the terminal boarding gate to the aircraft, or they may be stand-off bays that require passenger transport, such as buses. This latter option increases the complexity, time and cost of passenger handling, so there is clearly a trade-off to be made by the airline when considering which option is best for their operation.

Fuelling

In relative terms, common commercial aircraft fuel, such as JET-A1, is not a significantly volatile product. That being said, the sheer volume of fuel that is utilized, coupled with the very high temperatures of aircraft and GSE components with which it can come into contact, does pose a very real risk. A good example of this is an accident in 2007 involving a B737 that caught fire due to fuel leaking onto one of the aircraft's engine exhausts shortly after stopping at its designated parking bay at Naha Airport (Okinawa), Japan. Whilst fortunately no one was injured in the event, the aircraft was completely destroyed in a very short time; indeed, the time between the fire starting near one of the engines and the first massive explosion that engulfed the majority of the aircraft was three minutes and fifty seconds.[5]

Safety considerations for aircraft refuelling are primary and important considerations during ground handling, with state regulators imposing operational restrictions that differ globally. Some regulators, such as Australia's Civil Aviation Safety Authority (CASA) allow operators to conduct refuelling with passengers on board, provided appropriate risk controls are in place, such as, for example, ensuring passengers do not fasten their seatbelts during refuelling. Another consideration if refuelling is allowed with passengers on board is the risk to passengers embarking/disembarking from the aircraft via the tarmac, taking into account the emergency egress route of the fuelling equipment, particularly when both are occurring on the same side of the aircraft (usually the left-hand side). However, this practice is beneficial for airlines in terms of punctuality and efficiency as it removes refuelling from the critical path of the PTS (i.e., refuelling and passenger embarking/disembarking can be done in parallel, not in sequence). Other regulators, such as the Civil Aviation Authority of Vietnam, require a fire truck to be present during refuelling with passengers on board which, typically, is charged back to the airlines. Others still simply prohibit the practice.

Irrespective, there are other safety considerations from a ramp personnel perspective. Aircraft refuelling is provided by one of two means, either via a fuel hydrant truck that acts as a mobile pump, drawing its fuel from underground tanks, or via a fuel tanker truck. Effective sequencing of vehicular movement, and strict procedures for ramp personnel for driving in the vicinity of fuelling equipment (particularly fuel hydrant trucks, which will have fuel transfer hoses on the ground), are paramount. Given both fuel delivery systems require vehicles in very close proximity to or even under the wings of the aircraft they are serving, it is common practice to prohibit other vehicles from driving under aircraft wings. Furthermore, standard industry guidelines, such as those defined by IATA, specify a 'Fuelling Safety Zone' in which equipment performing aircraft servicing functions (e.g., aircraft loaders, baggage tractors) and any portable electronic devices (e.g., mobile phones, radios) should not be positioned or used within three metres of refuelling vehicles and aircraft fuel systems such as wing vents.[6]

Potable water and waste servicing

All commercial aircraft have a potable water uplift capability servicing the cabin and its associated amenities, and, depending on aircraft size, the total uplift volume can be over 2,000 litres. Access to safe drinking water is an essential human need, and as an industry, commercial aviation follows a consistent set of standards to ensure the source of potable water, potable water delivery systems and the aircraft storage tanks themselves are free from contamination. These standards are derived from the World Health Organization's guidelines for potable water. Local and individual airline standards define the testing requirements for water source, delivery systems and aircraft tanks to ensure the quality of potable water, with all three elements incorporating maintenance and cleaning programs. Aircraft potable water is delivered via mobile water tankers and although aircraft fittings vary, the process for potable water servicing is relatively consistent. The most fundamental requirement is ensuring that the delivery system is not contaminated from other servicing equipment or personnel, most notably those involved in aircraft waste servicing. Industry norms require that potable water is always serviced prior to the aircraft waste system. Furthermore, ground handlers are required to ensure segregation of potable water and waste servicing equipment when in storage; this is typically achieved by marking designated parking areas for both types of equipment. Aircraft waste servicing involves draining, flushing and replenishing the toilet waste tanks of the aircraft. Whilst considered an unpleasant element of ramp operations, failure to appropriately complete servicing an aircraft's waste system can lead (and has led) to toilets becoming unserviceable in flight, resulting in unnecessary in-flight diversions which impact on both operational cost and customer satisfaction levels. Waste servicing equipment involves either a waste truck or a servicing cart that is towed into place for smaller aircraft. For larger aircraft, a waste truck is generally required for two reasons: the capacity of the aircraft's waste system, and reaching the aircraft waste system's access panel, which is generally much higher off the ground, in some cases requiring a lift/hoist to access.

Departing aircraft

Pushback, remote controlled pushback, power out

At the end of aircraft loading and servicing activities, aircraft can dispatch from the gate through a variety of means. The traditional and most frequent approach is the process of aircraft pushback, using either a pushback tractor connected to the aircraft nose wheel via a tow bar or a 'tow-bar-less' tractor that connects to the aircraft nose wheel directly, usually lifting the nose wheel off the ground. In both circumstances, it is the pushback vehicle that provides the steering for the aircraft, not the aircraft itself. Once appropriate two-way communication with the flight deck has been established (either via intercom/headset or hand signals) and the aircraft has been given pushback clearance from Air Traffic Control (ATC), the pushback vehicle will reverse the aircraft onto the aircraft movement area/taxiway, before disconnecting from the aircraft and allowing it to manoeuvre under its own power.

Consistent with all ramp activities, there are a number of safety considerations to be accounted for during this process. The first is ensuring that the aircraft nose wheel steering system has been appropriately disabled to prevent inadvertent activation by the flight crew, which could result in either serious injury to dispatch personnel on the ground or damage to the nose wheel itself. This is commonly achieved through the installation of a 'nose wheel steering bypass pin' in the nose gear; a procedure actioned by the dispatch personnel. During the pushback itself, dispatch personnel (who may be engineering or ramp personnel) on the ground are responsible for ensuring the aircraft is clear of conflict with other aircraft, vehicles and personnel adjacent to and/or behind their aircraft. This is particularly important because the flight crew will have very limited to nil visibility of the aircraft's surroundings during this process, and are entirely dependent on the dispatch personnel for ensuring aircraft separation. Finally, dispatch personnel provide visual assurance during aircraft engine start procedures that systems are operating normally. With intercom/headset communication or hand signals with the flight deck, dispatch personnel are able to advise of signs of smoke, fire, fluid leaks or other abnormal conditions; often much faster than can be detected by aircraft systems or the flight crew.

An alternative method to the traditional pushback is the use of remote controlled pushback equipment that is connected to one of the aircraft's main gears. Such vehicles are available for commercial aircraft in size up to the larger single-aisle jet aircraft, such as the B737-900 or A321. In this circumstance, the aircraft's nose wheel steering is still enabled, with the flight crew providing the directional steering during the pushback on command from the ground dispatcher. These vehicles can be disconnected from the aircraft remotely at the completion of the pushback and subsequently recovered by the dispatch personnel once the aircraft has commenced taxi. This pushback method is appealing to many organizations, as it halves the minimum number of personnel to complete the pushback (i.e., traditional pushback requires a tractor driver and a dispatcher; remote pushback requires only the dispatcher) and removes the need for pushback tow bars (which have their own servicing needs). The downside is that unlike conventional pushback tractors, remote controlled vehicles cannot be utilized for other functions such as aircraft towing.

The simplest method available is known as 'aircraft power out', whereby the aircraft has sufficient room on the parking bay to move and turn around under its own power. Obviously if the aircraft has parked at a bay directly opposite the terminal and is serviced by an aerobridge, this option is unlikely to be feasible. However, it is a method readily used on stand-off bays. It is unsurprising that this is a preferred method for LCCs, as the capital investment needed is nil (i.e., no pushback tractors required) and process-wise it is very simple, typically requiring only one ground staff member to support the activity. Finally, and very rarely utilized today, is the method of aircraft power-back whereby the aircraft uses its own reverse engine thrust to reverse the aircraft away from the parking position under guidance from ground personnel. There are a number of significant safety considerations associated with such a practice, which has largely become prohibited, including the risks of foreign object damage to engines, the fuselage, the terminal itself or injuring ground personnel, and of course, there is unnecessary wear and tear on the engines.

Safety considerations for the ramp

Environmental conditions

The environment plays an enormous role in defining how activities on the ramp are performed. Whilst all industries that maintain outdoor activities are affected by the weather, the aviation industry is particularly affected because of the large open areas of airports, the size of the equipment being manoeuvred and the expected continuation of airport activity in nearly all scenarios. Whether it is a clear and sunny afternoon or at night in the midst of a snowstorm, the dynamic and often unpredictable nature of the weather is a risk which ramp personnel must constantly assess and adapt to. All airports and ground handling organizations will have a 'severe weather' policy and procedures that outline the activities that can and cannot be performed in particular weather scenarios, some of which are described below.

Strong wind

Strong wind is usually defined as a wind in excess of thirty-five knots (sixty-four km/h) and creates a variety of hazards to ramp personnel. First, all light or tall GSE needs to be either appropriately restrained or removed from the ramp environment to ensure they are not blown over or become projectiles/FOD around the airport. Examples include push up passenger stairs and Unit Load Devices (ULDs). The loading of aircraft should also cease for this very reason, as ULDs have been known to blow off the top of an aircraft loader. Rolling stock (ULD trailers/dollies) should be chocked to prevent movement. In strong winds special considerations are also needed for aircraft. All aircraft have limitations for the wind speed in which passenger and cargo doors can be opened and closed. Depending on the wind direction and the aircraft weight, aircraft may need to be tied down or additional wheel chocks positioned to prevent the aircraft from 'cocking' into the wind.

Thunderstorms

Personnel on the ramp are particularly vulnerable to lightning, with limited cover available and a variety of metal objects, including aircraft, to attract the lightning. In monitoring the position of thunderstorms, airport operators typically have a three-phased approach to operational stand-down to ensure all personnel in the ramp environment have opportunity to seek shelter prior to the arrival of lightning. A variety of methods are used to communicate the three phases to ramp personnel, including use of handheld radios, messaging on flight screens or through a lightning warning system installed around the ramp area.

- Phase 1 – Alert Phase – The Alert Phase is triggered when a storm with known lightning activity is within a specified distance from the airport, usually five to ten nautical miles. The Alert Phase is a monitoring phase, designed to alert personnel on the ramp that a shutdown of operations is possible.
- Phase 2 – Operational Shutdown – The shutdown phase begins when the storm is within five nautical miles and results in the cessation of all ramp activity, with personnel expected to seek shelter immediately. This includes passengers in the process of boarding or disembarking an aircraft. Furthermore, personnel using ground headset intercom systems with aircraft are required to cease using this method of communication, as the individual can act as a grounding point in the event lightning strikes the aircraft they are servicing.
- Phase 3 – Cancellation Phase – Once the storm has passed and is more than five nautical miles from the airport, operations can resume, but a monitoring phase is still in place in the event the storm changes direction.

Snow and ice

Snow and ice can make ground handling activities extremely difficult and hazardous. Airports that are susceptible to such conditions are typically well resourced to combat these conditions and ensure the airport remains open, including the use of de-icing treatments on apron surfaces. However, in terms of ramp operations, the hazard cannot be eliminated and so personnel need to alter driving and equipment handling techniques to account for the limited traction and high weights of vehicles and equipment. Snow and ice also makes many metal surfaces very slippery for personnel working at heights such as aircraft loaders and aircraft passenger stairs. Furthermore, it is likely that there will be times of reduced visibility on the ramp as snowstorms pass through, which further increases the risks in such a congested environment as the ramp.

Operational standardization

Historically, operational and safety regulations for ramp operations have been largely undefined, with the majority of ramp regulation left to individual airport authorities to determine policies and practices. This has led previously to significant variance across airlines, which makes operational consistency for ground handling organizations that support multiple airlines extremely difficult. Although aircraft manufacturers provide airlines with a framework for aircraft handling, it has been commercial aviation's principle organization, IATA, that has been the driving force behind operational standardization on the ramp. In 2003, the IATA Operational Standards Audit (IOSA) framework was formally introduced, with operational standards focusing on eight areas of operational safety for airlines:

- Corporate Organization and Management Systems
- Flight Operations
- Operational Control and Flight Dispatch
- Aircraft Engineering and Maintenance
- Cabin Operations
- Ground Handling Operations
- Cargo Operations
- Security Management.[7]

Although originally intended to satisfy codeshare arrangements by providing a consistent set of operational standards for airlines to be measured against, they have become an operational baseline that is almost universally accepted. With respect to ramp operations, the IOSA Standards and Recommended Practices detail requirements for management system elements to support ramp operations or specific ramp procedures, such as procedures for aircraft loading, fuelling, aircraft receipt and dispatch, de-icing/anti-icing, and emergency situations (such as fires).

Coupled with the IOSA Standards, IATA have developed the IATA Safety Audit of Ground Operations (ISAGO) program which is an 'internationally recognized and accepted system for assessing the operational management and control systems of an organization that provides ground handling services for airlines'.[8] Similarly, with IOSA, the standards provide the framework of ground handling consistency amongst organizations. Given their specific orientation towards ground handling, the ISAGO standards provide a far more comprehensive set of operational requirements than any other regulatory or industry standard available; and from a ground handling organization perspective are considered the 'gold standard' of operations.

Safety and quality management for ramp operations

The notion of an embedded Safety Management System (SMS) within an organization arose in the early 2000s, with the air transport industry initially focused on airlines and airport operators. Many of these considered the cost of implementation too prohibitive for all functions and support services such as ground handling organizations. However, as the former Chief Executive

Officer of Flight Safety Foundation, William Voss, once wrote, an SMS is simply designed to ask, and support answering, four questions:

- What are your key risks or what is most likely to be your next accident?
- How do you know they are your key risks?
- What are you doing about it?
- Is it working?[9]

In view of this, there is not only a practical and valuable need for such a framework, but for organizations that are either IOSA or ISAGO registered, an integrated SMS is mandatory. As SMS is touched upon in Chapter 18, it will not be detailed here, but specific to ramp operations, an SMS supports a number of key activities including:

- operational occurrence and hazard reporting
- investigation of incidents and accidents to identify causality and prevent recurrence
- assessing and defining of mitigation strategies for risks in the operation, at a local or organizational level (e.g., introduction of new ground service equipment or a new procedure)
- the establishment of an audit program to proactively identify issues in the operation of the management system
- a process to effectively manage change in the operation to ensure safety is not compromised or degraded with the change
- the implementation of a 'Just Culture' that recognizes human error is inevitable, with people being encouraged to identify and report errors without fear, while acknowledging that reckless violations will not be tolerated.

Conclusion

Ramp operations is a complex, high-hazard and varying environment that requires vigilance and a strong orientation towards coordination to ensure the reliable servicing of aircraft. Largely forgotten in the regulatory context, it has been left to the industry to strive for operational consistency and standardization. Whilst the efforts of industry bodies such as IATA have gone a long way to achieving this outcome, the frequency of ground accidents and personnel injuries demonstrates there is much further to go. As regulators and the aviation industry as a whole continue to propagate and mature safety management thinking, it is foreseeable that operations on the ramp will continue to improve. Considering the frequency of personnel injury and the costs of ramp accidents, continuous improvement of ramp operations and the organizations that conduct it is arguably a necessity.

Notes

1 Lacagnina M 2007, 'Defusing the Ramp', *AeroSafety World*, May 2007, Flight Safety Foundation, pp. 20–24
2 Cooperative Development of Operational Safety and Continuing Airworthiness (COSCAP) 1999, *Aerodrome Standards: Aerodrome Design and Operations*, International Civil Aviation Organization, Montreal
3 Also known as Visual Guidance Docking Systems or VGDS
4 International Air Transport Association 2016a, *Airport Handling Manual*, 36th edn, International Air Transport Association, Montreal
5 Japan Transport Safety Board 2009, *Aircraft Accident Investigation Report: AA2009-7, China Airlines B18616,* Japan Transport Safety Board, Tokyo
6 International Air Transport Association 2016a, *Airport Handling Manual*, 36th edn, International Air Transport Association, Montreal
7 International Air Transport Association 2016b, *IOSA Standards Manual*, 10th edn, rev. 1, International Air Transport Association, Montreal
8 International Air Transport Association 2016c, *ISAGO Standards Manual,* 5th edn, International Air Transport Association, Montreal
9 Voss, W 2012, 'SMS Reconsidered', *AeroSafety World,* May 2012, Flight Safety Foundation

14 Baggage processes

Rik Movig

Introduction

To understand the baggage handling process and its challenges, it is necessary first to understand what baggage is. In short, baggage is almost everything and anything a passenger brings on their flight. However, there are some restrictions. These are usually based on safety regulations and/or feasibility. For instance, it is not allowed (anywhere in the world) to bring explosive devices, chemicals, batteries, or anything else that can pose a fire or explosive risk for the aircraft. Exceptions like weapons are allowed under strict conditions. With regard to feasibility, it can be a challenge to fit a bicycle (non-foldable) or a wheelchair in the smallest types of aircraft. The passenger is more aware of the commercial restrictions of the airline such as the baggage allowance: how many bags, what weight is allowed as hold baggage, what the cabin baggage allowance is, and what the cost of excess baggage such as sports equipment, etc., is. Of course, the passenger will sooner or later become aware of the restrictions concerning battery-powered devices, such as hover boards and other appliances using lithium-based batteries.

Baggage categories

In the baggage handling process, it is common to distinguish between different types of baggage. These different types or categories are as follows:

- normal baggage
- hold baggage
- hand baggage, carry-on/cabin bags
- odd size (ODD)
- out of gauge (OOG)
- pets (animal vivant in hold – AVIH)
- wheelchairs, sports goods (bikes, surfboards, etc.)
- dangerous goods (weapons, chemicals, etc.)
- baggage taken/collected at the gate.

Normal baggage

Normal or regular baggage is considered to be luggage, suitcases, trunks, boxes or bags of a more or less rectangular shape, not being odd size (see below). Normal baggage can be rigid (hard-shell suitcase) or deformable within limits (duffel or equipment bags), and fits within the general dimensions applicable to each specific baggage handling area.

Hold baggage

Hold baggage, checked in by the passenger at the check-in desk, or baggage drop area, can be transported in bulk by a baggage handling system to its make-up location. This is the most efficient method of transporting and sorting all checked in (and transfer) hold baggage. Approximately ninety-five per cent of all baggage items is processed this way, and for baggage handling, it requires relatively few people to transport and sort numerous bags from an input area to an output area. Designing or developing a baggage handling system that allows for all types, sizes and weights of baggage to be handled is very expensive. Therefore, there are some restrictions with regard to which hold baggage can and cannot be transported by the baggage system.

Hand baggage, carry-on/cabin bags

All smaller items a passenger takes with them into the cabin is considered hand baggage, or 'carry-on' cabin bags. In general, there are restrictions as to weight and dimensions of these bags and to the number of extra items allowed to be brought along as hand baggage, and this varies considerably according to airline policy and/or type of aircraft. Also to be considered is the policy relating to inclusion or otherwise of items such as hairsprays, batteries, certain mobile phones, musical instruments, crutches, and even animals.

Odd size (ODD)

Odd-size baggage is hold baggage which cannot be transported by the automated baggage handling system. This includes anything that is obviously too large to transport by the conveyors, or which would not be appropriate to transport by conveyors, such as pets, sports equipment, wheelchairs, etc. Other examples include trolleys, buggies, (parts of) child booster seats, rolled sleeping bags, cans of paint, animal kennels, and unlocked, unsecured (tool) boxes. Odd size is simply anything that is either too small/light, too large/heavy, or too unwieldy for the automated baggage handling system to process. Further, odd-size baggage is baggage which clearly and visibly:

- may roll or run a risk of rolling on its own
- may open easily on its own

- has protruding or hooked edges
- contains live creatures
- contains liquids, chemicals, noxious/poisonous or flammable/explosive substances
- is fragile (i.e. the casing, not the contents)
- may damage personnel and/or the baggage handling system through sharp or pointed edges
- is constructed of multiple loosely attached items.

Odd-size baggage will be transported 'manually' from the check-in desk to the aircraft. The handler will have a process in place with personnel collecting odd-size items, and transporting them according to all regulations (such as security screening) to the destination location, which makes it a very labour-intensive and time-consuming process.

Out of gauge (OOG)

Out-of-gauge (OOG) baggage is normal baggage which either exceeds or falls outside the physical dimensions (length, width, height and weight) permitted for automated baggage handling. They are typically bags and trunks that *seem* to be transportable, but due to the specifics of the baggage handling system, are filtered out close to the entry point of the system. OOG items will typically be a little too long, too thick, too thin, or (much) too heavy. Out-of-gauge *hold* baggage is usually incorporated in the odd-size process.

Pets

Many passengers travel with pets. Pets can travel in the cabin or in the hold, but only pets which are checked in to travel in the hold of the aircraft are part of the baggage handling domain. They are considered 'odd size' as it is considered inappropriate to handle them through the automated baggage handling system. Pets also require specific loading in special holds to ensure their safety and comfort, and may need specific attendance during flight turnarounds, especially if they transit through ports on long-haul flights, and are exposed to very hot or very cold weather conditions.

Wheelchairs, sporting goods

Some specific types of odd-size baggage require manual handling from entry point to exit point, thereby bypassing the automated baggage handling system. They also have specific loading requirements, as they need to be tied down or loaded into special containers and/or holds. A special type of 'odd size' are wheelchairs, which can come in as many varieties as the passengers to whom they belong. Wheelchairs may become available for the baggage handling process at check in (odd size counter), or at the gate, should the passenger request to proceed to the gate in their own wheelchair. Battery-powered wheelchairs require specific loading instructions to comply with flight safety regulations.

Large odd-size items such as large sporting goods (bicycles, surfboards) may not fit into regular baggage containers and therefore require either special extra-large (XL) containers or need to be loaded separately in the bulk hold. However, smaller aircraft types will have restrictions as to the feasibility of transporting large odd-size items, which may have implications for the passenger's flight booking.

Dangerous goods

Items that may pose a risk on board an aircraft are not allowed in hold (or hand) baggage. There are exceptions to this rule, such as, for instance, weapons and specific chemicals, like medicines. These are items needing to be registered separately and packaged to conform with the rules of the airline and/or country. Also, they need to be accompanied by specific international transportation documents. These items are detected by screening machines, and passengers failing to comply will be confronted with the loss of these items and heavy fines.

Hand baggage and other items that can be taken to/collected at the gate

In some cases, passengers will bring hand baggage (carry on/cabin baggage) and several other items to the gate, most of which will be stowed in the cabin overhead bins or under the seats. Typically, strollers and baby carriers will be collected at the gate to be stowed in the bulk hold of the aircraft. Excess hand baggage can also be collected at the gate due to any discrepancy between stowage space in the cabin and the amount/volume of hand baggage for the specific flight. The process of collecting excess baggage, strollers and wheelchairs at the gate to be stowed in the hold is a combined effort by the handling teams at the departure gate and on the ramp.

The baggage handling process

The handling process commences when the handler (airline) takes the baggage from the passenger, and ceases at the moment the baggage is returned to them. The process generally is as follows:

- A passenger checks in a bag at the airport (self-service) check-in counter.
- Once the bag is tagged and registered, it is transported via conveyors to the 'make-up' location of the flight. This can be a lateral or a carousel from which a baggage handling employee will take the bag to put it into a cart or a container, but it could also be an automated loading unit of which there are several varieties.
- When all bags are loaded into carts/containers they are driven to the ramp/ apron to be loaded into the hold of the aircraft. Worldwide regulations require passengers and bags to travel together on the same aircraft to the

destination. While the aircraft is loaded and passengers are boarding, this requirement is monitored.

- At the *final* destination, bags are unloaded from the aircraft and transported to a baggage unloading quay – a conveyer that transports the bags to the reclaim area where the passenger retrieves his/her baggage from the reclaim belt. In the case of a transfer at a port, the bag is transported from an unloading quay to the make-up location of the next flight.

Exceptions to this process

There are many exceptions to the above process. For instance:

- The check-in and collection of the hold baggage of the passenger can take place at a remote location like a hotel, or a cruise ship. An extension to this is the 'door-to-door' service.
- A handler can also collect hand (carry-on) baggage from passengers at the departure gate which is then further processed as hold baggage. Odd-size items are handled separately from regular bags. Not only do they 'not fit' through the baggage handling system, but they often need to be loaded according to specific regulations too.

Baggage handling (sorting) systems

Most passengers do not travel to such remote areas that baggage handling consists of either the passenger or airport personnel carrying the bags to and from the aircraft. Most airports have *some* kind of baggage handling and/or sorting system. Its purpose is simply to automatically transport bags from one or more entry points to one or more exit points. In its simplest form one will see a conveyer directly connected to one output location, maybe even being part of a circular system, where the handler puts the bags on one end, and the passenger takes the bags off at the other end (or vice versa). This is a simple and faultless system that requires no intelligence to deliver the bag to the right location. This system is often seen in reclaim areas. However, where there are many flights of many airlines arriving and departing during the day, one will see more complex baggage handling systems that allow for transportation and sorting of bags from multiple entry points to multiple exit points. The technology of these systems is often similar to package sorting systems. In contrast to the previously mentioned 'simple' system, the more complex system requires in-built intelligence to continuously identify the bag and send it on to the correct location.

What happens at check-in?

Before the bag can be entered into the baggage handling system, several actions need to be taken. The first of these is to verify that the passenger has checked in for the flight. At that time, some basic checks as to transportability of the bag are also performed. The bag is weighed and with simple visual or other aids, its dimensions are checked. Possibly further precautions are taken to ensure proper transport of the bag, such as tying up straps or repacking of bags. If everything conforms, a label is printed and connected (correctly) to the bag, which is then inserted into the baggage system. If not, minor problems are taken care of, or perhaps excess baggage needs to be paid, or in case of issues with transportability through the baggage handling system (e.g., pets, surfboards) the passenger is sent to an 'Odd size' counter.

The baggage label contains information that enables both people and machines to deliver the bag to the right location. Preferably most bags are handled automatically so machines need to be able to 'read' the label. As a bag can be sent to any location anywhere in the world – not restricted to airports only – an international IATA (International Air Transport Association) standard (Resolution 740) defines the required information and layout of the label. All labels have a barcode (licence plate) as well as readable information like the destination code(s) of the bag. At present radio-frequency identification (RFID) is also available in printed labels but RFID-labels are more expensive than regular barcoded labels. Further, the read-success-rate of barcoded labels has improved so much that they are often considered almost as good as RFID. The latest development in baggage labels is 'home tagging': enabling the passenger to attach an electronic label to their bag at home, containing the correct information in the required standardized layout for the passenger's flight(s).

The following information is found on the baggage label (IATA Resolution 740):

- licence plate: this is a ten-digit numeric code on a bag tag issued by a carrier or handling agent at check-in. It is printed on the label in barcode form and in human readable form and is the 'identifier' of the bag during handling and transportation. It also links the bag to the BSM (Baggage source message) sent by a carrier's departure control system to the airport's baggage handling system. This message contains flight details and passenger information
- name of airport of arrival
- departure time
- IATA airport code of airport of arrival
- airline code and flight number
- name of passenger identified with the baggage (last name, first name)
- sometimes additional information such as 'priority', 'short connection', class of travel.

After check-in, the bag disappears into the baggage handling system. Behind the curtains, next to transportation of the bag, several specific processes can take place:

- screening (X-raying) the bag
- storage in an early baggage storage location
- make-up: loading the bag into a container or onto a cart ready for transportation to the aircraft.

Screening (X-raying for explosives)

At each airport, bags of departing passengers are screened for explosives and other dangerous goods before being loaded into the aircraft. Different screening protocols are used all over the world. Each bag carried by air to a specific country or area (e.g., the European union) must be checked according to the requirements of this country/area. However, there are countries/areas that accept each other's screening protocols which reduces the number of times a bag needs to be screened when travelling via multiple airports. These screening protocols and procedures are closely and continuously monitored by national and international agencies. Other screening protocols may also be required to check for agricultural items, drugs, etc.

Early baggage storage area

This is an area where baggage can be stored between the moment of insertion into the baggage system and the moment the bag is required at a make-up location. It is not always found in baggage handling systems, as it is expensive to build and relatively simple to avoid when not too many flights are to be handled at the same time. It is used when there is a lengthy time period between presentation of early bags by the passengers and baggage make-up, before being finally loaded on the aircraft. A passenger would typically find that the (hold baggage) check-in for a flight is (only) open from two or three hours before departure until (almost) scheduled departure time. All bags can be directly transported to the make-up location, loaded onto carts or into containers and driven to the ramp as soon as the aircraft is ready to be loaded. At larger airports where many carriers have flights departing simultaneously all day long, a process called 'common' check-in is used – as opposed to previously described 'dedicated' check-in, where the passenger is not restricted to a specific timeframe to check-in hold baggage, as long as it is checked in by a certain time before departure on the departure day.

As there is now a discrepancy between the time passenger bags are presented to the baggage handling system and the time the bags need to be loaded into containers and carts at make-up, the baggage needs to be stored somewhere in the system. This is when the bags are sent to the early baggage storage system. This also allows for a more efficient use of make-up locations (laterals and/or carousels). In theory, all bags for a specific flight can be collected in the early baggage storage and only when complete are sent to make-up during the minimal time required to load the bags into containers. A mix of dedicated check-in (only check-in during a specific time before departure), common check-in, use of early baggage storage systems and more or less advanced methods of loading bags at make-up will usually be present at each large airport.

Baggage make-up

As mentioned before, at make-up, bags are loaded into containers or onto carts, or other means of transportation to be taken from the baggage handling area to the ramp. In general, a make-up location (lateral, carrousel) is opened for a specific flight during a specific time before departure. Bags entering the system during opening time of the make-up location will be transported straight to this destination. Bags entered into the baggage handling system before opening time of the make-up location will be transported to the early baggage storage location. As soon as the make-up location for the departing flight is opened, the early baggage storage location will release all bags it has in storage for the flight. At the make-up location, loading of the bags is mostly done by manual labour. Around the world many initiatives are taken to minimize the strain on the human body, varying from lifting aids to fully robotized (automated) loading. Before a bag can be put into a container, several checks need to be performed.

- The most important is to verify whether the bag belongs to a passenger who has been checked in for the flight (baggage reconciliation). As a safety rule, bags must fly on the same flight as the passenger, so it is not allowed to load a bag into a container if there is no registration of the passenger check-in in the booking system.
- Separations/subsortations: Due to handling requirements at the destination station of the flight stage and/or requirements of the airline, separations may be required. For instance, all business class bags must be put in a separate container, or all bags that will make a transfer at the destination station must be loaded in another separate container. At the make-up location both reconciliation and separation can be combined. For instance, as a bag drops on the lateral, the handling agent scans the container, which will contain, for example, all economy bags travelling to the end destination, and then they scan the bag tag. The handheld appliance tells the handling agent that the bag is 'ok to load'. This means that the passenger has been checked in for this flight and the bag can be loaded into this container, because it belongs to an economy passenger travelling to the end destination.
- In the background, an IT system registers the fact that this bag is loaded in this container. This and other information is used to complete the baggage data on the load sheet and for advance information message(s) sent to the destination station(s). Another use of this information is for 'track and trace' apps: allowing the passenger to follow the status and location of his/her bag while travelling.

Transportation of bags to the ramp

At some time during the make-up process there will be several containers or carts filled with baggage. Often there is not enough space at the lateral or carrousel, or within the baggage area, to retain all full carts and containers. Space continuously needs to be created for new empty containers so that the process of filling the incomplete (half full) ones can be continued. Also one needs to account for the necessary time to load the containers or bags into the aircraft. Therefore, the full containers and carts must be transported to either the aircraft ramp or, if not available yet, an intermediate location. At the aircraft, the ramp officer will expect the baggage containers to be available at the ramp in time to enable an efficient and continuous loading process until departure. The ramp officer and their crew need time to position the containers correctly in the hold(s) of the aircraft, so most of the containers need to be available for the loading team at least thirty minutes before departure (depending on the size of the aircraft). The last few bags may be delivered shortly before departure but this can easily lead to delays.

The loading of the aircraft follows strict rules of weight and balance (see Chapter 16). The ramp officer/handling agent in charge of loading the aircraft will have instructions as to where to load cargo, baggage, live animals (pets), or wheelchairs, etc. The aircraft, depending on its size, will have several holds for cargo and baggage. The loading instruction report (LIR) serves to ensure the weight of cargo and baggage is evenly spread over these holds in such a way that the aircraft will be optimally balanced for take-off, flight, and landing. Within these restrictions there may be further requirements to enable efficiency in the unloading and further handling at the destination station. For instance, there may be a requirement that transfer baggage with a short connection at the destination station is loaded close to the door, so it comes out first. In general, in larger aircraft, air cargo will be loaded first. Cargo is usually less time-critical in the loading/unloading process than baggage, but one of the most important reasons is that many countries require bags to travel together with the passenger on board the same aircraft (some countries have very advanced screening machines, which allows exceptions to this rule).

As the ramp officer makes sure the containers are placed in the correct position, the passengers will start boarding the aircraft. During the passenger boarding process and as boarding passes are scanned, so the confirmation that all individual bags belong to actual boarded passengers is slowly completed. If all goes well, several minutes before departure all flight administration processes are finalized, resulting in a final load sheet which is sent to the captain of the aircraft. The final load sheet contains all information concerning the load of the aircraft: passengers, cargo and baggage, crew and fuel. Now all doors can be closed and the aircraft is able to depart. In case the finalization process shows a passenger (who has baggage loaded) 'is missing', meaning that they have not boarded the aircraft, the baggage must be offloaded. This means the ramp handling agent has to find the bag(s) of the missing passenger and remove it/ them from the aircraft. This can require a lot of unloading and reloading of bags which can cause a significant delay. Only after the bags of the missing passenger have been removed from the aircraft can the flight depart.

Arrival at destination

Unloading the aircraft doesn't follow such strict rules as loading, except for one major rule, which is to prevent the aircraft from tipping – literally! Therefore, the holds at the back will be unloaded first. Transportation to the baggage handling system(s) on arrival will be done according to the destination of the bags. If the bags are at their final destination, they will be transported to unloading quays for reclaimed baggage, otherwise they will be transported to unloading quays for transfer of baggage. The separations created at the make-up of the originating station allow bags to be handled according to priority rules. For instance, the premium class bags are unloaded and transported to reclaim first. Or transfer baggage with a (very) short connection time is collected and driven to its departing flight without passing through the baggage handling system (called 'tail to tail').

What can go wrong with baggage handling?

Baggage labels

To enable identification of the bag during the whole process the baggage label or bag tag is essential. After check-in of the passenger it is the first step in the process for baggage. The label contains all information linking the bag to its owner as well as to its flight(s) and destination(s). So the first and most difficult problem to solve is a missing baggage label. A label can go missing simply because during the handling process it was ripped off. Labels are made of strong paper and fixed securely to the bag, but can get caught behind protruding hooks in the baggage handling system or in containers and be ripped off due to the forces the bag undergoes in the system or during flight. Luckily this doesn't happen often. More common is misreading of the labels. In the baggage handling system, the labels are read automatically by barcode readers. This is at present the most commonly-used technique and has a success rate of approximately ninety-five per cent. The industry is moving towards labels with RFID-chips, which should have an even higher success rate, but these labels are much more expensive than barcoded labels. Labels can be misread due to problems in the printed barcode caused, for instance, by a faulty printer, or crinkled labels. Problems can also be caused by labels being handwritten, which may occur when there is no (functioning) printer available and therefore no barcode can be printed on the label. Finally, issues can arise due to the label-reading mechanism in the baggage handling system. In general, label readers will have been implemented around the conveyers to capture each label at any angle relative to the bag. This is often called 360-degree scanning. So even when the bag is lying on top of the label, the label is still scanned. In older baggage handling systems, this 360-degree scanning was not available, resulting in a higher percentage of misread bags. A misread label requires manual handling to solve the problem.

Solving the label problems

When a baggage label is missing or can't be read, the bag cannot be processed automatically. Therefore, it is rerouted to a location where a baggage handling agent solves the label problem. A system-read error can usually be solved by entering available label information into the booking system, such as passenger name and destination, or the barcode identifier. When a match is found, a new label can be printed, and the bag can be processed normally. In case of a missing label, the agent has to 'wait' until the passenger files a 'missing bag report' in which characteristics of both the bag (colour, type, etc.) and its contents are described. Based on these reports the bag is matched to its owner and returned.

Mishandled bags (too late/lost)

There are several reasons why bags can miss their flights. If the passenger also missed the flight 'there is no problem' (this does not necessarily reflect the passenger's viewpoint!). In this case, the passenger and baggage will be rebooked on another flight. If a *bag* misses the flight but the *passenger* does not, the bag is 'mishandled'. This mishandled bag contributes to the 'irrate' (irregularity rate) of the airline, which is an important performance indicator of the baggage handling process of that airline. Causes can vary from technical problems in the baggage handling system (bag can be stuck in the system due to malfunction), to too short a connection time to allow for timely processing, to 'lost'. Bags can get lost! They can fall off a cart, or from the conveyers of a baggage handling system, or they can get lost due to human error.

Solving the mishandling problems

As a rule, all 'lost' bags are (eventually) recovered. 'Too late' bags are bags that simply didn't make it to their flight in time, but were never lost. Both need to be returned to their owner. These bags will *not* travel on the same plane as their owner, the passenger, therefore a specific process is used called 'expedite baggage'. This process needs to ensure safe travel of the baggage on an aircraft and then the forwarding of it by a delivery service to the address of the passenger. Many airlines are working on early notification of the passenger in the case of mishandled bags, but it requires track and trace facilities worldwide as in parcel tracking systems. This technology is not widespread in baggage handling yet. In most cases the passenger finds that their bags are missing at their destination and reports to the baggage handling desk. At the desk the passenger needs to file a missing bag report, which contains a description of the bag and its contents to enable identification. Also the forwarding address information of the passenger will be required to enable delivery of the bags. The report is filed in a system called 'World tracer' which is used by airlines/baggage handlers all over the world to enable recovery and delivery of the lost and too late bag(s).

Damaged bags

Bags can get damaged during handling and transportation. The strains and mechanical forces bags endure during handling and transportation on the ground as well as in flight are pretty severe; specifically, when straps, handles, loops, etc., get caught around something. When the damage is discovered during the baggage handling process, the agents usually try to repair small defects, so the bag can continue its journey and the contents are not lost. More often the damage is discovered at the destination by the passenger. The passenger will claim this at the baggage handling desk, a report will be made, and the passenger will be compensated.

Not OK to load

Last but much more frequent than the aforementioned are the 'not ok to load' bags. This is usually a temporary status a bag gets on the baggage reconciliation device. It occurs at make-up or, at the latest, on the ramp during the loading of bags into the aircraft belly. It means that the bag cannot be loaded into the container or aircraft. Causes vary but in general it means there is no (through) check-in information available for the passenger from the booking system. This administrative problem often solves itself when the passenger check-in information becomes available. If not, the bag will not be loaded. A specific situation arises when the bag belongs to a 'selectee'. A selectee is a passenger who has been marked for closer examination by an authority. This person will be interviewed by that authority to verify their reasons for travel, and a physical baggage check may also be made at check-in inspection, in the presence of the selectee. Only when the selectee is cleared will the bag become 'ok to load'.

Baggage restrictions of the aircraft

Loading baggage into the aircraft follows strict rules due to the restrictions of the aircraft type. It is easy to imagine how the size of the aircraft will influence its ability to transport large items. But also the ability to heat up a hold and take into account the overall dispersion of passengers, their bags, cargo, fuel, etc., influences what can be realized in baggage handling. A number of these restrictions for baggage handling are briefly described below.

Maximum number of containers

In larger aircraft types, baggage is usually transported in containers. The absolute maximum number of containers that can be loaded is defined by the space in the holds of the aircraft. For many aircraft types only one or two types of containers are available. Size and shape of containers are highly standardized. Next to baggage there may be a shipment of cargo, some of which can be transported in containers and some that will be transported on pallets of varying sizes. For instance, an expensive car or an aircraft engine in a hold will take up the space of several regular sized containers. In the load-planning, a maximum allowed number of containers to be used for baggage will be given before the loading of bags at make-up starts. It will be based on the expected number of passengers, and what is known about their baggage. Regular hold baggage is estimated, but wheelchairs, large sport items, bicycles and pets will need special handling and need to be registered with the passenger booking. At make-up, the baggage handling agent will have to put all regular baggage in containers according to the required separation rules, but they cannot exceed the maximum number of containers allowed for the load planning of this specific flight. This can lead to necessary compromises in separations. For instance, the last economy bags may be added to the business class container.

Weight and balance

Loading the aircraft to achieve the optimum in weight and balance is necessary for safe and (fuel) efficient flying. The weight of baggage (containers) will be estimated, and together with all other available load information this will lead to instructions as to which hold and at which positions the baggage may be loaded, thus hopefully creating an optimum in safe and efficient flying and an efficient unloading process at destination. In smaller (non-containerized) aircraft, preferences to facilitate efficient handling at destination are often more difficult to realize, as compromises on safe flying are unacceptable.

Specific baggage items

Increasingly, passengers are bringing more items that need special loading such as pets and wheelchairs, which are subject to specific loading rules. Large (odd size) items like bicycles, surfboards, etc., are a challenge to transport to the aircraft, as they do not fit through the baggage handling system, but are relatively easy in loading. They can either be loaded into XL-containers (AAP), or in the bulk hold. Pets need to travel in heated holds or they will freeze to death, and not all holds can be heated! Pets are required to travel in benches that are large enough and sturdy enough for air transport. In the hold, the bench will be tied down to prevent it rolling and moving during flight. It is not allowed to stack other baggage immediately next to or on top of a bench containing a live animal. There needs to be some free space around the bench. Wheelchairs also need to be loaded and handled according to strict rules. Specifically, in the case of battery-powered wheelchairs, the battery can pose a safety risk.

15 Air cargo processes

Nicholas Donnison

Introduction

Many passengers may not be aware that below the aircraft floor, their baggage is also sharing space with air cargo. Air cargo can transport goods much more quickly than by sea or rail, and is vitally important for carrying goods both domestically and internationally. The types of goods that benefit from this speed can range from the latest technology such as smartphones, tablets or wearables, to medical samples, fresh produce or even large, heavy oil and gas equipment. This chapter will examine the players, infrastructure and processes which support the transportation of cargo by air.

Types of operators

Generally speaking, there are three types of air cargo operators: integrators, passenger airlines and cargo airlines. Together, they were responsible for the movement of 52.2 million metric tonnes of goods around the world in 2015 alone, which represents about thirty-five per cent of global trade by value.[1]

Integrators

Integrators typically offer a door-to-door service which includes pickup, packaging, air transportation, customs processing and delivery. Their services often carry time-sensitive documents or consumer goods purchased online, and generally offer a known transit time which is published by origin and destination. To facilitate this, the integrator often has their own network of aircraft and trucking services around the globe, which may be wholly owned, or contracted to other carriers. Sometimes integrators may transport their shipments on passenger or cargo airlines based on the trade lane, volume, cost and speed.

Passenger airlines

Passenger airlines sell the leftover space in the aircraft belly after all passenger bags are accounted for. This amount of space (expressed in volume or weight) can vary significantly based on aircraft, route, load factor and time of year but can generally be estimated by the carrier in advance. Many passenger airlines also operate a cargo airline which may be a division or subsidiary of the main carrier.

Cargo airlines

Cargo airlines operate all-cargo aircraft which can differ in size and capacity. They may exist in their own right, or be a part or subsidiary of a passenger airline. In terms of service, they may offer scheduled services, charter services or contract services on behalf of a customer, similar to an integrator. Ranging from small bulk-hold, narrow-bodied aircraft, to large containerized wide-body freighters, these aircraft are able to offer dedicated freight uplift. Some wide-body freighters such as the Boeing 747 offer nose cargo doors which facilitate the loading of long or oversized cargo. Whilst many purpose-built cargo aircraft exist, it is not unusual for passenger aircraft to be converted for use as a freighter aircraft in order to extend their useful life.

Types of cargo

Passenger and cargo airlines offer various products and services in order to differentiate them from the competition, and add value to their customers. These various products feature different rates, acceptance times, service or time guarantees and may require specialized equipment. Some of these products are described below:

- General cargo refers to any cargo that does not require special handling – for example textiles or books. Most airlines offer a type of general cargo product, which usually have lower rates and earlier cut-off times than their other products.
- Express cargo refers to any kind of urgent cargo – this could range from documentation to small spare parts for broken machinery. These products are typically guaranteed on a particular flight or the next available flight, have a later acceptance time (closer to the aircraft departure time) and a refund mechanism if they do not fly as booked.
- Perishable cargo refers to items such as flowers, or fresh or frozen meat that may be affected by the temperature or environment. These goods require additional and specialized handling such as storage in cool rooms or freezers, and loading segregation from other cargo such as animals or dangerous goods. Rules and regulations for the carriage of these goods can be found in the International Air Transport Association (IATA) Perishable Cargo Regulations.
- Pharmaceutical cargo products are medicinal goods which include either ingredients or finished products. These goods are very sensitive to temperature and are often transported in specially designed boxes, or airline containers with the aim of maintaining a constant temperature on the

ground and in the air. Airlines may provide temperature monitoring and tracking of these goods, and some may include temperature loggers that record the data during flight. Airlines may also utilize additional equipment such as thermal blankets or thermal trucks to maintain the condition of the cargo during transfer between flights – especially in hot climates.

- Live animal cargo can range from the transportation of pets, to day-old chicks, to racehorses. Airlines must ensure these shipments are suitably packed, segregated and loaded in an environment suitable for the kind of animal. Rules and regulations for the carriage of these goods can be found in the IATA Live Animal Regulations.
- Dangerous goods are goods which are dangerous or harmful to health and include various items such as acids, or flammable material. These goods must be specially packaged, and the documentation prepared and accepted by trained personnel. There are strict requirements in place for quantities, storage, build-up and loading on the aircraft. Rules and regulations for the carriage of these goods can be found in the IATA Dangerous Goods Regulations (DGR).
- Specialized carriage refers to over-dimensional or heavy cargo that airlines may also handle as some form of expert solution. This could include items such as helicopters, long pipes, generators or heavy machinery for the oil and gas industry. These shipments typically need a lot of preparation and care in terms of both build-up and loading on the aircraft.
- Secure cargo refers to valuable or secure cargo such as banknotes, jewels and blank credit cards. Airlines need to ensure their safety from tampering or pilferage from acceptance to delivery.

Airline equipment

Aside from the aircraft itself, the major equipment required for the transportation of cargo is the Unit Load Device (ULD) and associated equipment such as tie-down straps. ULD can refer to both a flat pallet and a container. ULDs enable the airline to combine cargo into an easily moveable and transportable unit, and also to secure the unit inside the aircraft. By doing do, the airline can load and unload the aircraft more quickly and more efficiently, allowing for a faster turnaround time. Many different shapes and sizes of ULDs are available, allowing the ability to load different sizes, shapes and weights of cargo across various aircraft types. Speciality ULDs are also available, such as ULDs that can provide heating and cooling (useful for perishable or pharmaceutical shipments), or horse stalls for the carriage of horses. ULDs are more commonly used on wide-body aircraft. Most narrow-body aircraft are generally only bulk hold-able (loose cargo), although there are some exceptions such as the AKH container for Airbus A319, A320 and A321 aircraft. As ULDs are built to standards and require certification, as such they are an expensive asset for an airline to own, manage and repair. As a result, some airlines engage the services of ULD pooling companies which offer ULD provision, management and maintenance services.

Shippers

Shippers are the manufacturers or primary producers of goods. They sell their goods to a consignee, which is generally the buyer of the goods. The requirements of preparing goods for air transportation are complex, involving many legal and logistical requirements. As these are not the primary focus of a shipper, nor does the airline have time to explain these to multiple shippers, there exists a body between the shipper and airline known as a freight forwarder.

Freight forwarders

Freight forwarders are experts in the movement of cargo from the shipper to consignee. The freight forwarder is responsible for ensuring that goods move from origin to destination at the right place, right time, in good condition and at the most economical price. Freight forwarders add value to the air cargo transportation chain by providing expertise in logistics, regulatory compliance, risk management, and finance and payment. Typically, a freight forwarder will have established relationships with various airlines, enabling them to offer multiple products, prices and timeframes to their shippers. Their choice of airline could be based on many factors, which include the commodity being shipped, expertise of the air carrier, space availability, transit time and cost. However, before a freight forwarder can do business with an airline, there are many steps needed to become an appointed agent. Whilst these vary by airline, the typical requirements would include the following:

- provision of a bank guarantee or some sort of financial guarantee; this is to protect the airline's interests in case of default or bankruptcy, as the cargo is generally carried on credit terms and settled at a later date. Depending on jurisdiction, this bank guarantee may be between the forwarder and airline, forwarder head office and airline head office, or the forwarder and IATA
- forwarder business plan highlighting the major trade lanes and projected tonnages
- evidence of training of their staff, such as Dangerous Goods Awareness Training
- agreement to use air waybill stock.

Once the above are satisfied, the forwarder would sign a contract or agency agreement in order to begin business with the airline. Once the shipper and freight forwarder have established their business relationship, they are ready to begin trade.

Cargo Terminal Operators

A Cargo Terminal Operator (CTO) can refer to both a facility in which cargo is accepted, stored and built-up ready to transport, as well as the company that provides this handling. If the handling is provided by another company within the cargo terminal, they may also be known as a Ground Service Provider (GSP). CTOs vary from large companies with presence in various continents, to smaller operators that may only be present in one port. The size and level of sophistication may vary based on location as well as cargo volume. In large transfer hubs, the facilities may be larger and include multiple aspects of automation in terms of the movement and storage of cargo. In other locations, the terminals may be nothing more than a small building or shed. Some airlines may also choose to build and operate their own cargo terminal in their home base.

The IATA Operational Safety Audits (IOSA) Standards Manual[2] lists the standards and recommended practices that are required to be documented and implemented by IATA member airlines. According to this manual, member airlines are required to have a contract or agreement in place with external service providers. This contract or agreement outlines what each party is responsible for and covers items such as acceptance, storage, build-up, transfer of information and dispatch of cargo. The manual also recommends that airlines ensure cargo terminals are equipped with facilities appropriate for storage of certain types of special cargo such as live animals or valuable goods. The availability of these facilities may determine which products the carrier is able to ship from each location. Significant equipment is required to handle air cargo. From a CTO's perspective, this would include weight scales, special facilities such as cool-rooms and secure storage, forklifts, slave pallets for the build-up and transportation of cargo, and ULD storage areas.

Cargo process: shipper and freight forwarder

Once the shipper and freight forwarder have established their business relationship, they are ready to send their first shipment. In handling the cargo, the general process of the freight forwarder includes the following nine steps.

Choice of carrier and reservation

The choice of carrier will depend on the type and size/weight of cargo to be carried, the airline schedule and space availability as well as the cost.

Collection of goods from the shipper's premises

The freight forwarder will arrange collection of goods from the shipper's premises. Depending on the setup, these goods may be transported directly to the CTO or may be transported to the freight forwarder's facility for consolidation or build-up. Sometimes this task may be outsourced to a trucking or cartage company.

Ensuring the goods are suitably packaged, marked and labelled for air transportation

Transportation by air can involve being loaded, unloaded and stored in various locations – the packaging used must be able withstand these activities. Special cargo, such as dangerous goods or live animals, has more requirements, which may be found in IATA Dangerous Goods Regulations or IATA Live Animal Regulations.

Ensuring all the required permits and permissions for export and import are in place

Special cargo may require specific types of permits for export and import based on the origin, transit point and destination.

Consolidation with other shipments to the same region or destination

One of the advantages a freight forwarder can provide a shipper is that they may offer a lower rate by consolidating multiple shipments from more than one shipper into a single consignment. As airlines' per-kilogram rate is less at higher weights and volumes, this can result in significant savings to both parties.

Build-up into pallets or containers, if required

Freight forwarders may tender cargo as 'loose' to the airline, or built up onto ULDs. If consolidating cargo, there may be savings in time or money to be made tendering as a ULD versus tendering the cargo loose, due to lower terminal and/or airline charges.

Provision of security requirements

In some jurisdictions, security requirements will be completed before tendering at the CTO – whilst in other jurisdictions they may take place at the CTO. The freight forwarder will document the security status on the master air waybill.

Preparation of the air waybill

The master air waybill is a contract between the shipper and the airline for carriage of the goods between origin and destination. In the case of a consolidation, there may be multiple house air waybills between the freight forwarder and the shipper, which acts as their contract. The air waybill may be in paper or electronic form, depending on the airline and origin/destination.

Delivery to the cargo terminal by the cut-off time advised by the airline

The cargo must be delivered to the CTO by the agreed cut-off time between the airline and the freight forwarder in order to be accepted for carriage. Whilst this provides a basic outline of the steps taken to handle cargo by a freight forwarder, there are naturally more complicated examples when taking into account special cargo such as dangerous goods.

Cargo process: Cargo Terminal Operator/airline

Once the cargo has been lodged at the Cargo Terminal, the CTO is responsible for ensuring the goods are ready for carriage, stored, built-up and dispatched to the aircraft ramp. In completing these tasks, the CTO will generally refer to the airline's operations manual, but may also need to refer to industry documentation such as the IATA DGR. The IATA Cargo Handling Manual (2017) also contains general procedures for cargo handling, which include:

- physical inspection of cargo
- inspection of documentation
- inspection of special cargo
- storage
- build-up.

Physical inspection of cargo

The CTO will first ensure the cargo has been accepted by the cut-off time advised to them by the air carrier. They will then conduct a ready-for-carriage check, which verifies that all information is consistent with the physical shipment, and ensures that applicable embargoes, operational restrictions and country and carrier specific rules are complied with:[3]

- **Counting** – ensuring the amount of physical cargo tendered matches the documented total. Accepting less cargo than is documented may result in wasted time tracing the goods at destination, and could result in claims against the airline.
- **Inspection of the cargo or ULD for signs of damage** – damaged boxes may result in damage to the cargo itself, or even collapse of cargo on/in a ULD. If not identified at acceptance, damaged ULDs may cause costly aircraft damage.
- **Inspection of the cargo or ULD for signs of tampering/pilferage** – if the goods appear to have been tampered with or pilfered, they may need further security controls.
- **Weighing and measuring** – as airlines' charging mechanisms are by actual and chargeable (volumetric) weight, the weight and volume checks are important to guard against revenue leakage.
- **Determining contour (for ULD)** – pallets can have particular contours which describe their height, width or length. These are used by the load controller to plan how to place the cargo in a suitable position on the

aircraft. If the contour is incorrectly recorded, this could cause loading problems leading to the offload of the cargo.

- **Inspecting marking/labelling** – this ensures the shipment is identifiable by the airline and CTO, as well as highlighting any special handling requirements. This is also an opportunity to identify any marking or labelling which may indicate items which may not be correctly declared (e.g., hidden dangerous goods).
- Matching cargo against the contents declared on air waybill.
- Reviewing security status – the security status on the air waybill will determine whether the cargo can be transported on a passenger or cargo aircraft, or at all. The absence of this status will require the cargo to be screened.

Inspection of documentation

The air waybill details must be inspected in paper or electronic form. The checking of this data is important for a couple of reasons: identifying potentially hidden dangerous goods that may be listed under an innocuous description, and the need for accuracy given that the air waybill concludes a contract for the carriage of goods.

Inspection of special cargo

Specialist types of cargo such as live animals, valuables or dangerous goods require more stringent inspection before acceptance than general cargo, generally with the aid of a checklist.

Storage

Depending on what time the cargo was lodged, the CTO may need to store the cargo until build-up begins, or, in the case of a ULD, until it is ready for dispatch. Special cargo may require storage in specific locations, such as live animals which need to be placed in a quiet, well-ventilated area, which is protected from adverse weather conditions.[4]

Build-up

Loose cargo to be built on/in a ULD will usually follow a load plan provided by the airline to the CTO. This could either be in the form of a detailed plan listing which shipments to load, or could be as simple as the maximum number of ULDs available for use. Regardless, the CTO needs to ensure the cargo is loaded appropriately based on its size, weight, destination and segregation requirements. For example, cargo that will directly transfer flights at a hub airport would generally not be loaded with cargo destined for that airport as its final destination. Segregation requirements may be a matter of regulation (such as dangerous goods) or based on airline practices described in their operational manual. The build-up includes the following steps:

- **Selection of the ULD** – the ULD required may have been advised on the airline load plan. Regardless, a ULD suitable for the aircraft type must be selected to ensure compatibility.
- **Inspection of the ULD to ensure it is serviceable** – damaged ULDs must be identified to prevent aircraft damage. The damage limitations can be found placarded on the ULD, and also in the airline's operational manual.
- **Distribution of the weight appropriately across the ULD** – there are limitations in terms of the loading on the ULD floor which may require the spreading of cargo on wooden spreader boards or other devices. This is to prevent excessive load in one particular part of the ULD, which may result in its failure or difficulty in loading. As a general practice, heavier cargo should be loaded towards the bottom rather than on top to prevent damage and collapse.
- **Securing of the cargo with nets and/or straps** – the cargo must be restrained to prevent movement inside the aircraft so that neither the cargo nor the aircraft get damaged.
- **Closing of the ULD** – this involves ensuring the contour is met, and closing the door or netting the cargo to the pallet which is important to ensure the cargo is secured.
- **Weighing the ULD** – the ULD must be weighed so as to determine whether it has exceeded its maximum certified value, and so that the information can be transmitted to the load controller for weight and balance planning.
- **Attachment of the ULD tag** – the ULD tag must be completed so that the ULD and port of unloading are identified.

Loose cargo for the bulk hold or for bulk hold-able narrow-body aircraft will not require build-up on/in a ULD, but will require weighing.

Communication of information to load control

The CTO is required to transmit certain information to the load control office, to allow for weight and balance calculations and the delivery of a load sheet. According to the IATA Cargo Handling Manual, these include the ULD identification, gross weight, special handling or hazard codes and complementary information, bulk load pieces and weight, airport of unload, and the Notice to Captain (NOTOC).[5] All of the above information is very important to ensure the load controller is able to load the aircraft in accordance with the airline weight and balance requirements. For example, the contour codes will assist in placing freighter main-deck cargo in the correct locations, whilst dangerous goods codes will allow for correct segregation. The NOTOC provides dangerous goods and other special load information which will assist the crew in the case of an emergency.

Transport from facility to aircraft

Depending on the agreements made by the airline, transportation to the ramp may be completed by the CTO or the Ramp Handling Agent (RHA). This involves inspecting the cargo or ULDs, ensuring transportation equipment is serviceable and the cargo is protected from adverse weather conditions. Some cargo items such as valuables or live animals may be delivered to the aircraft ramp closer to departure, to prevent them from pilferage or distress.

Offloads

Not all the cargo accepted for the flight may be able to travel on the flight. Known as an offload, this may occur due to a number of reasons. For example, a change in weather may require an increase in the amount of fuel required, resulting in less available payload. A ULD could collapse due to improper build-up, or more passenger baggage could be accepted than planned. Airlines may also accept more cargo than that for which there is space or weight availability, in the chance some passengers may not arrive for their booked flight and payload becomes available. Regardless of the reason for the offload, the cargo needs to be returned to the CTO and stored appropriately, the agent notified and the shipment rebooked.

Transit

Whilst some cargo may travel on one flight from origin to destination, other cargo may transfer to another flight or another airline at an intermediate point. When transferring to the same airline, the airline will have instructed their CTO to build the cargo in a means to facilitate this (e.g., combined in a ULD, or bulk-hold) as well as advising their RHA to effect the transfer. For longer transit periods, the cargo will be towed back to the CTO and may undergo additional processing or build-up/breakdown. Regardless, it is important to store the cargo in a location appropriate for its type. Some cargo may transfer airlines, and a transfer manifest will be provided to the receiving airline.

Destination

At the destination, a similar transportation process will occur from the aircraft to the cargo terminal. The handling after this point depends on whether the cargo was pre-packed by the agent in a ULD, or as loose cargo. Shipper-built ULDs are not normally broken down in the facility and are usually delivered along with the ULD to the consignee. The loose cargo needs to be broken down from ULDs and stored as loose in appropriate locations. The ULDs will generally be broken down in a particular order – with special cargo such as perishable or express handled before the general cargo. The steps involved in the breakdown include:

- **Checking the cargo against the load plan** – this is necessary to ensure the right cargo and the right amount of cargo is received. If the wrong cargo or a short amount of cargo is received, the airline should be notified and tracing will commence.
- **Checking the cargo for damage or pilferage** – these will need to be recorded and informed to the airline and consignee.
- **Storing the cargo** – the cargo will be stored in an appropriate place based on the type of cargo and local customs requirements.
- **Inspecting the ULD and return equipment for storage** – any damaged ULD will need to be segregated and the airline informed. Loading equipment such as tie-down straps need to be returned to the appropriate storage location for reuse. ULDs in proper condition should be sent to an appropriate storage area where they will be protected from damage.

After these processes are completed, the consignee will be notified that their cargo is ready for collection. In order to collect the shipment, documentary evidence of the following must be provided – that the person is authorized to collect the cargo, customs clearance is completed, and all fees and charges accounted for. The latter is particularly important in cases of charges collect shipments, or shipments not collected within the CTO's published timeframe, which may have incurred storage charges. After this, there will be a joint check of the amount of contents and their condition, a delivery receipt signed, and if the cargo was in a ULD, a unit control message in order to update the airline and/or ULD pooling company that the freight forwarder is in possession of the ULD.

Cargo process: freight forwarder

The process for the cargo freight forwarder at the destination is generally the inverse of the origin – ensuring customs clearance, collecting the goods from the terminal, in the case of pre-packed cargo – breaking down from ULD, and finally delivering to the consignee. For pre-packed cargo, the ULD must then be returned to the airline or ground handler within the agreed time as per the unit control message.

Notes

1 IATA, (2016). *Value of Air Cargo: Air Transport and Global Value Chains*. [Online] developing trade consultants, Foreword. Available at: http://www.iata.org/publications/economic-briefings/value-of-air-cargo-2016-report.pdf [Accessed 29 Dec. 2016].

2 IOSA Standards Manual, (2016). 10th ed. Rev 1. Montreal: IATA, pp. CGO 6 and 12.
3 IATA Cargo Handling Manual (ICHM), (2017). 1st ed. Montreal: IATA, pp. 23, 25, 31, 51, 52, 53, 63, 69, 105.
4 IATA Cargo Handling Manual (ICHM), (2017). 1st ed. Montreal: IATA, pp. 23, 25, 31, 51, 52, 53, 63, 69, 105.
5 IATA Cargo Handling Manual (ICHM), (2017). 1st ed. Montreal: IATA, pp. 23, 25, 31, 51, 52, 53, 63, 69, 105.

16 Aircraft load planning and control

Paul Avery

Introduction

Aircraft Load Planning and Control is the result of a diverse group of activities, involving many different areas of an airline's ground and flight operations with the end result being the aircraft loaded in a safe and efficient manner. The culmination of the Load Control process is a safely loaded aircraft and the accurate determination of both the aircraft weight, and aircraft centre of gravity (CG). On the day of operation, Load Planning and Control interacts with many different areas of an airline operation, and relies on timely and clear information, both incoming, and outgoing. Cargo, baggage, passengers, catering, cabin services and fuelling all provide essential information for the Load Control process. Conversely, Load Control provides essential information to cargo, flight planning, ramp and baggage services. In fact, the subject of Load Control can be divided into two main activities:

- Load Planning, where the Load Controller takes into account all of the requirements for the particular day's operation, and plans where each item is to be loaded on the aircraft
- Load Control, where the resultant load, plus any variations, are taken into consideration during the calculation of the aircraft weight and centre of gravity. In this chapter, it is assumed Load Control encompasses both activities.

The chapter includes introductions to the concepts used in Load Control, regulation, documentation, and process.

Aircraft weight

On the day of operations, the aircraft weight must be determined so that:

- flight crew can calculate appropriate take-off and landing performance, taking into account field lengths, obstacle clearance, and take-off, approach and landing speeds; this includes the opportunity for reduced thrust take-off

- operations/flight planning/flight crew can calculate appropriate fuel requirements for the flight
- the loaded aircraft remains compliant with manufacturer's limitations.

Aircraft weight definitions and limitations

Each aircraft manufacturer publishes a Weight and Balance Manual (WBM), in which all information regarding aircraft weight, balance and loading are defined. Some of the items defined are the maximum structural weights for the following aircraft configurations. These are:

- Zero Fuel Weight (ZFW) – the weight of the aircraft, loaded, but without fuel
- Taxi (or Ramp) Weight (RWT) – the weight of the aircraft before pushback and engine start
- Take-Off Weight (TOW) – the weight of the aircraft at the commencement of take-off roll
- Landing Weight (LDW) – the weight of the aircraft at landing.

The maximum weights for each of these configurations (MZFW, MRWT, MTOW, MLDW) are the maximum weights that the manufacturer certifies the aircraft will achieve safe and controllable flight in the hands of a competent pilot. An important part of the Load Control process is to ensure these weight limitations are not exceeded on any flight. In order to achieve this, the weight of passengers, baggage, cargo, fuel, crew, catering, and finally, the weight of the aircraft when empty must be known. Aircraft are weighed at regular intervals as determined by the local regulatory authority, and, together with a mechanism for tracking weight changes resulting from any engineering activities, the aircraft empty weight and CG can be calculated and monitored. If the changes in aircraft empty weight or CG exceed the acceptable figures defined by the operator's regulatory authority, then new aircraft empty weight documentation must be reissued. This calculation of the aircraft empty weight and CG become the starting point for the calculation of aircraft weight. Note: there are many definitions of aircraft empty weight. Different operators consider different items to be part of the aircraft empty weight, but as a general guide the starting point of Load Control calculations fall into one of two categories – Dry Operating Weight or Basic Weight.

Dry Operating Weight (DOW)

Dry Operating Weight is the weight of the aircraft before passengers, baggage, cargo and fuel is added. This weight may vary depending upon differing factors, such as crew complement, catering requirements, and any other adjustments. DOW operators normally publish an extensive table which covers every possible combination of crew and catering. This method was popular when the Load

Control process involved more intervention and calculations, because it gave the Load Controller a start point which did not need to be calculated. However, the effort involved in maintaining large quantities of data can be burdensome. For example, a small change to a catering load would lead to the recalculation of all DOWs/Dry Operating Indices.

Basic Weight (BW)

Basic Weight is the weight of the aircraft without crew, catering or adjustments. Dependent upon the operational requirements of the flight, different crew, catering, and adjustments are added to provide a DOW for each flight. In this way, crew are provided with a DOW, itemized to show exactly what is loaded onto the aircraft for each flight. Although this calculation must be performed for each flight, the use of Departure Control Systems (DCSs) has automated the task. In addition, there is minimal effort in maintaining BW data, because each DOW is calculated for each flight and therefore there is no need to publish tables of aircraft weight data.

Limiting weight

Having calculated the DOW of the aircraft, payload (defined as any load carried that provides revenue) is added and the result is the ZFW: the weight of the laden aircraft without fuel. To this is added the fuel, and the result is the RWT of the aircraft: the weight of the aircraft prior to pushback from the ramp. Some fuel is burnt during engine start and taxi to the commencement of the actual take off. The weight of the aircraft at this point is the TOW. The estimated fuel burn is subtracted from the TOW to calculate the LDW. During the Load Control process, each of these weights is compared against the manufacturer's maximum certified weights, and the minimum difference becomes the limiting weight for a flight. This is also the payload available for the flight; that is, the maximum amount of load that can be added before the first of the manufacturer's limitations is reached. (See Figure 16.1. In this example, the difference between the aircraft ZFW and MZFW is the smallest amount, so for this flight, ZFW becomes the limiting weight.) In the example, the ZFW is the limiting weight for this flight (373,000 – 341,272 = 31,728kg) vs TOW (510,000 – 436,643 = 73,357kg) vs LDW (395,000 – 362,052 = 32,948 kg).

Aircraft centre of gravity

On the day of operations, the aircraft centre of gravity must be determined so that:

- flight crew can set appropriate stabilizer trim settings
- the aircraft handling characteristics in flight and on the ground are compliant with the manufacturer's limitations

Basic Weight:		288 193	104.70 IU
+ Pantry:	G	8 047	3.90 IU
+ Crew:	2/24	2 680	* -0.72 IU
+ SWA:		0	0.00 IU
+ Ballast/Trapped Fuel:		0	0.00 IU
DOW		298 920	107.88 IU
+ Traffic Load:		42 352	
⊚ ZFW:		341 272	MZFW: 373 000
+ Usable Fuel:		96 751	P
- Taxi Fuel:		1 380	
TOW:		436 643	MTOW: 510 000
- Trip Fuel:		74 591	
LDW:		362 052	MLDW: 395 000

Actual Underload	35 069
- To Come Weight	3 341
Predicted Underload	31 728

Figure 16.1 Example of limiting weight calculation

Aircraft CG is the point at which the aircraft would balance if set upon a pivot. Aircraft manufacturers define all longitudinal locations as a distance from their datum Station 0. See Figure 16.2.

The calculation of the balance effect of load can be expressed a number of ways. The balance effect of load in engineering terminology is Weight × Distance, called a Moment, with units defined by the weight and distance (e.g., kgmm). Summing all these moments together, and dividing by the total weight will provide a total CG Balance Arm expressed as a unit of length. See Equation 16.1.

Aircraft CG is normally expressed in terms of Mean Aerodynamic Chord (MAC). See Figure 16.3. LEMAC is the Leading Edge MAC.

Conversion of the aircraft CG from Balance Arm to a %MAC is derived using the equation shown as Equation 16.2.

Calculating CG of aircraft using the Moment method results in large and unwieldy numbers, so a simpler method is required. An Index Unit is the expression of aircraft CG in terms of a Reference Station (nominally around

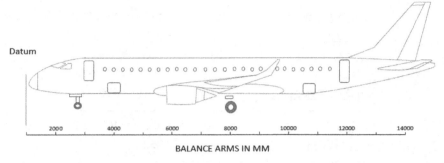

Figure 16.2 Balance arms from Station 0

$$CG = \frac{Wt1 \times Dist1 + Wt2 \times Dist2 + Wt3 \times Dist3 + Wt4 \times Dist4 + Wt5 \times Dist5}{(Wt1 + Wt2 + Wt3 + Wt4 + Wt5)}$$

Equation 16.1 Moment calculation

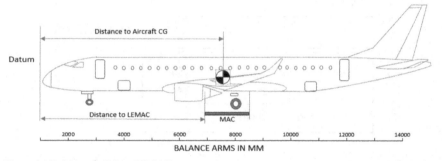

Figure 16.3 Aircraft CG as %MAC

$$\%MAC = \frac{(CG\ Bal\ Arm - LEMAC)}{MAC} \times 100$$

Equation 16.2 %MAC calculation

the centre of the aircraft), and a divisor, called the C Constant. Calculated using this reference, the balance effect of load forward or aft results in a negative or positive value, where negative equates to a 'nose-down' effect, and positive equates to a 'nose-up' effect, resulting in a simple method of expressing the balance effect of items loaded. See Figure 16.4.

When considering the CG of the entire aircraft, an optional constant to make all calculations positive, called the K Constant, is used. The resultant calculation gives a simple figure as shown in Equation 16.3 and Figure 16.5.

Most manual balance charts (see later in this chapter) use the concept of Index Units to determine the CG of a loaded aircraft. See Figure 16.6.

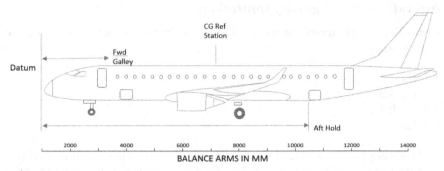

Figure 16.4 Index effect of load

$$IU\text{ effect} = \frac{(Bal\text{ Arm} - Ref\text{ Sta}) \times Weight}{C\text{ constant}}$$

Equation 16.3 IU effect calculation

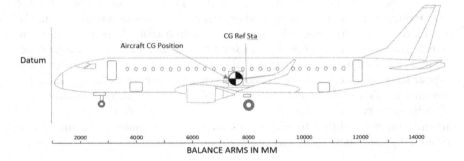

Figure 16.5 Aircraft CG as an expression of Index Units

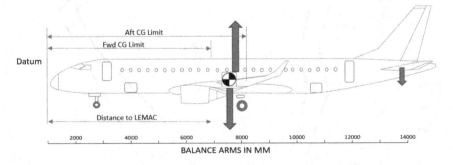

Figure 16.6 Aircraft CG limits

Aircraft centre of gravity limitations

In the WBM, each manufacturer also defines CG limits for the following aircraft configurations:

- taxi
- take-off
- in-flight
- landing.

These are known as 'Certified CG Limits', and are the CG limits that the manufacturer certifies the aircraft is safe and controllable in the hands of a competent pilot for take-off and landing, and also in-flight. A very important part of the Load Control process is to ensure these CG limitations are not exceeded on any flight. The operator must therefore make some assumptions to include the uncertainties of day-to-day operations, and apply the results of those assumptions to the manufacturer's certified CG limits. See Figure 16.7.

These certified CG limits are defined through a combination of aerodynamic analyses and confirmed through flight testing. They must be adjusted for the uncertainties that occur in everyday airline operations. These uncertainties could be variations in the distribution of load in a hold or within a pallet/container, the way in which passengers are distributed throughout each cabin section, or the differences in fuel distribution due to changing fuel densities. There are many of these adjustments for uncertainties to consider, and if appropriate, they are applied to the manufacturer's Take-Off and Landing CG limits. These are called 'curtailments'.

Adjustments for occurrences during flight are also applied to the manufacturer's certified In-Flight CG limits. An example is the movement of aircraft components, such as landing gear, flaps and slats, where significant

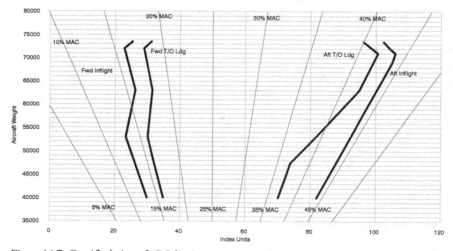

Figure 16.7 Certified aircraft CG limits

weights are moved during the aircraft flight. Another example could be changes due to the in-flight movement of passengers and crew. Although these may at first sound insignificant, consider the movement of two flight attendants plus a full catering trolley from the aft galley to the most forward row, or the movement of passengers throughout the cabin. In these situations, several hundred kilograms of weight are being moved from one end of the aircraft to the other.

The Take-Off and Landing adjustments are applied to the certified Take-Off and Landing CG limits, and the In-Flight adjustments are applied to the certified In-Flight CG limits. The worst (most constrictive) points become the Operational Take-Off and Landing CG limits. These are the CG limits used on manual balance charts, and in some cases, Load Planning Systems. Through analysis of fuel loading, these Operational CG Limits are then, in turn, used to define a set of ZFW CG Limits. Therefore, if an aircraft is within CG limits with zero fuel, it will always be within CG limits for take-off and landing. It is these Zero Fuel, and Take-Off/Landing CG Limits, that provide the structural and aerodynamic constraints that, first and foremost, drive the Load Control process. Operating an aircraft outside these limits can have serious or fatal consequences, so Load Control is an essential part of an airline's safety procedures.

Regulation

All airworthiness authorities regulate the requirements and standards for the safe loading of aircraft to which all operators must comply. These regulations also define the documentation required for flights to safely depart. In addition, regulations regarding the engineering management of aircraft weight and balance define how aircraft weight and CG are determined and tracked, and provide instruction on aircraft weighing. Further, regulations defining Load Controller training and certification requirements exist to confirm Load Controllers continue to have the skills and knowledge to perform their duties.

Documentation

The Load Control process results in a calculation of the aircraft weight and centre of gravity for each flight, and this information (along with some additional data), is transferred to the flight crew using a load-sheet. The load-sheet is the official statement of the aircraft's weight and centre of gravity for the flight.

Documentation – load-sheet

There are many types of load-sheet, which have been developed to support the many different ways airlines operate, and the individual requirements of each airline and regulatory body. Most airlines base the format of the load-sheet on the International Air Transport Association (IATA) standard as defined in the IATA Airport Handling Manual AHM516 (for manual) and AHM517 (electronic data processing (EDP) version). See Figure 16.8.

```
L O A D S H E E T              CHECKED        APPROVED         EDNO
ALL WEIGHTS IN KILOS       A.LOADCONTROL                        02


FROM/TO FLIGHT      A/C REG  VERSION       CREW       DATE     TIME
AAA BBB XX666/01    ABCDE    14F/76J/427Y 2/25      01JUN16 0929


                    WEIGHT          DISTRIBUTION
LOAD IN COMPARTMENTS    24190    1/  3466  2/  6430  3/  7500
                                 4/  6668  5/   126  0/     0


PASSENGER/CABIN BAG     19451 139/105/  7/  2 TTL 253 CAB 0
                            PAX  11/ 53/187    SOC   0/  0/  0
                            BLKD  0


**************************************************************
TOTAL TRAFFIC LOAD       43641
DRY OPERATING WEIGHT    298134
ZERO FUEL WEIGHT ACTUAL 341775 MAX 373000  L    ADJ
TAKE OFF FUEL            83600
TAKE OFF WEIGHT  ACTUAL 425375 MAX 510000       ADJ
TRIP FUEL               72600
LANDING WEIGHT   ACTUAL 352775 MAX 395000       ADJ


BALANCE AND SEATING CONDITIONS   .   LAST MINUTE CHANGES
DOI       109.0    LIZFW    77.2 .DEST SPEC CL/CPT WEIGHT/IND
LITOW     146.9    MACZFW   32.3 .
MACTOW     39.5                  .
BASED ON FUEL DENSITY .796 KG/LTR .
A55.E11.B61.F43.C48.G10.D23.     .
CABIN AREA TRIM                  .


UNDERLOAD BEFORE LMC       31225  .        LMC TOTAL
BALANCE LIMITS AT TOW BEFORE LMC MAC   FWD 33.2 AFT 41.4
**************************************************************
LOADMESSAGE AND CAPTAINS INFORMATION BEFORE LMC


-BBB.139/105/7/2.0.T24190.1/3466.2/6430.3/7500.4/6668.5/126.PAX
/11/53/187.PAD/0/0/0.ACT/23R.PES/15R


SI PAX WEIGHTS USED M85 F70 C38 I10
Weight Report : 56B
-L/S AS PER LIRF EDNO 1
SERVICE WEIGHT ADJUSTMENT WEIGHT/INDEX
ADD
NIL
DEDUCTIONS
NIL
PANTRY CODE  G
NOTOC Required
TRIM TANK FUEL 12900
BBB C   15022 M       0 B   306/  5386 O     941 T        0
END OF LOADSHEET
```

Figure 16.8 Load-sheet (AHM517 – EDP version)

Documentation – Load Instruction Report (LIR)

Just as the load-sheet is the document used to transfer aircraft weight and CG information to the flight crew, the LIR is the document used to transfer loading requirements to ramp staff. It is the result of the Load Planning activities. The LIR will show ramp staff exactly where the Load Controller requires each load item. This document can be in many formats but, again, most are based on the IATA recommendations as defined in the IATA Airport Handling Manual as AHM514 or AHM515. All LIRs include areas into which ramp staff can record any variations to the final loaded aircraft compared to the Load Controller's instructions. See Figures 16.9 and 16.10.

Documentation – Notice to Captain (NOTOC)

The NOTOC is a statement of all Dangerous Goods (DG) and Special Load (SL) on board the aircraft for the particular operation. Some regulatory authorities require a NOTOC for each flight, even if there are no Dangerous Goods or Special Load on board. Some authorities require only a statement on the load-sheet. An example EDP Format NOTOC is shown in Figure 16.11.

Load Planning vs physical loading

As stated earlier in this chapter, Load Planning is the action where, given certain requirements or constraints, the Load Controller plans exactly where each piece of load allocated for uplift on a flight will be positioned on the aircraft. There are many factors to be taken into account, and depending upon each airline's requirements and procedures, the importance of each type of load is assessed, and its priority and position planned accordingly.

Load Planning – baggage

Different requirements will consider the operational and commercial factors. High priority/high value items, such as premium class baggage and courier load, need to be positioned close to the door, to allow easy access for ramp staff to unload upon arrival. If the flight is in transit through a port, consideration of the ramp process at the transit airport needs to be taken into account. For these types of flights, different airlines have different methods, ranging from loading all transit load in a forward, or aft hold, meaning ramp staff at the transit port only need to access one door. Other airlines load transit load on the side of the aircraft opposite the cargo door.

Load Planning – cargo

A potential source of revenue for airlines is the carriage of cargo, and, similar to baggage, different commercial factors will determine how much cargo can be

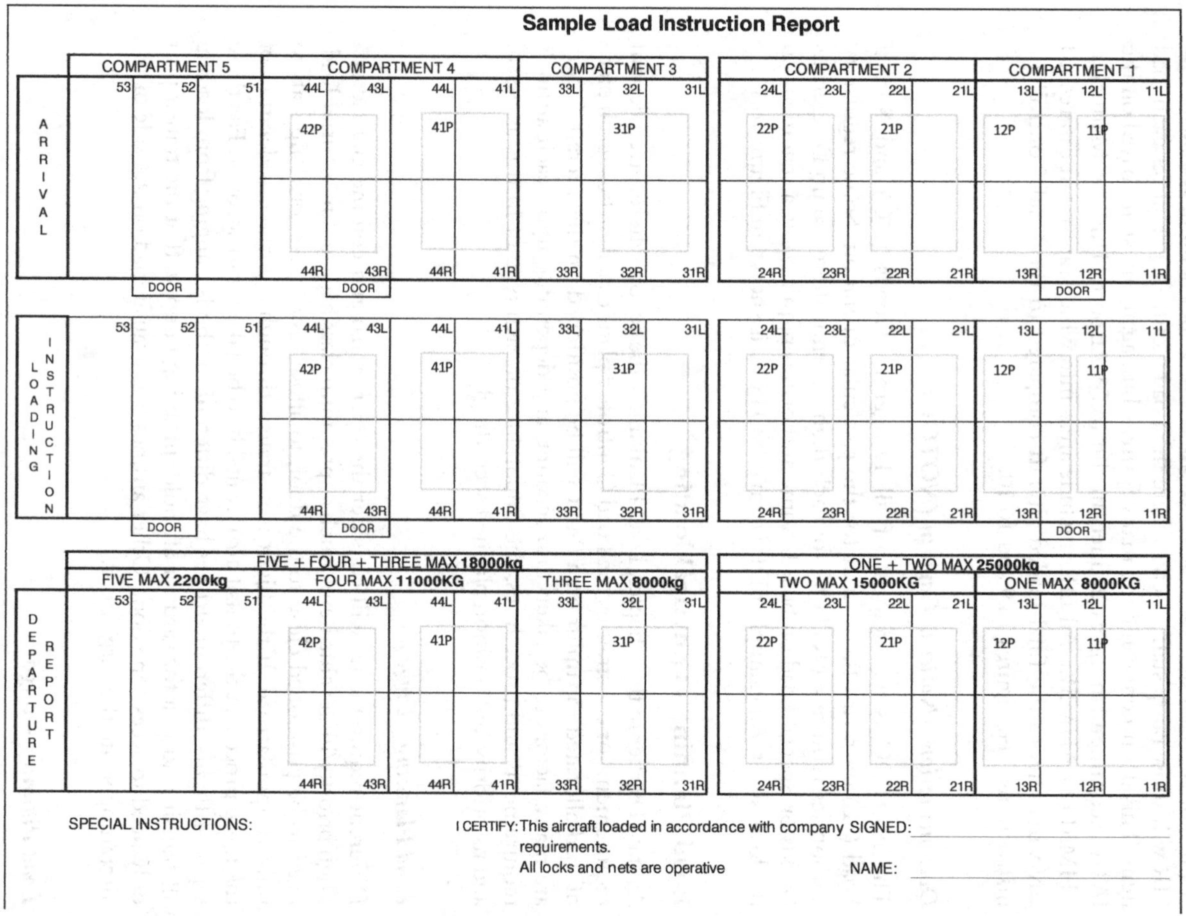

Sample Load Instruction Report

Figure 16.9 Load Instruction Report – manual version (AHM515)

```
LOADING INSTRUCTION/REPORT    PREPARED BY
ALL WEIGHTS IN KG             RADIO NBR TETRA-6257/TDMC01        2
FROM/TO FLIGHT    A/C REG      VERSION    GATE TARMAC  DATE      TIME
                              A380-888   7                23MAY16  1322
PLANNED JOINING LOAD
BBB       F 7    J 76   Y 275  C 2189   M 0       B 8879
JOINING SPECS:    SEE SUMMARY
ACTUAL
WEIGHT
LOADING INSTRUCTION                                           IN KGS
*******************************************************************
CPT 1      MAX 15870
:11L  AKE46660             :11R  AKE18391           :
:ONLOAD: BBB C/160         :ONLOAD: BBB Q/599        :
:SPECS: NONE               :SPECS: NONE              :
:REPORT:                   :REPORT:                  :
:                          :                         :
-------------------------------------------------------------------
:12L  AKE47   *            :12R  AKE18229           :
:ONLOAD: BBB X/80          :ONLOAD: BBB Q/578        :
:SPECS: NONE               :SPECS: NONE              :
:REPORT:                   :REPORT:                  :
:                          :                         :
-------------------------------------------------------------------
:13L  AKE48   *            :13R  AKE49   *          :
:ONLOAD: BBB X/80          :ONLOAD: BBB X/80         :
:SPECS: NONE               :SPECS: NONE              :
:REPORT:                   :REPORT:                  :
:                          :                         :
-------------------------------------------------------------------
:14L  AKE42   *            :14R  AKE46   *          :       D
:ONLOAD: BBB BT3/113*      :ONLOAD: BBB BT3/97*      :       O
:SPECS: NONE               :SPECS: NONE              :       O
:REPORT:                   :REPORT:                  :       R
:                          :                         :
-------------------------------------------------------------------
:15L  AKE50   *            :15R  AKE46478           :
:ONLOAD: BBB X/80          :ONLOAD: BBB D/62/28PCS   :
:SPECS: NONE               :SPECS: NONE              :
:REPORT:                   :REPORT:                  :
:                          :              CPT  1 TOTAL:
*******************************************************************
```

Figure 16.10 Load Instruction Report – automated version (AHM514)

carried (see Chapter 15). Using the available payload figure calculated earlier, cargo with high priority/high value can be lodged onto the flight. Other cargo with lower priority can be assigned to the flight, and if payload is available, can be loaded to the flight. As with baggage, if the flight is in transit through a port, consideration of the ramp process at the transit airport needs to be taken into account.

Load Planning – passengers

For large airline aircraft, the location of passengers is not under the influence of Load Control. Passengers are free to choose whichever vacant seat they desire, and the balance effect is calculated either by the row location, or the cabin section. For smaller aircraft and aircraft with a long fuselage (e.g., Dash 8-Q400) with partial passenger load, some restrictions on which seats can be occupied may occur.

```
SPECIAL LOAD    NOTIFICATION TO CAPTAIN
FROM FLIGHT                    DATE            A/C REG
AAA  XX666                    01JUN16          ABCDE
*** LOADED EX AAA ***
DANGEROUS GOODS
PROPER SHIPPING NAME
  TO    AWB    CL/DV UN/ID SUB PCS QTY/TI RRR PKG IMP CAO   POS
              COMP  NBR   RSK            CAT GRP CODE     ULD CODE
001.RESIN SOLUTION
BBB 63058214     3 UN/  *** 1  0.2LT         RFL          32P
                1866                     II  PMC73648EK
                                     DRILL  3L
002.LITHIUM METAL BATTERIES CONTAINED IN EQUIPMENT
BBB 63058214     9 UN/  *** 1  0.5KG         RLM          32P
                3091                         PMC73648EK
                                     DRILL  9FZ
003.DRY ICE
BBB 65670404     9 UN/  *** 1  10KG          ICE          11R
                1845                         AKE19082EK
                                     DRILL  9L
004.DRY ICE
BBB 65670426     9 UN/  *** 1  12KG          ICE          11L
                1845                         AKE43846EK
                                     DRILL  9L

*** LOADED EX AAA ***
OTHER SPECIAL LOAD
  TO    AWB        CONTENTS       PCS  QTY  IMP   POS
                                            CODE ULD CODE
BBB    63088782 PHARMACEUTICALS    1   70KG  ACT   23R
                                            RKN60176EK
BBB    63052323 LIVE BROWN CRABS  33   651   PES   15R
                                            AKE18119EK
SI
WHENEVER POSSIBLE DURING TRANSPORTATION AND STORAGE
THERE IS NO EVIDENCE THAT ANY DAMAGED OR LEAKING PACKAGES
CONTAINING DANGEROUS GOODS HAVE BEEN LOADED ON THE AIRCRAFT
AT THIS STATION
LOADED AS SHOWN              CAPTAINS SIGNATURE

EMERGENCY TELEPHONE NUMBER 004 0 7778621684
01JUN/07.45.48Z
```

Figure 16.11 Notice to Captain (NOTOC – AHM382)

Load Planning – aircraft limitations

Loading limitations of the aircraft hold itself must also be considered during the planning process. For bulk loaded aircraft, the strength of the cargo compartment floor determines how much load can be assigned to each bulk area. Often, netting is required to restrain bulk load. In addition, there are also combined limitations of different holds and compartments. For containerized aircraft, the aircraft manufacturer determines the maximum weight and type of Unit Load Device (ULD) that can be loaded to each position of the aircraft, and these will vary according to the distance of the load location from the centre of the aircraft. In containerized aircraft, particularly Boeing aircraft, the ability to restrain ULDs using the aircraft in-hold locking system can have implications on the load planning process. For all containerized aircraft (except the B787 series), Boeing specify a layout for the ULD locking system, which allows a series of containers to be locked into position. In the example in Figure 16.12, containers must occupy all of the positions within the groups defined (A, B, C, etc.). With these aircraft, the consideration of container locking becomes a significant factor in planning the load.

Airbus aircraft use a different concept, where any ULD can be locked into any position, so the aircraft in-hold locking system does not restrict the potential loading options to the Load Controller.

Load Planning – Dangerous Goods/Special Load (DG/SL)

The carriage of Dangerous Goods and Special Load (DG/SL) is the most obvious consideration when planning the loading of an aircraft. The IATA Dangerous Goods/Special Load Manual defines types and groups of items and provides airlines and ground handlers with recommended practices for loading these items. Some DG/SL items are not permitted to be loaded on passenger flights at all, some items cannot be loaded within the same compartment, whilst some can only be loaded when there is a minimum distance between them. There are also restrictions on the amount and location of some types of goods (e.g., radioactive) that can be loaded. In addition, aircraft manufacturers may restrict the type of load that can be loaded onto an aircraft. As an example, there will be restrictions on carriage of livestock/pets into cargo compartments that have ventilation and heating. Further restrictions also apply to the carriage of live animals and dry ice in the same compartment. All of these requirements must be considered in planning the load on an aircraft, and any Load Controller must also complete Dangerous Goods/Special Load training to ensure these loads are carried safely and securely.

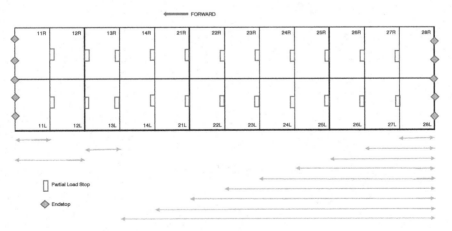

Figure 16.12 Sample in-hold locking system

Load Planning – fuel

The aircraft manufacturer defines the volume and balance arm of each fuel tank, the sequence in which fuel is to be loaded, and the sequence in which fuel is to be burnt. Fuel has a variable weight per given volume, dependent upon temperature. This is known as the fuel density, and depending upon the type of aviation fuel, this can vary between 0.76 kg/ltr to 0.85 kg/ltr. This variation has a significant effect on the distribution of fuel through an aircraft's tanks, and must be taken into consideration during the Load Control process, particularly on larger aircraft with tanks distributed throughout the aircraft. Although the Load Controller cannot directly influence the position of fuel (aircraft fuelling systems control this), the balance effect of fuel distributed across the tanks in use must be calculated at RWT, TOW and LDW.

The aircraft CG at Take-Off, is the CG position at pushback, and includes the balance effect of fuel burnt during taxiing. This is calculated according to the fuel usage instructions in the manufacturer's WBM. There are occasions where fuel is trapped in a particular tank. The fuel is therefore unusable, and must be accounted for as part of the aircraft DOW. There can also be occasions where fuel is carried as ballast, and is therefore unusable and must be considered as part of the aircraft DOW.

Load Control – interactions

Figure 16,14 shows the interaction of Load Control with the other parts of a full-service airline, and the times when these occur will vary depending upon the type of operation.

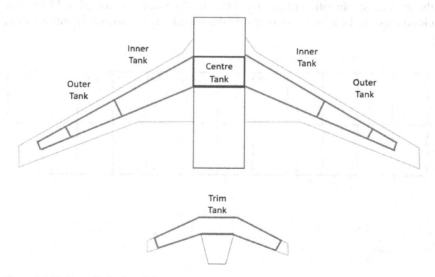

Figure 16.13 Sample fuel tank layout

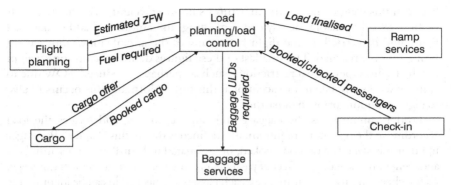

Figure 16.14 Load planning and control interaction

Load Control – a typical flight

The following describes the activities involved in the processing of a long-haul flight from a Load Control perspective. It assumes a full-service carrier, utilizing modern airline Departure Control and ancillary systems. The flight is created from information in reservation systems, usually seventy-two hours prior to departure. At this time, it is highly unlikely that a specific aircraft registration will be assigned to the flight, so an average aircraft empty weight and CG will be used. Passenger and baggage weights, based on booked passenger figures are then added.

Based on historical passenger data (the weight and number of bags per passenger), the number of baggage containers required is calculated, and the information is sent to the Baggage make-up area (see Chapter 14) so the correct number of baggage containers can be prepared. The volume of containers (and sometimes the average number of bags to fill a container) is data stored within Load Control systems. For a bulk-loaded aircraft, an estimate on the amount of hold volume for baggage will be calculated. This event occurs approximately twenty-four hours prior to departure.

Once the amount and weight of baggage have been determined, this weight can be added to the weight of passengers, which in turn, is added to the DOW. The difference between this and the limiting weight for the flight is the amount of payload available for cargo uplift (see Chapter 15) on the flight. This is sometimes referred to as the 'cargo offer', and is sent to the Cargo department approximately twenty-four hours prior to departure. This allows cargo to be prioritized and lodged onto the flight.

There is now a relatively accurate estimate of the ZFW of the flight, and dependent upon the particular airline's processes, this weight is transmitted to Flight Planning systems. Here, taking into account all the operational requirements of the flight, weather, winds, flight tracking, fuel reserves (see Chapter 17), the fuel uplift for the flight and the fuel burn is calculated. The fuel uplift is added to the ZFW to calculate an RWT, TOW, and LDW. The difference between this weight and the manufacturer's limiting weights is calculated. This is the payload available, or payload remaining, the amount of additional load that could be carried on the flight before any of the aircraft maximum weight limitations are reached. The smallest of these figures defines the limiting weight for the flight. Operational restrictions, such as, perhaps, a reduced TOW due to runway works, are taken into account at this time. Normally this occurs twelve to eighteen hours prior to departure.

Load Planning takes the baggage and cargo estimates, and locates the load according to the operator's requirements (defined earlier in this chapter). Passenger uplift at this stage is based on booked, or 'estimated to board' passenger numbers and, generally, the balance effect of passengers is not taken into account at this stage. As the check-in process commences, each passenger checked in can be identified as male/female/child/infant (some airlines do not differentiate between male/female, and use an adult passenger weight), and each passenger is added to the 'checked' numbers and removed from the 'booked' passenger count. Further, from a balance viewpoint, the location of each checked passenger on the aircraft is now known, and an accurate calculation of their balance effect can be made. Check-in at the airport generally commences four hours before departure, but the balance effect of on-line check-in and passengers checked in from connecting flights will be calculated up to twenty-four hours before the flight. During this time, the Load Controller is consistently working to assign and locate baggage and cargo according to whatever operational requirements may be in place for that particular flight.

Approximately ninety to sixty minutes prior to departure, a final judgement is made, and the Load Controller will issue an LIR. This is the official communication to ramp staff, and they will begin to load the aircraft based on this document. If there are any items that need clarification during the aircraft loading, ramp staff will contact Load Control. In some cases (such as a damaged ULD), the Load Controller will need to re-plan, and reissue this document. Loading continues until the last bags accepted for the flight, or last-minute cargo, are finally loaded. At this point the ramp leader checks that all load is correctly positioned and secured (for containerized aircraft, this means all ULDs are secured using the aircraft in-hold loading system), and any changes from the latest LIR are communicated back to Load Control, so that the weight and balance effect of the final load can be calculated.

The Load Controller makes the final adjustments and issues the final load-sheet to the flight crew. Using this information, the flight crew make final calculations of take-off speeds, and take-off stabilizer settings, and the flight is ready for departure. After departure, there are numerous tasks which also must be completed. An arrival LIR must be sent to the next port, so that the ramp staff there can plan how to unload the aircraft. A Load Message (LDM) must be sent to the next port. If the aircraft is containerized, a ULD Control Message listing the serial numbers of all ULDs on the flight is sent. Finally, a Deadload (term for Cargo or Freight) Uplift/Offload (DUO) message is sent to Cargo Departments, advising which load was carried on the flight and which load (if any) was unable to be loaded on this flight. See Figure 16.15 for a timeline applicable to Load Control.

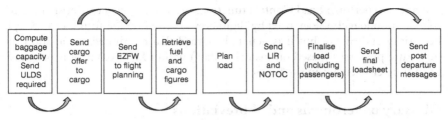

Figure 16.15 Simplified Load Control timeline

Evolution of Load Planning and Control

Like all day-to-day functions of airline operations, Load Planning and Control has changed as a result of continual evolution of airline efficiency improvements, (the efficiency of Load Control is generally measured as the number of flights processed per Load Controller per shift). The other driving factor in the evolution of Load Control has been the introduction of new technologies. In the early days of airline operations, Load Planning and Control was performed by dedicated individuals at each port using manual load-sheets to calculate aircraft weight, and manual balance charts to calculate aircraft centre of gravity. The task required extensive knowledge and training, both of the concepts, and the documentation and tools used.

As time progressed and competition increased, airlines developed different strategies to increase the efficiency of Load Control. Some airlines combined the task of Load Control into other departure functions and responsibilities at each port to create a Departure Controller role. Other airlines refined the role, leading to even more specialized staff at each port. The advent of computerized DCSs relieved Load Controllers of the manual calculation aspects of the task (although manual procedures are still the 'back up' option if computer systems fail), and some efficiency gains were generated as part of this. However, these were offset by the greater training requirements of the new DCS spread over each port.

Due to high staff training costs, there has been considerable focus on Load Control costs and staffing. Developments in communication technology, both internally within an airline, and to/from the aircraft itself, have enabled airlines to consider centralizing Load Control functions in either single or key locations throughout the globe, and even outsourcing this centralized function to specialist ground handling providers. Adding to this, the introduction of mobile computing technology and almost universal wifi access has allowed the load finalization process to be carried out at the ramp, enabling a more refined departure process and minimization of delays. Some low-cost carriers have pushed the Load Control responsibilities to the operating crew, who perform aircraft weight and CG calculations using aircraft manufacturer software embedded in Electronic Flight bags (EFB), or even locally developed applications. Currently, most full-service carriers use a centralized model, increasingly utilizing third-party providers to perform Load Control functions, whilst low-cost carriers generally rely on mobile technology used by flight crew. Predicting the future can always be a risky endeavour, but it is generally agreed that continued automation of departure processes (based on historical data) within Load Control is one way of gaining efficiencies in the future.

Glossary of acronyms and abbreviations

AHM	Airport Handling Manual
BW	Basic Weight
CG	Centre of Gravity
DCS	Departure Control Systems
DG	Dangerous Goods
DOW	Dry Operating Weight
DUO	Deadload Uplift/Offload
EDP	Electronic Data Processing
EFB	Electronic Flight bag
IATA	International Air Transport Association
LDM	Load Message
LDW	Landing Weight
LEMAC	Leading Edge Mean Aerodynamic Chord
MAC	Mean Aerodynamic Chord
MLDW	Maximum Landing Weight
MRWT	Maximum Taxi (or Ramp) Weight
MTOW	Maximum Take-Off Weight
MZFW	Maximum Zero Fuel Weight
NOTOC	Notice to Captain
RWT	Taxi (or Ramp) Weight
SL	Special Load
TOW	Take-Off Weight
ULD	Unit Load Device
WBM	Weight and Balance Manual
ZFW	Zero Fuel Weight

17 Dispatch and flight following

Gene Kim

Introduction

Often referred to as the 'Captain on the ground', the Flight Dispatcher plays a vital role in airline operations. This chapter will explore the world of dispatch and flight following as it pertains to airline operations, primarily from a US perspective. Depending on airline and country, a Flight Dispatcher may also be known as an Aircraft Dispatcher, Flight Controller, Flight Operations Officer, or Flight Superintendent. For the purposes of this chapter, Flight Dispatcher will be used as an all-encompassing term to cover all the industry variations in title. Flight Dispatchers are licensed airmen certificated by Federal Aviation Administration (FAA). They are tasked with flight planning and flight following each flight under their control.

The flight planning process begins with the Flight Dispatcher becoming thoroughly familiar with the weather and airport conditions at the departure, en route, and at the destination points. From there, they will plan the flight route and fuel load by taking into account payload, aircraft performance, restrictive aircraft Minimum Equipment List (MEL) items, en-route winds, and any known or potential Air Traffic Control (ATC) delays and restrictions. When the flight plan is complete, the Flight Dispatcher will file the flight plan with ATC to include proposed departure time, route of flight, altitude, estimated time en route, and aircraft type and registration.

Once a flight becomes airborne, the Flight Dispatcher monitors the progress of the flight, issuing any new or revised information relevant to the flight to the Captain. This is known as flight watch or flight following. As the flight progresses, changes to the original route of flight are not uncommon due to changing weather conditions or ATC delays. When this occurs, the Flight Dispatcher will replan the flight with the new variables to ensure the flight has enough fuel to complete its trip legally and safely. The flight following process continues until the flight has arrived at its intended destination. One of the most important aspects of the Flight Dispatcher's job is that they share joint legal responsibility with the Captain for the safety and operational control for each flight they oversee.

The US Federal Aviation Regulations (FARs) define Operational Control, with respect to a flight, as the exercise of authority over initiating, conducting, or terminating a flight. While the airline or air carrier certificate holder assumes ultimate responsibility for operational control, the Captain and Flight Dispatcher are jointly responsible for the pre-flight planning, delay, and dispatch release of a flight in compliance with appropriate regulations. Additionally, the Flight Dispatcher is responsible for monitoring the progress of each flight, issuing necessary information for the safety of the flight, and cancelling or re-dispatching the flight if, in the opinion of the Flight Dispatcher or the Captain, the flight cannot operate or continue to operate safely as planned. No person may start a flight unless a Flight Dispatcher specifically authorizes that flight.

Historical perspective

During the early days of commercial aviation, airlines primarily carried mail and airfreight. The first Flight Dispatchers worked for the Post Office Department providing flight following services and weather observations to pilots via airmail radio stations along the routes of flight. The growth of commercial aviation in the 1920s and 1930s was fast paced and tumultuous. As air commerce grew, so did the number of high profile aviation accidents. In 1938, President Franklin D. Roosevelt signed the Civil Aeronautics Act, which created the Civil Aeronautics Authority (CAA) whose focus would be on air safety and regulation of the airline industry. Regulations were created for the formal certification of airmen which included the Flight Dispatcher. This also brought about the operational control concept.

Figure 17.1 Airline dispatcher

Source: Airline Dispatchers Federation (ADF) website – www.dispatcher.org/dispatcher/early-dispatch-history

Over the years, positions such as Crew Schedulers and Aircraft Routers augmented the Flight Dispatcher in managing the daily airline operation. Additionally, advancements in technology changed the way Flight Dispatchers flight planned and flight followed their flights. The job functions of the Flight Dispatcher started to include additional responsibilities such as managing fuel costs, working with ATC to manage traffic delays, and dealing with increased security measures. Today, the typical Flight Dispatcher works in a high-tech control centre using sophisticated tools to plan, track, and communicate with each of their flights. Despite additional responsibilities and a change in tools, the basic role of the Flight Dispatcher remains unchanged – to be the airman on the ground who shares operational control authority of a flight with the Captain.

Facilities

Depending on airline size, facilities for Flight Dispatchers could range from simple office space to a large Operations Control Centre (OCC). Regardless of size, the dispatch office or OCC is the operational nerve centre of the airline. Massive amounts of data flow in and out of these facilities as they orchestrate the airline's daily operation. While smaller airlines may only require Flight Dispatchers, medium to larger airlines add more team players to help manage the operation. These additional team players usually include Aircraft Routers, ATC Coordinators, Customer Service Coordinators, Crew Coordinators, Flight Followers, Load Planners, Maintenance Controllers, and Meteorologists. Some of these positions may be organized into Planning Units to help manage the commercial aspects of the operation. This is done intentionally to allow the Flight Dispatchers to focus on safety and the regulatory aspects of the operation.

Medium and large airlines utilize an OCC where multiple operational disciplines work side by side under one roof due to the size and complexity of their operations. These are secure facilities with controlled access and often include a 'Bridge' (oversight working area) where a senior leader such as an Operational

Figure 17.2 Southwest Airlines Network Operations Centre

Source: Southwest Airlines

Duty Director may be located with other centre leaders. The hierarchy of such systems uses the Bridge for overseeing the entire airline network, with the Planning Units assigned to oversee various regions of the airline network, and the Flight Dispatchers overseeing the individual flights assigned to them.

Flight Dispatcher business process

As long as there is a flight in the air for an airline, a Flight Dispatcher must be on duty. Since most airline operations run 24/7, Flight Dispatchers are assigned to shifts. Typically, these shifts can be broken down into day, afternoon, and overnight shifts. While workload varies from airline to airline, each Flight Dispatcher usually flight plans thirty to sixty flights per shift and flight follows ten to twenty flights in the air at any given moment. When irregular operations occur, Flight Dispatchers can experience high levels of stress as their workload suddenly spikes up. The Flight Dispatcher's role is unique in that it is both strategic and tactical at the same time. A strategic approach is used as the Flight Dispatcher plans flights several hours out, interpreting forecast weather data, airport conditions, ATC delays, aircraft performance, payload limitations, and any other factor that may affect the flight being planned. This strategic thought may be interrupted by a tactical situation such as a call from an airborne flight that has been rerouted, placed into holding by ATC, experiencing an emergency, or some other irregularity. The Flight Dispatcher may also receive calls from operational personnel at the airports informing them of payload increases or changes in fuel loads. In all cases, the Flight Dispatcher must stop what they are doing and tend to the situation needing immediate attention. Multitasking, organizational, and prioritization skills are critical for the success of the Flight Dispatcher.

At the start of their duty, oncoming Flight Dispatchers will receive a briefing, or 'shift turn-over', from the outgoing Flight Dispatchers. This is to highlight any issues or situations the oncoming Flight Dispatcher needs to know. After the shift turn-over, the Flight Dispatcher will assess and familiarize themselves with their sector or geographical area that their flight assignments operate. Additionally, they will check on their airborne flights making sure any outstanding needs are addressed. Once all this is complete, the Flight Dispatcher's 'nest' is made and they now turn their attention to flight planning flights on their worksheet. Flight Dispatchers look for three primary goals when flight planning:

- safety
- service
- efficiency.

Together, these factors ensure a high probability of an on-time arrival which incorporates all known and anticipated factors. For example, flight planning for safety means planning for known hazards. Understanding where any adverse weather is expected to be when a flight reaches an affected area, rather than where it is now and then having to anticipate changing conditions, is crucial to safe flight planning. Flight planning for service means meeting customers' expectations. Obviously, passengers want to arrive at their planned destination on time. Further, Flight Dispatchers will look for routes and altitudes that offer the proper balance of speed and comfort. Passengers may not consider arriving on time a pleasant travel experience if they have been 'tossed about' by turbulence the entire flight. Finally, Flight Dispatchers flight plan for efficiency. This means planning the right amount of fuel for the conditions to be encountered. After optimizing routes, speeds, and altitudes, Flight Dispatchers will consider any potential delays that could result in airborne holding or en-route deviations.

Prior to the 1990s, many Flight Dispatch offices were strategically located at bases throughout an airline's network. There, Flight Dispatchers in each office would compile the flight plan, weather information, load manifest, and pertinent company information into a packet to be given to the Flight Crew. The Flight Dispatchers would conduct face-to-face briefings regarding the flight plan with the Flight Crews. After the 1990s, airlines began to consolidate Flight Dispatch offices back to their headquarters or in a single Operations Control facility. With Flight Dispatchers then being physically removed from line operations, flight plan briefings were conducted over the phone with Flight Crews. Some flight planning systems allowed for a Flight Crew briefing sheet to be added with the dispatch packet.

Today, Flight Dispatchers use computerized flight planning systems to optimize routes, calculate performance, calculate fuel load, apply MEL restrictions, and file flight plans with ATC. Technology has now become a part of every aspect of the Flight Dispatcher's job. Aircraft Situational Display (ASD) is used to graphically depict where each airborne flight is geographically. Weather overlays such as radar summaries, satellite imagery, lightning strikes, Pilot Reports (PIREPs), and Significant Meteorological (SIGMET) information provide enhanced situational awareness for Flight Dispatchers as they flight follow their airborne flights. Flight Dispatchers and Flight Crews routinely communicate with each other via a texting system known as the Aircraft Communications Addressing and Reporting System (ACARS). Automated ACARS messages from the aircraft also provide Out, Off, On, and In (OOOI) times so flight tracking systems have the latest times of every flight.

Some of these new tools, such as a graphical ASD, help Flight Dispatchers flight follow their flights once airborne. The power of these tools is significant, since they can not only track where their flights are, but they can also see traffic flows of all aircraft into or out of an airport to better understand the potential of delays. Some of these ASD tools are sophisticated enough to zoom down to the taxiway level at selected airports so the Flight Dispatchers can see the aircraft movement on the surface. This gives them an idea of how long taxi-out or taxi-in delays may be or observe the progress of clearing a runway of snow and ice.

As flight conditions change, Flight Dispatchers undertaking flight following will advise the Flight Crews of those changes and make any necessary modification to the plan. Sometimes, these modifications are minor, requiring only confirmation of change in fuel burn and flight time. At other times, the modification can be so significant that the flight will have to land at an intermediate airport for additional fuel or divert to an alternate airport due to severe weather or an unexpected airport closure. In either case, the Flight Dispatcher is always in direct contact with the Flight Crew. Communication is performed via ACARS or, for more complex discussions, through voice radio contact. An important factor in flight following is the necessity for the Flight Dispatcher to maintain rapid and reliable communication with all their flights at all times.

Direct communication may not always be about the flight-planned route. In some cases, it could be about an inflight medical emergency. The Flight Dispatcher will typically 'patch in' an on-call doctor from a hospital the airline has contracted to provide medical advice for their flights. If the situation is severe enough, a diversion may be necessary immediately, to accommodate the ill passenger. The Flight Dispatcher coordinates emergency services to meet the flight upon arrival for speedy transport to the nearest medical facility. Other cases may involve security issues such as inflight passenger disturbances. Depending on the level of threat, a diversion to the nearest airport may be required, or there may be a need for law enforcement officials to meet the flight upon arrival at the intended destination. Sometimes, Flight Dispatchers coordinate communication with the Flight Crews and Maintenance Control if an aircraft system anomaly were encountered during flight. Regardless of the reason, Flight Dispatchers are the primary communicators between the airline and the Flight Crews.

In addition to the Flight Crews, Flight Dispatchers have the ability to directly communicate with ATC. This can range from discussing routine changes in flight plan, to coordinating delays due to irregular operations, to requesting special handling of flights in dealing with an emergency situation. Within many OCCs, specially classified Flight Dispatchers work as ATC Coordinators or ATC Specialists. These positions act as a liaison between flight dispatch and ATC to coordinate ATC initiatives throughout the National Airspace System (NAS) and minimize impact to the airline.

Flight Dispatchers may also be categorized as Domestic and International Dispatchers based on the geographical area they are assigned. The reason for the separation is due to the differences in regulations and requirements between Domestic and International (Flag) Operations. Some Flight Dispatchers may have a Training classification to provide training and hands-on guidance to new-hire Flight Dispatchers, or to be a Subject Matter Expert (SME) on new initiatives or policies and procedures. Other specialized classifications of Flight Dispatchers may include Dispatch Specialists or Key Users who maintain the operational systems used by Flight Dispatchers and others within the OCC. Additionally, Fleet or Sector Managers control the daily activities within a region of an airline's network. These positions are usually headed up by a Planning Unit comprised of other operational disciplines to manage the commercial aspect of the daily airline operation. Chief Dispatchers provide direct guidance, oversight, and supervision to the Flight Dispatchers. These specialized positions may be found in whole or in part, depending on the airline's size and complexity of operation.

Specialized flight planning requirements

ETOPS

Depending on operation and geographical region, some specialized flight planning may be required. For example, flight planning over oceanic regions requires special procedures such as Extended Operations (ETOPS). ETOPS rules govern the operation of turbine-powered aircraft beyond sixty minutes of an adequate airport. Originally, ETOPS was defined as Extended-range Twin-engine Operations. However, in 2007, the FAA broadened the definition to Extended Operations to include aircraft with more than two engines. This chapter will use the term 'ETOPS' as it pertains to twin-engine operations.

Flight planning ETOPS routes requires additional oversight from the Flight Dispatcher. The route selected must fall into the airline's approved ETOPS operation time limits (i.e. sixty, seventy-five, 120, 138, 180 minutes). The portion of the route that is beyond sixty minutes of flying time at the approved single-engine inoperative cruise speed from the nearest adequate airport is the ETOPS portion of flight. Under the ETOPS portion of flight, the route must be within the approved ETOPS operational diversion time limit at the approved single-engine inoperative speed from the nearest adequate airport or ETOPS alternate airport. The ETOPS alternate airport must have appropriate and available airport facilities, Approach Navigation Aids, Aircraft Rescue and Firefighting (ARFF) services and appropriate weather conditions to allow for a safe approach and landing with a single-engine and/or systems inoperative. For example, a flight that is operating under 120 minutes ETOPS means the ETOPS portion of flight is always within 120 minutes diversion time to an ETOPS alternate airport. The approved single-engine diversion time creates a 120-minute operating radius around the ETOPS alternate airport. The increase in ETOPS time results in a bigger operating radius around the selected ETOPS alternate airport.

In Figure 17.3a, a route from KJFK (New York JFK) to LFPG (Paris Charles De Gaulle) without ETOPS would have to remain within sixty minutes of an adequate airport. This is the upper sixty-minute non-ETOPS route. For reference, a great circle route is depicted south of the sixty-minute non-ETOPS route to illustrate the savings in distance and flying time. However, since this route goes beyond sixty minutes of an adequate airport, ETOPS authority would be required to fly it. Note: The sixty-minute radius rings around each adequate airport appear different in size due to the fact the chart used is a Mercator projection.

By applying 120-minute ETOPS using CYQX (Gander), BIKF (Keflavik), and EINN (Shannon) as alternate airports, the flight is able to take advantage of the optimal route as shown in Figure 17.3b.

By increasing the ETOPS operation time to 138 minutes (see Figure 17.3c), the same route can be flown using just CYQX and EINN as alternate airports.

Once the ETOPS route of flight has been determined, Equal Time Points (ETPs) are calculated to determine the location along the route of flight where diversion time between two selected ETOPS alternate airports is equal. In still air, the ETP would be equidistant from each ETOPS alternate airport. However,

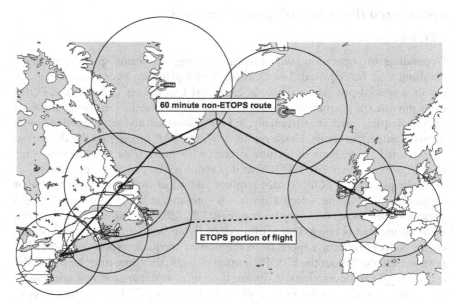

Figure 17.3a ETOPS Planning (60 minutes)

Source: Gene Kim

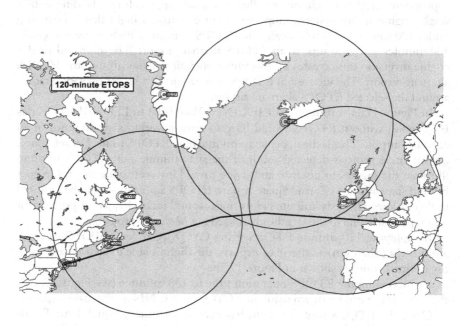

Figure 17.3b ETOPS Planning (120 minutes)

Source: Gene Kim

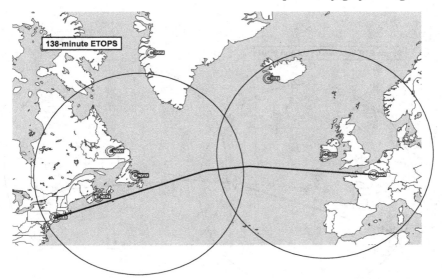

Figure 17.3c ETOPS Planning (138 minutes)

Source: Gene Kim

once winds aloft are factored in, the location of the ETP varies along the route of flight based on the wind velocity. When only two ETOPS alternate airports are listed, only one ETP would exist as in Figure 17.3d.

In Figure 17.3d, due to the winds, the ETP is not equidistant between CYQX and EINN. However, the time it would take to divert to either airport from the ETP would be the same. When more than two ETOPS alternate airports are listed, there will be multiple ETPs as shown in Figure 17.3e.

In the last example, the ETP 1 is between CYQX and BIKF. If the flight experienced an engine failure prior to ETP 1, it would divert to CYQX. After ETP 1 and prior to ETP 2, the flight would divert to BIKF. After ETP 2, the flight would divert to EINN. The ETPs and diversion scenarios apply only while the flight is in the ETOPS portion of the route. Once the flight enters the portion of the route that is within sixty minutes of an adequate airport, diversion would be to the nearest suitable airport in point of time. Flight Dispatchers also need to calculate Critical Fuel Required (CFR) at each ETP to ensure there is enough fuel to divert to the appropriate ETOPS alternate airport assuming additional factors such as:

- fuel burn rate for single-engine loss
- decompression
- single-engine loss *and* decompression
- APU fuel burn
- headwind adjustment
- drag induced by ice accretion on the aircraft
- aircraft performance fuel bias
- possible holding prior to landing.

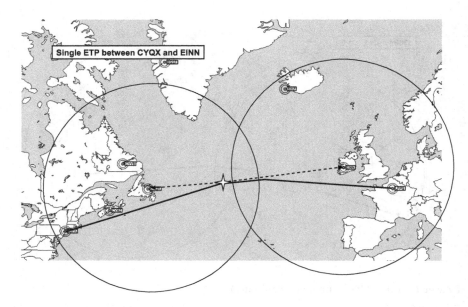

Figure 17.3d ETOPS Planning (ETPs)

Source: Gene Kim

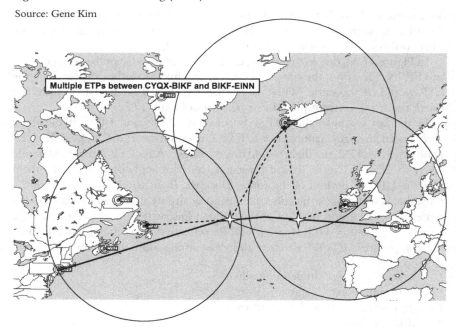

Figure 17.3e ETOPS Planning (Multiple ETPs)

Source: Gene Kim

Due to the critical importance of ETOPS alternates, Flight Dispatchers keep a close eye on weather and airport conditions throughout an ETOPS flight. Each ETOPS alternate airport has a validity period to determine the earliest and latest possible arrival time at that airport in the event of a diversion. During the flight, if an ETOPS alternate airport's weather conditions deteriorate below landing minimums during the validity period, the Flight Dispatcher and Captain must exercise good judgement in evaluating how to proceed. Decisions for the safest course of action include substituting the ETOPS alternate with a different ETOPS alternate if one is available within the fuel range of the aircraft, returning to the departure airport or diverting to another airport that is available within the fuel range of the aircraft, or continuing on the planned route. Because communication is vital to the success of flight following ETOPS flights, normal Very High Frequency (VHF) radio channels are augmented with High Frequency (HF) radios, and in many cases, Satellite Communication (SATCOM) radios. Voice communication protocol may be slightly different from VHF communication. This is especially true of HF communication where voice contact is usually done through a Radio Operator from a third-party radio network such as Rockwell Collins/ARINC.

Planned re-dispatch

Another example of specialized flight planning is Planned Re-dispatch. In Flag (International) operations, FARs dictate a flight may *not* take off unless there is sufficient fuel to accomplish the following:

- fly to and land at the destination airport
- fly for an additional period of time based on ten per cent of the planned time between departure and destination airports
- fly to and land at the most distant alternate airport specified in the dispatch release
- fly for thirty minutes at holding speed at 1,500 feet above the alternate airport (or destination airport if no alternate is required) under standard temperature.

Additionally, if a Flag operation flight is scheduled for more than six hours, a destination alternate airport must be added regardless of weather conditions at the destination airport. Often referred to as Contingency Fuel, the ten per cent additional fuel based on the planned time between departure and destination airports can be considerable as shown in Figure 17.4.

In Figure 17.4, the Estimated Time En route (ETE) is ten hours. Based on Flag fuel requirements, the flight must carry an additional sixty minutes or one hour of fuel (ten per cent of ten hours). The 10% Contingency Fuel requirement came from an era when there was limited ability to forecast weather across the oceans as well as human error associated with celestial navigation. Today, advancements in meteorological forecasting provide enhancements

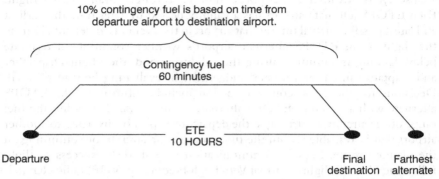

Figure 17.4 Contingency fuel calculation

Source: Gene Kim

such as satellite imagery and pseudo radar. Modern aircraft employ substantial redundancy in their very sophisticated navigational equipment such as Inertial Reference Units (IRUs) and Global Positioning Systems (GPS).

Planned re-dispatch is flight planning to an intermediate destination with a plan to recalculate fuel required while en route to allow the flight to continue on to the final destination. This procedure reduces the amount of fuel needed to meet the 10% Contingency Fuel requirement. Flights under planned re-dispatch essentially operate with two flight plans. The first is the original flight plan from origin departure airport to the intermediate destination airport, and the second flight plan is from a re-dispatch fix or waypoint to the final destination airport. While en route, the Flight Dispatcher will recalculate the flight plan from the re-dispatch fix to the final destination based on the latest wind models. During the recalculation, if the final destination airport weather is VFR (Visual Flight Rules), the destination alternate airport may be eliminated from the flight plan allowing for additional fuel savings. At the re-dispatch fix, if the flight has enough fuel on board to meet the requirements of the final flight plan, the flight overflies the intermediate destination and continues to the final destination. If there is insufficient fuel on board at the re-dispatch fix to meet the requirements of the final flight plan, the flight lands at the intermediate airport where it will be refuelled to continue ultimately to the final destination airport (see Figure 17.5).

Special Fuel Reserves

Some airlines have special authority to conduct another type of specialized flight planning known as Special Fuel Reserves. Special Fuel Reserves planning is used to lower the amount of 10% Contingency Fuel carried by requiring it only during the portion of the flight where the aircraft's position cannot be reliably fixed at least once an hour from any land-based navigational facility. Further, the

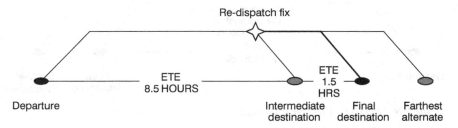

Figure 17.5 Re-dispatch fuel calculation

Source: Gene Kim)

Flight Crew must utilize long-range navigation procedures. Therefore, in our ten-hour example flight, if long-range navigation is only required for five hours, the 10% Contingency Fuel can be reduced from sixty minutes to thirty minutes as shown in Figure 17.6.

Performance-Based Contingency Fuel (PBCF)

Another special authority some airlines may possess is Performance-Based Contingency Fuel (PBCF). This allows the carrier to maintain an approved landing fuel program where actual fuel consumption of the airline's fleet is monitored and the occurrence of flights landing below planned arrival fuel is negligible. If approved, the carrier may replace the 10% Contingency Fuel value with a statistical value of not less than five per cent. Therefore, if our ten-hour flight had a PBCF of five per cent, the total amount of Contingency Fuel would be thirty minutes, or five per cent of ten hours (see Figure 17.7).

Combining Special Fuel Reserves and PBCF

In some cases, airlines have combined Special Fuel Reserves and PBCF to achieve significant savings from the original 10% Contingency Fuel. In cases where Special Fuel Reserves and PBCF are combined, 5% Contingency Fuel would be carried only during the portion where Long-Range Navigation procedures are used. For our ten-hour example flight, that means sixty minutes of Contingency Fuel can be reduced to fifteen minutes. If only five hours of the flight is operated using long-range navigation procedures and a five per cent PBCF is used during those five hours, the required Contingency Fuel would be fifteen minutes as shown in Figure 17.8.

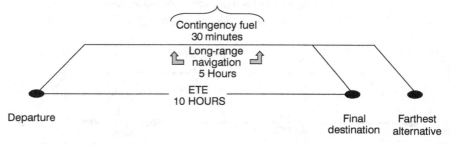

Figure 17.6 Special fuel reserve calculation

Source: Gene Kim

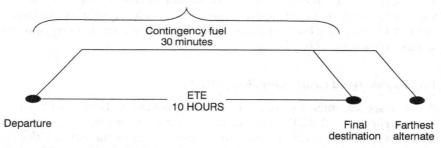

Figure 17.7 PBCF fuel calculation

Source: Gene Kim

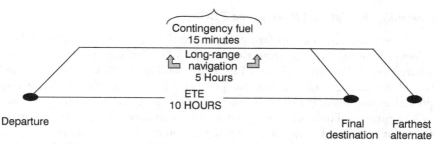

Figure 17.8 Combined special fuel reserves and PBCF calculation

Source: Gene Kim

Conclusion

Although they do not wear uniforms and are virtually unknown to the airline passenger, Flight Dispatchers play an important role in flight operations acting as a Flight Crew member on the ground. Tasked with the safe and efficient flight planning of a flight to ensuring its safe operation while airborne, the Flight Dispatcher and Captain share a unique relationship that is unlike any other in the airline industry. While technological advances and the focus of airlines on efficiency may have changed the business process for the Flight Dispatcher, the core role remains the same – to be the teammate on the ground for the Captain in the air.

Glossary of acronyms and abbreviations

ACARS	Aircraft Communications Addressing and Reporting System
ADF	Airline Dispatchers Federation
ARFF	Aircraft Rescue and Firefighting
ASD	Aircraft Situational Display
ATC	Air Traffic Control
BIKF	Keflavik
CAA	Civil Aeronautics Authority
CFR	Critical Fuel Required
CYQX	Gander
EINN	Shannon
ETE	Estimated Time En route
ETOPS	Extended Operations
ETP	Equal Time Points
FAA	Federal Aviation Administration
FARs	Federal Aviation Regulations
GPS	Global Positioning System
HF	High Frequency
IRU	Inertial Reference Unit
KJFK	New York JFK
LFPG	Paris Charles De Gaulle
MEL	Minimum Equipment List
NAS	National Airspace System
OCC	Operations Control Centre
OOOI	Out, Off, On, and In
PBCF	Performance-Based Contingency Fuel
PIREP	Pilot Report
SATCOM	Satellite Communication
SIGMET	Significant Meteorological
SME	Subject Matter Expert
VFR	Visual Flight Rules
VHF	Very High Frequency

18 Operational safety

John Frearson

Aviation in itself is not inherently dangerous. But to an even greater degree than the sea, it is terribly unforgiving of any carelessness, incapacity or neglect.[1]

Introduction

This chapter is written to provide operations managers, training managers and line crews with a perspective on the issues central to the delivery of safe operations on a day-to-day basis. Its premise is that there are few 'new' accidents; simply replays of accidents or causal elements that have happened before and which a mixture of forethought and 'speaking up' might well prevent. An operator's Safety Management System (SMS), the fostering of a safety-oriented culture and good crew training programmes are the principal methods of ensuring that lessons are learned and that crews are well-trained and empowered to 'speak up' not just in principle but in practice. This chapter focuses mainly on flight crews. But the content can equally apply to ground crew, engineers, cabin crew and even an airline's catering division. Wherever safety critical events happen it is essential that management lays down clear policies and procedures and line employees feel empowered to 'speak up' and be heard before bad things happen.

Is hij er niet af, die Pan American?' ('Is he not clear that Pan American?') These were the last words of Dutch Flight Engineer William Schreuder. Moments later, in heavy fog, his KLM 747 collided with a Pan American 747 still on the runway at Tenerife in the Canary Islands. His captain had not delayed the take-off to properly answer Schreuder's question. The accident was the worst in aviation history. 583 people died.[2]

Definition of operational safety

Australia's Civil Aviation Safety Authority (CASA) defines operational safety as that level of safety relating to activity in one or more of the following work areas:[3]

- flying an aircraft
- cabin crew operations

- dispatch of aircraft or crew
- development, design, implementation and management of flight operations safety-related processes (including safety investigations)
- any other duties prescribed by an AOC (Air Operator's Certificate) holder as flight operations safety-related work.

Background

The Tenerife accident, together with a 1978 United Airlines DC-8 crash in Portland,[4] marked the beginnings of the 'CRM era' where Crew Resource Management (CRM) took its first steps to develop alongside technological advances and take its place at the centre of aviation's safety focus. Over the next thirty years, CRM in its various manifestations was taught as a growing and necessary skill set, but largely not embedded in training and licence requirements. As CRM was slowly embedding itself into the fabric of aviation thinking, an array of technological advances (such as Ground Proximity Warning Systems, fly-by-wire, Global Positioning System (GPS) navigation, simulators, collision avoidance systems, etc.) were the drivers of significant improvements in safety outcomes.

The array of 'non-technical skills' which constituted CRM training, morphed into 'TEM' – Threat and Error Management, a systems approach to safety resting on individual skill development and systems design. In 2008, thirty years after Tenerife, a Colgan Air Bombardier Q-400 crashed after stalling in icing conditions on approach to Buffalo, New York.[5] The causes of this widely publicized crash were found to include non-adherence to Standard Operating Procedures (SOPs), crew management, command judgement, flying skills and fatigue. This accident and its aftermath effectively marked the end of the passive 'CRM era' and heralded a series of changes that introduced new standards in licensing and training.[6] Complementing the 'in-cockpit' training and awareness of the human element in safety, as from January 2009, the International Civil Aviation Organization's (ICAO) Annex 6 required ICAO member states to implement acceptable SMSs for their flight operations. In response to this requirement CASA published a suite of advisory publications (known as CAAPs – Civil Aviation Advisory Publications) aimed at introducing SMS into Australia's aviation standards and procedures.

In 2014 CASA took this forward with the introduction of Civil Aviation Safety Regulation (CASR) Part 61 which introduced mandatory training in Multi-Crew Cooperation (MCC) for pilots of aircraft certified for multiple flight crew members.[7] Competency requirements for MCC training include the following:

- MCO.1 – Operate effectively as a crew member
- MCO.2 – Demonstrate effective leadership and authority
- MCO.3 – Maintain situational awareness
- MCO.4 – Make effective decisions.

These competencies can be demonstrated within the following range of variables:

- activities are performed in accordance with published procedures
- operations may be Visual Flight Rules (VFR) or Instrument Flight Rules (IFR)
- approved flight simulation training device or aircraft
- normal and simulated non-normal flight and ground operations
- simulated hazardous weather conditions
- simulated interaction involving ground and Air Traffic Control (ATC) personnel relevant to aviation activities.

In addition, MCC trainees must have a good knowledge of:

- Air Transport Pilot Licence (ATPL) human factors (in Schedule 3 of the Part 61 Manual of Standards)
- TEM principles, with particular emphasis on multi-crew operations.

Part 61 also introduced the requirement for applicants for the ATPL to have completed a course of training in MCC.

Introduction to practical operational safety

By the time the pilots and cabin crew reach their aeroplane for a flight, most of the foundational elements of safety should be well in place. The operator's SMS exercises active safety oversight of the whole operation and the airline's operations and dispatch functions are monitoring weather and airport availability on a 24/7 basis for all their routes and diversion airports. Ideally the aircraft will be well maintained, the crew well trained, well rested and in good health, and safety equipment all in place. The dispatch office will have prepared flight plans, the pilots will have been well briefed on the weather along the route and issued with the latest information on their destination and alternate airports.

Ground handling crew will have safely packed the holds with bags and freight, potentially dangerous cargo items will have been screened and properly handled, and security personnel will have ensured that unsafe items and people have been excluded from the flight. Yet despite all this preparation and the safety-oriented structural and procedural measures, accidents do happen – and not just the accidents that fill the front pages of newspapers, news programmes and sensationalist documentaries. Of far more interest to industry professionals and safety analysts are the 'nearly happened' events; situations where the safety margins were below acceptable limits. For every accident that does get to the headlines there are usually many similar events where the safety margins are close to but not quite below acceptable limits. It is in this database, a far bigger set of events, that analysts, regulators and aviation safety managers can find out what's really happening in the area 'too close' to the edge of the desired safety margins. It is an industry truism that 'there's no such thing as new accident; just people with short memories'. That saying should properly be expanded to include the words: '...and people who didn't quite look hard enough'. Good pilots are those who are well trained and well supported by management, and bring 'chronic unease' into the cockpit as their way of managing their flight.[8]

Among the first outcomes following the establishment of the ICAO in 1944 was the development of a comprehensive suite of Standards and Recommended Practices (SARPs) for the operation of international aircraft. These were adopted by ICAO's Council on 10 December 1948 in accord with the provisions of Article 37 of the Convention on International Civil Aviation (Chicago, 1944). The SARPs were contained in a document designated as Annex 6 to the Convention, the name by which they have been known ever since. SOPs are contained in the various manuals and training programmes used to prepare crews for their daily operations. Standard calls and procedures are a very important part of SOPs. They have been carefully planned to give pilots the maximum assistance in difficult and normal situations. Standard calls are designed so that all pilots, even if it is the first time they have flown together, know how to operate together in normal and abnormal situations. These SOPs are followed, and are adequate to cope with respect to, the situations that arise on a very high proportion of flights, hence the good aviation safety record that has been developed since the 1944 Chicago Convention.

Culture

'The way we do things around here' is an enormously important factor in the actual safety outcomes achieved on a flight-by-flight basis. It characterizes the underlying culture that affects everything that happens in daily operations. Ideally the culture of the operation will be reflected in the training programmes and operations manuals, which allows the training and assessment systems to focus resources in a way that will reinforce the desired culture. The problem facing airline managers is that in many accidents, crew do not behave completely as they were trained. It is a common finding in accident investigation that the pilots involved successfully passed their most recent simulator checks and were well regarded by their managers and peers.

If the operator's crews develop their own unwritten procedures they become, in whole or in part, self-regulating. It is for that reason that standardization and benchmarking capabilities such as Line-Oriented Safety Audits (LOSA) and data analysis through a Flight Data Acquisition Program are so critical, as they provide evidence as to how SOPs are actually followed, with a relatively high degree of reliability. Operators willing to spend the small cost to ensure they do 'look hard enough' are the operators most likely to identify problems and threats before they happen. It is often said that a characteristic of a good safety culture is a level of 'chronic unease'; a desire to find out what they don't know but don't want to find out too late. That might sound a little strange but it is the hallmark of a good manager.

Ideally, training programmes will be continually upgraded to match the actual challenges faced by crews. The process of upgrading training programmes is increasingly proceeding under the banner of Evidence Based Training (EBT), an International Air Transport Association (IATA) and ICAO initiative using formalized programmes aimed at utilizing the vast amounts of data captured every day from line operations and training programmes to generate the required focus of training and procedures.[9] The recent development of Upset Prevention and Recovery Training (UPRT)[10] is an example of how the industry is reacting to some recent well-publicized accidents where crews lost control of the aircraft in flight.

But refining the training focus to ensure the best intra-cockpit culture and practice is only part of the solution. Even the best-trained and motivated crews are subject to another set of factors in daily operations. As stated above, 'the way we do things around here' is very important and the way that crews perceive and respond to management is just as critical as the way they respond to each other on the flight deck. In an ideal world, crews would be free to make the best decisions without any fear, real or imagined, of some form of negative reaction by management. A crew delaying a flight because of a passing thunderstorm would simply note in a delay report that the flight was held until the weather improved, and operations management would note the cause, add it to training scenarios if needed, and add that item to the lists of elements tracked in the on-time performance monitoring software and the airline's SMS.

Further than this though, lies the area of mistakes and lapses in judgement. Crews who find themselves in this arena face a dilemma. To admit to and confront their error and, after landing, report the incident through the proper channels (usually an air safety report) or possibly attempt to somehow cover-up, inevitably makes things worse. Human Factors expert Sidney Dekker was one of those influential in developing the concept of 'Just Culture'.[11] This approach centred on the development of a 'restorative' rather than 'retributive' focus to be the organizational response to mistakes and violations of standard procedures and regulations.

Neither retributive nor restorative justice let people 'off the hook'

Both retribution and restoration acknowledge that a 'balance' has been thrown off by the incident and its consequences. Both acknowledge reciprocity, or an 'evening of the score.' But they differ on the 'currency' to rebalance the situation. Both impose accountability. But they go about it in different ways:

- Retributive justice achieves accountability by looking *back* on the harm done. The community can demonstrate that it does not accept what the person did (it would not accept such actions from *any* of its members), and demonstrates that it makes the person pay.
- Restorative justice achieves accountability by looking *ahead* to meet the needs and repair the trust and relationships that were harmed. It wants to understand why it made sense for the person to do what they did. For this, they [offer] an account; a story. People

are accountable by reflecting on their actions and understanding *what* was responsible for producing it. This also gives them the opportunity to express remorse. The community decides whose obligation it is to meet the needs that arose from the incident, and agrees how to do this.[12]

In a truly 'just' world, crews (and indeed all those staff whose daily decisions and possibly mistakes can affect operational safety) would find a management response to mistakes and violations based on an understanding of why the people concerned did what they did. In this way, crews can make decisions and acknowledge, correct, and report mistakes and errors without fear. This has the very desirable effect of ensuring that crews and other operational staff can make the decisions and acknowledge mistakes free of the fear of overt or even covert retribution. This is one of the best defences against data that shows that accidents often happen when a missed approach, rejected landing or safe diversion, at little cost, to a more suitable airport could readily have been made.

Missed approach

Much aviation industry research has focused on reducing 'the frequency and severity of approach and landing accidents and incidents'.[13] Boeing focuses much of its research and preventative activity on runway overruns during landing.[14] The decisions to call for and execute a missed approach or rejected landing are the primary method of ensuring flight safety when:

- the approach is unstable
- required aircraft or ground equipment fails or there is doubt about its status
- weather conditions on the approach or at the airport exceed acceptable levels
- for any reason there is uncertainty about the safety of a continued approach and landing.

The decision to execute a go-around is the responsibility of the pilots. When needed, it is what the passengers pay for and what the airline, the regulatory authorities, common sense and professionalism demand. It may not always be an easy decision to make, just as the decision to delay a take-off is not always easy to make. A go-around is no indication of poor crew performance. But even with good planning and procedures, mistakes, unexpected air traffic control changes and other problems do sometimes happen. Pilots should assess the approach at a height above terrain where safety margins are good. The landing briefing should ensure that crew members understand before the approach commences that a missed approach or rejected landing is the primary method of ensuring flight safety if errors are made (such as false glide slope capture, speed exceedance, early descent, high sink rate, etc.) or if air traffic control instructions or weather create problems. A briefing which is done by memory and doesn't address the specifics of the approach about to be flown is potentially a waste of time.

All crew members in the cockpit need to know that is unacceptable to attempt to continue an approach which has already encountered a significant unintended or unplanned deviation from the briefed approach. If the criteria for a stabilized approach cannot be established and maintained, the best strategy is the execution of an immediate go-around. As D.P. Davies, author of 'Handling the Big Jets' suggests:

> Make an assessment of the criticality of the operation and then stand by your decision. If, having thought the whole thing out, you decide in your responsibility as commander of the aeroplane that it would be imprudent to take-off or land – then don't! Delay the take-off, delay the landing or divert. Don't let the fact that your competitors might be operating cause you to change your mind. If you should bust something the fact that someone else got away with it a few minutes before or after will be little consolation to you, your company, the passengers or the accident investigation people.[15]

But there remains the problem of crew communications. In many accidents, at least one crew member in the cockpit had some concerns about the safety of the continued flight path. The concerns don't have to be based on fact or readily available evidence, though they might well be. Few pilots would ignore a fire warning; no airlines would expect them to. But pilots can have those 'did I leave the stove on?' fears and the real test of how communications work is whether or not fears turn out to be groundless, are enunciated by the crew member concerned, and acted upon by the pilot in command. A crew, where one member is not sure of the safety of continuing (for example a take-off or landing) is, for that moment, divided and dysfunctional. And safety cannot be found in reassurances from one crew member to another that fears or concerns are groundless or in the simple overriding of a junior crew member by a more senior crew member. All airlines proudly announce that safety is their first priority. Yet as Admiral Nimitz wrote: *'Nothing is more dangerous than for a seaman to be grudging in taking precautions lest they turn out to have been unnecessary'*.

Referring to approach/landing accidents and over-runs, Davies wrote the following message to pilots nearly fifty years ago:

> If you have assessed the approach as 'critical' but nevertheless have decided to make it – a perfectly proper decision – this is your last chance to salvage what could be a mess. Proceed with the landing only if you are absolutely satisfied with your flight conditions at the threshold. If you are not absolutely satisfied, don't hesitate; open up and go around at once. If you are high and/or fast you are taking a chance. If you proceed and slide off at 50 knots and smash the aeroplane – and survive, your first reaction will be 'What wouldn't I give to have that last 5 minutes of my life over again' (Who hasn't said that at some time in their life?). Well now, at the threshold you have that five minutes so think about it.

Remember that once you are down and start aquaplaning there is very little you can do about it on a tight runway.[16]

It is thus vital to the maintenance and improvement of air safety for crews not to feel any real or imagined management or peer pressure as they make such decisions.

Lessons from the sea

The aviation community can learn many lessons from the sea, from the thousands of years of history of seafaring. Perhaps the most vivid demonstration of these lessons and the consequences that can follow came during World War 2 in the Pacific. The summarized extracts below tell their own story:

On 18 December 1944, vessels of the Pacific Fleet, operating in support of the invasion of the Philippines in an area about 300 miles east of Luzon, were caught near the center of a typhoon of extreme violence. Three destroyers capsized and went down with practically all hands; damage was sustained by many vessels, from Fleet Carriers down to Destroyer Escorts. Some 146 planes on various ships were lost or damaged beyond economical repair and 790 officers and men were lost or killed.

A hundred years ago, a ship's survival depended almost solely on the competence of her master and on his constant alertness to every hint of change in the weather. Ceaseless vigilance in watching and interpreting signs, plus a philosophy of taking no risk in which there was little to gain and much to be lost, was what enabled him to survive.

Obviously no rational captain will permit his ship to be lost fruitlessly through blind obedience to plan or order, since by no chance could that be the intention of his superior. But the degree of a ship's danger is progressive and at the same time indefinite.

The safety of a ship against perils from storm, as well as from those of navigation and maneuvering, is always the primary responsibility of her commanding officer; but this responsibility is also shared by his immediate superiors in operational command since by the very fact of such command the individual commanding officer is not free to do at any time what his own judgment might indicate.

In conclusion, both seniors and juniors alike must realize that in bad weather, as in most other situations, safety and fatal hazard are not separated by any sharp boundary line, but shade gradually from one into the other. There is no little red light which is going to flash on and inform commanding officers or higher commanders that from then on there is extreme danger from the weather.

The time for taking all measures for a ship's safety is while still able to do so. Nothing is more dangerous than for a seaman to be grudging in taking precautions lest they turn out to have been unnecessary. Safety at sea for a thousand years has depended on exactly the opposite philosophy.[17]

Lessons for pilots

No one was born a pilot. Everyone learned what they know from experiences in their own career or, importantly, from someone else. Ever since flying began, pilots have been gathering to exchange ideas, information, stories and questions. 'Hangar talk' was a very important source in the development of airmanship. Many older Captains learned their airmanship skills 'the hard way' in difficult military or civil environments a long way from the world of 'glass cockpit' airline flying.

'Airmanship' describes the personal and professional skills good pilots use in their daily work. Airmanship is not just adherence to procedures. It is an attitude, a way of thinking, of practising alertness, preparing for the unexpected, being observant, knowledgeable and practised in good CRM, flying skills, situational awareness and contingency planning.

> Airmanship is the consistent use of good judgment and well-developed skills to accomplish flight objectives. This consistency is founded on a cornerstone of uncompromising flight discipline and is developed through systematic skill acquisition and proficiency. A high state of situational awareness completes the airmanship picture and is obtained through knowledge of one's self, aircraft, environment, team and risk.[18]

Good CRM is a part of good airmanship and good airmanship is a part of CRM. All pilots make mistakes. That is why in most air transport operations there are two pilots on board and why checklists are used instead of just memory. It is important that pilots learn from their mistakes. That's one of the best ways to learn and build on initial training and qualifications, making experiences count for something. After every flight (or every day's flying) pilots should spend some time critically appraising their performance. Here they will have to be 100 per cent honest if they have made a mistake. Even if they do not think it is very important and may not even have been noticed by the other pilot, they should tell them what has happened. It may affect the operation of the flight in ways they do not understand. Acknowledging mistakes is a critical part of good CRM procedures. Admitting where mistakes may have been made and making notes as to what happened will assist intentions to prevent it from happening again. Preparation for the challenges ahead in flying will be assisted by the training department, by the aircraft's capabilities and systems and by fellow crew members. But much of the task of being a professional rests on the pilot's own shoulders.

> The demand of jet transport flying can best be met by enthusiasm. Personal enthusiasm for the job is beyond value because it is a built-in productive force, and those who have it do not need to be pushed into practice and the search for knowledge. Enthusiasm thus generates its own protection. This is the frame of mind which needs to be developed for the best execution of the airline pilot's task.[19]

Appendix: Safety Management Systems

Safety Management System (SMS) goes beyond a traditional Quality Management System (QMS) by focusing on the safety, human and organisational aspects of an operation. Within an SMS, there is a distinct focus on operational safety, and the human element in the system. This underlines the importance of integrating human factors through all parts of the SMS.[20]

ICAO had for some years referred to various elements of safety management in a number of its Annexes, and in 2006 formally initiated the process of developing a specific Annex covering SMSs. ICAO's Annex 6 to the Convention on International Civil Aviation (usually referred to as 'Annex 6') was amended to include reference to safety management and contained updated materials on the concept of acceptable levels of safety.[21]

In 2013 ICAO drew together material from existing Annexes as well as some new material relating to State safety oversight programmes and published Annex 19, titled Safety Management.[22] As with all other ICAO Annexes it contains a number of SARPs.

As from January 2009, Annex 6 required ICAO member states to implement acceptable SMSs for their flight operations. In response to this requirement Australia's CASA published a suite of advisory publications (known as CAAPs) aimed at introducing SMS into Australia's aviation standards and procedures. These advisory publications followed the foundational changes in Civil Aviation Orders 82.3 and 82.5:

- January 2009 CAAP SMS-1(0) Safety Management Systems for Regular Public Transport Operations
- January 2009 CAAP SMS-2(0) Integration of Human Factors (HF) into Safety Management Systems
- April 2011 CAAP SMS-3 Non-Technical Skills Training and Assessment for Regular Public Transport Operations.

CAAP SMS-1(0) was designed to provide guidance on the introduction of SMSs into regular public transport (RPT) operations. The CAAP covers operations in the two categories of RPT operations:

- low capacity, covered by Civil Aviation Order (CAO) 82.3; and
- high capacity, covered by CAO 82.5.

High capacity is defined in paragraph 2.1 of CAO 82.0 as an aircraft certificated as having a maximum seating capacity exceeding thirty-eight seats or a maximum payload exceeding 4,200 kilograms. Appendix 2 to ICAO Annex 19 specifies the framework for the implementation and maintenance of an SMS. The framework comprises four components and twelve elements as the minimum requirements for SMS implementation:

Safety policy and objectives

- Management commitment and responsibility
- Safety accountabilities
- Appointment of key safety personnel
- Coordination of emergency response planning
- SMS documentation.

Safety risk management

- Hazard identification
- Safety risk assessment and mitigation.

Safety assurance

- Safety performance monitoring and measurement
- The management of change
- Continuous improvement of the SMS.

Safety promotion

- Training and education
- Safety communication.

Advisory material on the implementation of an SMS is contained in ICAO Document 9859, the Safety Management Manual.[23]

Glossary of acronyms and abbreviations

AOC   Air Operator's Certificate
ATC   Air Traffic Control
ATPL   Air Transport Pilot Licence
CAAP   Civil Aviation Advisory Publication
CASA   Civil Aviation Safety Authority
CASR   Civil Aviation Safety Regulation
CRM   Crew Resource Management
EBT   Evidence Based Training
GPS   Global Positioning System
IATA   International Air Transport Association
ICAO   International Civil Aviation Organization
IFR   Instrument Flight Rules
LOSA   Line-Oriented Safety Audit
MCC   Multi-Crew Cooperation
QMS   Quality Management System
RPT   Regular Public Transport

SARPs Standards and Recommended Practices
SMS   Safety Management Systems
SOPs   Standard Operating Procedures
TEM   Threat and Error Management
UPRT   Upset Prevention and Recovery Training
VFR   Visual Flight Rules

Notes

1 Lamplugh, Captain A.G. A widely-distributed quote from the 1930s, framed copies of which may be seen in numerous flying clubs and training organizations. Viewed 12 December 2016, https://www.raes.org.au/index.php/accreditation
2 FAA *Lessons Learned*. Viewed 12 December 2016, http://lessonslearned.faa.gov/ll_main.cfm?TabID=1&LLID=52&LLTypeID=2
3 Civil Aviation Safety Authority (CASA) 2009 *Civil Aviation Advisory Publication CAAP SMS-1*
4 United States National Transportation Safety Board (NTSB) 1978 viewed at 12 December 2016, http://www.ntsb.gov/investigations/AccidentReports/Reports/AAR7907.pdf
5 National Transportation Safety Board. 2010. *Loss of Control on Approach, Colgan Air, Inc., Operating as Continental Connection Flight 3407, Bombardier DHC-8-400, N200WQ, Clarence Center, New York, February 12, 2009.* NTSB/AAR-10/01. Washington, DC. Viewed 28 June 2017 http://www.ntsb.gov/investigations/AccidentReports/Reports/AAR1001.pdf
6 United Kingdom CAA 2002. There are numerous resources that provide the history of the development of human factors in aviation. One of the first documents in this area was originally published by ICAO in 1989 and can be found at http://www.skybrary.aero/bookshelf/books/890.pdf. Viewed 12 December 2016. The current ICAO reference is ICAO Document 9683 Human Factors Training Manual, 1st edn., 1998.
7 MCC competency requirements are contained in Schedule 2 of the Civil Aviation Safety Regulations Part 61 Manual of Standards. Viewed 12 December 2016, www.legislation.gov.au/Details/F2016C00540/Html/Volume_2#_Toc393120492
8 The term 'chronic unease' is most commonly attributed to Professor James Reason. It is best explained in this extract from consultants Risktec: 'This term *actually appeared earlier in the literature than other related terms such as mindfulness, restless mind or safety imagination, when Professor James Reason introduced it as a 'wariness' towards risks as far back as 1997... Put simply, chronic unease is the opposite of complacency. It is a healthy scepticism about what you see and do. It is about enquiry and probing deeper, really understanding the risks and exposures and not just assuming that because systems are in place everything will be fine. It is not just believing in what you see or what you hear or what the statistics tell you. It is about resetting your tolerance to risk and responding accordingly and continually questioning whether what you do is enough'.* Viewed 20 February 2017, www.risktec.co.uk/knowledge-bank/technical-articles/chronic-unease---the-hidden-ingredient-in-successful-safety-leadership.aspx
9 IATA 2013 *Evidence Based Training Implementation Guide,* 1st Edn and ICAO 2013 *Manual of Evidence Based Training* 1st edn
10 International Civil Aviation Organization 2014 *Document 10011 Manual on Aeroplane Upset Prevention and Recovery Training* 1st edn
11 Dekker, S. *Just Culture.* Viewed 12 December 2016, http://sidneydekker.com/just-culture/
12 Dekker, S. *Just Culture.* Viewed 12 December 2016, http://sidneydekker.com/just-culture/

13 Flight Safety Foundation *ALAR Toolkit*. Viewed 12 December 2016, http://www.skybrary.aero/index.php/Flight_Safety_Foundation_ALAR_Toolkit

14 Boeing Aero Magazine, 2012 Reducing Runway Landing Overruns. Viewed 12 December 2016, http://www.boeing.com/commercial/aeromagazine/articles/2012_q3/3/

15 Davies D.P. 1968 *Handling the Big Jets,* Air Registration Board, Brabazon House, Redhill, Surry, England. 2nd edn, p. 216

16 Davies, D.P. 1968 *Handling the Big Jets,* Air Registration Board, Brabazon House, Redhill, Surry, England. 2nd edn, pp. 190–191

17 Nimitz, Admiral C. 1945. *Pacific Fleet Confidential Letter 14CL-45.* Viewed 12 December 2016, www.history.navy.mil/research/library/online-reading-room/title-list-alphabetically/p/pacific-typhoon-18-december-1944/admiral-nimitzs-pacific-fleet-confidential-letter-on-lessons-of-damage-in-typhoon.html

18 Kern, T. 1996 *Redefining Airmanship* McGraw-Hill, New York

19 Davies, D.P. 1968 *Handling the Big Jets,* Air Registration Board, Brabazon House, Redhill, Surry, England. 2nd edn

20 CASA 2009 CAAP SMS-1

21 ICAO 2010 *Annex 6 (Operation of Aircraft) to the Convention on Civil Aviation. Part 1, International Commercial Air Transport — Aeroplanes,* 9th Edn (usually referred to as simply 'Annex 6'). References to the safety related changes and requirements are found in Amendments 30 (2006) and 33A (2009) in the list of amendments to Annex 6, page xxii

22 ICAO 2013 *Annex 19 (Safety Management) to the Convention on International Civil Aviation,* 1st edn

23 ICAO 2013 *Annex 19 (Safety Management) to the Convention on International Civil Aviation,* 1st edn

19 Operating a flight
A pilot's perspective

Nathan Miller

Introduction

The role of airline Captain has always been that of ultimate accountability for the aircraft, its passengers and crew, but the role has evolved significantly over the last century since the first pilots carried passengers for reward across Tampa Bay on January 1, 1914.[1] Early pilots had perhaps more in common with pioneers than the image attributed to them today. Pilots flew in many cases by the seat of their pants. Reading Ernst K. Gann,[2] one can hardly relate to the modern-day commander.

Early beginnings

Over many years, aircraft have become more sophisticated, with piston engine power plants driving propellers in the De Havilland Dove through to the Douglas DC3 and culminating in the mighty Lockheed Constellation. This gave way to gas-turbine-powered aircraft in the 1950s with the advent of the ill-fated De Havilland Comet, followed by the hugely successful Boeing 707. With this sophistication came a number of fundamental changes for those who commanded and flew these aircraft. Early piston aircraft were, by modern standards, unreliable; their piston power plants stretching the limits of the technology of the time, they experienced numerous engine failures and other mechanical perturbations. Furthermore, systems aboard these aircraft were, by modern standards, rudimentary. Previous generations of aircraft were literally 'Fly by Wire', with a direct connection between the pilots' control columns and the control surfaces, via cables. Aerodynamic design, power, weight and speed all contributed to how the aircraft flew and how the pilots interpreted the aircraft through the control columns.

Early navigation and radio communications were conducted by dedicated professionals, namely the navigator and the wireless operator. Long since forgotten, these roles were necessary in order to carry out the complex tasks associated with operating early aircraft wireless communication systems and navigating using maps, dead reckoning, and celestial navigation. More recently, the retirement of aircraft such as the Boeing 727 and 747-300 saw the role of flight engineer, the trusted expert tasked to manage the complex systems associated with modern aircraft, become redundant.

The advent of the Jet Age in the 1950s welcomed in a new era in aircraft sophistication, speed, size and reliability. Whilst the early Pratt & Whitney JT3D-1 engines of the B707-120B were, by modern-day standards, underpowered, inefficient and relatively unreliable, these power plants brought with them a new age for air travel. Very quickly, modern technology, from transistor to digital and computer, saw the removal of the flight wireless operator, with this role now absorbed by the pilots. Next, with the new INS (Inertial Navigation System) technology, the navigator's role came to an end with the introduction of aircraft such as the B747-100. Finally, with the advent of FADEC (Fully Automated Digital Engine Control), further improved engine reliability, and enhancements such as digital engine monitoring and displays, the flight engineer was removed in aircraft such as the B747-400. The cockpit, having been reduced from perhaps five persons, is now a cosy two (excluding augmented crew operations). Compared to the swashbuckling explorer days of Ernst Gann, today's pilots are not expected to discover or learn or 'pioneer' – far from it. Now, airlines, and by far most of their passengers, expect a flight to be a far more sombre, calm and repetitiously banal affair.

The modern airline Captain and his crew are tasked with just that: to ensure that the flight departs on time, avoids even the slightest hint of danger and travels uneventfully to its destination, where it touches down on time. Sophisticated systems are only part of the trick to this. Decades of honed procedures, relentlessly trained into skilled professionals using leading training techniques ensure that the Captain and crew are able to offer the sound contented monotony which today's air travel demands. This chapter will discuss the ways in which the modern airliner and its flight crew come together in a detailed and intricate system to perform repeatedly, a complex, highly-synchronized routine, the result of which is predictably safe, routine and ultimately successful.

Role and responsibility of the Pilot in Command (PIC)

Whilst the intention of this chapter is not to engage in a detailed description of the role of the PIC, it is, however, necessary to at least bring to life the core legal concerns of the PIC in terms of their day-to-day responsibility:

- legal civil aviation legislation, including Civil Aviation Regulations (CARs) and Civil Aviation Orders (CAOs)
- safety
- disposition of the aircraft
- security.

Customer interaction

The modern-day Captains cannot ignore their role in terms of the customer. In general terms, this has been one area where little demonstrable progress has been made. Arguably, in the post-9/11 world of locked cockpit doors and heightened security, modern flight crew are more isolated from their passengers than ever before. Prior to 9/11, many Captains would enjoy inviting passengers into the cockpit or even, for a lucky few, up for a landing in the jump seat.[3] Many an aviation career was born through a fortuitous invitation to witness a landing from immediately behind the controls. The interactions between today's flight crew and the customer are limited to visibility whilst walking through the terminal and occasionally, time permitting, during disembarkation in addition to the venerable public announcements (PAs). Today however, the PA must be carefully considered. PAs prior to departure can be a useful tool to both provide the Captain's reassurance as well as to convey flight and destination information. These, however, are made time permitting. PAs during flight are becoming less effective as passengers are engaged with either their own portable electronic devices, such as tablets, smartphones, etc., or the aircraft's in-flight entertainment, in which case, an unfortunately timed announcement during a critical phase in the movie can irritate, rather than inform. As the role of the flight attendant has become far more sophisticated in meeting the customers' expectations (see Chapter 20), pilots have lacked this training and in many cases still believe their primary role – to conduct a safe flight – is sufficient in and of itself.

Initial recruitment and training of pilots

Airline employment programs are typically cyclical, with two key drivers:

- airline expansion
- pilot attrition.

Airline expansion

Historically, this meant the acquisition of additional airframes, achieving net growth in fleet size. There can be numerous drivers for this, ranging from commercially driven opportunities to nationalistic and politically driven ones. Whilst fleet renewal and replacement can and does create a temporary increase in crew demand, due to the need for additional crew in training (and therefore not yet operating), overall this is not a permanent state. More recently, as airlines have sought to increase profitability and ROIC (return on invested capital), one key lever has been to increase aircraft *utilization*. During the period from 2012 to 2016, both Qantas Airways and Virgin Australia announced increases to fleet utilizations.[4] Once any latent crew capacity is absorbed, further increases to fleet utilization will increase crew demand and therefore recruitment.

Pilot attrition

Pilot attrition (pilots leaving the airline) has two core components:

- resignations
- retirements.

Whilst a third driver – redundancies – also exists, it is not a recruitment driver.

Recruitment of pilots

Airlines, having identified a requirement to recruit, will typically commence the process with a detailed analysis of their crew requirements in terms of crew ranks: Captains, First Officers or Second Officers. For the majority of established airlines, pilot contracts force strict adherence to systems such as the North American Seniority system. As such, new pilots are recruited to the lowest ranks and placed at the bottom of the list. In exceptional circumstances, such as a lower pool of experience, or immediate demand for experienced crew, these airlines will recruit directly into more senior roles. An example of this in Australia was a Qantas Airways recruitment campaign in 2001 for direct entry B767 and B737 First Officers to alleviate the gap created following the collapse of Ansett Airlines. Many of the non-legacy airlines are not constrained by Seniority and will therefore seek to recruit pilots to the positions required. Examples of this include Middle Eastern carriers who continue to employ experienced Direct Entry Captains.

Airlines will set minimum experience criteria associated with the recruitment of new flight crew. Generally, these requirements are set by the Flight Operations team, having regard for factors such as the overall experience levels in the airline, capabilities of the training system, and simple supply and demand. Aviation Insurers' requirements can also be a factor in flight crew selection. Having defined overall numbers required, minimum experience levels and ranks to recruit, the airlines will then be in a position to place advertisements for crew. From there, an initial screening process will comprise the first cut. This will include a review of relevant biodata such as education and experience levels. There are many different variances on the overall themes. However, in general terms, most airlines will employ a three-part selection process post initial screening, which includes:

- psychometric testing
- flight testing
- interview.

Aspiring airline pilots are sourced from four main backgrounds:

- general aviation
- military
- smaller niche airlines and charter companies
- airline-sponsored cadet programs.

Following initial selection, new recruits will enter an intensive training program, which will take place over a period of up to five months or more, depending on initial aircraft type, the airline's training system, and recruits' experience levels. The stages of training will initially include the ground training elements, such as:

- orientation
- aircraft type technical training (Ground School)
- systems training
- flow or scans training
- Fixed Base Simulator training
- Full Flight Simulator training
- Emergency Procedures training.

Each of the above stages will be assessed, with particular emphasis on the crucial Full Flight Simulator assessment. Following the ground training elements, recruits will commence 'Line Training', which will consist of a minimum number of sectors. The exact number of sectors will again vary by airline and pilot experience, i.e., cadets will receive substantially more training. As a guide, First Officers on narrow-body jets will require a minimum of eighty (checked) sectors, whereas training for other ranks will generate different requirements. Line training will be conducted by an airline's qualified Training (or Check) Captains. Following the completion of the minimum sectors required, a final check will be carried out by a suitably qualified Check Captain. This check is commonly referred to as the 'Clearance to Line', upon successful completion of which a new recruit is cleared to operate with a line Captain, performing typical line duties.

Recurrent training and checking

In order to maintain quality assurance, ensure continuous improvement and provide training opportunities for new systems, policies or procedures, airlines will schedule pilots to attend a number of training and assessment sessions in an accredited Level D simulator. The task of training and quality assuring pilots is handled by the airline's Training and Checking[5] Department, sometimes referred to in Australia as the 'CAR 217' in reference to the regulations governing Training and Checking. The CAR 217 will be led by a HoTAC (Head of Training and Checking), whom the Civil Aviation Safety Authority (CASA) or equivalent national aviation authority (e.g., Federal Aviation Authority (FAA) in the USA) approve. The HoTAC is responsible for the Training and Checking Department's policies and procedures, including details of the airline's pilot training and checking program (usually a cyclic program), as well as Emergency Procedures Training and Checking for both Flight and Cabin Crews. This will be documented in the airline's Training and Checking Manual, which must be approved by the Regulator (e.g., CASA or FAA). In regulatory terms, The Civil Aviation Act (or equivalent) regards the HoTAC as responsible to the Accountable Manager (Chief Executive Officer – CEO).

Once checked to line, all pilots can expect four simulator session days each year. This can take the form of either a one-day check each quarter, or two days, comprising a training day and a checking day. The simulator provides an opportunity to practise, review and repeat specific exercises in a safe and cost effective manner, whilst simultaneously facilitating a learning environment in which maximum training value can be extracted. Regulation CAO 82.0 requires the use of Flight Simulator Devices for aircraft with more than twenty passenger seats. Simulators must be certified as appropriately representing the aircraft type to an acceptable level of fidelity. Sessions will normally encompass a range of exercises, as determined by the approved training matrix, and will usually include a selection of non-normal procedures such as system malfunctions, as well as emergency procedures (e.g., engine failures and fires).

Flight simulator sessions carry a degree of jeopardy, depending on the airline's Training and Checking Department policies. For example, pilots who are unable to pass a particular exercise after a predetermined number of attempts (usually with retraining in between) may be let go by the airline. In addition to Simulator Checks, pilots are also required to pass an annual Line Check, which is an observation of normal operations, conducted either from the aircraft's Flight Deck supernumerary, or jump seat, or a control seat. Finally, both flight and cabin crew are required to attend an Emergency Procedures (EPs) assessment – for pilots, this is an annual requirement. These requirements, covered under CAO 20.11, ensure that all crew are proficient in such things as the operation of normal and emergency exits for an evacuation on land and water, location and operation of on-board equipment, as well as crew duties in an emergency. Both the pilots' annual Line-Check and the Emergency Procedures training must be passed and will therefore carry a level of jeopardy, like the simulator checks.

Standard Operating Procedures – purpose and role

Prior to any discussion of a typical airline flight, the concept of Standard Operating Procedures (SOPs) must be understood. A SOP is a documented set of accurate and detailed instructions which articulate specific ways to perform a process or procedure. Their purpose is to ensure that the procedure is performed in a standardized manner, i.e., the same way, every time by every person. The absence of SOPs would inevitably lead to well-intentioned individuals performing tasks with degrees of differentiation, thereby introducing potential risk. Well-communicated and understood instructions ensure that, irrespective of background and experience, all those performing a task or procedure do so in the same manner. Much can be said of the background and history of SOPs. Suffice it to say here that a key learning outcome from aviation accidents has been that adherence to a set of SOPs provides an effective safety control. The US FAA defines the scope and contents of SOPs.[6] The SOPs defined in AC 120-71 includes items related to:

- general operations policies (i.e., non-type-related)
- airplane operating matters (i.e., type-related).

Further, AC 120-71A lists the mission of SOPs as being 'to achieve consistently safe flight operations through adherence to SOPs that are clear, comprehensive, and readily available to flight crew members'. According to Airbus, strict adherence to suitable SOPs and normal checklists is an effective method to:

- prevent or mitigate crew errors
- anticipate or manage operational threats; and thus, enhance ground and flight operations safety.[7]

Without strict adherence to SOPs, the implementation of good Crew Resource Management (CRM) practices is not possible. SOPs are recognized universally as being basic to safe aviation operations. Effective crew coordination and crew performance are two central concepts of CRM, and depend upon the crews having a shared mental model of each task. That mental model, in turn, is founded on SOPs.

Flight crew pre-flight – up to twenty-four hours prior

Rosters

The nature of most flying operations, particularly RPT (Regular Public Transport), dictates that the allocation of work to pilots is done via rosters. Rosters are generated by the requirements of the airline's schedule and take in to account various factors for the pilots including:

- CAO Flight Time Limitations (CAO48.0)
- industrial agreements
- airline schedule constraints
- crew fatigue.

Pilot rosters are published generally for a 14-, 28- or 56-day period with most crew being provided their roster at least seven days in advance. The roster will detail all of their work periods, their days off, standby days and any other duty periods. In accordance with the regulator's legislation, the airline is required to roster in accordance with the Flight Time Limitations (see CAO48.0), as well as to constantly monitor pilots' duty and flight times to ensure they are within the legally prescribed limits.

Readiness for work

Fatigue has become a more of a feature in recent years, as research and accident history have shown that the presence of fatigue in a pilot (or indeed any individual) has a demonstrable effect on their performance. Existing Flight Time Limitations are based on a prescriptive format which seeks to ensure safe operations through limitations on duty and flight times – on a per-duty as well as cumulative basis, minimum rest periods, frequency of late night and 'back of the clock' operations and other such limitations. In contrast, a focus on fatigue aims to understand the underlying impact of the work being performed, together with quality of rest and individual factors in order to gauge and predict an individual pilot's ability to perform the rostered duty safely and within acceptable limits of mental alertness. In the lead up to a pilot's duty, careful consideration needs to be given to managing rest appropriately to ensure that any flight duties can be performed with the highest levels of mental alertness, thereby helping to avoid fatigue-based errors. Regional and low-cost airline pilots, in particular, can find balancing the repetitious nature of their flying, with many days on-duty, and ability to ensure quality rest in the home environment with all of the ensuing distractions, challenging. It could be argued that the practice of multi-day trips, more common in full-service airlines which employ optimum 'customer driven' schedules, can facilitate a more consistent and undisturbed rest period, particularly for those pilots with a family life at home.

Arrival at the airport

Pilots will arrive at the airport at or prior to 'Sign-on time', the time that they are required to report for duty. At their home or at major ports, this will generally be in a crew room, where the company will provide the necessary facilities for their pre-flight preparation. Duties performed at sign-on will commence with obtaining the company-supplied briefing material, which includes:

• Flight Standing Orders, INTAPs (Internal Notice to All Pilots), MELs (Minimum Equipment Lists)
• weather
• NOTAMs (Notice to Airmen)
• flight plans.

Most airlines now provide mobile solutions for documentation and manuals, held and presented on tablets such as iPads. Pilots will therefore be required to ensure that the documentation and programs held are the most recent version.

The crew will gather the required information and then review it individually. Then, in accordance with good CRM practice, they will then discuss what they have observed. Ultimately, the crew is seeking to make informed flight planning and fuel decision, taking into account the serviceability of the aircraft itself (and any MELs) and any restrictions that may impact their operations. This could also relate to the nature of the destinations themselves and any restrictions on them such as runway closures or airspace limitations as advised by NOTAM, and any weather, both en route and at the destination. The weather in particular will play a part in influencing the ultimate fuel decision.

The presence of thunderstorms over a destination or the need to plan for an alternate airport will place a requirement for the aircraft to carry up to an additional sixty minutes of fuel. The consequence of this additional fuel may result in commercial penalties (cost) and/or operational requirements (possible offload of passengers or freight, or even rerouting of the flight). At the conclusion of the Pre-Flight Briefing, the crew will decide, the Captain having the ultimate decision authority, on an appropriate fuel figure, and this will be passed to the company and the refuellers.

Completion of Flight Planning also serves as a suitable time to decide which pilot will be the Pilot Flying (PF) on particular sectors and which pilot will be the support pilot or Pilot Monitoring (PM). In simple terms, the PF will be responsible for flying the aircraft, either using the autopilot or manually through the aircraft's joystick or control column, whilst the PM will support the PF with tasks such as checklist calling, secondary control selection (flaps, landing gear, etc.), radio operation, to name a few. Either pilot can be PF or PM, however the Captain will always be 'in charge'. Ultimately, the Captain will decide, taking into account factors such as crew experience, weather, aircraft serviceability and airport restrictions, etc., as it is the Captain who is legally responsible for the disposition of the aircraft, its passengers and crew.

PIC pre-flight briefing to cabin crew

Having reviewed all the relevant information to the day's flying, the Captain (or delegated flight crew member) will conduct a briefing to the cabin crew. This briefing can be to the entire crew, typical in smaller narrow-body aircraft, or to the Cabin Manager and/or deputy in the case of larger aircraft, who will in turn, brief the remaining crew. This is an opportunity to provide operational information to the cabin crew, and to gain understanding of any issues from their perspective. It also helps to build rapport as a basis for sound CRM.

An example of the type and format of information passed on is the 'ISTOP Threats' format below:

I   Introduction

S   Status of the aircraft (any relevant MELs) and to confirm crew is 'fit to fly'

T   Turbulence/weather

O   Operational considerations such as, for example, boarding via rear stairs, curfew considerations

P   Passwords

Threats   Any threats not identified above, along with mitigation strategies.

Once the cabin crew briefing is complete, the pilots will proceed to the flight deck.

Flight deck preparation

Initially, a preliminary cockpit preparation is completed to ensure that the flight deck (cockpit) and aircraft are in a suitable initial state to commence set-up. This will start with a basic safety check prior to the continuation of set-up procedures and will include items such as the positioning of important switches and levers such as landing gear (and pins), seat belt sign position (e.g., 'OFF' during refuelling), etc. The Captain will also conduct a review of the aircraft's serviceability which will include a review of the maintenance or technical log. Following the preliminary preparation, each pilot will continue with their own tasks. These tasks will be dependent on whether that pilot is Flying (PF) or Monitoring (PM). Like most of the normal procedures from this point on, the pilots will follow a 'scan' or 'flow' pattern which will define the order in which they perform their tasks. An example of a cockpit preparation flow pattern is presented in Figure 19.1.

Flight Management System set up

It is worth mentioning here the importance and programming of the Flight Management System (FMS). The FMS is an essential component of the

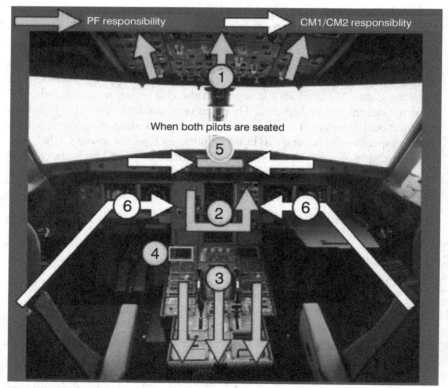

Figure 19.1 Cockpit preparation flow pattern

modern airliner and is a dedicated computer system which performs numerous aircraft functions including navigation, performance, and aircraft operations. The heart of the FMS is a computer 'brain' (Flight Management Computer or FMC), and a number of display units, MCDUs (Multifunction Control and Display Units) or DUs (Display Units), which the pilots will use to program the FMS. The FMS automates a large number of tasks which would previously have been performed by a flight engineer or navigator. The FMS comprises four main components:

- an FMC
- the Automatic Flight Control System or Automatic Flight Guidance System (AFCS or AFGS)
- the Aircraft Navigation System
- an Electronic Flight Instrument System (EFIS) or equivalent instrumentation.

Aircraft navigation is a primary function of the FMS. Utilizing Global Positioning System (GPS) and Inertial Reference System (IRS) inputs, the FMS calculates aircraft position and maintains Flight Plan track when required. The FMS sends this information for display to the EFIS, Navigation Display (ND), or Multifunction Display (MFD). Given the importance of the FMS, accurate programming is essential. Other essential checks that will be performed prior to each and every flight are first, the exterior walk around, where a Flight Crew member conducts an external check of the aircraft, its critical components and systems, and second, the oxygen check procedure, where each operating crew member will ensure that his/her crew station oxygen mask is operating correctly. This is essential in the event that the aircraft experiences a decompression.

During this preparation, once any required refuelling is complete, the fuel system will be checked, correct gauge quantity independently verified, and the seat belt sign ensured to be in the 'on' position. It is at this point, where all necessary programming and checks have been completed by each individual pilot, according to the requirements of their function (PF or PM) that the Flight crew will come together for the first time in the aircraft and verify each other's critical inputs as well as forming a 'united crew understanding' of the flight.

Checks and briefings

The final checks and briefings will be conducted at an appropriate stage prior to departure. Items discussed will include:

- aircraft status and serviceability
- fuel quantity and checks
- flight plan check
- Airways Clearance request and check
- briefing
- aircraft data check.

Flight plan check

This is a check that the flight plan, as discussed at pre-flight briefing, has been correctly entered into the FMS and that the FMS data matches the 'paper' flight plan data (i.e. with respect to waypoints, distance, etc.). This is a critical function for aircraft navigation, as the information carried in the FMS represents the direction that the aircraft will designate the pilot, or autopilot to fly. An incorrect entry may place the aircraft in a potentially dangerous conflict scenario. This check is conducted by both pilots.

Airways Clearance request and check

The PM will request an 'Airways Clearance' via the radio and record the information. This will then be confirmed as correctly set in the FMS, that the correct cleared altitude is set in the aircraft's 'altitude window' instrument, and that the correct transponder code is set. This will be verbally read back by the PF, and verbally cross-checked by the PM.

Briefing

The briefing is critical to ensuring that all flight crew share a common understanding of the intended flight path, method and modes of operation proposed for the aircraft – in other words the plan of action. The briefing is normally performed by the PF. However, it may be permitted to delegate it to another flight crew member when considered appropriate. There are various forms that the briefing may take. Many airlines do not specify a structure, but all will specify a minimum content.

Pushback and engine start

Once all the checks, briefings and required cabin preparations are complete, the crew will complete the 'Before Start Checklist'. If the aircraft is parked in a position where it is required to push backwards prior to taxi, then a 'pushback clearance' will need to be obtained. Once engine start and pushback (if required) are complete, the crew will commence another scan to ensure that the aircraft is now set to the required configuration. This may differ by type. For example, the Airbus type aircraft will at this point be configured for the take-off configuration, as per the example in Figure 19.2.

Once the scan is complete, the PM will request a taxi clearance (usually) from Air Traffic Control (ATC) and the PF will taxi the aircraft to the cleared position. In most aircraft over approximately thirty seats, this will be using a small tiller positioned near the Captain's left hand (First Officer's right hand if a second tiller is fitted). During the aircraft's taxi to the take-off position, the cabin crew will complete the passenger briefing whilst the flight crew will complete any required 'Pre-take-off' checklists. The aim is to have all crew

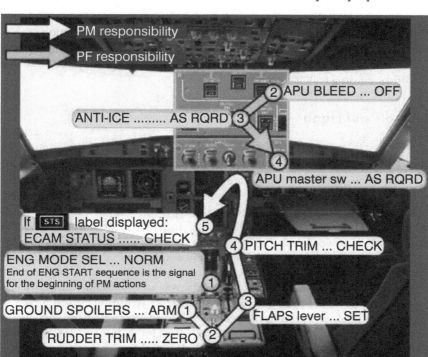

Figure 19.2 Take-off configuration flow pattern

checks completed by the time the aircraft reaches the holding point such that the crew can advise the Control Tower that they are 'Ready' for take-off.

Sterile flight deck policy

To minimize crew distraction and ensure that both pilots are focused on the critical flight operations, a sterile cockpit policy limits conversation/comments, etc. to matters directly relating to the operation of the aircraft during the following periods:

- on departure, from last door closed until the seat belt sign is switched off
- on descent, from transition level[8] (e.g., 11,000 ft in Australia, 18,000 ft in US airspace) until the aircraft arrives at the gate.

Furthermore, most airlines will incorporate policies restricting cockpit contact by cabin crew, generally during the following periods:

- take-off – *limited contact* between door close to application of take-off thrust; *no contact* from take-off power application to landing gear retraction
- landing – *limited contact* from commencement of descent or passing 20,000 ft to landing gear extension; *no contact* between landing gear extension to end of the landing roll.

Take-off and climb

Take-off

Upon receiving take-off clearance, the crew will complete any remaining checklist items, confirm that they are entering or on the correct runway, check any critical settings, then commence the application of power. Most modern transport aircraft engines (jet and turboprop) use FADEC to control the engines. FADEC is effectively 'fly by wire' for the aircraft thrust levers (for jet aircraft) or power levers (for turboprop aircraft). FADEC ensures that the application of power through the levers will result in the desired thrust being developed by the engines without exceeding any limitations (e.g., temperature/torque). FADEC's introduction in the 1980s was an important feature used to reduce crew workload managing engines, particularly during critical phases of flight, and therefore enabling the reduction of crew complement such as the flight engineer. Whilst the PF will move the thrust levers initially, at some point, the FMS (for aircraft fitted with this) will 'take over' the fine-tuning of power, ensuring that the preprogrammed thrust settings are achieved. Simultaneously the PF will use the aircraft rudder pedals to guide the aircraft down the runway to the take-off speed and rotation point. The PM will monitor the correct engine and other instrument settings, aircraft systems and tracking.

At this point, some explanation of 'V' speeds is required. V speeds are standard terms given to **defined** airspeeds critical or important to the aircraft's operations. Whilst there are numerous V speeds used, for the purposes of simplicity, only the most useful for the take-off manoeuvre are shown below:

- V_1 (pronounced Vee one)
- V_R
- V_2.

These are explained according to definitions provided below by Airbus.[9]

V1: Decision speed

V_1 is the maximum speed at which a rejected take-off can be initiated in the event of an emergency or as required by ATC or the pilots. V_1 is also the minimum speed at which a pilot can continue a take-off after an engine failure. If an engine failure is detected after V_1, the take-off must be continued. This implies that the aircraft must be controllable on ground.

VR: Rotation speed

The rotation speed ensures that, in the case of an engine failure, lift-off is possible and V_2 is reached by a height of 35 feet (ft) at the latest. (Note: therefore, at 35 ft, the actual speed is usually greater than V_2.) The rotation of the aircraft begins at V_R, which makes lift-off possible at the end of the manoeuvre.

V2: Take-off safety speed

V_2 is the minimum speed that needs to be maintained up to acceleration altitude, in the event of an engine failure after V_1. Flight at V_2 ensures that the minimum required climb gradient is achieved, and that the aircraft is controllable. V_2 speed is always greater than VMCA (Velocity Minimum Control Air – that is, the lowest speed directional control can be maintained in the air), and facilitates control of the aircraft in flight.

As the aircraft accelerates, it will achieve V_1 speed first, from which point there is no longer discretion to reject the take-off, so the crew will resolve any failures or abnormalities only when airborne. To signify this, the Captain, whose right hand remains on the thrust levers up to V_1, will then remove it from the levers. This is to prevent uncertainty of continuing the flight. An audible call will be made at this speed, simply with the PM stating 'V_1'.

At the speed of V_R, another call will be made of 'rotate' and the PF will commence a steady pull force on the controls, pitching the aircraft up at a rate of three degrees per second. Depending on the aircraft type, thrust settings, etc., the final pitch angle will normally be around thirteen to seventeen degrees nose up. As the aircraft moves away from the runway, the PF will call for the landing gear to be retracted, and as the aircraft reaches a safe height, or 'acceleration altitude' of around 1,000–3,000 ft, the flaps will be retracted. As the aircraft accelerates to climb speed, a scan will be performed by the pilots to ensure that the aircraft is in the correct climb configuration, and the 'After-take-off' checklist will be performed.

Climb

As the aircraft continues its climb, the crew will be given a series of clearances from ATC, for both altitude changes and for tracking, eventually clearing the aircraft to its planned cruising level. At 'Transition' the crew will set the aircraft's altimeters to a standard setting of 1,013 hPa (hectopascals) thereby ensuring vertical separation standards are maintained with aircraft in their vicinity. During the climb, crew workload begins to reduce, such that the crew will turn their focus primarily to navigation and weather updates for both the destination and alternates, as well as any en-route weather considerations. Once the seat belt sign is switched off, the cabin crew will commence service and passengers may move around the cabin. This also signifies to the pilots that they will need to apply additional consideration to turbulence and the possible reactivation of the seat belt sign.

Cruise

With the aircraft entering the cruise phase, the aircraft's systems will conduct the performance and navigation functions as programmed. The role of the pilots is then to monitor systems and confirm that the aircraft is flying according to plan, and act accordingly if not. This may include navigational adjustments for winds, track shortening or rerouting to avoid severe weather such as thunderstorms. The crew may also climb (or descend) in order to better optimize performance or to avoid turbulence. They will also maintain communications with ATC, either through Very High Frequency (VHF) or High Frequency (HF) radio, satellite phone or datalink. During this phase the crew will continue to monitor weather at the destination and alternates.

Descent

As the aircraft approaches approximately 180 nautical miles (NM) from the destination, the crew will commence final preparations for descent and approach. The preparations will commence with the crew obtaining the weather information for the destination, from a service known as the ATIS (Automated Terminal Information Service). This will be obtained either through the VHF radio, electronically via the Aircraft Communications Addressing and Reporting System (ACARS), or broadcast via a navigational aid at the airport. They may also gather information on any alternates nearby. Where the arrival airport is 'uncontrolled', meaning that there is no Air Traffic facility, weather information may be obtained via AWIS (Automated Weather Information Service). Similar to the activities in the departure phase, modern transport category aircraft are designed to allow the crew to preprogram as much information as possible into the aircraft's Flight Management System. This will include the approach routing, or STAR (Standard Terminal Arrival Route), the approach method, be that either a visual approach (by sight) leading to a circuit or an instrument approach, and of course the runway to be used. In most modern transport category jet aircraft, the FMS can also be set up to include information about an alternate runway and approach.

Also programmed will be all necessary data to give appropriate landing speeds, including aircraft configuration (flap setting), and winds on descent and at the aerodrome. The above information will normally be programmed in anticipation of an ATC clearance. Once this is obtained, the crew will verify the entries into the FMS as correct. By programming in advance, the crew are relieved of some of the workload which would otherwise be experienced in the busiest part of the descent and approach. Once all the programming is complete and the clearance is obtained, the crew will commence a briefing. Similar to the departure briefing, the aim of the arrival briefing is to ensure that all crew members have a shared mental model of the intended approach and landing as well as any likely threats and contingency plans. The briefing also serves as a valuable opportunity to cross-check the programmed plan against the briefed plan. The briefing will normally be performed by the PF.

Finally, when within radio range, the crew may seek to obtain from the company representatives at the airport information such as gate number and details of the aircraft's next flight. Modern jet transport aircraft descents follow a similar pattern. At the calculated descent point, the engine thrust will be reduced to idle and the aircraft will commence a controlled gliding descent. As a rough rule of thumb, modern jet aircraft descend approximately 3 NM per thousand feet. Adding approximately 20 NM for deceleration, a typical jet flying at 35,000 ft will commence descent at approximately 135 NM. Various factors may have some effect on this distance, including aircraft weight and winds. Descent speeds will vary, but a speed of about 280 knots is a general guide. In contrast, modern turboprop aircraft will also reduce power for descent, however not to idle. Therefore, their descents will be somewhat shallower.

At some point just prior to, or during the descent, the crew will notify the cabin crew of the need to commence preparing the cabin for landing. As the aircraft approaches 11,000 ft (transition level in Australia), the crew will commence the scans for the approach checklist. This will include activation of the seatbelt signs, landing lights and, in Australia, the setting of the aerodrome QNH (a Q code representing atmospheric pressure, adjusted to sea level at a particular station). The crew will then normally conduct a checklist to confirm these actions are complete. By 10,000 ft the aircraft will normally be slowed to 250 knots. In most jurisdictions, this is a maximum speed for operations below 10,000 ft. As the descent continues, the crew will be in continuous contact with ATC in the case of a controlled airport, or listening and communicating on the Aerodrome's CTAF (Common Traffic Advisory Frequency) at an uncontrolled aerodrome. At around 20 NM to touchdown, the aircraft should be approximately 5,000 ft above the airfield and will commence a deceleration to the approach speed. This deceleration will be continuous, with the crew aiming to have the aircraft at 210 knots or less by 3,000 ft, with 10 NM to run to touchdown.

Landing

The point of 10 NM and 3,000 ft marks the significant point of entry for most approaches to land. It is by this point that the crew will have commenced configuration for landing. This will include at least the first stage of extending flaps, as well as further deceleration. The aim is to achieve a continual descent towards a stable approach and landing. The stable approach refers to a situation whereby the aircraft is fully configured, i.e. landing gear extended, flaps set for landing, engines set for the correct thrust and the aircraft at the landing speed and descending at an appropriate rate, all by 1,000 ft above the aerodrome. The theory, based on numerous studies into aircraft accidents by organizations such as the Flight Safety Foundation, is that an aircraft flown in a stable approach will have far less chance of a landing incident, such as a runway overrun, or the need to conduct a go-around, where the aircraft aborts the landing, and positions again for a subsequent approach.

By at least 1,000 ft, the crew should have completed all instrument scans required for landing, as well as the landing checklist itself. By 500 ft, the crew will typically make a final call on the stable approach, ensuring that the aircraft remains stable. In the event that this no longer remains the case, the crew must conduct a go-around. For the final 1,000 ft, the pilots will continue to fly the aircraft towards the runway, following either a visual guidance system located on the runway, known as a PAPI (Precision Approach Path Indicator), or following an electronic 'glide path' indicated in the cockpit. Generally speaking, for approaches being flown in visual conditions, i.e. where the pilot can see the runway from at least 1,000 ft, the pilots may elect to disconnect using an autopilot and manually fly the aircraft from this point on. For most runways in Australia, depending on the accuracy of the instrument approach being flown, the pilots will need to disconnect the autopilot by somewhere between 750 and 200 ft. Whilst many aircraft are equipped with auto-land systems, in Australia the opportunity to use these systems is limited in poor weather, due to limitations in the physical airport environment.

As the aircraft approaches the runway, at around 30 ft the PF, using visual cues from the runway markings and environment, will manipulate the aircraft to reduce airspeed by gently raising the nose and holding the aircraft (the flare) at a particular attitude for touchdown. Various corrections will need to be made to adjust for wind and other atmospheric perturbations. Just after the aircraft main wheels touch down, braking will commence, either through the aircraft's autobrake system or manually by the PF, and the aircraft reverse thrust system and spoilers on the wings will be deployed. The aircraft will be slowed to taxi speed, the reversers stowed and ATC contacted for further instructions as the aircraft commences the taxi to the gate.

Taxi to gate

As the aircraft taxis to the gate, the crew will again perform scans to 'clean the aircraft up' by raising the flaps and configuring the aircraft to taxi. This will include starting the Auxiliary Power Unit (APU), to enable electrical power and air conditioning once the aircraft's main engines are shut down. As the aircraft approaches the gate, the Captain will either be marshalled or follow an electronic guidance system to the correct parking position. Once parked, engines will be shut down and a further scan and checklist performed. Any unserviceabilities will be entered into the aircraft's maintenance log and engineers contacted as required for rectification. At this point the crew will either commence preparations for a further sector or complete their duties and exit the aircraft. Crew completing their duties will be given a sign-off period of fifteen to thirty minutes to allow for completion of all duties. The completion of this period will mark the end of their duty period, which will be added to their previous periods to ensure that the crew member continues to operate within the legal limits of flight and duty times.

Glossary of acronyms and abbreviations

ACARS	Aircraft Communications Addressing and Reporting System
AFCS	Automatic Flight Control System
AFGS	Automatic Flight Guidance System
APU	Auxiliary Power Unit
ATC	Air Traffic Control
ATIS	Automated Terminal Information Service
AWIS	Automated Weather Information Service
CAO	Civil Aviation Order
CAR	Civil Aviation Regulation
CASA	Civil Aviation Safety Authority
CEO	Chief Executive Officer
CRM	Crew Resource Management
CTAF	Common Traffic Advisory Frequency
DU	Display Unit
EFIS	Electronic Flight Instrument System
EPs	Emergency Procedures
FAA	Federal Aviation Authority
FADEC	Fully Automated Digital Engine Control
FMC	Flight Management Computer
FMS	Flight Management System
ft	foot or feet
GPS	Global Positioning System
HF	High Frequency
HoTAC	Head of Training and Checking
hPa	hectopascal
INS	Inertial Navigation System
INTAP	Internal Notice to All Pilots
IRS	Inertial Reference System
MCDU	Multifunction Control and Display Unit
MEL	Minimum Equipment List
MFD	Multifunction Display
ND	Navigation Display
NM	Nautical Mile
NOTAM	Notice to Airmen
PA	Public Announcement
PAPI	Precision Approach Path Indicator
PF	Pilot Flying
PIC	Pilot in Command
PM	Pilot Monitoring
ROIC	return on invested capital
RPT	Regular Public Transport
SOP	Standard Operating Procedures
STAR	Standard Terminal Arrival Route

V_1	Decision speed
V_2	Take-off safety speed
V_R	Rotation speed
VHF	Very High Frequency
VMCA	Velocity Minimum Control Air

Notes

1 Smithsonian – National Air and Space Museum (2007) America by Air (Online) available at https://airandspace.si.edu/exhibitions/america-by-air/online/early_years/early_years01.cfm. Accessed 28 June 2017
2 Gann, Ernest K. (1986). *Fate is the Hunter*. Simon & Schuster, USA
3 Jump seat – an additional seat provided in the cockpit, usually behind and between the pilots, from which the crew's actions can be observed
4 Company Annual Reports
5 The term Training and Checking is used for consistency, but may also be known as 'Checking and Training' or 'Check and Training'
6 Advisory Circular (AC) 120-71
7 Airbus FOBN (Flight Operations Briefing Note): FLT_OPS – SOP – SEQ 01 – REV 04 – SEP. 2006
8 Transition level in Australia is 11,000 feet for descending aircraft transitioning from Flight Levels to Altitudes (and setting local QNH), but 10,000 feet for climbing aircraft transitioning from Altitudes to Flight Levels (and setting the standard atmosphere of 1,013 hPa)
9 Airbus FOBN (Flight Operations Briefing Note): FLT_OPS -TOFF_DEP-SEQ07 -REV01-AUG. 2004

20 Operating a flight

A flight attendant's perspective

Jamie Horswell

Introduction

Airline customers are subjected to various service experiences offered by airlines. The standards and quality of these services, particularly those offered in the cabin, form customers' appraisal and discriminatory judgement of the overall travel experience. As mentioned previously, the FA's role has become progressively mandated and regulated around safety. The interpretation of air safety regulations by an airline is important when defining their own policy settings. However, standard operating procedures can present contradictory elements between service and safety within the day-to-day execution of the Flight Attendant role. The suggestion is that both these elements are inherently complementary, they link back to historical attributes, and are set around a competitive/marketing-driven indoctrination, which can be found within many airlines.

While fundamental differences exist in the hard product between airlines including aircraft type, cabin configurations, seat choice, inflight entertainment (IFE), lounges and food and beverage provisioning, it is the quality, appearance, timeliness and overall performance of the Cabin Crew and indeed the safety and service tasks they perform, which become the major evaluative measure of an airline's customer experience success – particularly those airlines that offer a premium versus low-cost experience. Over time the airlines have become progressively attentive to the importance of inflight service, safety and the operational performance of Cabin Crew. This has a direct impact on the airline's stature in the marketplace.

Flight Attendant role – historical attributes

In the eyes of the flying public, the Flight Attendants are the airline.[1]

In the eyes of the regulator, a Flight Attendant is responsible for the safety of aircraft occupants. An airline's product is not necessarily just the physical infrastructure, but also encapsulates the 'soft' service consumable that takes place during the flight. This includes the functional, psychological and aesthetic aspects of service and provision of safety and security. In addition to this, and increasingly importantly, the service exchange includes the perceptive operational reliability aspects attributable to the look and feel of the Cabin Crew. Indeed, the marketability of an airline product, in the majority, is based on the perceptions and judgements made by customers of the inflight experience. This includes timeliness of performance, impressions of safety, reliability and care, and inflight soft service provisioning.[2] Cabin Crew are indeed the 'face of the airline'.[3] Edwards and Edwards[4] found that commercial airline passengers hold preconceived impressions and service level expectations which they hold for an airline and use this paradigm to benchmark and ultimately judge an overall inflight experience, the basis of which is primarily built on Cabin Crew interactions.

The role of a Flight Attendant for an airline has historical links to service, which over time have become progressively mandated and regulated around safety. The importance of inflight care for aircraft occupants dates back to 1912 when the first Flight Attendant, Heinrich Kubis, was hired by the world's first airline, Deutsche Luftschiffahrts-Aktiengesellschaft (DELAG).[5] Twenty-five years later, Kubis led the evacuation from the ill-fated LZ 129 *Hindenburg* airship, which was destroyed in a horrific accident while attempting to land at New Jersey. Fortunately for the world's first Flight Attendant, after assisting many of his passengers to safety, Kubis was able to jump away from the burning aircraft subsequently surviving the event without injury.

By the early 1920s under the name 'Cabin Boys', fourteen year olds weighing in at 40 kilograms were tasked with serving passengers thermos tea and pre-made cut sandwiches on the world's major airlines.[6] By the late 1920s, as the food provisioning became more lavish and the galleys on aircraft became more sophisticated, uniformed males held concurrent roles as flight engineers and inflight service facilitators. Cases of inflight illness, uncomfortable conditions for occupants and issues with passenger wellbeing came into focus. This was due to the nature of flying at the time, where one in four passengers became unwell due to flying conditions.[7] United Airlines responded to these concerns by employing trained female nurses as Flight Attendants, with the first, Ellen Church, hired in 1930 to work aboard the Boeing 80A aircraft. It wasn't until the late 1930s, which followed a period of rapid development in aircraft technology, that airlines with fleets of airships and flying boats began offering services that resembled luxury cruise ships with sleeper cabins, separate dining areas with hot meals and observation decks with more Flight Attendants on each sector.[8] Following some high-profile accidents, and with persistent issues around passenger care, the need existed for a more dedicated, skilled crew to attend to the cabin and its occupants. By the late 1940s, British Overseas Airways Corporation (BOAC) employed a combination of Stewards and Stewardesses, tasked with cooking and serving meals, cabin presentation and passenger well-being, all in addition to some specific cabin safety responsibilities.[9] These crew would change from a formal blue uniform used to perform safety orientated tasks, into a white mess-style serving jacket used for the meal service – a process that continues to this day on some airlines.

With the advent of mass passenger travel in the late 1950s and into the 1960s, the industry witnessed the so-called 'glamour' years of flying. This saw a strong uptake of Stewardesses to the profession, continuing into the 1970s. 'The image of the air stewardess epitomised the excitement of travel for a whole generation of young women'.[10]

The late 1970s and 1980s saw significant upscaling of the world's airline system, with an increase in the volume of passengers carried and major developments in cabin provisioning including new levels of service and comfort, and newly-mandated responsibilities for the Cabin Crew, which also included crew being used for advertising the airline brand. The use of Cabin Crew as the prima facie image and the embodiment of the Flight Attendant as the airline's marketing icon is best illustrated with the 'Singapore Girl'.[11]

With the advent of deregulation in the 1990s and a move to a low-cost versus premium full-service experience, along with industry consolidation, the role of a Flight Attendant diversified to different skill-set and work tasks. Many domestic airlines sidelined their meal services, with some airlines choosing to replace them with inflight sales of refreshments and concessionary items. Other airlines sought to minimize the crew-to-customer ratio in an effort to reduce costs.

Regulatory attributes

Following the Chicago Convention of 1944 and the formation of the principle agency of civil aviation governance, the International Civil Aviation Organization (ICAO), rules became mandated and standards called for Cabin Crew to be appropriately skilled and trained for civil-operated, multi-seat aircraft to facilitate occupant safety. A passenger could become unwell or sustain an injury related to the operation of the aircraft, or the aircraft could suffer a technical fault possibly involving a full-scale emergency requiring a crew-driven response. In all of these circumstances it is the response of the Cabin Crew and their ability to take the appropriate course of action to protect and maintain safety for all those aboard which ultimately determine the subsequent outcome. It is this critical safety function that regulatory authorities require airlines to pay attention to and thus sanction the role.[12] Under the auspices of the United Nations, ICAO issues articles, annexes and procedural standards governing civil aviation, the framework for which sovereign states oversee regarding their respective airline industry. The responsibility for governance and compliance therefore rests on the legislative instruments of each sovereign state, and airlines are assisted with rule making and interpretation by an industry association.

The International Air Transport Association (IATA) is the main association which represents the airlines' technical, operational and commercial interests, coordinating information, resources and discussion amongst its members. It disseminates this via guidelines including 'recommended best practices' that establish aviation standards in operator policy and procedures for the airlines to implement.[13] In accordance with Annex 6 – Operations of Aircraft – as published by ICAO,[14] the role of the Cabin Crew is to attend to passengers on aircraft and complete the following duties: provide safety, comfort and cabin services, ensure cabin articles and in-cabin baggage is secured as required, enable passengers to conform with customs, immigration and health requirements, and ensure passengers are briefed on the safety equipment and egress procedures, etc. Cabin Crew need to maintain competency in aircraft emergency equipment and aircraft systems. They also need to be competent and current in conducting aircraft evacuations and dealing with inflight emergencies including safety, security and medical incidents. Furthermore, Cabin Crew need to maintain a high level of dangerous goods awareness.

The regulatory definition as prescribed by IATA,[15] suggests a Flight Attendant or the Cabin Crew are assigned to perform safety-related duties in the passenger cabin in accordance with operator and regulatory requirements. They are required to be qualified to perform specific functions and carry out procedures which ensure the safe evacuation of occupants from an aircraft when required. Cabin safety is now a critical activity impacting greatly across the air transport industry with Cabin Crew contributing to effective and efficient operational safety performance in normal, non-normal and emergency situations.

The paradox within the role – safety versus service

The roles and responsibilities of Cabin Crew are twofold: safety and/or service. At times there can be a contradiction between the two very different functions or modes. Although it can be argued that the best service given to any aircraft occupant is safety itself, the role of the Flight Attendant has a rich history of hospitality, which is very different from the safety function. According to Lashley and Morrison,[16] hospitality is a state where the guest experiences the host demonstrating feelings of regard for that guest, including demonstrating a genuine desire to please each guest. The commercial air transport system whilst, by definition, belonging to the transportation industry, is implicitly a highly competitive, service-driven, people-focused, hospitality industry, where all the players are desperately trying to outdo each other for comfortable, attractive, courteous, genuine levels of hospitable service, aiming to please their guests the best they can. According to Paradis, service is '[t]he most important thing an airline has to sell'.[17]

Although safety is the primary function of a Flight Attendant, in most of the world's airlines the role of the Flight Attendant is typically dominated by functions and tasks that emanate from the airline's marketing department.[18] Even with this being the case, the effective handling of an inflight medical emergency, cabin fire, violence/air rage incident, or aircraft emergency evacuation, requires a special set of skills and well-practised knowledge. These differ from the skill-sets displayed by Cabin Crew and seen by passengers day-to-day. Unlike Heinrich Kubis aboard the *Hindenburg*, a typical Flight Attendant may complete an entire flying career without ever having to use the unique skills they are repeatedly trained and drilled in. These skills are often only ever used in simulation, practice and during the course of recurrent training. In day-to-day operation, a

Flight Attendant must be in a position to instantly exhibit these emergency skills and change suddenly from a smiling, welcoming hospitality/service provider to an assertive safety leader who specializes in aircraft occupant survivability. This is despite the major component of their substantive work tasks being concerned with non-statutory, hospitality/service and, increasingly, sales/marketing-related tasks. To meet this capability, a Flight Attendant is typically recruited and trained to a standard that allows them not only to understand, but also to manage the paradox within their role with the ability to switch between mind-sets at very short notice.

Each and every airline will have its own style, custom, legacy, capability and standards of operational policy. Edwards and Edwards[19] suggest these are all determined by cultural, historical, geographic and economic factors, and the importance of safety versus service culture and brand deliverables within the role as perceived by the given airline.

Recruitment, training and role facilitation

The role of Flight Attendant is one of the most sought-after roles in the aviation industry with thousands of applicants for every position. Working as a Flight Attendant for a major airline is often perceived to be a glamorous and exciting job, although this is considered to be a misconception by those already employed in the industry.[20] The role is physically fatiguing and emotionally demanding. There are the effects of travelling across multiple time zones and being away from home for extended periods. There are atmospheric effects from spending long periods of time in the air. There are the physical effects of spending extended periods of time on one's feet, and the role involves manual handling and manoeuvring in confined spaces at risk of injury, while working with potentially dangerous equipment. The working hours are often arduous and inflexible; they often involve lengthy stints, across public holidays, long weekends and at unsociable hours. Conversely, the ever-changing work environment, the variety of work colleagues, the chance to interact with a wide range of people, travel to local or global destinations, the lifestyle opportunities, the industry benefits and the rewarding nature of the role, are unparalleled.

The profession therefore remains highly desirable and ultra-competitive for placement.[21] To be recruited from the large pool of applicants, a Flight Attendant candidate will need to be seen as a professional, immaculately groomed, assertive yet approachable, genuine, a good communicator with excellent interpersonal skills and with a highly engaging and enthusiastic disposition.[22] Employer airlines will typically have physical requirements including height and proportionate bodyweight due to space restrictions and ceiling/locker heights, etc. Other airlines require a certain smart corporate look where there is no evidence of visible tattoos, piercings or issues with complexion. These and other qualities, physical attributes and overall physical fitness are normally prioritized over academic qualifications, although some airlines do require candidates to have a second language. A tertiary qualification or university degree is therefore not a requirement, but this and previous experience can be an advantage, particularly if there is evidence of customer service, teamwork and time spent in public-facing roles. These can be gained from nursing, travel, tourism, hospitality or as an emergency responder. The recruitment process can include telephone and recorded video interviews, assessment days, panel interviews, etc.[23]

A recruitment process is undertaken by an airline to ensure that workforce levels, known as the crew establishment, match the flying schedule requirements. This could be a reflection of additional aircraft being purchased, extra or new flying opportunities with network expansions, increased aircraft utilization, changes to the flying plan and or staff turnover. A range of preliminary training courses and interview preparation programs are available to help prepare would-be crew. These also introduce would-be candidates to the recruitment processes, and the necessary skills and role attributes, before recruitment. Such courses often have useful links to major recruiters and can be an advantage, but do not guarantee entry to the profession. Initial and recurrent raining for Cabin Crew is critical to the ability to fulfil their function.

On start-up, Cabin Crew would typically undergo extensive initial training. Over the course of their career they would also be exposed to recurrent training which is sanctioned by IATA and the State regulator. This is so they retain their knowledge and practice in the performance of their skills.[24] The duration of a training course may be impacted on by many variables – full-service or low-cost business model, product and brand knowledge, and fleet type certifications as required. Most airlines require Flight Attendants to complete this training upon entry to the organization and are then placed out on the flying line on a probationary basis while being monitored for performance feedback. Some Cabin Crew will have difficulty actually passing the initial training, particularly if not prepared. Some airlines will go to great lengths and great expense to ensure training is delivered to a high standard to ensure the best for their crew.[25] This is the case at airlines such as Qantas Airways, rated the world's safest airline, where Cabin Crew receive a significant amount of training in aircraft safety, emergency procedures (EPs), aviation medicine and medical procedures (AVMED), security procedures, galley equipment operation, aircraft systems, door operation, aircraft familiarization, brand awareness, customer service, galley management, and food and beverage delivery.[26]

An initial Flight Attendant training program may last up to six weeks, which concludes with supernumerary or coached flying. This training is typically conveyed via classroom lessons and practical exercises, and is further simulated in mock-up cabin environments, and coached inflight. EPs are a major component, and include the management of events that require a specialized response such as an aircraft depressurization, inflight fire, turbulence, an unruly passenger event, emergency evacuations and remote survival skills. 'Cabin Crew need to have a strong commitment to safety and security and understand their role and contribution in the event of an emergency'.[27] Service training too is a significant part of both initial and recurrent training for a Flight Attendant. This covers standards of inflight service delivery, food and beverage standards, service recovery, grooming and uniform, company attributes and strategic vision including corporate ethos and brand values.

For member airlines, training successfully completed by Cabin Crew needs to comply with the requirements specified by the IATA Operational Safety Audit (IOSA) program and the applicable state regulations appropriate to that country. The training needs to meet a high standard of competency-based measurement and be supported by efficient record-keeping in accordance with ICAO policy, ensuring procedural alignment. Airlines provide their Cabin Crew with a suite of documentation covering all procedural aspects and emergency requirements of their role. This can be done via hard copy or via electronic distribution. These documents need to reflect some prescribed IATA and regulator-sanctioned material and be kept updated with an amendment system as required by the regulations. An example of the documentation and amendment suite used by Cabin Crew at Qantas Airways includes:

- Cabin Crew Safety Management Systems (CCSMS)
- Aircrew Emergency Procedures Manual (AEPM)
- Cabin Crew Operations Manual (CCOM)
- Customer Announcements Manual (PAM)
- Operations INTAM (Internal Notice to Airmen)
- Galley Management Guide (GMG)
- Work Health and Safety (WHS) Manual
- Cabin Standing Orders (CSOs)
- Service Guide
- Style on Q (grooming guide).[28]

Procedural compliance is essential to ensure continual safe and effective operations. Many airlines prioritize this, as well as the message of safety, as a core brand value, for example, 'Safety is our first priority'.[29] There are typically two types of inspections or oversight regimes used by airlines to determine operational safety compliance and subsequent violations by Cabin Crew. These include the check/inspection process of upholding mandatory standards and the operational audit program known as Line Operational Safety Audit (LOSA), predominantly with a view of the Human Factors (HFs) and behavioural elements observed within the interaction of the crew, their environment and the various systems/ standard operating procedures. LOSA has the objective of observing behaviours in both full and reduced narrative, recording, coding, sanitizing and collating data from observational audits of crew performance over regular flight stages. In accordance with the Threat and Error Management (TEM) framework, this data is used to evaluate and measure procedural effectiveness, safety compliance and organizational efficiency. To this extent, based on final analysis of the data, procedural variations are monitored and can lead to prescribed changes in future and/or amendments to existing company policy. LOSA forms part of audit compliance under the standards and controls of the IOSA program, where member airlines register these activities as part of their IATA compliance, forming part of their risk identification and management strategies within the airlines safety management system.

Cabin Crew employed by IATA member airlines are required to be certified and hold type endorsements on each aircraft type operated, be a minimum of eighteen years of age and undergo and successfully complete training as defined by the relevant regulations. Cabin Crew must be medically fit to operate and carry out their duties whilst employed. Cabin Crew are issued with a uniform that complies with IATA standards, they are obliged to be familiar with the laws, regulations, relevant procedures and company policy, and are required to indicate compliance prior to duty.[30]

Aircrew rostering, crew complement and chain of command

Cabin Crew work to scheduled activities which are listed in sequence and typically come in two different formats: allocated rosters or 'bidline' schedules. These generally fit into thirteen 28-day or six 56-day roster/bid periods per year. Activities assigned may include: pattern rotations or tours of duty, rest/base turnaround, training, ground duties, transitions (carry-in/carry-out), leave, non-assigned available days, union leave days and, for reserve/blank line holders, airport and/or home standby spans.[31] The availability of rosters from 'bidline' schedules vary from airline to airline, with 'bidline' being one of the most commonly used systems particularly in North America, Europe and Australia. Some Cabin Crew prefer bidding for particular preference destinations and elect certain preferred days to work, and this is facilitated within the rostering system following either a rotational preference, seniority, or other type of preferential bidding system. Duty hour lengths and rest periods are built into the published schedule in accordance with regulations, airline policy and applicable industrial agreements. Rest lengths are dictated by these agreements and regulations, and through the review and management of risks as reported and monitored by the airline's own Fatigue Risk Management System (FRMS).

While individual sovereign state regulators dictate the minimum number of Cabin Crew needed to be assigned to a particular flight, in accordance with the Air Operator's Certificate, ICAO Annex 6, Chapter 12 *Operation of Aircraft* requires a minimum of one qualified Flight Attendant for every fifty passengers.[32]

> An operator shall establish, to the satisfaction of the State of the Operator, the minimum number of Cabin Crew required for each type of aeroplane, based on seating capacity or the number of passengers carried, in order to effect a safe and expeditious evacuation requiring emergency evacuation.

It is the airline's own product, service promise, length of the flight sector and the relevant industrial agreements that determine the actual operating ratio or crew complement on a particular fleet and flight above the minimum regulatory requirement.[33]

The typical chain of command for aircrew within a given crew complement according to IATA is as follows:

1st   Pilot in Command (PIC)/Captain/Commander

2nd   Supernumerary Captain/Check Pilot/Supervisory Pilot/Senior Check Captain

3rd   First Officer

4th   Relief Pilot/Non-Flying Pilot/Second Officer

5th   Senior Cabin Crew Member (SCCM)/Chief Purser/Flight Service Director/Cabin Manager/Customer Service Manager

6th   Second Senior/Cabin Supervisor/Customer Service Supervisor

7th   Cabin Crew/Flight Attendants (in order of seniority)

8th   Deadheading Aircrew.[34]

The PIC maintains full responsibility for the operation of the aircraft and the control of all of the crew while ensuring the safe conduct of the flight. The SCCM is appointed accountable to the PIC and is responsible for the conduct and duty of care for all the Cabin Crew. The SCCM oversees all passenger services on the aircraft including crew performance in normal, abnormal and emergency situations in accordance with the airline's procedures manual. They are there to provide leadership to the crew, liaise between the Flight Crew and the Cabin Crew, brief the Cabin Crew on relevant operational and safety-related information, apply all safety, security and service standards as outlined by the airline operator, manage incidents and accidents or safety violations affecting the aircraft, fellow crew and passengers. They also report and log defective aircraft items/components in the aircraft's technical or cabin condition log, in harmonization with the PIC.[35]

Cabin Crew sign-on and pre-flight briefing activities

The operating duty for a Flight Attendant begins when the crew reports for sign-on at a designated base or domicile. Airlines vary the number of crew base domiciles they operate, and many crew choose to be based from these domiciles while some commute from other locations for the purposes of commencing the duty. The propensity to commute is an idiosyncrasy of Cabin Crew, generally due to the accessibility of heavily discounted air travel. One of the first duty tasks for a Flight Attendant is to sign-on. Cabin Crew are typically required to complete this sixty to seventy-five minutes prior to flight departure when operating a long-haul/international sector, and forty-five to fifty-five minutes when operating a domestic sector. With recent technology advancements, sign-on is typically done electronically, with the Flight Attendant accepting the duty and the various pattern parameters. This electronic acceptance forms part of compliance acknowledgement and alerts the Crewing Department/Operations of the Flight Attendant's physical attendance for the duty. This also includes compliance with relevant statutory requirements for the duty, such as customs, crew documentation, passport validity, current identification, valid/recent qualification, acceptance of latest revisions/amendments and/or updates to operational cabin standing orders, service and/or port-related briefs, etc. This allows the airline to be assured that the Flight Attendant is suitable and qualified to operate the duty and is accepting the duty with the latest information, and is good governance. Following the sign-on, a Flight Attendant may be notified and subsequently be required to attend a procedural compliance test, also known as a line readiness check.

Prior to each operating duty, a pre-flight briefing is conducted by the SCCM. The objective of the briefing is to ensure all Cabin Crew members are aware of information relating to the duty stages. The pre-flight briefing is a critical component of the preparation for flight and promotes rapport amongst the crew while aiding effective team cohesion and performance.[36] Whilst there are mandatory/regulated aspects, the briefing typically covers updated miscellaneous company information, customer specifics, special handling, meal service timings, crew rest schedules, crew work position assignment, flight deck access, emergency communications, major operational/safety changes, aircraft operational information, aircraft system differences and door usability. As an added benefit, the pre-flight briefing can be joined by the Flight Crew. The briefing can take anywhere between ten and fifteen minutes to complete, and at the conclusion the crew make their way out directly to the aircraft gate. When downline (at other ports), this briefing is often shorter and can be quickly delivered at sign-on in a hotel lobby, on transport or aboard the aircraft itself.

Pre-boarding – aircraft emergency equipment and security checks, Flight Crew briefing and cabin preparation

When the Cabin Crew arrive at the aircraft gate, they interact with the ground handling agent and discuss the departure sequence, aircraft status and special handling requirements for the flight. The crew then make their way down to the aircraft and move to their assigned work position. There are three types of operational work position assignments on an aircraft, notwithstanding the particular category assignment of Flight Attendant, i.e., Manager or Attendant, or their service role such as 'cabin' or 'galley'. Furthermore, Flight Attendants have zonal responsibilities for their assigned area within the aircraft. There is the important operational assignment of Door Primary – this is a Flight Attendant who is accountable for a particular door/exit location on the aircraft. This is arguably the most important role for a Flight Attendant as they may be required to open their door in an emergency and conduct/lead an evacuation.[37] The Door Primary has the responsibility for the door mode selection, door opening/closing in routine and non-routine circumstances and station inter-phone communications. The second operational assignment is Auxiliary or Assist – this Flight Attendant is to assume the role of an incapacitated Door Primary. They will also have specific vigilance and operational/safety functions depending on their respective operating category and station location. The third operational assignment is the Supernumerary Flight Attendant, who is either there to check or be checked supplemental to the operational crew complement. An example of this is a Cabin LOSA auditor conducting an audit observation on the flight, a new Flight Attendant coming onto the line for the first time, or a Manager or Attendant commencing in an upgraded category.

Upon boarding, the Cabin Crew are required to stow their in-cabin baggage and proceed directly to their assigned stations. Cabin Crew stations are fitted with crew 'jump seats' and emergency equipment, typically in proximity to an exit, as specified in accordance with the aircraft type and relevant regulatory requirements. The Cabin Crew are required to conduct a pre-flight emergency equipment, door status and security check as soon as possible after initial aircraft enplanement. This check reviews the presence, appropriate stowage and operational status/serviceability of emergency equipment including inter-phone operability. Cabin Crew seat and restraint system serviceability and door condition, including door mode checks such as armed or disarmed, are checked. The security check reviews the security of the cabin, galleys, waste bin stowage, crew rest areas, lavatories, stowage compartments and other concealed areas, thus ensuring that no prohibited articles are present prior to passenger boarding. On flights to some jurisdictions there is an additional requirement of an enhanced security check of the aircraft to be conducted prior to crew arrival by a statutory or airport-endorsed authority. Unserviceable or missing equipment and/or security threats identified are reported via the SCCM to the PIC for action. In the case of equipment, a cross-referencing occurs with the Minimum Equipment List (MEL) for that particular aircraft type and the sector to be flown before the aircraft is dispatched. The completion of the check follows an inter-phone call-back for verification, typically made by the SCCM. All Door Primaries respond to the call and, depending on company procedures, can be sequenced right to left, aft to forward. The SCCM will report the results of the checks to the PIC during the Flight Crew briefing.

The Flight Crew briefing occurs between the PIC and SCCM and includes the following provided by the PIC: review of applicable INTAM, taxi information, expected flight time, aircraft serviceability/inoperative/hold items, forecast weather, refuelling status, flight deck security procedures and flight crew catering requirements. The SCCM will typically brief the PIC on the following: Crew complement, Cabin Crew assignments, passenger uplift, results of pre-flight checks, special handling information and boarding clearance, etc. The relationship between the Flight Crew and the Cabin Crew is critical and is often facilitated by good professional relations between the PIC and SCCM. 'Great team performance depends in part on synergy'.[38] It's very much a team approach with collective goals and the shared leadership of the crew. Communication at this level is essential for safe and effective outcomes, and can determine the success of the flight. The appropriate application of Crew Resource Management (CRM), where all available resources are used, and a full, unrestricted flow of information between the crew is fostered, creates an environment that is effective for communication, cooperation and teamwork. Consequently a safe operation is the outcome.

Meanwhile, Cabin Crew ensure the cleaning and presentation of the cabin is completed to the required standard, and they prepare the cabin and galleys for service-related functions, effectively after which clearance is given for passenger boarding. While cabin operators move through preparing the cabin, ensuring the passenger seats are presented correctly, amenity items are organized, newspapers and magazines are updated, coat hangers and cloaking tickets are ready, bathrooms are stocked and the headsets are placed, concurrently the galley operators are busily checking on catering uplift, ensuring ovens are serviceable, beverages are chilled and service equipment is loaded, all while checking-off items with a Catering Checker. Following all the pre-flight checks, the aircraft cabin becomes a 'sterile' (meaning secured) environment, placed under the continual surveillance of the Cabin Crew, while access by unauthorized persons is prevented until passenger embarkation commences.

Passenger embarkation and pre-departure checks

Passenger embarkation is the busiest period with the highest workload for Cabin Crew and in particular for the SCCM. Vigilance, situational awareness, safety compliance and service interactions are all part of the Cabin Crew's responsibilities during boarding. Before passenger embarkation begins, the minimum operating complement of Cabin Crew is required to be present and in position, and the aircraft is declared 'sterile'. The SCCM needs to be satisfied with the safety, security and readiness of the aircraft prior to approval being sought via the PIC to commence passenger embarkation. This approval by way of 'clearance to board' is then conveyed to the ground handling agent responsible for the departure. Following this, passenger embarkation commences.

One of the primary responsibilities of the Cabin Crew during this time is to check the boarding pass of each passenger at the boarding door to ensure correct flight and date. Customers are then directed to the appropriate aisle/stairs or directly to a seat, as the case may be. Cabin Crew positions for embarkation and disembarkation are specified around the ability to block or reach to operate the nearest exit, monitor passenger flow, assist passengers with special needs, maintain aisles and exits clear of obstructions and remain in position.[39] Cabin Crew are required to maintain a disciplined approach to situational awareness of the aircraft status and passenger compliance during this critical phase. This includes the monitoring of passengers for oversized baggage, dangerous goods compliance, safety compliance, fitness-to-fly/suitability, possible intoxication, correct seating assignments, seating restrictions and possible factors pertinent to the timing of aircraft refuelling. This occurs while ensuring service interactions are in line with the marketing/brand promise and the scheduled departure time is maintained. Pre-boarding may be enacted when the SCCM gives clearance. This process generally caters for passengers with reduced mobility or those requiring special assistance.

Passenger embarkation can occur while the aircraft is connected to an aerobridge or at a stand-off/remote bay. During passenger boarding, the Cabin Crew are not just conducting a number of visual checks on suitability of passengers to travel, compliance with seating restrictions and enforcing overall safety compliance, etc. They are also required to maintain situational awareness of the aircraft status. The aircraft status may change, i.e. the aircraft may be refuelling, alternative service doors may be opened and closed as required by ground staff, live engine runs could be conducted, etc. All of these situations would require a different arrangement in terms of where the crew are to be positioned around the aircraft and their mode of response, i.e. safety or service – otherwise known as 'transit requirements'. The Cabin Crew would also be distributing extension seat belts, conducting safety briefings to passengers with special needs, completing over-wing or other self-help style exit briefings to passengers adjacent to exits and offering support to stow or find approved stowage for carry-on baggage. There could be a double seat booking, or a requirement for the crew to conduct a headcount, resulting in passengers needing to be off-loaded, which again will require a different form of Cabin Crew response. The crew are further assessing customer suitability to travel in their zones, are ensuring that the lavatories are unoccupied prior to pushback, and are ensuring that electronic device compliance is met.

One of the most important combined service/safety-related duties during this busy and critical stage is the welcoming public announcement (PA). This is normally executed as the final customer boards and is usually conducted by the SCCM or via a selection using the aircraft's Prerecorded Announcements and Music (PRAM). These announcements are typically designed to meet the requirements of the state regulator and fall under the published recommended practices of IATA.[40] Depending on aircraft type, this PRAM can be activated via a Flight Attendant Panel (FAP) or equivalent. This is a trigger point informing the Cabin Crew that departure is imminent and to ensure the cabin is secure for pushback. The Cabin Crew carry out a sweeping check of the aircraft cabin including the following:

- ensuring passengers are seated
- seat belts fastened
- infant restraints are fitted
- seat backs upright
- all carry-on articles stowed
- overhead lockers closed and secured
- tray tables and other deployable items, including bassinets, stowed
- window shades up
- electronically dimmed windows set to 'full clear'
- galleys secured
- carts and galley load units latched and secured
- cabin dividers and cross-over curtains restrained
- passenger portable electronic device (PED) use is observed to be in the appropriate mode
- aisles, exits and crossovers are clear ready for door closure and subsequent pushback.

Before the final passenger entry door is closed, all ground support staff are checked that they have vacated the aircraft and a copy of the manifest or passenger information list (PIL) is handed over to the SCCM by the ground agent. This forms part of a regulatory requirement when operating on international flights and is good practice on all others.

Precision timing schedule/door closure

Depending on airline operator procedures, the final passenger door closure occurs in consultation with the flight deck, and the authority to do so typically comes from the PIC. The decision to close the final door is made once passenger boarding has ceased, special briefings are complete, aircraft documents including the maintenance release, load sheet, PIL, flight plan and fuel load are aboard, all passengers are seated and all stowages are secure. Procedures for door closing, whether initiated by the Cabin Crew or the ground agent, vary amongst operators and between aircraft types. An example of a final door closing sequence on an Airbus Industrie A380-800 aircraft operated by Qantas[41] is initiated by the Cabin Crew. The Cabin Crew provide a verbal clearance to close the final door to the ground staff, who subsequently remove the safety shoe from the door underside and secure the exterior door handle. The door is then closed internally with the Flight Attendant pressing and holding the electronic Door/Slides Indication Panel (DSIP), then rotating the door operating handle to close when the door is moved into the door frame. The reopening of an aircraft door prior to pushback brings increased risk and can only be done safely with the approval of the PIC. This can be initiated by a ground agent or the SCCM depending on airline procedures. If the request is generated from the ground, the PIC is typically notified over the aircraft radio via the airline's Movement Control Centre. Consideration is given to the aircraft/flight schedule, airport slot constraints, air traffic congestion, loading requirements and airport gate requirements as to timeliness of door closure. Also known as the precision timing schedule (PTS), the decision timing for final door closure is critical within this sequence. An example is for door closure to occur at three minutes before scheduled flight departure time ('minus three minutes').

Pushback, taxi-out, take-off and top-of-climb

As the aircraft pushes back from the gate, or pushes back or performs 'aircraft power out' from the hardstand (where stand-off procedures are implemented), and the stairs are withdrawn from the aircraft, the Cabin Crew are instructed to arm their designated doors, check their doors and in most cases, cross-check an adjacent door. Door arming call-back occurs across the cabin requiring the Door Primary Flight Attendant at each station to respond to confirm the door arming status. This call-back response is completed typically right to left, aft to forward. Verification can be sought by both the SCCM and PIC via the aircraft's electronic cabin monitoring, in some cases removing the need for the call-back altogether, depending on operator process. The door arming procedure is essentially switching the mode of the door from Manual to Automatic. This is done using a door arming lever or by manually attaching a girt-bar to the door bracket, dependent upon aircraft type. A girt-bar mechanism extends to the door bustle or fuselage and is attached to an embedded escape device/slide/slide-raft. Depending on aircraft type and door, this is in turn physically attached to the doorframe. This facilitates the immediate deployment of the escape device once the door handle is rotated to the automatic/armed mode, and on larger aircraft this typically involves a power-assist feature. The Cabin Crew at this stage remain in close proximity to their designated armed door, to prevent any inadvertent slide deployment (ISD).

Prior to every take-off, Cabin Crew provide a general safety briefing to all aircraft occupants independently or via a combination of demonstration, audio or video. It is recommended by IATA[42] that Cabin Crew be assigned a designated demonstration position, at the very least to indicate the nearest exit. The following safety information should be conveyed in a safety briefing:

- passenger signs
- seat belt use
- escape path lighting
- nearest exits
- review of the 'passenger safety on board' card
- life jackets
- oxygen systems.

Cabin Crew use this time to assess the suitability of occupants as Able-Bodied Passengers (ABPs) who may be able to assist in an emergency, and to monitor compliance to the safety messaging. They then move through to ensure the cabin and galleys are cross-checked and secured for the take-off phase. The Cabin Crew then take up assigned crew seats at their nominated stations, secure themselves, adopt the relaxed brace position and either partake in a 'cabin secure for take-off' call-back or immediately observe a sterile cabin period until the seat belt signs are extinguished after take-off. Discussion amongst crew and with passengers at this stage is minimized to safety-related matters only. This period is also known as 'silent review', where an appraisal of potential responses to an emergency is commenced. This would include the notation of aircraft type, the operation of the emergency exit, location of important safety equipment, impact drill, suitability of ABPs and non-ABPs, brace position, evacuation signal and appropriate commands. The review is aimed at focusing the Cabin Crew's uninterrupted attention on safety and their responsibilities should an unexpected emergency occur during this period.[43] The period is similarly timed with what is regulated and known across the industry as 'Sterile Flight Deck'. This is a time of limited contact with or between the Flight Crew – unless it is a safety-related matter – and of zero contact during the actual take-off roll, until the aircraft becomes airborne.[44]

Cruise, customer management, inflight service, service recovery

After take-off, and once the seat belt sign is extinguished, the Cabin Crew will ensure lavatory doors and exit row seats are unlocked. One of the first roles of an SCCM or other senior crew member in most airlines is a personal welcome by way of a 'meet and greet' with customers, with priority being given to premium/commercially important customers and those customers with special needs or tight connections, etc. The Cabin Crew focus their attention on providing inflight customer service throughout the flight aligned with the airline's service standards and policy settings. The Cabin Crew ensure flight crew are provisioned and a plan is put in place for the length of flight for meals and controlled rest periods. The Cabin Crew remain available to provide relief to the flight crew ensuring mandated flight deck minimum occupancy requirements are met. Typically, the Cabin Crew would contact the flight deck every twenty to thirty minutes, never exceeding an hour unless controlled rest on the flight deck is being observed. With customers and crew free to move about the cabin unrestrained, Cabin Crew will conduct regular cabin and lavatory patrols, ensuring equipment is not interfered with and passenger safety compliance. Cabin Crew patrols go on all flight, throughout the cabin. This cabin presence is complemented by call-light response following activation from passenger seats and lavatories. Crew respond to these with urgency in case passengers require urgent medical assistance, or in case there may be a possible safety-related incident. More often than not call-light requests are regarding a service-related request.

It is widely accepted that customers spend more time with Cabin Crew than with any other role or employee group within the airline.[45] Therefore, the airline industry is inundated with the latest customer service programs, which typically harness inflight service quality and conformity to stringent standards and specifications. Holloway found that it all comes down to the quality of the service offered inflight and the value proposition that airline customers use to benchmark a given airline's service promise against their own perceptions.[46] Customer service promise and product tangibles affected by Cabin Crew can include:

- the physical attributes, presentation and serviceability of the facilities/seats/ cabin and presentation of crew
- crew responsiveness, including the enthusiasm and disposition of the crew to help and provide efficient services and smile
- assurance, including experience, confidence, empowerment, knowledge, deportment and crew approachability and trustworthiness
- empathy including the genuineness and caring nature of the crew when providing service or recovering a service shortfall.

The service offered in flight by Cabin Crew will have a significant impact on the likelihood of the customer repeating their custom with that airline. The delivery of services through a personal connection is considered to provide the edge over competitors. The conundrum for an airline's service department is whether to focus on the transactional elements of the service, such as the competency and standards of the service skills themselves, or on the interactional elements, which deal more with the rapport or relationship between the Cabin Crew and the customer. The requirements around a more interactional service call for Cabin Crew to be attentive, ready to assist, warm, friendly and approachable. Further, they must be polite, flexible, have diplomacy and tact in difficult situations, and understand what it means to be treated, and how to treat people, individually. Importantly, they must know how to *smile*. Delivery of an airline's flight service policy is therefore an important function of Flight Attendants, which they are highly trained to deliver. Each inflight service policy is accompanied by a set of procedures, which set out the standards of delivery and the procedures to follow for achieving delivery. Meal, beverage, duty-free and ancillary/concessionary services will differ greatly between airlines. With this being the case, typical service activities across different classes of travel can follow defined sequences. A generic example can be explained across different classes of travel:

- First Class – a more sophisticated, exclusive, tailored/individualized service offering with classic tones, fine dining, fine crockery, fine wines, sommelier service, table d'hôte and à la carte style meal services depending on customer preference. First class amenities are highly prized, and the sleep service offered by airlines includes luxurious bedding and a turndown service, and, more recently, on-board shower facilities.
- Business Class – can start with a pre-meal drink service, followed by order-taking of small and larger courses, followed by a cabin-wide lay-up of the tray tables, then meal and beverage service delivery, followed by replenishments, then collection, and finally dessert with a combined sweets–hot drinks trolley service.
- Premium Economy – akin to business with economy class food and business class beverage provisioning, somewhat similar across most carriers, dedicated crew format and a slightly scaled-up amenity.
- Economy – on most airlines Cabin Crew will work from a cart and deliver meal and drink services to passengers during main meal services. The Flight Attendant will remove the tray or box of food from the cart, placing a hot or cold meal choice in the tray/box as per customer preference, offer a drink then move on to the next customer.

The service expectations of customers must be understood by airlines in order for them to effectively deploy service strategies with the goals of addressing and meeting customer needs, being consistent with delivery, and being competitive. Holloway found consistency to be the big challenge for most airlines due to the complex nature of providing customer service across remote workgroups.[47] There are many variables sited around intangibility within the service interface, such as variability in employees, experiential dynamics, the psychosocial state of the customer, and now, more importantly, the corporate culture within the service organization. Where a service shortfall occurs, airlines have developed strategies for recovering customers. Service recovery is an important strategy deployed by the Cabin Crew as part of their role to ensure customer retention and to avert a negative word of mouth situation from arising following the receipt of a complaint.

During the cruise stage of flight, the Cabin Crew may be confronted with a number of occurrences which will have to be managed concerning the provision of normal service delivery, crew rest, and ongoing cabin safety surveillance. Medical events in particular require the urgent attention and oversight of the Cabin Crew should one arise at any stage during the flight. The responsibility typically rests with the SCCM or delegate to ensure such situations are handled correctly and a care plan is in place for the passenger(s) involved. A key part of the role is to deliver emergency first aid in response to a variety of conditions, provide treatment, administer medication and/or oxygen and importantly communicate with medical experts, either on board or from the ground via a satellite communications link.

Turbulence is another threat that Cabin Crew face, coming in two formats: anticipated or unanticipated. In times of anticipated turbulence, the crew will have notice to secure the cabin and themselves prior to the onset of the turbulence. Unanticipated turbulence can present an immediate safety hazard, requiring the crew to quickly secure both service equipment and themselves.

Cabin Crew rest can vary across carriers, depending on flight sector length, industrial agreement, regulatory requirements and the provisioned crew rest amenity on the specific aircraft being operated. In long-haul/transoceanic flying, crew rest facilities are typically recumbent, with a horizontal, curtained bunk, and with high comfort seating for meals/smaller breaks. These facilities are needed to rest the crew due to the lengthy duty times involved in this type of flying. On a fourteen-hour sector, it's not uncommon for a long-haul Flight Attendant to receive three rest breaks, for example, a twenty-minute meal break, followed by ninety-minute rest break, and then a 180-minute sleep break.

Disruption/diversion management

During a disruption or diversion, the Cabin Crew are key to providing comfort, information and presence to passengers both on board and in the gate lounge or other customer hosted areas within the airport terminal. In some cases, Cabin Crew typically remain with customers during a significant disruption, to attend to their needs and assist with relocating them to hotels or rebooking them for onward connections. A disruption response is often managed by the SCCM who would liaise with ground authorities and the PIC. They would implement the most appropriate customer-focused approach depending on the airline's disruption management processes. It is critical that timely information relating to the status of and reasons for the disruption are given to passengers at frequent intervals throughout. The management of passengers with specific needs, or indeed premium or commercially important customers, is typically given priority and can be more personalized in some circumstances. Disruptions usually occur when an aircraft is out of position or is late inbound and is unable to operate the flight in accordance with the schedule. Causes include tight scheduling, airspace/airport congestion, weather-related events, maintenance and aircraft serviceability requirements. Diversions can also lead to disruptions and predominantly occur due to weather-related events. They can, of course, also occur for other reasons, such as technical problems, fuel management issues, or to provide a deplaning opportunity during an on-board medical emergency.

Descent, landing and aircraft on blocks

Prior to arrival, and in the moments leading up to the descent, Cabin Crew provide some arrival information and instruct customers on international flights on the arrival process and border control arrangements for the arrival destination. At the time of 'Top of descent', the crew are typically clearing remaining items away in both the cabin and galley and readying the aircraft for the landing phase. Prior to landing, it is a safety requirement to ensure that all passengers are prepared and that safety ordinance signs are observed.[48] Different airlines have different ways of notifying their Cabin Crew that the cabin needs to be prepared. One example is that of Qantas, where the announcement by the Flight Crew is to 'prepare the cabin for landing'.[49] This is a verbal instruction to the Cabin Crew which may also require a call-back receipt by the SCCM, followed by an instructional announcement by the SCCM to passengers to prepare the cabin for landing. This marks the end of inflight service and the beginning of safety-related duties for the Cabin Crew, including ensuring that passengers are seated, seat belts are fastened, cabin baggage is stowed, overhead lockers are secured, tray tables are upright, foot rests are stowed, in-arm entertainment screens are stowed, bassinets are stowed, curtains/dividers are secured, window shades are open, the flight deck is cleared of service items, service items are stowed, galley benches are clear, galley electrical equipment is switched off, galley stowages are secured, aisles, cross-overs and exits are clear, and PEDs are in 'flight mode', or switched off, depending on the airline's requirements.

Cabin Crew then take up their assigned seats for landing and, depending on the procedure, may be required to undertake a 'cabin secured for landing' call-back once secured. This is where the sterile cabin and sterile flight deck procedure recommences; the 'no contact' period starts when the gear is lowered and the aircraft is on final approach and remains in place until the aircraft comes to a stop or taxis off the active runway.[50] As the aircraft taxis into the gate, arrival announcements are typically made by the SCCM. The crew remain seated ensuring passenger compliance with safety. During the closing minutes, as the aircraft moves into final position, the Cabin Crew are requested by the flight deck to disarm doors and cross-check. Again, this refers to the Cabin Crew changing the mode of the door from automatic to manual, to prevent ISD when ground staff approach the aircraft doors for access. The aircraft arrives at the gate and manoeuvres into its final parking position either at a stand-off/remote bay or at an aerobridge under its own power or perhaps pulled by a ground tug. This is when the aircraft is known to be 'on blocks' and is the conclusion of the flight.

According to IATA, the crew are required to use standard signals to indicate approval for an aircraft door to be opened.[51] This is done with a firm two knocks on the door by the ground agent and a 'thumbs-up' return signal by the Cabin Crew as a response when the door is clear to be opened. Cabin crew may be required only to give clearance for the door to be opened by the ground staff, but in some cases they may actually crack the door, and then open it, depending on the airline's procedures. Stand-down time for the crew can be between fifteen and thirty minutes after the block time is recorded to facilitate passenger disembarkation.

Disembarkation, flight closure and slip port arrangements

Cabin Crew typically farewell their passengers as they disembark while offering assistance to those customers with special needs such as persons with reduced mobility/ambulant passengers/unaccompanied minors and/or persons in custody. Prior to Cabin Crew departing the aircraft to end their duty, they secure the aircraft by ensuring sensitive equipment stowages are locked, the cabin and surrounds are considered unoccupied and no passenger belongings are left behind. The flight close-out, or flight wrap as it is also known, is a process which includes recording any significant events and forwarding these through to the relevant stakeholder area within the airline. Safety, medical and security reporting back to stakeholder areas with the airline should occur within twenty-four hours of the incident in accordance with IATA requirements.[52]

Cabin Crew travel for a living, and spend an exceptional amount of time away from home. This is typically compensated for by additional downtime at the end of the duty in slip port or back in home base. A long-haul Flight Attendant is away from home approximately half the time. Self-discipline, waking up on schedule, downline sign-on and slip port activities require a great deal of attention from the Flight Attendant. Downtime in slip ports enables the crew to recuperate and rest in usually high-quality accommodation. Here they can enjoy one of the many benefits of the profession: seeing the world and meeting new people. The length of these times is typically dictated by rest provisions as stipulated in the applicable industrial agreements and/or relevant regulations around crew rest and fatigue risk management principles. Meal allowances are also provided by most airlines, and may be a cash payment of an amount representing the various meal periods during the layover period paid in the local currency, a per-diem, hourly amount paid to the Flight Attendant for the total time spent on tour from sign-on to sign-off, or a meal voucher/meal credit system with the specific hotel.

It is important during the slip time that crew manage their consumption, rest and physiological state, as loneliness and substance abuse are recognized occupational threats. A recent study into health concerns for Flight Attendants found that deaths attributable to suicide are 1.5 per cent higher, and those attributable to alcoholism are 2.5 per cent higher, than the general population.[53]

To mitigate these risks Cabin Crew are encouraged by airlines to manage their slip port activities appropriately, by regulating their sleep/wake schedules, avoiding excessive alcohol consumption and exercising regularly. Crew can be encouraged to reach out to employee-counselling and assistance services where needed, and in some cases these can be at the company expense.

Conclusion

It is the impression and presence displayed by the Cabin Crew that resonate most in the customers' overall airline experience. Thus, the perceptive value placed on various standards of safety, operational performance and service experience will invariably define the customer journey. Customer expectations are typically driven by the reliability of the Cabin Crew performance concerning safety, on-time performance and inflight service dependability. Historically, the role can be attributed to a hospitality/service purpose, with the importance of the role changing over time. This importance increased as the industry upscaled, and the role became progressively more regulated to ensure airlines provide Cabin Crew of a recommended standard for aircraft occupant safety. In addition to recently introduced brand/marketing-related functions, Cabin Crew are required to facilitate safety and service-critical tasks as specified by the airline's manual suite which is assembled to benchmarked industry standards. This can create a unique paradox between the two modes – safety and service – which a Flight Attendant is trained to manage. It remains a highly sought-after role, and airlines go to great lengths to recruit, train and facilitate the right Cabin Crew to match their brand. A Flight Attendant's perspective begins with understanding the basics of the day of operation from pre-flight, to pre-boarding to cruise, to top of descent followed by disembarkation, with all things 'safety and service' in-between. This includes a comprehensive understanding of the airline's service promise, customer disruption guidelines and service recovery process. Critically, a Flight Attendant's perspective concludes with an understanding of the crucial safety-related components that make up, and indeed mandate, the requirement for the role in the first place.

Glossary of acronyms and abbreviations

ABP   Able-Bodied Passengers
AEPM   Aircrew Emergency Procedures Manual
AVMED   aviation medicine and medical procedures
BOAC   British Overseas Airways Corporation
CCOM   Cabin Crew Operations Manual
CCSMS   Cabin Crew Safety Management Systems
CRM   Crew Resource Management
CSO   Cabin Standing Orders
DELAG   Deutsche Luftschiffahrts-Aktiengesellschaft
DSIP   Door/Slides Indication Panel

EPs   emergency procedures
FAP   Flight Attendant Panel
FRMS   Fatigue Risk Management System
GMG   Galley Management Guide
HFs   Human Factors
IATA   International Air Transport Association
ICAO   International Civil Aviation Organization
IFE   inflight entertainment
INTAM   Internal Notice to Airmen
IOSA   IATA Operational Safety Audit
ISD   inadvertent slide deployment
LOSA   Line Operational Safety Audit
MEL   Minimum Equipment List
PA   public announcement
PAM   Customer Announcements Manual
PED   portable electronic device
PIC   Pilot in Command
PIL   passenger information list
PRAM   Pre-recorded Announcements and Music
PTS   precision timing schedule
SCCM   Senior Cabin Crew Member
TEM   Threat and Error Management
WHS   Work Health and Safety Manual

Notes

1 Wensveen, J.G. 2007, Air *Transportation: A Management Perspective*, 6th ed. Ashgate, Aldershot, England, p. 237
2 Yu, G. 1998, *Operations Research in the Airline Industry*, Kluwer Academic Publishers, Boston
3 Wright, C. 1985, *Table in the Sky: Recipes from British Airways and the Great Chefs*, W.H. Allen & Co. London, England
4 Edwards, M. and Edwards, E. 1990, *The Aircraft Cabin: Managing the Human Factors*, Gower Technical, Hants, England
5 Grossman, D. 2010, The World's First Flight Attendant, http://www.airships.net/blog/worlds-first-flight-attendant/ Accessed 28 June 2017
6 Wright, C. 1985, *Table in the Sky: Recipes from British Airways and the Great Chefs*, W.H. Allen & Co. London, England
7 Jones, P. 2004, *Flight Catering*, 2nd ed. Elsevier Butterworth-Heinemann, Oxford, England
8 Lovegrove, K. 2000, *Airline Identity, Design and Culture*, Laurence King Publishing, London, England
9 Wright, C. 1985, *Table in the Sky: Recipes from British Airways and the Great Chefs*, W.H. Allen & Co. London, England
10 Lovegrove, K. 2000, *Airline Identity, Design and Culture*, Laurence King Publishing, London, England, p. 34
11 For further details see https://www.singaporeair.com/en_UK/sg/flying-withus/our-story/singapore-girl/

12 ICAO. 2010, Annex 6, to the Convention on International Civil Aviation, Operation of Aircraft, International Standards and Recommended Practices Montreal, Canada

13 IATA. 2015, Cabin Operations Safety Best Practices Guide 2015, International Air Transport Association, Montreal, Canada

14 Op.cit.

15 Op.cit.

16 Lashley, C. and Morrison, A. 2001, *In Search of Hospitality; Theoretical perspectives and debates*, Butterworth-Heinemann, Oxford, England

17 Paradis, A.A. 1997, *Opportunities in Airline Careers*, VGM Career Horizons, Lincolnwood, IL

18 Wensveen, J.G. 2007, *Air Transportation: A Management Perspective*, 6th ed. Ashgate, Aldershot, England

19 Op.cit.

20 Wright, C. 1985, *Table in the Sky: Recipes from British Airways and the Great Chefs*, W.H. Allen & Co. London, England

21 Wright, C. 1985, *Table in the Sky: Recipes from British Airways and the Great Chefs*, W.H. Allen & Co. London, England

22 Ward, K. 2014, *The Essential Guide to Becoming a Flight Attendant*, King Printing, Lowell, MA

23 Wright, C. 1985, *Table in the Sky: Recipes from British Airways and the Great Chefs*, W.H. Allen & Co. London, England

24 IATA. 2015, *Cabin Operations Safety Best Practices Guide 2015*, International Air Transport Association, Montreal, Canada

25 Paradis, A.A. 1997, *Opportunities in Airline Careers*, VGM Career Horizons, Lincolnwood, IL

26 Qantas Airways Limited, 2015, *Cabin Crew Operations Manual*

27 IATA. 2015, *Cabin Operations Safety Best Practices Guide 2015*, International Air Transport Association, Montreal, Canada, p. 16

28 Qantas Airways Limited, 2015, *Cabin Crew Operations Manual*

29 Qantas Airways Limited, 2015, *Cabin Crew Operations Manual*

30 IATA. 2015, *Cabin Operations Safety Best Practices Guide 2015*, International Air Transport Association, Montreal, Canada

31 Gamache, G. and Soumis, F. 1997, 'A Method for Optimally Solving the Rostering Problem' in G. Yu (ed.) *Operations Research in the Airline Industry*, Kluwer Academic Publishers, Boston

32 ICAO. 2010, *Annex 6, to the Convention on International Civil Aviation, Operation of Aircraft, International Standards and Recommended Practices*, Montreal, Canada

33 Clarke, P. 2012, *Buying The Big Jets: Fleet Planning For Airlines*, 2nd ed. Ashgate, Surrey, England

34 Op.cit.

35 Op.cit.

36 IATA. 2015, *Cabin Operations Safety Best Practices Guide 2015*, International Air Transport Association, Montreal, Canada

37 Wright, C. 1985, *Table in the Sky: Recipes from British Airways and the Great Chefs*, W.H. Allen & Co. London, England

38 IATA. 2015, *Cabin Operations Safety Best Practices Guide 2015*, International Air Transport Association, Montreal, Canada, p. 42

39 IATA. 2015, *Cabin Operations Safety Best Practices Guide 2015*, International Air Transport Association, Montreal, Canada

40 Op.cit.

41 Op.cit.

42 Op.cit.

43 IATA. 2015, *Cabin Operations Safety Best Practices Guide 2015*, International Air Transport Association, Montreal, Canada

44 IATA. 2015, *Cabin Operations Safety Best Practices Guide 2015*, International Air Transport Association, Montreal, Canada
45 Wensveen, J.G. 2007, *Air Transportation: A Management Perspective*, 6th ed. Ashgate, Aldershot, England
46 Holloway, S. 1998, *Changing Planes: A Strategic Management Perspective on an Industry in Transition Vol. 2. Strategic Choice, Implementation and Outcome*, Ashgate, Aldershot, England
47 Op.cit.
48 IATA. 2015, *Cabin Operations Safety Best Practices Guide 2015*, International Air Transport Association, Montreal, Canada
49 Op.cit.
50 Qantas Airways Limited, 2015, *Cabin Crew Operations Manual*
51 Op.cit.
52 Op.cit.
53 National Institute for Occupational Safety and Health (NIOSH), 2012, *Health Concerns for Flight Attendants*, Centre for Disease Control (CDC), US

21 Operating a flight

A passenger's perspective

Frank Zimmermann

Introduction

A multitude of complex pieces comes together to create a successful flight but, just as in everyday life, the chaos of the uncontrollable, i.e. the flying public, ultimately contributes to the success of the airline as much as the staff, crew and the aircraft itself. Although the success or failure of an airline may well be assessed based on the economic indicators, those indicators are not completely under the control of the expert management but are also affected by public sentiment based on past experience. Unfortunately for the airlines, given the random nature of human responses, the airlines cannot always plan or predict human behaviour.

Selecting fares and tickets

From the moment a passenger is faced with the need (or desire) to travel, there are vast differences in the approach they will take to purchasing a ticket – choice of destination, routing, timing, pricing, and carrier. Most business travellers have their arrangements handed to them, and some are afforded little choice when the corporate travel staff organize their flights and accommodation. Most tourist or holiday travel is organized by the individual and that is the moment the excitement begins. Long before the pilots or flight attendants are even aware of their working roster, the aircraft is filling with bookings from travellers many months out, and often, travellers are researching every little detail about their flight. The difference between airlines is great and the services and prices they offer can be a little overwhelming. If the passenger is flexible with date and time, chances are they will find a much better fare than having to travel on a specific day. The airlines monitor the aircraft loads constantly so as the flight gets close to departure, the airline will make adjustments to availability of airfares, or may offer different airfares based on the aircraft type operating the flight.

The airline frequent-flyer programs have had a substantial effect on choice of airline, and if a person flies frequently, consideration of which loyalty program is offered may become a valid question. Many of the frequent-flyer programs have status levels. A passenger with a high status level (e.g., Platinum/Gold) may find themselves in a 'buy-two-get-one-free' situation due to the many bonuses they can be offered, which of course, can have a huge impact on their decision to travel with a specific airline.

It is easy for travellers who are organizing their airfares to find the best deals on the internet. With an abundance of websites offering a search and price comparison facility, not just between cities but between regions or even countries, finding the cheapest fare is not that hard. The complexity is in understanding what the airfares include. For instance, once the passenger has purchased the ticket, the airline may still charge them for any multitude of services. Airlines are generally categorized into broad groups such as low-cost carrier, regional or full-service airline. There are certain expectations under each of these banners. However, this is by no means prescriptive; the airlines will behave in a manner that the market will tolerate.

Once the ticket has been purchased, the airline may still charge extra fees for services not covered by the purchase price of the seat. For example, they may charge for luggage – effectively the ticket may only cover 'the seat'. Some airlines charge for carry-on luggage, some airlines include meals while others only sell meals. In some extreme cases airlines charge to use the lavatory and there is a fee for not checking in on-line, while at the other end of the spectrum, depending on airline and class of travel, airlines will provide limousine transfers and lounge access with spa treatments. The travelling public are faced with a barrage of options and while some decisions based only on point-to-point travel can be quite easy, value for money is not always as simple as the price shown on the computer screen.

Preparing for travel

Tickets purchased, the passenger should also now have an understanding of any visa or vaccinations they require for travel to their destination. These need to be organized well before departure. In many cases countries allow tourist visa applications to be done on-line, and while the process may still take time, it is not an onerous one. The smart traveller will also have researched all their travel insurance options. There are almost as many insurance options as there are airlines. Policies that are written as short-term, long-term, annual, multi or single use, individual or family, with or without frequent-flyer miles, or with a range of discounts and inclusions, will cause endless confusion even amongst the most ardent consumers and frequent travellers. Travel insurance is however essential, especially medical cover. Horror stories of hospital costs in the USA, or stranded tourists in Asia who cannot leave without paying their medical bills are frequent, and no one wants to find themselves in that position. Once the traveller has their tickets and documents in order, their luggage is packed (under the weight limit and hopefully not in a black hard-shell suitcase), they are ready for departure.

The day of departure

It is hard to imagine that many of the DC-3 aircraft that were flying post WWII actually had fully flat beds and there were no classes of travel. Also, the fare was inclusive of all services. It was the DC-3 that first enabled airlines to serve hot meals. (One European airline served pre-heated meals as early as 1928 but the DC-3 was the first aircraft to allow airlines to heat the meal on board.) Over time, single class travel came to an end and the airlines introduced First and Tourist Class. Although throughout the years and up to the present day, there have been a variety of travel cabins, the Jet Age did not only deliver much faster aircraft and shorter travel times, but also provided larger aircraft which were more economical to run. This started a trend which continues today – an ever-widening chasm between the Economy or Tourist class of travel at lower airfares and the luxury offered by some First or even Business Class cabins.

Checking-in

The passenger arrives at the airport and enters a maze of check-in counters, food and retail outlets and signs overflowing with informative and/or cryptic information directing passengers and other visitors to a myriad of services. From this point forward, as with almost everything on this day of travel, most things the passenger experiences will be based on their class of travel or frequent-flyer status. At check-in, the traveller is directed by the many signs into a line generally speaking according to their seating class. Economy, Business and First Class are sorted into lines and while the First Class passengers 'breeze' through check-in generally in a matter of minutes, it can become a very stressful experience to be stuck in a check-in line for upwards of an hour with 350 other people trying to check in for a fourteen-hour flight on a mega jumbo.

Once check-in is complete, the traveller will most likely feel a sense of excitement return as their mind goes back to the anticipation of what to expect on the aircraft and the adventure that lies ahead. If travelling internationally, the passenger will need to complete the customs and immigration processes before being allowed to fly. Usually this takes the form of a passport check, and once the officials are convinced the passenger is authorized to leave the country and travel, the passenger then moves to the security checks.

Make no mistake – never underestimate the security process. This is an absolute requirement for all the travelling public and something intended to keep everyone safe. As mentioned earlier, even this process in most airports is linked to class of travel. There are 'express lanes' for 'Premium-class' travellers or 'pre-checked' travellers. The greatest benefit to the people able to use these express lanes is speed of processing, which isn't necessarily due to the fact that all the users are from the premium cabins, but generally, they are experienced travellers who know exactly what they need to remove from their persons to get through security quickly. First-time travellers will often slow down the processing dramatically as they walk through the scanners multiple times having forgotten to take off their belts, or to empty their pockets, or have left their laptop in their case, did not take off their shoes, forgot to take off their jacket, were carrying bottles of water... the reasons are endless, as are the delays.

Once finally through security the passenger has entered the sterile part of the terminal and is now free to move about the departure area, generally lined with retail outlets, or may proceed to one of the many airline lounges available. Lounge access is one of the perks of being a loyal frequent flyer or a Business or First Class passenger that gives great value to the passenger. The standard of the lounges varies greatly, based on location and airline, but generally lounges are a quiet, relaxing environment with light snacks and beverages provided. Internet access and a business centre are usually standard, and some lounges also include restaurant dining, spa treatments, and movie theatres. Some even offer limousine transfers from the lounge (often a separate building) to the aircraft, even having their own security process. A frequent flyer or someone travelling in the premium cabins will almost always consider these services when making a reservation. Much like the early days of aviation, airlines will compete on service at these higher fare levels versus the fare itself in Economy or Tourist Class.

Boarding

The ground crew scan the passenger's paper or electronic boarding pass and the passenger is welcomed to the flight. Walking through a secure doorway and down the jetway or aerobridge builds the excitement. This is the moment where the passenger has almost 'left the land to board the vessel'. Approaching the light at the end of the tunnel, the silhouette in the doorway is revealed as that of the flight attendant reaching out and welcoming the passenger into the aircraft. Stepping forward and passing through the imposing doorway, the passenger is now in an alternate world. At this point, some passengers are excited, some are bored, and some are perhaps a little apprehensive as they hand control to the pilot and other crew while they sit back and allow the experience to envelop them. Depending on the aircraft type, some passengers may turn left on boarding into what many airlines try to describe as some sort of utopian sanctuary in the sky. Some airlines manage to deliver on that description, but some fail dismally. Regardless, whatever is going on to the left of the boarding door is a lot more comfortable than the middle seat in row 62!

On-board

On a long-haul flight, an airline may have a concierge showing the passenger to their suite. Normally a First Class seat, this configuration may be named a 'suite' by the airline as the sliding door enables the passenger to close themselves off from everything around them. Once inside their suite, the passenger may find many luxuries to pamper them on their journey. Most long-haul First Class suites and seats include a duvet, an additional mattress and designer toiletries bag, and a much larger touchscreen monitor. The assortment of entertainment in some cases may consist of hundreds of viewing and gaming options, even live TV from around the planet.

Some airlines manage to make their suites even more special by offering large widescreen televisions (in addition to a handheld video device providing a second viewing option), a complimentary minibar and refreshments, a range of skincare and spa products to help the passenger relax, a menu with a large range of meals all available at the passenger's leisure and finally, a pair of pyjamas. Often, before boarding is even complete, these passengers may have changed into the airline-supplied pyjamas and settled in for the thirteen-hour flight to the other side of the globe.

In First Class the lavatories and in some cases showers and bathrooms provide luxury to the extreme. In contrast, the lavatories in the economy cabin are usually small and cramped. Compliments of US Department of Transport Law, all carriers flying into the US must now have lavatories that can accommodate a wheel chair, which has helped provide a little extra room in at least one lavatory. But in First, changing into those pyjamas then becomes easier. Shower time is generally limited. However, the ability for passengers in the First Class suites to take a shower during the flight is very welcomed. Chapter 20 spoke about operating a flight from the flight attendants' perspective, but in some cases an airline also employs spa attendants who make sure that after each passenger the facility is immaculately maintained and all the skin and body treatments are refreshed and ready for use.

Although the configuration of aircraft varies greatly depending on aircraft type and services offered by the airline, generally located behind the First Class cabin is Business Class. Business Class was introduced at the end of the 1970s as a compromise between First and Economy Class, although originally it was made available to those passengers who had paid a full Economy fare as distinct from discounted Tourist fares. The Business cabin soon developed into a premium product as competition between airlines became more aggressive.

Originally Business Class provided no more than extra legroom and a better quality meal service. Over time, the Business Class product has been constantly upgraded. In the 1990s many airlines introduced lie-flat (albeit angled) seats to enable passengers to sleep. Not long after their introduction, the angled seats were upgraded to 180-degree flat sleeper seats. Two seats together by the window are now considered to be the lesser configuration with many airlines now offering direct aisle access from all Business Class seats. Thus, the configuration is often 1-2-1 across the Business cabin. The introduction of Business Suites is only a matter of time.

The biggest difference between a First Class and Business Class seat is space, although direction of travel may also vary. In order to fit in as many seats as possible into the Business Class cabin, some airlines have chosen a design where half the seats face backwards. The concept is easy enough to imagine. Generally, passengers want to lie flat. They need more space for their upper torso than they do for their feet. Imagine the body shape as a V. By putting rows of seats, alternating between forward and backward facing, the V shape can be pushed closer together. The Business Class passenger is provided a menu with a variety of meal options, often with variable serving times, service by plate instead of the economy tray and a selection of beverages include wine and spirits.

As the boarding process continues and passengers move further to the back of the aircraft they sometimes pass through a small Premium Economy cabin and finally the Economy Cabin. With each new improvement to the First and Business Class cabins, some airlines chose to drop the First Class cabin completely and focus on the Business Class product. When the cost of travelling First and Business Class rose, it was clear a mid-range product was again needed between Business and Economy. This led to the introduction of Premium Economy. Initially Premium Economy (especially in the case of some US carriers) was nothing more than extra legroom, but over time, airlines started to introduce improved seating for Premium Economy and an improved meal service. In some cases, airlines will offer free seating in the Premium Economy cabin for high tier-level frequent flyers as a perk for their loyalty.

There was a time when all air travel was considered to be a special event, when flying was considered an adventure, even glamorous. Although this excitement and sense of adventure lives on in many people and is sometimes provided by the airlines in the premium cabins, the airlines themselves do little to preserve the joy of travel in their economy product offerings. It is common to hear of passengers complaining about the trauma of flying Economy. Passengers will tell stories of poor quality meals, bad service, or cramped seating, but there are many ways to improve the experience and some options to improve the overall experience.

Walking through the premium cabins to get to the Economy cabin, passengers should remind themselves that the airline probably wants the travelling public to turn green with envy in the hope that next time they fly, they will pay for an upgraded seat. It is worth noting that a Business Class ticket can cost three or four times the Economy Class fare and the First Class ticket can be up to fifteen times the Economy fare. The costs associated with the levels of luxury may be prohibitive and with a bit of forward planning the Economy traveller can make their experience a little more comfortable.

When booking a premium cabin, advance seat selection is included. When travelling Economy, this is not always guaranteed and depending on airline and airline operating model, the Economy passenger may not even be able to select a seat. The status of a passenger in the airline's loyalty programme is also a large factor in seat selection. Some airlines block seats in all cabins for their top tier frequent flyers, some allow free seat selection to Economy top tier members, while others release most seats to all passengers about seventy-two hours out from departure, knowing this assists many passengers in securing a slightly more desirable seat in Economy. Some airlines will charge extra for exit-row seating or seats with more legroom, but the savvy traveller will have researched this extensively. Regardless, some passengers seek the window seats to offer them a little privacy and less disturbance, as no one will have to climb over them to get to the aisle.

On-board amenities

Noise-cancelling headphones can be a huge asset to any traveller and, in particular, to an Economy traveller. The noise, clutter, presence of children, or the droning of the engines can all be blocked out with a pair of quality headphones. The headphones are a great method for the passenger to cocoon themselves away from the occasional chaos of Economy. However, they can also have the opposite effect for fellow travellers. Passengers who sometimes put on a pair of noise-cancelling headphones, because they cannot hear any noise, seem to think no one else can. Often people who raise their voices or laugh so loudly that both ends of the aircraft can hear them, are wearing noise-cancelling headphones. One must also consider those passengers who have a head cold and who may also disregard others in the immediate surroundings. Some airlines are now offering 'quiet zones' – for an extra fee, passengers can book seats in the quiet zone, which excludes young children.

An experienced Economy traveller will make sure they bring their own refreshments (within security allowances). On a long-haul flight, some may even bring their own blankets and slippers or a neck pillow to help with more comfortable sleep. These small items will help make the journey a little more personal and comfortable, although in some cases, airlines will offer extra services in busy peak periods. For example, flights between major airports on a weekday may provide passengers with free alcohol.

Finally, everyone is seated and the flight is ready to depart. The Cabin Crew will complete their pre-departure checks, using strange terminology such as 'Boarding Complete' – everyone is on the plane and an indication that the ground crew should leave, 'Doors Armed and Cross-checked' meaning that the doors are armed for the journey. For a traveller who is not used to this environment, or a little anxious, some of these announcements can be a little daunting – but, as been said so many times before, flying is safer than driving a car.

In-flight

Once the plane is in flight the Flight Attendants start their service. The format of a meal service in each cabin of the plane is usually quite different. For example, in the premium cabins the passengers may receive a beverage and hors d'oeuvres service prior to their main meals. The number of Flight Attendants generally available will also vary, such that there is a much lower ratio of passengers to Flight Attendants in the premium cabins, and therefore also a much less rushed or cluttered atmosphere.

The meal service may sometimes be interrupted by turbulence. If this is not too severe, the Flight Attendants will continue their service, albeit perhaps withholding hot beverages, but in more severe instances the Flight Deck will ask the crew to be seated until the aircraft has cleared the turbulence. For a nervous flyer, turbulence can be a traumatic experience. The sight out the window of the giant engines oscillating on the wing, or the wing flexing up and down, can be more than a little disconcerting, but is nothing that they were not designed for.

Most aircraft are now equipped with in-flight internet. By enabling the passengers to connect with their smartphones, laptops or other devices, they enable the business traveller to continue to work, and the leisure traveller to be in contact with people at home or just pass the time researching their destination.

Arrival

Several movies later and the aircraft is descending to its destination. The First Class passengers are changing from their pyjamas back into their day clothes; all passengers have perhaps just finished their breakfast service if it was overnight flight, and are starting to restow all their belongings ready for landing. Flight Attendants begin at this stage to clean up and prepare the cabin, stowing curtains, ensuring passengers re-set their seats and tray tables to secure positions, and opening the window shades, etc.

If the passengers are arriving on an international flight, many countries around the world have very strict quarantine rules, and some spray the inside of some or all inbound aircraft with pesticides to prevent the introduction of any foreign insects or contaminants into their country. This is a fairly unusual process and is often the cause of delays disembarking the aircraft while local authorities undertook this process. The now more common process of 'residual disinsection' (see Chapter 12) is an alternative which doesn't delay disembarkation. Once disinsection (if performed) is complete, the passengers are free to disembark and legally enter the country.

Almost the reverse process to departure is now underway as Immigration procedures are undertaken, before the crowds (off perhaps numerous flights that have just arrived) gather at the luggage collection belts. Baggage collected, the passengers queue again, to present pre-completed documentation for quarantine purposes, maybe being subject to final quarantine inspections of luggage and/or person, before being permitted to leave the arrivals hall to join meeters and greeters, catch an array of transport into the city, or even transit to other flights.

Unfortunately, although rare, luggage is sometimes misplaced. An airline will almost never use the word 'lost' (even though most airlines have a 'lost luggage' department), but if the luggage fails to arrive, the airline will sometimes say it has been delayed. Usually this is true, and most delayed luggage appears within twenty-four hours. However, in the rare event that the luggage has lost its tags or a passenger's details have somehow been separated from the bag, the passenger will be asked to fill out a description of their luggage. The majority of luggage carried by an airline is in the form of a black wheeled suitcase; in the United States alone, that is approximately ninety per cent of 400 million bags per year. Smart travellers will at least tie a yellow ribbon on their luggage, but truly experienced travellers will have egg yolk yellow or spinach green suitcases; anything to stand out amongst the nearly 400 million black wheeled suitcases.

The passenger's journey comes to an end and everything that the passenger has enjoyed or endured during the trip will be part of the lasting impression of that airline. There is an abundance of options available to the travelling public, and the airlines' offerings are always being updated. From the passengers in First Class who have enjoyed a luxurious night's sleep, to those in Business Class who have watched endless entertainment and relaxed on their flat beds, to the first-time flyer who sat in Economy, amazed and excited by the adventure of flight and simply looking out the window, all three groups will have formed an opinion and have a story to tell.

Part IV
Operational disruption management, performance, and the future

Peter J. Bruce

The previous part considered the events that take place in normal operations of flights. Unfortunately, though, not all goes to plan every time an aircraft is operating or is about to operate a flight, despite the rigorous planning and effort that precedes this stage. With so many stakeholders' interests and significant costs involved, managing an airline in such a large, highly complex, diverse and challenging environment is difficult to say the least. All kinds of disruptions can impact the operation of a flight or series of flights from things like seemingly trivial buttons or switches that may not work, failures of large systems, operations in inclement weather, or even insufficient loading of bread rolls on an aircraft. The task of this final part is to explore the myriad of problems that airlines regularly encounter and the effects that these problems may have on individual flights and beyond.

The ways in which airlines mitigate these problems vary enormously, according to size, type and business model of the airline, managerial policies, extent of the problem(s), considerations of partners and even competitors, the range of alternative solutions, and the time available for decision formulation and solution implementation. No two airlines have the same equipment, schedules, facilities, staffing, or processes, etc. So, when problems occur, finding satisfactory solutions is very much a process of adopting appropriate responses tailored to the requirements of the specific airline. Disruption or recovery management also differs markedly between Domestic (within country) operations and International Operations, and this is elaborated further in the first two chapters of this part.

Disruption Management has largely been a manual process, drawing upon the vast experience and expertise of many people across the industry. Operations Control Centres (OCCs) traditionally brought some of these people together in order to assist information sharing and dissemination but also importantly to capture the expertise for efficient problem-solving. More recently, the reformations of OCCs into Integrated Centres (IOCs) or Network Operations Centres (NOCs) have drawn upon a greater field of resources (now including social media specialists), enabling multidisciplinary teams of decision makers to come together, thus providing far more synergy than ever before. This, combined with technological advances that use intelligent systems to assist what has been largely a manual problem-solving process, has airlines realizing significant future benefits for disruption recovery, with consequential flow through to the airlines' passengers.

22 Operational disruptions
Causes, strategies, and consequences

Peter J. Bruce

Introduction

As alluded to in the introductions to Parts II and III, normal operations should reflect the conduct of a series of flights that operate according to published schedules that passengers, other stakeholders, and staff expect. Unfortunately, it is rare that on any given day an airline would operate a series of flights without the interruption of some problem. Such interruptions are known as off-scheduled, disrupted or irregular operations (IROPS). This chapter examines the wealth of problems that airlines experience, strategies that the IOC[1] may use to mitigate them, and the consequential effects. In Chapter 8, the IOC was described and its key purpose and functions explained. The current chapter describes the problems faced daily by the IOC, while the following chapter explains in further detail specific management approaches and tools to solving operational problems. These three chapters together should provide the reader with a fairly comprehensive understanding of the ways in which an airline's IOC aims to provide the expected level of service.

Operational complexity

Aviation is a highly complex industry – it is very exciting but also very challenging. The IOC is provided each day with a set of schedules. As described in the first parts of the book, the airline has also painstakingly formulated plans and amassed resources to reflect the intention of operating flights according to these planned schedules. So, there should be a fleet of fully prepared aircraft (appropriately maintained and legally permitted to fly), sufficient crews (Technical, Pilots, and Flight Attendants) who are licensed, trained, rostered and adequately rested, airport and terminal resources, an air traffic system ready to accept and progress the flight through relevant airspace, and so forth. This will help to ensure the flight departs, flies and arrives according to the schedule.

Add to this the multicultural complications of flying through several countries, changing time zones, enduring fatigue, communicating across different cultures, or being faced with a host of challenges, and it can be appreciated just how difficult the task of operating these flights can become. A significant characteristic of the aviation industry is the nature of its unpredictability.[2] What is expected to happen with the amount of planning and preparation that takes place, often bears little resemblance to actual events unfolding. IOC controllers with many years' experience still encounter situations they have not come across before. Sometimes this may be a feature of operating new aircraft equipment, operating into new regions or airports, or coming across a scenario they had never previously faced.

Nature of domestic operations

Domestic schedules – those planned to operate within a single country – have a number of characteristics of relevance to IOCs. They tend (with exceptions) to exhibit the following:

- There is a high frequency of flights between city-pairs, and spread over the domestic network.
- The high frequency of flights implies that there are several backup flights between city-pairs, which provide options for recovery in the event of IROPS, and help to retain passengers within the network.
- Aircraft may fly eight to ten sectors per day.
- Many aircraft are of a low to medium capacity (i.e., often narrow-bodied aircraft such as the B737 or A320).
- Aircraft performance problems (taking into account airport restrictions, payload and fuel limits) are less likely.
- There is a high level of connectivity among flights.
- Flights are generally contained within the calendar day, with some exceptions of overnight (redeye) flights.
- Maintenance servicing bases are dispersed around the network.
- Maintenance work is generally conducted overnight when the majority of the fleet is not flying.
- The utilization of these aircraft is tight, in order to optimize the fleet units extensively, and due to the generally small size of aircraft, short turnaround times (e.g., thirty-five minutes[3]) can be scheduled.
- Crewing bases are dispersed around the network so replacement crews are readily available.
- Backup or standby aircraft may be available in some airlines that market, for instance, city-to-city shuttle services.

These characteristics give rise to a number of issues for domestic controllers in IOCs. There may be quite a degree of flexibility given the access to numerous aircraft in or passing through certain ports. However, the complexity of operation and sheer volume of flying builds an intensity in the network that requires close attention to the dynamic performance of the network and significant speed required for problem assessing and solving, and actioning of solutions in the event of IROPS.

Nature of international operations

Compared with domestic schedules, international schedules have quite different characteristics and tend to exhibit the following (again, with exceptions):

- There is a low frequency of flights spread between city-pairs with fewer backup flights, so competitors' operations may contribute more to recovery solutions in the event of IROPS.
- Aircraft may only fly one to two sectors per day, but these are often of longer duration (e.g., PEK–LHR), requiring 'heavy' crews (additional pilots due to required rest breaks).
- Aircraft are often large wide-body types (such as the A350, B777) operating longer-range flights with higher weights (payload and fuel).
- Some operations (e.g., ETOPS – extended operations – very long range) are marginal, especially operating long range into destinations with weather problems (e.g., fog).
- Subject to the carrier, there may be significant network connectivity, or relatively little. For example, major carriers with a sizeable international hub such as Emirates or Singapore rely heavily on connectivity for international on-carriage, with networks such as Qantas or Air New Zealand less dependent on international connectivity but very much reliant on international/domestic connections.
- Maintenance bases are limited and maintenance assistance may be sought from other airlines.
- Maintenance work may be conducted at any time of the day subject to aircraft availability.
- Longer turnaround times are required on the ground to service, fuel and maintain the larger aircraft.
- Crewing bases are dispersed around the world so replacement crews may be difficult to access.
- In very large aircraft such as the A380, many customers are involved, so any disruptions involving accommodation and/or buses become considerable.
- There is a high reliance on third-party contracts for most activities (not only engineering and ground handling, but areas such as check-in staff, etc.). As part of a third-party contract, there are often clauses around disruption management support and ways in which the contract may be influenced by the rosters and staffing levels of third parties.

Problem-solving and decision-making for controllers dealing with international IROPS is therefore quite different from those dealing with domestic IROPS. With less access to maintenance labour and parts, and fewer available crews, there is less flexibility for recovering from IROPS events, so the options for instigating various recovery plans are fewer. While the timeframe for decision-making is greater than for domestic problems, the more limited solutions can have significantly greater impact on a set of flights and passengers.

In some cases, the pattern of flying planned for the aircraft may be of several days' duration, and an IROPS event may affect the pattern across this extended time, with implications for future flying patterns planned for that aircraft.

Schedule integrity and robustness

The readiness of a day's network schedules for handover to current-day operational control (i.e., the IOC) implies that, barring any disruption whatsoever and assuming no detrimental environmental, human or organizational interference or any other conditions apply to the operations, all flights are potentially capable of operating to schedule with the booked passenger, cargo and any other loads. In this ideal world, the IOC would act as a monitoring station only, with little need for interjection. Of course, in the real world, such a state does not exist. Because of this, several contingencies are built into the airline system. Crew reserves are rostered in case of sickness or unavailability, spare parts are located strategically around a network, and additional fuel is carried to cater for changes in air traffic, weather or other requirements. Some airlines (usually large ones) are fortunate enough to have an operational spare aircraft or two that can be called upon if needed. This additional asset becomes very useful if it can be deployed into an area of significant disruption provided other support such as crews are also available. But it also carries with it the cost of an aircraft not scheduled for revenue earning. Thus, there is a commercial versus operational dilemma for airline management to consider.

An airline's schedules are often built with excess block time included (time measured from off-blocks to on-blocks, as distinct from flight time) in order to absorb minor delays to a flight, enabling a late departing flight to arrive at its destination on or ahead of the scheduled arrival time. This buffering creates a greater robustness in the schedules and a better on-time performance for the airline, and as airspace and airports have become increasingly congested, the buffering of schedules has also increased. The downside of this, however, is some loss in utilization of the fleet as fewer flights can be allocated into a specific pattern.

Attention now turns to the myriad of problems that cause airline disruptions. The materials on causation are presented in two parts to demonstrate differences between problems that may occur before an aircraft departs and those that may occur when the aircraft is airborne.

Causes of disruptions – pre-flight

There are numerous causes of disruptions prior to departure that can lead to IROPS. Subject to the location around the world, the season of the year, the time of day and so forth, probably the most challenging cause of disruptions is weather. Arguably, the next significant causes are likely to be due to maintenance, crewing and Air Traffic Control (ATC) influences. Often it is not a matter of a single event delaying a flight, rather it is that one event might be the root cause, which results in a series of problems that compound the disruption. For example:

During flight planning, an en-route issue is anticipated, requiring a new plan to be produced that reroutes the flight via another airport. In turn, this causes the crew to exceed their duty hours and the first available replacement crew results in a delay of several hours, which prompts an alert that the last flight of the pattern would then break curfew at the final destination!

Weather

Weather causes the most disruptions largely due to severity of problems. Forecasting conditions such as fog, winds, high temperatures, thunderstorms, tornados, cyclones, etc. has become extremely accurate, such that airlines can plan around these events in many cases. However, their occurrence is still likely to interfere with operations and often the duration or severity of the occurrence exceeds expectations. With sufficient warning, IOCs develop a series of plans to manage such events.

Fog

Fog is probably the most difficult condition to predict accurately, especially its formation and dissipation rates. Sometimes cloud exists above the fog, increasing the time for fog to be 'burnt' off. Departing airports with fog is not so much a problem provided minimum visibility requirements (such as number of visible runway lights) on the ground are met. But for a flight about to operate into an airport with forecast fog, IOCs have a number of options. Depending on the above factors, the IOC may elect for the flight to depart on schedule, but uplift additional fuel such that the aircraft is able to make a normal approach if conditions permit, or have sufficient fuel to hold (over or near the airport) until conditions improve. The fuel carried would ideally permit holding for a specified time (e.g., one hour), perhaps including an attempted approach or two, then diversion to a nominated airport. Another option for the IOC is to hold the flight on the ground at the origin port until the fog has begun to dissipate or at least until an updated forecast predicts the fog dissipating at a given time. The costs of holding and burning fuel often determine the preferred action, but sometimes the forecast cannot predict events as desired.

Winds

Winds cause operational problems in a number of ways. Aircraft commonly take-off and land using a runway best oriented to prevailing wind conditions where possible (subject to aircraft performance, runway availability, runway length, etc.). So strong winds aligned with the runway direction do not generally pose an operational problem. However, strong winds in the vicinity of airports may cause up- or downdrafts resulting in wind shear, in which case aircraft may not be able to operate at the airport. Airlines develop policies and contingencies in the event of wind shear. For instance, this may consist of having one attempt at an approach and an immediate diversion if wind shear is detected.

Crosswinds, however, can cause problems as each aircraft has a maximum tolerance (prescribed by the manufacturer) for operating in these conditions. In operational control terms, if an airport has a selection of runways that overcome crosswind restrictions, then flights can operate normally. However, if the airport has a single runway, and crosswinds exceed the maximum tolerance, an aircraft may not be able to use the airport. This is exacerbated if the airport is a remote airport, especially with the closest alternate airport some considerable distance away. In Australia, for example, Alice Springs and Mount Isa are two such airports. Even in main, large airports, if the wind directions negate the use of the cross runways (i.e., reduce to single runway operations), the normal ATC flow rates or operating traffic capacity of the airport may be cut by as much as fifty per cent.

Strong en-route headwinds that are forecast and hence taken into account during flight planning stages may also be a source of operational disruption. There may be a number of options in this case. The longer planned flight time may require the aircraft to uplift additional fuel with or without a compensatory payload offload so the flight can still operate direct (as scheduled). The decision whether to do this by offloading cargo, baggage or even some passengers is debatable. An alternative option may be to operate the flight via an interim port without any offloads. This option may preserve the payload, but the schedule will be compromised, with possible consequence for downline flights and passenger and crew connections.

Thunderstorm activity

For flights yet to depart, isolated thunderstorms at the origin, en route, or at the destination may cause some disruption to schedules, and additional fuel (determined at the flight planning stage) would usually enable the aircraft to avoid the storms by diverting around them and/or holding for short times either on the ground or in the air. However, significant lines of thunderstorms in systems that are several kilometres wide, high and deep will influence the decision as to whether or when aircraft can operate in the locality. Certainly, planning for such operations will entail additional fuel requirements and selection of alternate routes and diversion airports that will enable aircraft to operate, subject to the extent of the systems. Lightning in the vicinity of airports usually mandates the cessation of all ground activities, including all unloading and loading. Thus an aircraft can be held on-gate or, worse, off-gate whilst lightning persists.

Snow

Extensive snow events are usually predictable and, as such, airlines will have already put into place significant contingency plans at least the day or some days before. These plans are formidable, often removing numerous patterns of flying from the schedules. Lighter snow events on the current day may result in snow-clearing processes along runways and taxiways. Operational delays then become a function of the resources available and efficiency in keeping the airport open. In some cases, unseasonal or rare snowstorms may close airports which have less capability to maintain full operations. The necessity to operate in snow- or ice-affected airports invariably means increased congestion, as aircraft may have to de-ice or wait for snow-clearing tasks to be completed. Thus, delays to these flights are likely and the IOC's mission becomes one of trying to minimize the effects on a broader scale.

Typhoons, hurricanes, cyclones

These events are also usually forecast several days ahead of the operating day as meteorology personnel (sometimes located in IOCs) track their paths. Their severity dictates the action taken by airlines and, again, contingency plans are likely to have been put in place prior to the day of operation. With severe events such as these, aircraft safety is of highest priority, followed by customer comfort. So, any operations that are still being conducted in these locations are subject to decisions to continue or abandon the flights. This presents IOCs with a 'wait and see' approach, but similar to some other operational events, this may be the best option at the time. Clearly, many uncertainties exist in situations such as this.

Acts of God

Acts of God mainly include events such as sudden volcanic eruptions. If unforeseen, these can require, at short or no notice, an aircraft to divert hundreds of kilometres off-course. If the event is taking place and is known, the IOC will have to schedule severely changed routings to avoid the ash cloud. At worst, an airline can, in effect, be totally grounded until the ash cloud passes.

Maintenance (also called Technical or Mechanical)

Chapter 10 discussed, among other topics, aircraft serviceability and reliability. With the complexity of aircraft systems and components, and the meticulous attention to maintaining fleets, one would imagine that disruptions due to technical or maintenance issues would be minimal. However, disruptions can occur for various reasons. An airline's Network Scheduling Department liaises with Maintenance Planning to allocate time for maintenance to be conducted. Aircraft that re-emerge into flying patterns after having been in the hangar for periods of time ranging from overnight, a few days, or sometimes months, are anticipated to return to flying on a particular day and in time for a particular flight departure.

Sometimes, though, the maintenance processes take additional time such that delays may still occur. Operation of an aircraft naturally causes wear and tear on its components. Besides regular servicing, aircraft undergo a plethora of maintenance work tasks such as engine changes, instrument changes, control surface changes, carpet repairs, windscreen replacements and so forth, any of which may result in inability to meet scheduled flight commitments on completion. Occasionally, aircraft land heavily, land overweight due to some unforeseen reason, or are struck by lightning while flying in storm activity. These events require specific maintenance checks to be carried out, and in some cases, aircraft may be grounded awaiting such inspections.

Crewing

By the time a flight is ready to operate, the Crew Scheduling department in nearly all cases will have ensured that all the day's flights are crewed appropriately. Disruptions can occasionally be attributed to crew sickness or late sign-on at work. In an outport, where an airline typically may not have spare or reserve crews, crew sickness may have significant impact on a flight. Subject to the type of operation, the full complement of crew members is normally required to operate a flight, in which case a sick crew member may effectively ground the flight until a replacement is found. Chapter 9 described the rostering and pairing practices undertaken by airline Crew Scheduling departments. In most cases, and for many reasons, crews (both Pilot and Flight Attendant complements) and aircraft do not all follow the same patterns. Thus, crews may need to transfer from one aircraft to another during their duty time. This can be quite complex, with several crew members transferring from any number of inbound flights. This means that should one or more of these inbound flights be running late, one or more outbound flights to be operated by another aircraft (tail number) may have to be delayed while the crew members transfer across, unless crew commitments can be changed on the day. This is quite a common occurrence and a cause of many delays during IROPS. During significant disruptions, an airline may simply run out of crews that have sufficient duty hours or have no other operational restrictions, resulting in the cancellations of flights.

ATC

Delays may be incurred due to a variety of ATC requirements or procedures on the ground, often caused by congestion or reduced runway availability due to prevailing weather conditions. Traffic congestion in the airspace around an airport, or through which a flight is planned to operate, may also be the source of delayed pushback or flight clearances, and in some parts of the world onward clearance to fly through a region may result in, perhaps, a sixty-minute hold at the departure port. In the USA, the ground stop program (see Chapter 23 for further detail) can also cause widespread disruptions across a network, as can the invoking of non-planned slot times, in which case departing and/or arriving aircraft must operate in line with the slots that become available at those airports.

Ramp

In peak times especially, the volume of traffic on the ramp may create its own congestion issues. The ramp frequently operates at a frantic pace with the combined movements of aircraft, ground service vehicles and people. Delays may be caused, for example, by having to push back and tow aircraft clear of this area for engine start-up, or may be due to several aircraft movements, both inbound and outbound, competing for limited apron space. Times of inclement weather and poor lighting bring into play additional safety concerns. If flights become off-schedule, then the levels of planned resources and equipment may become stretched, having a further effect on handling of flights.

The efficiencies of sound aircraft bay planning are important for well-run ramp operations, but in a disrupted environment, off-scheduled arriving aircraft may be allocated bays some distance from other aircraft to which there may be transhipping (connecting) passengers, cargo and crews. An airline may 'own' its own gates and bays at an airport, which gives it a considerable advantage in planning. However, at many airports the airport authority owns the gates and bays and is the final arbiter for their allocation. The airport may also have different priorities to the airline's IOC.

Late aircraft and lost block time

Despite efforts to maintain schedule, flights do run late and with the compactness of most flight patterns, there is often little that can be done to arrest the late operating patterns. Other than cancelling selected flights to 'free up' some of the utilization (which upsets passengers more than being late), the delays will often just propagate during the day. In addition, congestion on the ground at the departure port, headwinds en route, or slowed ATC procedures on arrival can all lengthen the block (schedule) time. This in turn is likely to exacerbate the delay of subsequent flights unless some preventative action can be taken.

Late passengers

Passengers for a flight may be late due to any number of reasons. Passengers caught up in road traffic congestion or road accidents may be late by a matter of five minutes, or as much as several hours, and with technologies such as remote passenger check-in, it has become far more difficult for airlines to establish exactly what proportion of passengers may have arrived at an airport in time for boarding their flights. Passengers may be arriving as tranships from a late inbound flight. The decision as to whether to hold the outbound flight(s) may depend on the numbers of passengers involved, the durations of the flights, choices of alternative uplift and so forth. Passengers are sometimes late from the lounges, not aware of public announcements, or lose their way to the appropriate gate. At times, passengers wander away from the gate-lounge area in which case they can be difficult to locate. If they cannot be located in time for departure, the airline must remove their baggage from the aircraft, which guarantees a delay. Ticketing issues, check-in system problems, power supply problems, as well as congestion in the terminal, and slow lines through security and immigration are all additional factors that may contribute to flight delays. Flights can also be specially booked or even chartered in connection with Cruise-Fly package holidays, which makes some airline flight departures subject to ship schedules and subsequent transport from the dock. Numbers of passengers from cruise ships can be quite high, and the late berthing of a ship can impact flights to several destinations.

Cabin service and catering

Similar to other planning activities before the day of operation, cabin service and/or catering sections or organizations roster teams for servicing aircraft cabins and providing the supplies and equipment required for a number of flights (including handling the airline's own flights and others if contracted). More often than not, these activities are now outsourced to specialist organizations. But vehicles can deliver to, or service, the wrong aircraft, equipment or staff shortfalls occur, and highly congested ramps, with off-scheduled operations, mean that the level of service may simply fall behind time.

Fuelling

The refuellers also have a specific series of flights to service in their shift. Refuelling delays may be related to equipment, gaining efficient access to the aircraft, the time taken to load high volumes of fuel, or handling off-scheduled aircraft. Should higher fuel figures be required by several aircraft, due to weather or other operating circumstances, this may also be a cause of delays. On rare occasions, fuel may not be at the correct specification, therefore being deemed unusable, the supply may run low, or a power failure may prevent pumping. Any of these could be significant issues for airlines which may then need a strategy such as a fuel policy to uplift fuel from alternative sources (i.e., airports) until some resolution is reached. This is called 'tankering' fuel, and the consequences may include reduced revenue payload and higher costs as tankered fuel may not be from contracted sources.

Industrial

Disruptions caused by industrial unrest can have significant effects on the airline. For example, some countries experience industrial action by ATC organizations, which has the effect of closing airspace for defined periods, and occasionally Crewing or Engineering (Mechanic) unions conduct industrial action. However, as disruptive as it is, if sufficient notice is provided, and the action can be contained to known timeframes, an airline is usually able to amend its flight schedules before the operating day. Industrial action on the day of operation is more disruptive, of course. Should refuellers or pushback tug drivers, for example, stop work, aircraft may be instantly stranded without fuel or not have the capability to push back from the terminal. Although there may be means for resolving these problems, delays are inevitable in this situation, and likely to snowball with increased airline movements through the airport.

Airport availability

Similar in a sense to airspace availability, airports sometimes become unavailable on an operating day, perhaps due to a disabled aircraft or damage that has been caused to a runway. In such cases, flights may need to be delayed to avoid the restricted time, or even be rerouted (i.e., with a new flight plan before the flight has departed) to operate to an alternate airport.

Other

Disruptions are subject also to power or computer system outages, sometimes resulting in the need for manual processing systems. These systems can affect key areas in the airport such as check-in, baggage systems, and load control. Staff are trained in the event of outages such as these, but reversion to manual processes usually creates backlogs due to the lack of automation and speed.

Causes of disruptions – in-flight

Once a flight is airborne, several factors can determine its progress, whether these are during the cruise phase or on approach and landing phases.

Weather

Weather problems such as thunderstorms or turbulence encountered en route do not usually require operational decisions to be made other than crews electing to divert their tracks around the event or make changes to altitude or speed. In most cases, little disruption to the flight or onward flights would be expected, although flying through storms can result in hail damage to the aircraft, or in rarer cases lightning strikes can be experienced. More common though, are headwinds that may be in excess of the forecast strength, creating the need for the crew (and dispatcher/flight follower) to conduct in-flight replanning to ensure that fuel is sufficient to reach the destination, or if not, decide what other actions may be necessary such as diverting to another airport.

Marginal or deteriorating weather conditions at the destination, though, are more likely to be disruptive. This typically consists of fog, snow, heavy rain, high winds and turbulence, and thunderstorm activity in the vicinity of the airfield or on the approaches to landing. Should the destination airport close due to weather conditions, calculations are made quickly to determine if inbound aircraft are able to hold near the airport for a time, or whether and if so when, they might need to divert to a nominated alternate port. For long-haul flights (especially international long haul) where fuel margins may be far more critical, decisions to divert may need to be made earlier.

Maintenance

Aircraft can only depart an airport in a serviceable condition. In laymen's terms, they are 'fit to fly'. This means that everything related to the safety of the operation works as designed. Occasionally, though, components develop faults in service. If the failure does not affect the safety or efficiency of the operation, the flight normally continues. If necessary, the crew may elect to divert the flight and land at another airport. Inspection of the component on arrival by maintenance engineers will then determine what may need to be carried out to make the aircraft fully serviceable again. On determining the fault, the efficiency of recovery may then rest on the availability of appropriate licensed engineers (e.g., airframe, engine, avionics) and if necessary, spare parts. Sometimes the aircraft may be grounded awaiting repair.

Customer[4]/medical emergencies

Circumstances such as medical events or customer-related emergencies occur occasionally. If these are minor events, or can be contained sufficiently on board, the flight normally continues to its destination. Otherwise, the crew may elect to divert the aircraft to the nearest suitable airport, for example one with a hospital.

ATC

ATC delays related to airborne aircraft are normally due to traffic congestion in or around the destination airport. Procedures to manage this often include slowing down inbound aircraft, adjusting their tracks, or placing aircraft into holding patterns. In addition, marginal weather conditions may require specific instrument approaches, sometimes reducing the volume of traffic flow substantially. In these situations, IOCs are interested in the locations and estimated landing times of all their inbound aircraft. Thus, communication with ATC or some intermediary becomes crucial. Based upon anticipated landing and hence arrival times, IOCs can predict the consequences to outbound flights or take a series of actions to lessen the effects of the disruption.

Airport unavailability

Airport unavailability can influence operations in a number of ways. The sudden unavailability of a destination airport, or at least main runway, is likely to result in an inbound aircraft either holding or needing to divert to an alternate airport, as the fuel carried is not normally sufficient to allow for such an event. Should an airport that is being used as an alternate airport during ETOPS (or extended diversion time operations, EDTO) become unavailable (see Chapter 17 for further details), the flight may not be able to continue as originally planned.

Crew duty/hours

During IROPS, flight patterns can be severely disrupted and crews' duties extended to operate as much of the schedule as possible. This may result in crew hours becoming exhausted and flights having to be cancelled. In the event of long-haul international flight diversions, crews may well run out of duty hours in the diversion port such that either continuation of the flight will be subject to the crew taking a rest break (e.g., ten hours), or a replacement crew being positioned to retrieve the flight and continue to the destination.

Operational decision philosophy

The aim of operational control is to ensure that scheduled operations are carried out safely and as close to the published schedule as possible. In terms of IROPS, the aim is to monitor operations, identify and assess deviations from the plan and take corrective action(s) as necessary. Part of this process involves the gathering of information and using it to make decisions. Errors come about when information is unreliable or insufficient, or a decision is made too late to be effective. The problem is that the environment is highly complex, dynamic and uncertain. So information changes quickly and new information may only become apparent at an inopportune time, often too late for effective use.

In addition, decisions made in IOCs are based on a combination of reliable information and informed communications, high levels of expertise and experience, historic solutions, and company policies. All this is done in the context of legal frameworks, and all underpinned by the safety of operating. Criticism of operational decisions or lack thereof from the flying public or from within the airline itself, may sometimes be well meaning but often unfounded. No one else in the airline has the oversight of the network, nor the resources to judge and action problem solutions, and while decisions affecting specific flights may seem 'unjust' or 'uncaring', the IOC is charged with ensuring higher order objectives are met across the network. One of the key objectives is efficient and effective communication between all parties in a disruption. This is a two-way process, as the IOC relies on timely and accurate information upon which to make decisions, and its outward communications are as important as the actual recovery plans. The next section of this chapter describes the various strategies that can be implemented in the course of disruption management.

Operational strategies and consequences

Given the variety of problems that may occur, IOCs have at hand a number of strategies for preventing or at least mitigating the effects of the disruptions. The costs of IROPS in monetary terms, or perhaps passenger loyalty scores, are enormous, so selecting the optimum strategy to solve a problem is the key to efficient IROPS management. In a complex IROPS situation, the resolution strategies could have quite substantial snowballing or downline (consequential) effects that may impact the current day, or beyond into the next day. This is particularly the case with international operations.

Delaying flights

Nearly everyone who has travelled will be familiar with presenting themselves at an airport only to find that their flight has been delayed. Despite efforts to maintain scheduled departure and, hopefully, arrival times, flights do run late. Delaying a flight or a number of flights is not desirable, but unless opportunities enable other actions to be taken, sometimes there is little alternative. Besides effects on passengers, delays can also affect time-sensitive cargo, especially perishable goods, which include fresh produce, flowers and even items such as newspapers. If delays do occur, IOCs will endeavour to isolate them within a time period, or isolate a particular pattern of flights, or attempt to keep the delays within a geographic region so as not to spread problems around the network. However, this may not be possible if, for example, there are transhipping passengers from one flight (aircraft) to a different aircraft. In this case, the delay can spread to both the pattern of the aircraft originally running late as well as the aircraft awaiting the tranships. Delaying flights can lead to further problems, such as threatening to breach curfew times or requiring the negotiation of alternative slot times into or out of an airport. Delays can also affect some catering uplift that is time limited due to its freshness and shelf-life limits. In this case, the Catering supplier may have to replan catering uplift or even cancel the planned uplift.

If flights need to be delayed awaiting inbound crews from another flight, this may also be a source of spreading delays. In addition, the later operation of flights has an impact on airports and resources simply because they are late, such that the ground resources which had been so carefully preplanned and optimized, are suddenly handling off-scheduled movements. Should flight bookings be compatible, IOCs may be able to remove (i.e., cancel) some of the flights from the network, thus freeing up space in aircraft patterns and enabling them to use the time to get back on schedule. In peak times of the day or week, or when weather or other influences cause more widespread network delays, *many* patterns run late and recovery becomes far more difficult.

The extent to which IOCs disseminate information through various systems to the travelling public or even staff in relation to anticipated delays is a great point of conjecture. Much of this is due to uncertainty or changing circumstances which are characteristic of the operation. For example, if a particular pattern were running late (e.g., a remote pattern running two hours behind schedule) and there was virtually no chance of resurrecting the operation by taking any other action, then a delayed schedule may be broadcast publicly, such that passengers at each subsequent port could be advised well in advance of an impending delayed departure time. However, when other options (such as swapping aircraft patterns, or cancelling some flights) present themselves, there is no certainty at all that future flights will be delayed. All it needs, sometimes, is another disruption to occur, for which the solution resolves both that disruption and the originally delayed pattern. The key in the IOC is to recognize actual and potential problems and identify the options that may be used to mitigate them. The set of skills needed for this often reflects the levels of experience and expertise of personnel in the IOC.

Swapping aircraft (tail numbers) – within type

This is the simplest aircraft swap and involves swapping two similar aircraft at some point during their flying patterns. Each aircraft would then fly the remainder of the pattern of the other aircraft (unless further swapping brought about more change). The simplicity is due to the similarities in ground handling, use of the same Pilots,[5] Flight Attendants, catering equipment, fuel loads, and (very similar) weights and performance. Delays may or may not be incurred as a result of the swap, or the swap may be enacted to stop further delays to a pattern. Operational considerations could include changes to parking positions and gate lounges, changes of aircraft for crews and passengers, and possibly disrupted maintenance work due on one of the aircraft that no longer matches with the planned maintenance base. Caution is also exercised even when swapping derivatives of one aircraft type (e.g., B777-300 for a B777-200). It may be that crew who are not endorsed to fly the larger 300 aircraft cannot operate it following an aircraft change, which may then deem the aircraft grounded (awaiting another crew). Even aircraft of identical type may not have an identical interior configuration, for instance in seating. This may result in reservations and check-in personnel having to reallocate passengers with a higher risk of passenger dissatisfaction, for instance if loved ones cannot be allocated adjacent seats.

Swapping aircraft – type changes

This change is more complex, as different types of aircraft generally require different Technical Crews (Pilots[6]) and Flight Attendants who are endorsed on type. If up-gauging (to a larger) type, extra Flight Attendants will be required. In addition, baggage and cargo containers and loading/unloading procedures may differ, as well as catering requirements and on-board equipment, particularly if narrow-body and wide-body aircraft changes are envisaged. Down-gauging could result in passenger offloads on some of the flights operated either on the current day, or, if the patterns affected included overnight displacement, the next day. If overnight bases are changed, then the same maintenance considerations apply, as well as changes to accommodation requirements for the crews. The implications of these factors are that should the changes be required in a short timeframe, there are likely to be delayed flights incurred to incorporate the additional handling involved.

Diverting flights

Diverting a flight can be quite messy and very costly. In the case of *planning* a flight diversion prior to departure (perhaps better termed *rerouting* rather than *diverting* a flight), airport staff and other key personnel at the unscheduled airport can be advised well ahead of the anticipated arrival time. Therefore, refuellers, cabin service including catering, and other ground handling services will be prepared for the additional aircraft movements. In contrast, flights that divert due to unforeseen circumstances (such as weather or perhaps a medical emergency on board) are unplanned and therefore unresourced. If a major airport were to close quite suddenly due to storm activity, for example, and several aircraft divert to a common nominated alternate airport, the resulting congestion at the alternate port will cause significant parking, handling, and fuelling problems as well as disruption to passengers and crews. It may even result in the need for overnight accommodation should the flights involved be at night-time. Decisions to divert a flight may be made by a Dispatcher in collaboration with the Aircraft Captain or Commander. In the absence of the Dispatch role, the Captain may make their own decision to divert, or if time permits and communication is possible with the IOC, questions may be asked as to which diversion port would be preferred. This provides an opportunity for IOC input in spreading diversions more evenly and taking advantage of any operational benefit, such as cancelling or combining other flights. A further consideration relates to any aircraft that becomes 'out-of-position', where an aircraft may have diverted to a particular port but then becomes 'owed' to another port. If there are multiple diversions, there may well be numerous aircraft (and passengers and crews) caught out-of-position. Recovering this situation is discussed below. Of course, this situation may also result in foregone scheduled maintenance work with downline ramifications. Any diversion is likely to result in the loss of perishable cargo, which may be unable to be transhipped to other carriers before its due time.

Cancelling flights

As implied above, cancelling flights generally disrupts passengers the most as their original plans for flying between origin and destination are changed. Airlines would obviously prefer to operate flights as planned for this very reason, but at times, the option to cancel a number of flights may be the preferred choice in order to prevent wider network disruption. Cancelling flights also carries a number of consequential effects. Crews who may have been rostered for the cancelled flight and then other commitments may now be out of position, requiring some rerostering of crews, or having to change (even cancel) other flights as well. Cancelling flights in one direction (e.g., MAN–CDG) usually implies that some other action is needed to restore the balance of aircraft. In this case, solutions could include cancelling the opposite direction CDG–MAN, or positioning (ferrying) another aircraft either from MAN or from somewhere in the airline's network into CDG to operate the next flight. This may create another gap that may need to be filled where *that* aircraft was supposed to operate. The situation becomes far more challenging with cancellations of long-haul flights, with large numbers of passengers usually being booked, and solutions to problems being more difficult.

Adding flights

As a means for continuing operations during or after IROPS events, airlines sometimes need to reposition aircraft. These flights are often non-revenue (or ferry) flights, as they may not carry Flight Attendants, in which case they cannot carry passengers. Ferrying aircraft is, of course, very costly, but in the overall picture of a significant IROPS event, where multiple cancellations may have taken place to keep the network flying, positioning aircraft can be a useful and necessary strategy to ensure aircraft can recover future flying patterns, perhaps later in the day, or for the next day. It also serves as a means of utilizing the crew who position the aircraft to continue flying. Selecting the appropriate time to position an aircraft is also a strategic decision. If an aircraft is required to ferry to a port to operate a scheduled flight out of that port, the ferry flight is usually conducted as late as possible (allowing for a standard turnaround time prior to operating the scheduled flight) just in case further disruptions negate the need for ferrying at all. However, this must be weighed against any potential operating problems such as weather (especially fog) which may further disrupt the ferry itself. Thus, a ferry flight is usually conducted as a last resort.

Conclusion

This chapter has built on Chapter 8, which introduced readers to the IOC, and also used the foundation chapters in Part II describing 'normal current day operations' as a basis for exploring what happens when 'normal' isn't being achieved. The next chapter considers domestic and international IROPS, especially in terms of seasonal problems that occur, particularly in the USA.

Notes

1 The term IOC will be used as a reference to the Integrated Operations Control Centre. Other terms used in this text include NOC (Network Operations Centre), AOC (Airline Operations Centre), AOCC (Airline Operations Control Centre), SOC (Systems Operations Centre).
2 Bruce, P.J. (2011) *Understanding Decision-making Processes in Airline Operations Control*, Ashgate, Aldershot.
3 Less in the case of some airlines such as LCCs.
4 The term 'customer' is preferred in many airlines but 'passenger' is still commonly used.
5 Note: Pilots can be multi-endorsed to fly 'families' of aircraft such as B737-700, -800, -900 or A320/319/321 aircraft but normally endorsed to fly A320/A330 or B737/B777.
6 See note 5.

23 Operational disruption management

Charles Cunningham

Introduction

Managing daily operations at a major domestic carrier is much like trying to manage a large beehive. Domestic airline operations are a frenzy of carefully organized and choreographed activity that appear chaotic from the outside. It seems impossible that an operation comprised of millions of moving parts spread from coast to coast can be coordinated, yet major carriers do it every day. Passengers, airline and airport employees, airplanes, de-icing trucks, belt loaders, pushback tugs, provisioning trucks, even airport shuttle vans all play an important part in daily operations. It does not take long working in the domestic air carrier industry to realize the schedule only operates as it should if all of those parts are moving when and where they are supposed to. Any disruption can cause flights to back up, and if left unchecked the operation can quickly become unmanageable.

Irregular operations

These disruptions are what cause irregular operations, known as 'IROPS'. The IROPS themselves are a combination of cancellations, aircraft swaps, overflies, and controlled delays (metering). They are the airline's attempt to reset the schedule back to normal. There is no perfect solution when dealing with schedule disruptions or the IROPS that follow. When dealing with a major disruption, airlines are faced with a bad situation. All of the likely outcomes cause some degree of passenger and employee inconvenience. Finding the solution that causes the least passenger inconvenience is optimal for crews and crew pairings, in order to deliver the impacted station a schedule they can safely operate which is as close to perfect as airlines can achieve. In other words, airlines try to find the least bad solution to operational disruptions.

The term 'irregular operations' is widely used but is somewhat of a misnomer. IROPS occur almost daily at major carriers somewhere in their network, making the irregular a rather regular occurrence. What IROPS really means is that one or more airports are not operating in a way that allows them to support the robust schedule published by the airlines, especially at the largest airports where gate utilization is at its highest and employee and equipment resources are stretched to their limits. Domestic airline operations is a highly competitive sector of the industry, so carriers publish schedules that can be challenging on good days and seek every advantage that can help ensure a profit. While there are many domestic carriers in the U.S., according to U.S. Department of Transport statistics, the vast majority of passengers are moved by four major carriers: Southwest, American, Delta and United. These four giants handle roughly eighty per cent of passengers travelling within the United States.

Lately, one of the areas in which airlines are seeking an advantage is the management of IROPS. There are almost as many causes of IROPS (see Chapter 22) as there are ways to manage them. The most common causes stem from some type of weather disruption, which is often compounded by an Air Traffic Control initiative. There are both IROPS that can be foreseen or forecast, such as major winter storms, and IROPS that happen very suddenly and without warning, such as a disabled aircraft on a runway or an airport security breach causing delays and diversions. In these types of IROPS, airlines are attempting to manage the situation while still attempting to gather facts. In cases like these, airlines rely heavily on the knowledge, expertise and experience of their employees, and managing both types of IROPS has become something of a science.

Proactive and reactive disruption management

There are two dramatically different ways of dealing with disruptions to the network: proactive and reactive. Proactive management is far more desirable and is characteristic of situations where a forecast event may enable the airline to get ahead of any potential disruptions, often reducing the schedule to some degree. Prevailing wisdom is that making a proactive decision and being wrong is better than doing nothing and subjecting the airline to unnecessary risk. Making decisions regarding potential disruptions early is much better for all concerned. Many IROPS recur seasonally with similar scenarios playing out year after year. Each season brings unique challenges, and may call for different strategies, just as each airport is handled differently. Many airports have operational constraints beyond simply landing minimum requirements and facilitating efficient and safe approaches.

Managing domestic disruptions

Seasonal operations – fall and winter

Winter is unique not only due to the possibility of heavy snow or freezing precipitation, but because of potentially extensive de-icing delays. Meteorologists have become very accurate in their ability to predict with a high level of confidence not only when snow will begin, but what type of accumulations can be expected, as well as whether the snow is likely to be wet or dry. Airlines can use that information to reduce or suspend operations, depending on the severity of a storm. Safety is always an airline's highest priority, but ensuring an acceptable level of passenger experience is also important. There are many reasons for which an airline would reduce its schedule at one of its larger airports, but here is one example. An airline has four de-icing pads. With two crews working on each pad in moderate snow, de-icing might average fifteen minutes per aircraft, one aircraft per pad. That means the best throughput they can expect is four aircraft per pad per hour, or sixteen departures per hour, as a best case. Even if the rate were reduced to sixteen per hour, it is important those sixteen are staggered as much as possible to minimize delays. If all sixteen arrive in a bank and then push back at roughly the same time, the delays will be much longer than desired. If they are scheduled at a rate of twenty arrivals per hour, it will not take long for the delays to become unacceptable not only to the airline, but to its passengers.

Often the source of disruption in snow events is the amount of time it takes to de-ice an aircraft. Those times vary based on the intensity of the snow, outside temperature and wind velocity. There are strict guidelines that must be followed during freezing precipitation events regarding de-icing. Pilots and ground personnel must adhere to those guidelines to meet the specific conditions, then follow either a 'holdover' chart for snow and other freezing precipitation or an 'allowance' chart if ice pellets are involved, to see how long they have from the time de-icing begins until the aircraft takes off. If many aircraft start exceeding their holdover or allowance times and return to the de-ice pad to be retreated, then even a throughput of sixteen aircraft per hour may be far too optimistic. There is far more than just simple mathematics in play when determining a realistic and manageable rate.

Other factors come into play during winter operations. Human factors, such as the maximum time agents can be exposed to the cold, must be considered. Some airlines provide warming huts to give personnel a chance to warm themselves during extreme winter operations. Others schedule ramp workers to rotate through outdoor duty quickly, giving them a chance to go inside and warm up at designated intervals. Wind speed can also slow or stop the de-icing process, and carriers have a limit as to how strong the winds can be during de-ice operations. This is for the safety of the employee in the de-ice bucket (that services the aircraft), as well as to avoid potential damage to the aircraft. Metering can often provide relief in de-icing situations. Depending on the airport's scheduled arrivals, flights can often be delayed deliberately hour by hour to even out the throughput rate to a manageable number. This technique is best used when there are busy arrival hours, followed by hours where recovery is possible. Figure 23.1 shows an airport's arrival spikes at 1200, 1700 and 1900 with recovery time in the following hours which makes delaying hour to hour a viable option.

When using this approach, care must be taken to ensure the optimal flights are delayed. This would normally be flights that have the fewest passengers and crews connecting in the city being metered, and have the fewest downline flights remaining on their line or flying pattern. Cancelling down to a desired rate is another option. Figure 23.2 shows a snow event in DEN (Denver). The combination of snow and de-icing made operating the schedule as published unrealistic.

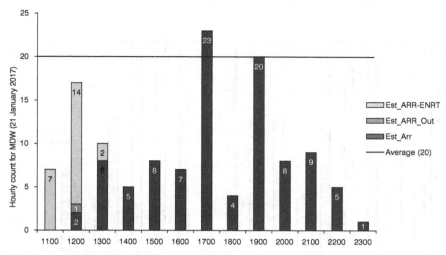

Figure 23.1 Airport arrival spikes

Source: Charles Cunningham

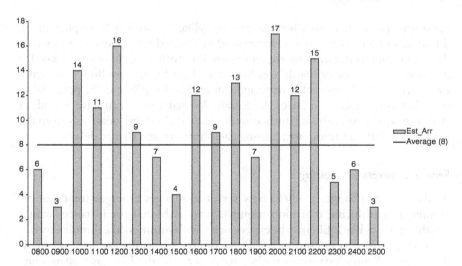

Figure 23.2 Arrival spikes during a snow event at Denver

Source: Charles Cunningham

Station leadership can be a valuable source of information in situations like this, as they can provide insights regarding their staffing, airport conditions and city infrastructure. Figure 23.3 shows the arrival rate at Denver post schedule reduction.

After the schedule reduction, the station is left with a level eight arrivals per hour, and fewer arrivals in the hours that were *already* scheduled with fewer than eight arrivals. This proactive strategy set the station up for a successful recovery from

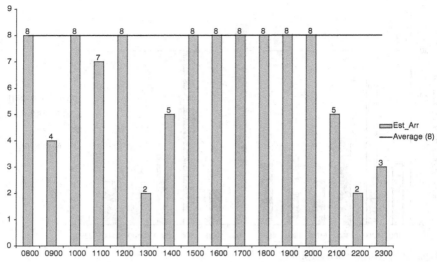

Figure 23.3 Arrival spikes (after schedule reduction) during a snow event at Denver

Source: Charles Cunningham

the storm. The earlier that schedule reductions like this one can be implemented, the more options there are to reaccommodate affected passengers on alternative flights. During winter months, the jet stream dips further south causing delays for flights which operate primarily westbound, and for flights travelling eastbound, early arrivals. Both are problematic and can lead to IROPS and the potential of over-delivering at large airports. A centrally-located airport can have a bank of arrivals from the east arriving thirty minutes late, while a bank of arrivals from the west arrive thirty minutes early, causing gate shortages and tarmac delays.

Seasonal operations – spring

As the seasons change, a whole new set of challenges emerges for domestic airlines. Often during transition months, such as March for instance, winter weather in cities like DEN may be experienced, with summer-like thunderstorms, sometimes severe in the southeast of the country. Generally speaking, spring is when lines of thunderstorms may be observed across the U.S., as well as some isolated 'pop-up' storms. Lines of thunderstorms are more predictable in terms of speed and movement, and it is easier to forecast when they might impact a critical airport or begin interfering with ATC (Air Traffic Control) flows. There will be more on ATC and its role in IROPS later in this chapter.

As the line of storms progresses, airlines are able to time the arrival of their flights to arrive either ahead or behind this line. Once flights can no longer arrive ahead of the line of storms, they are delayed or sometimes cancelled to allow the storms to pass, with remaining traffic rescheduled to arrive behind the worst of the convective activity. Landing during heavy storms is sometimes possible, but introduces new hazards. Lightning strikes, hail damage and wind shear are all possible, as well as strong crosswinds caused by shifting winds beneath storm cells. Again, an airline's first priority is safety, so the days of landing in any conditions have passed. Wind shear manifests itself to the passengers and flight attendants in the form of turbulence, which makes for an altogether unpleasant experience, and brings unnecessary safety risks.

Seasonal operations – summer

The heat of summer brings a plethora of operational problems. Lines of thunderstorms persist. In addition, summer heating brings 'convective popcorn' thunderstorms that can develop suddenly. On the downside, this type of storm is less predictable than solid lines of storms but, often, flight crews are able to fly around them more easily than they could a solid line. This type of operational disruption is common during summer months. The heat also brings other challenges. Aircraft do not perform optimally in high temperatures and ATOG (Allowable Take-off Gross Weight) issues often arise which may restrict payload or otherwise affect the routing of the flight. The excessive heat also takes a toll on employees, and staff health considerations can be an issue due to the handling requirements of high passenger and bag numbers and weights. To counteract this, ramp employees must take more breaks to avoid heat-related problems.

Fog

As with most weather-related disruptions, fog can occur at any time of the year, and some geographic areas are more prone to it than others. Fog can settle in and stay for hours. It is less of a problem at larger airports with more sophisticated equipment and lower take-off and landing minimums. But even those airports can dip below limits. Getting an accurate forecast for fog is challenging. It is nearly impossible to accurately forecast a fifty-foot difference in the ceiling or a couple of hundred feet of visibility on the runway; yet that is what it often comes down to. The difference between operating and not being able to operate often comes down to minimal differences in visibility or ceiling. These periods of marginal weather are a time when, especially if loads are light, airlines often choose to hedge their bets and reduce the number of arrivals, greatly reducing the number of potential diverted flights. This strategy makes the worst-case scenario (the weather going below landing limits) more manageable. Thinning the published schedule mitigates some degree of risk and ensures that, at a minimum, there will be fewer diversions if the weather does not cooperate!

Mandates that changed IROPs (for the better)

In April 2010, the U.S. Department of Transportation addressed a series of incidents that left passengers stranded on aircraft, unable to get off, during a disrupted operation. The new rule would prohibit U.S. airlines operating domestic flights from permitting an aircraft to remain on the tarmac for more than three hours without deplaning passengers. Airlines that violated this rule would face heavy fines, potentially as much as $27,500 per passenger on board. There were also requirements that passengers be provided food and water within the first two hours of the delay, and have toilet facilities made available. While this new rule sent shock waves throughout the industry, in the end it forced airlines to re-evaluate the way they had been doing business and provide their passengers a better experience.

In January 2014, airlines were forced to deal with another major change in regulations: FAR Part 117. This regulation addressed flight time limitations and rest requirements, and marked the first changes to pilot duty limitations in sixty years. Prior to the changes brought about by FAR Part 117, airline pilots were classified as 'legal to start, legal to finish', meaning that if they were legal for their last flight leg when it departed, they were legal to finish the leg even if it diverted or took extensive delays after departing from the gate. The new Part 117 included an approach to determining a rigid time the pilots must be at the gate. In the event of a diversion, there was now a good chance the cockpit crew would be illegal to continue out of their diversion city. Airlines have adjusted and are able to formulate new strategies and contingency plans, such as diverting to a city where crews are available.

These two rules forced airlines to become more proactive in the way they deal with IROPS. Even if they chose to operate flights very late, airlines are simply no longer able to absorb extensive delays due to the risk of crew hours running out and the possibility of extensive tarmac delays. This has led to more proactive approaches by airlines when they have a station under duress. Airlines have had to make difficult changes to the way they operate, but in the end the overall passenger experience has improved.

Managing international disruptions

While the focus of this chapter is domestic airline IROPS, it is worth at least touching on some of the complexities of international IROPS. Airlines strive to protect their international operations for several reasons. Many of the large international destinations are slot controlled. Airlines are expected to arrive within fifteen minutes either side of their scheduled arrival time to suit their slot, as parking is often limited. International flying is also very lucrative for the airlines, so they take precautions to ensure they maintain the integrity of their international operation. International service is often operated almost as an entity separate from the rest of the airline – an airline within an airline. Adjustments like additional ground time and padded block times help ensure the integrity of the schedule. Despite airlines' best efforts though, factors beyond their control occasionally come into play, leading to international IROPS.

Communication is crucial when faced with an international IROPS situation. Communication cannot be overdone and there are many more parties involved in the communication process. Different governments have different policies regarding matters such as, for example, shipping parts in to repair an out-of-service aircraft, but extensive coordination is required with the country's customs and border service. Crew legalities become more critical unless the airline has a crew base in the city where the IROPS are taking place. If diversions are necessary, often airlines are forced to divert to a city they do not serve. This is called an off-line diversion, and requires coordination and communication with contract companies to handle aspects such as parking, refuelling and secure passenger areas. There are vendors who help airlines with just this sort of complex coordination effort.

There are many different factors to consider when diverting internationally. For example, should an International flight conduct an 'air return' to the U.S., having been unable to land at its scheduled destination, due care must be taken to ensure the flight goes to another International Gateway city, to ensure U.S. Customs is available. Another consideration arises when flying to particular state, and circumstances dictate a diversion to a foreign country. In this case, passengers may not have passports or visas for the country, in which case there will be a need to ensure they are sequestered. There will also potentially be restrictions regarding the other servicing requirements for the aircraft such as, for instance, removal of trash and taking on potable water, depending on the country.

Operations in the future

Every passenger who flies regularly will eventually experience some form of IROPS. The complexity of major airline networks, regulations and restrictions, and an infinite number of events that could disrupt those complex schedules, make chances of getting to the destination on time seem slim – but there is cause for optimism. Major carriers have established Network Operations Control (NOC) Centres or Integrated Operations Control Centres (IOCs). The idea is to bring representatives from all major operating groups within the airline together in one room. These representatives are not only a tremendous resource for others in the NOC, but having all stakeholders together helping to devise an operational game plan ensures that details are not overlooked and that everyone with a stake in the operation has a voice. Commonly now, major carriers bring together representatives from Meteorology, Flight Operations, Inflight Services, Crew Scheduling, Dispatch, Proactive Customer Support, Safety and Security, Customer Service, Maintenance, Social Media, etc. Various members of the leadership of these and other groups meet several times daily to debrief on the prior day's operation and formulate a plan for the current and future days. Leadership from the airline's largest cities and many other members of senior leadership often join via teleconference. This type of setup not only ensures all stakeholders' concerns are heard, but the plan going forward is communicated to all at the same time.

One by one, each department is given the opportunity to make others aware of challenges they may be facing. For example, Meteorology will provide a national weather brief, focusing on areas of concern, station (port) managers discuss staffing, equipment and facility concerns, and Dispatch Managers share their operational plan for the day, including any proactive actions that may be required. This has proven an excellent way of avoiding or minimizing the impact of IROPS. Major carriers tend to retain employees, therefore decision makers are highly experienced and have an excellent grasp of what operations are feasible, as well as realizing when the need for reducing or suspending operations may be the best option.

New philosophies have allowed airlines to 'isolate the passenger pain' in the event of any type of disruption. This may involve the prevention of delays propagating to downline flights, mitigating or solving delays by optimizing ground time utilization, rerouting flights by overflying ports, or cancelling downline flights. Cancelling flights is not the only way to repair the schedule. A simple aircraft swap which delays one flight, while getting three others on-time is a successful strategy for both the majority of the passengers and the airline's On-Time Performance (OTP). Handling disruptions in that manner keeps delays isolated to the fewest number of passengers possible and protects the remainder of the network.

Technology

This is a very exciting time in aviation, specifically when it comes to IROPS management. Airlines and vendors alike have realized the tremendous value in having the ability to effectively manage IROPS. There are both hard and soft costs associated with IROPS, and combined they have a staggering effect on the airline's bottom line. Hard costs encompass expenses such as crew time, fuel, passenger misconnections and compensation, agent overtime, hotel rooms and the effect on the all-important OTP. Soft costs come in the form of passenger satisfaction, goodwill towards the brand and repeat business. Airlines monitor passenger satisfaction with information such as a Net Promoter Score (an index ranging from minus 100 to plus 100 that measures the willingness of customers to recommend a company to others), and have seen a direct correlation between the soft costs and the way in which IROPS are managed.

Airlines and vendors have invested heavily into exciting new tools and optimization engines that have proven to be game changers. The keys to managing IROPS are proactivity and communication. The further ahead airlines can look at potential disruptions, the better the likely result for passengers and employees alike. Airlines are also rapidly abandoning operating systems that generate isolated departmental solutions. Tools that are integrated and communicate with other systems facilitate cohesive management of IROPS. Many major carriers are developing sophisticated optimization engines, customized to mimic their best manual practices typically used to handle proactive reductions and/or major schedule shutdowns. The benefits are many. Shutting down a major station is a process that can take five or six hours to complete manually. The cancellations are relatively easy, however rebalancing the fleet is very complicated. Often the solution(s) needs to take into account a combination of further cancellations and positioning of ferry (non-revenue) flights, ensuring that every flight has a properly equipped aircraft with enough seats to accommodate the bookings (and perhaps additional bookings due to the original problem). This is a mind-numbing manual process, during which other departments such as Ground Operations, Customer Service and Crew Scheduling are forced to wait until a final solution is complete. There is no sense in attempting to solve crew issues until it is known which flights are actually operating, and where crews will ultimately be needed. The algorithm in a powerful optimization engine can complete that task in a very short time. In addition, optimization engines have the ability to reveal crew and passenger misconnections, maintenance requirements on particular aircraft that may need to be rerouted, curfew issues, etc. Investments in tools like this have paid off manyfold, improving OTP and customer satisfaction, while reducing total cancellations and aircraft swaps. Continued investment and advances in technology, as well as integration of key operating systems, will surely improve the overall passenger experience and enable airlines to anticipate further ahead of disruptions.

Innovative advances in fleet management have the potential to dramatically reduce the number of unscheduled aircraft swaps. Predictive tools and alerting systems are also being developed. New technology for managing crews and optimizing their pairings, and more sophisticated and dynamic flight-planning engines will also help airlines manage and recover from IROPS. This type of multipronged approach by airlines and vendors, along with system integration, will have a significant impact, improving the product airlines are able to deliver to their passengers.

ATC

Our air traffic control system can both contribute to making minor disruptions worse, as well as in some cases help to alleviate problems. Anticipating how ATC will react to storms can be challenging. Airlines often have groups of people with knowledge and experience in ATC and therefore understanding of procedures and processes that will assist them in handling disruptions. At a minimum level, the airline will be aware of, and can plan for, large ATC initiatives. Ground Stops (aircraft held on the ground at their origin) become likely during dense fog events, or when thunderstorms force the closure of one or more arrival approaches at a large airport. In some cases, this saves airlines from having to hold their own flights bound for a problem city; in others it triggers the need for the airline to take action in the form of IROPS.

Ground Delay Programs are another common ATC initiative, used when demand exceeds an airport's acceptance rate. The acceptance rate fluctuates based on the weather, winds and other factors. Airlines often look for ways to reduce their delays through cancellations early in the disruption, or utilize less critical lines or patterns of flying to absorb delays. In a major program with extensive delays, the number of passenger misconnections and crew issues created can be a deciding factor in addressing a problem. Airspace Flow Programs, or AFPs, allow flights to take their delays in the air. They can be used to meter traffic or divert traffic away from an over-saturated ATC centre. While essential to avoid overwhelming an airport or ATC centre, these ATC initiatives can also exacerbate a carrier's efforts to mitigate an IROPS situation, and at a minimum must be considered.

Summary

Weather events are often the root cause for IROPS. ATC initiatives can sometimes be the cause, but are more often a contributing factor. As mentioned earlier, in some cases, ATC initiatives can even be of help to airline operators in stopping the flow of traffic to a problem airport. There is no single triggering event for IROPS – the root cause of an IROPS event can be any number of things. Essentially, it can be any disruption that causes one flight to back up into another, or one bank of flights to back up into another. It is anything that causes a deviation from the airline's published schedule. Airline operations are fluid, and must keep moving. Much like a small waterway overflows its banks when its flow is disrupted by impediments, when an airline's flow is disrupted, airports quickly have more aircraft than they can handle. Technological advancements and the development of specialized tools, as well as the overall shift towards proactivity and focus on communication, will certainly provide additional relief to airlines and their passengers in the near future. The mystery of solving IROPS is within the grasp of carriers.

24 Changes to the operating environment

Mark Palmer

Introduction

The aviation environment has remained fairly stable in operations over the last fifty years, with only minor changes in the way it operated. Although incredible increases in technology have occurred, they have not greatly changed the operational environment. In the coming years, the pressure that is being put on this environment from saturation of airports and airspace, rapid growth and new technology will both force and enable dramatic changes.

Airport saturation

Saturation of airports is the first significant challenge that is already changing the way the system operates. An ever-increasing number of airports have reached capacity during peak periods and the period of capacity overload is growing continually. A lot of these airports cannot increase the number of runways, as they are now surrounded by the ever-expanding cities to which they are attached. The first technology solution to this problem arrived when the super jumbo aircraft such as the Airbus A380 entered service. However, at the same time, passengers started to desire more frequent direct flights to their destinations. This change in attitude, and the limitations of operating these aircraft, has restricted the effect of this solution in reducing capacity issues especially in peak periods.

There are two major issues with increasing capacity of a runway: wake vortices and runway occupancy time. These two limitations will both have to be reduced to enable more aircraft to land in a given period of time. One solution is to have aircraft with lower wake vortex effects. If new aircraft types could reduce the wake vortex they create, more aircraft could land in the same period of time. The second limitation is runway occupancy time, or the time the aircraft spends on the runway before being clear. At most airports today this is close to, or lower than, the wake vortex separation, although not at all airports. As aircraft reduce their wake vortex separation limitation, this will quickly become the limiting factor and therefore must be considered. New technology like 'brake-to-vacate' is already available to improve this, and combined with the addition of rapid taxiway exits, can also be used to reduce the runway occupancy time.

As the difference between aircraft runway occupancy times and wake vortex separation times increases, there is one other limiting factor that must be addressed. Today most airports operate on a strict first come, first served basis. Unfortunately, this principle does not allow the airport to optimize the capacity numbers of aircraft. Aircraft are given a weight classification which is then used to determine separation during landing. Currently aircraft are given a 'Light', 'Medium', 'Heavy' or 'Super Heavy' classification. The time separation required between aircraft on approach is different for each type. For instance, the sequence of Heavy, Light, Heavy, Light will take a similar amount of time as a sequence of Light, Light, Light, Heavy, Heavy. However, this second sequence increases the capacity of aircraft numbers using the runway. To utilize this increase in capacity, we need to change the way we operate at airports, stopping the strict first come, first served approach and moving to a capacity-optimized approach. This will add a level of difficulty into the operations and complexity into airline operational planning.

Many methods for improving traffic sequencing are being considered today. However, it is clear that airline operations will have to adapt to these differences in traffic flow management. Initially, this may be in the form of strict planning and the need to meet arrival sequence times. The penalties for not meeting the planning will be significant. To enable greater flexibility, airline operations will also potentially have to accept and manage aircraft being delayed for the greater good of the capacity of the system. Aircraft will be sequenced to maximize capacity and therefore some aircraft will have to move back in the sequence. A loss one day will be a gain the next, with an overall gain in efficiencies in the system, but this will increase the complexity of operations.

The capabilities of the aircraft will also have to be considered when airline operational planning is performed. Aircraft with certain technological abilities like brake-to-vacate, or having lower wake vortices, will have priority during periods of high capacity. This will add a significant level of complexity, especially into mixed fleet airline operations.

Another method that will evolve is the ability to prioritize some aircraft over others. During a situation where aircraft are being delayed, modern systems will allow the airline to protect some aircraft in the sequence. This will allow the airline to limit the delays on key aircraft, for example, those with large numbers of transfer passengers, or short turnaround requirements for the aircraft, while potentially increasing the delay on less key aircraft. Again, while this will bring improvements to the overall system, it will also add further complexity into airline operations. Airlines that have the operational capability to manage this 'on the fly' will benefit greatly.

Airspace limitations

While airports are an obvious area of capacity limitation, more and more often, airspace is also suffering from capacity limitations. These are largely caused by the limitation in the number of aircraft that can be handled by an Air Traffic

Controller using the current methods of control. Today, several factors limit the number of aircraft that can be handled by Controllers. This limitation, despite the improvements in technology, has largely remained the same for the last fifty years. The fact that most communications are largely still performed by voice results in a Controller only able to command a limited number of aircraft at one time, as communication is via voice commands over a single voice channel. At present, controllers look after a specific area of airspace, and consequently there can only be a limited number of aircraft inside this area. Aircraft wishing to fly through or into such an area can therefore be delayed or routed around the area if capacity is exceeded.

In addition, the number of voice commands that need to be sent to, or received from, the aircraft further limits the number of aircraft that can be controlled. In airspace where aircraft are manually vectored, the number of commands to aircraft is significantly increased and therefore the number of aircraft that are allowed in the area is significantly reduced. Clearly, one way to increase capacity is to reduce the amount of manual intervention that is required of the controller. To do this, the first requirement is to be able to fully plan the trajectory of the aircraft in advance. This is the concept of trajectory operations.

The airline, air traffic control system, or a combination of the two, first develops a very accurate plan that takes into account all other aircraft in the system to ensure the planned trajectory is capable of being flown without the need for change. To reduce the workload on the controllers and therefore increase capacity, the airline must then fly the trajectory as planned. The greater the number of aircraft that do not fly the planned trajectory, the higher the workload in the system, and if too many aircraft do not fly the planned trajectory, the system breaks down and reverts to manual operations. This is an important point for future operations – airlines must fly the operations as planned and Air Traffic Controllers must control operations as they are planned.

In theory this seems like a simple solution to the current capacity problem. However, in practice there are a lot of reasons that this is much more difficult than it first appears. One key element that needs to be addressed is weather. Today, weather causes a significant amount of change during operations compared with the planned operation. On many occasions problematic weather is encountered en route by aircraft, causing pilot-driven requests for changes to the flight plan. This type of activity causes a significant increase in the workload of the Controller. It can potentially cause a reduction in capacity within an area of airspace, because the controller has to increase their workload above the safe level given the large amount of manual intervention required. The solution to this is twofold:

• First, better weather forecasting at the planning phase will enable more complete weather information to be taken into account for the planned trajectory. Weather forecasting is improving every day, and can now significantly improve flight planning capability. This capability needs to be both in the airline operations system planning the flight and also in the Air

Traffic Control or Air Traffic flow management system. If it is not in both these systems, flight planning cannot be accurate.

- The second part of the solution is to have better situational awareness during the flight. Situational awareness of the weather should be common and shared amongst all participants – airline operations, pilots and Air Traffic Controllers. With this improved situational awareness, actions can be taken as early as possible and with limited manual intervention. A change to the flight plan can be planned and requested by airline operations early enough to make the simplest and most efficient change. This allows the pilot (or in the future, airline operations) to make one simple change request, compared with possibly many changes needed at the last minute if problematic weather is encountered en route.

Today, to increase airspace capacity the normal solution is to divide the airspace into smaller and smaller areas, therefore allowing more aircraft in the sky. However, this increases the number of Air Traffic Controllers required, which increases the cost of flying through the airspace. However, it is not possible to linearly divide the airspace to create more capacity forever. Another current issue is the handing over of aircraft from one sector of airspace to another, as in most cases, this is a manual process that includes voice communications. There is, therefore, an ever-decreasing benefit from dividing airspace to the point where the handing over and receiving of aircraft is the limiting factor.

This factor also currently limits the capacity to move between airspace controlled by two different systems. At the present time, the hand over from one controller to the next in the same system can be largely automated, reducing the workload of the controller. However, when handing over between two different systems in different countries, the process is much more workload-intensive and manual. This is due to the systems not sharing their information in an effective and real-time fashion. By not fully sharing the information, the process of accepting an aircraft from one airspace to the next involves a set of deliberate manual actions by the controller. The resulting capacity limitations for flying certain routes have caused significant delays to operations.

Future technologies

In the future however, the introduction of the SWIM (System Wide Information Management) will provide the technology to allow systems to fully share the current situation. Once neighbouring systems are updated to fully take advantage of this technological change, the workload of the receiving controller and therefore the capacity of aircraft to move between adjoining airspace will be significantly increased.

This concept of sharing information regionally to reduce the workload on controllers is only part of the answer to improving operations on a regional basis. The other step that needs to be taken is to introduce regional-based flow management. Here the flows of aircraft are managed on a regional basis and not just an individual airspace basis. With regional-based flow management, aircraft operations can be planned effectively to allow full trajectory-based operations up to a particular time. It is not seen as practical to fully manage the complete duration of each operation today. It may become so in the future, but at the moment the thinking is to manage three hours out from arrival. This is due largely to the accuracy of weather information as mentioned above. As weather prediction improves, so will the ability to manage trajectory operations for longer periods of time. In many regions of the world this means the possibility of flights that travel over multiple countries and airspace. Without a regional approach to the management of these flows, it will not be possible to have trajectory-based operations in the region.

As mentioned above, a limiting factor is the use of voice communications. Therefore another way to increase capacity in the future is to increase the use of 'datalink', which is currently still very limited. However, in the future there is no reason why it cannot become the primary method of communication, with voice becoming a backup method. When this change occurs, it will enable significant reductions in the controller workload, as the Air Traffic Control system can become responsible for creating and sending the message. This will significantly reduce the controller's workload and therefore provide a means of increasing their ability to handle more aircraft. It will also reduce the number of errors that occur with voice communications, which also contribute to the workload of the controller.

The use of datalink also allows the controller or Air Traffic Control system to give much more complex instructions to the aircraft, therefore enabling the use of more complex types of solution to resolve issues. Rather than using vectoring, or manoeuvring aircraft through designated points when a change is needed, with datalink it is possible to use free flight principles and provide the most efficient solution possible. For instance, if an aircraft were required to divert around some bad weather, today that would need controllers to transmit several vectoring commands or a change of route involving a few new designated points. With datalink, however, it is possible to give the aircraft a set of latitude and longitude points, which would be too complex to communicate via voice, thus allowing the aircraft to fly a more efficient solution to the issue.

The use of datalink between the aircraft and Air Traffic Control system is not the only significant change in method of communication that will become available to aircraft in the future. With every reduction in satellite communication costs, eventually voice commands between the controller and aircraft will change from being radio-based to being satellite-based methods of communications. This will allow for significant reduction in the ground equipment required and will eliminate areas where voice communications are not possible or are too difficult. However, this will require a significant change in operational procedures, as aircraft will no longer be handed from controller to controller through the changing of radio frequency. This change will modify the ways in which both pilot and controller work, potentially reducing the workload on both. Currently, pilots also monitor all instructions given to surrounding aircraft as a safety measure. If this is eliminated, other means will be required to compensate for this safety measure, such as satellite communications broadcast. However, thinking differently and utilizing technology such as Automatic Dependent Surveillance–Broadcast (ADS-B) in order to enable the pilots to have this situational awareness would be a real step forward.

Connectivity

Aircraft today are increasingly being more and more connected to the ground, not just by datalink and satellite voice communications, but also by high-capacity internet links. This connectivity enables the aircraft to have a much better situational awareness in terms of the current weather situation and the forecast. This allows the pilots to better manage the flight, and plan changes earlier. It also enables an aircraft to send details of the weather it is currently experiencing to the ground, virtually empowering every aircraft to be a weather station in the air. This is particularly useful in airline operations, as aircraft frequently follow each other and the information of an earlier flight can be used to better plan any trailing flights.

With a connected aircraft, it is also possible for the aircraft while in flight to utilize the power of ground-based computing. Concepts such as Big Data, machine learning and artificial intelligence can now be used in-flight. The possibilities of these technologies are endless, and are changing at such a high speed that they will revolutionize the ability to predict, optimize and improve operations. The ability of a ground-based system that has all the weather information, together with flight plans of surrounding aircraft, to produce an optimized solution to an in-flight problem is significantly greater than any capability on board. As this is increasingly introduced into operations, airlines will be able to gain significant operational advantages from utilizing this type of technology.

Airlines in the future will also improve their ability to interact directly with Air Traffic Control and flow management systems. They will be able to prioritize aircraft that are key to their operations and communicate these priorities to the Air Traffic Control and flow management systems. Thus, airline operations will be able to negotiate and solve problems directly using these systems. Airlines will also be able to see the future plans, issues and restrictions of the Air Traffic Control systems. Some Air Service Navigation providers are already proposing that any changes that are required by an aircraft that is not pushed back be performed by airline operations directly into the flow management system of the air service provider. Even if this is not universally accepted, it is certain that in the future the airline operations system will be much more integrated with the Air Traffic Control and flow management systems.

Conclusion

The future will bring significant capacity problems that will need to be solved. However, technology will deliver the airlines a far greater capability to optimize their operations. As capacity is increased through these methods, there will be an increased need for airlines to run very accurate operations, with severe consequences for flights leaving later than scheduled. This increased need for sticking to precise schedules, and the increased operational capabilities, will, however, increase the complexity of airline operations in the future, forcing the use of increased automation in the operations.

Index